"OPERATION JACKDAW"

That was the code name given to the secret pipe-
line of defectors and informers who provided
author "Richard Deacon" with much of the data
for this book—some of it is still classified TOP
SECRET in Red China!

Including: Nuclear Espionage—The Kidnapping
of Sun Yat Sen—The Opium Wars—"Two-gun
Cohen"—Taiwan and the CIA—The Art of Brain-
washing—The four rival Secret Services—The operation that flooded Viet Nam with drugs—aimed
at hooking U.S. servicemen!

THE CHINESE SECRET SERVICE
By Richard Deacon

"A SWIFT-MOVING HISTORY OF ORIENTAL
INTRIGUE . . . ENOUGH CURIOUS ANEC-
DOTES OF ESPIONAGE TO PLEASE DEDI-
CATED SPY WATCHERS."
—*Publishers Weekly*

Also by Richard Deacon:

A HISTORY OF THE BRITISH SECRET SERVICE

MADOC AND THE DISCOVERY OF AMERICA

JOHN DEE

THE PRIVATE LIFE OF MR. GLADSTONE

THE CHINESE
SECRET SERVICE

Richard Deacon

BALLANTINE BOOKS · NEW YORK

Library of Congress Catalog Card Number: 74-5817

ISBN 0-345-24901-1-225

This edition published by arrangement with Taplinger Publishing Co., Inc., New York

Manufactured in the United States of America

First Ballantine Books Edition: May, 1976

Contents

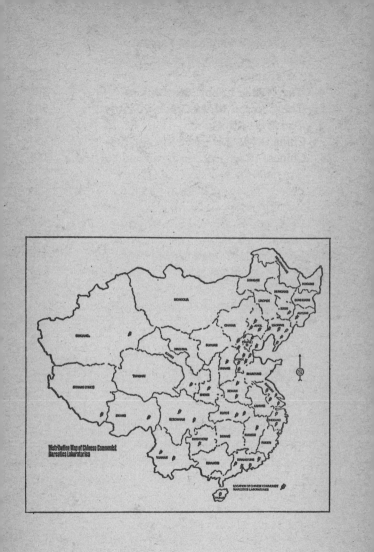

Distribution Map of Chinese Communist
Narcotics Laboratories

LOCATION OF CHINESE COMMUNIST
NARCOTICS LABORATORIES

1

Introductory

Hostile armies may face each other for years, striving for the victory which is decided in a single day. This being so, to remain in ignorance of the enemy's condition simply because one grudges the outlay of a hundred ounces of silver in honours and emoluments is the height of inhumanity.

Sun Tzu

To assert with any authority who first started a formal system of espionage in the world would be rash indeed. The most primitive people have indulged in the craft of spying. Nevertheless there is no doubt whatsoever as to who first studied the whole question of espionage as an intellectual exercise, who analysed it, developed certain axioms concerning it, worked out a complete system of espionage and set it down in a text-book.

His name is Sun Tzu, the reputed author of the *Ping Fa,* or *Principles of War,* which is believed to have been in circulation as early as 510 B.C., though this is by no means certain. But this book is without question the earliest known text-book on espionage and the arts of war generally and on the organisation of a Secret Service particularly.[1] What is even more remarkable is that it is still regarded as one of the aptest books ever produced on the subject and has been respected even by Mao Tse-Tung as something verging on Holy Writ.

The principles and methods of espionage laid down by Sun Tzu have not only been compulsory reading for Chinese generals down the centuries, but were being studied by the Japanese Army from the late nineteenth century up to the time of Pearl Harbour. Indeed, it has been claimed that the Japanese tactics prior to Pearl Harbour were borrowed almost intact from the works of Sun Tzu.

When I first set out to trace the development of the Chinese Secret Service down the centuries I was told by a scholarly foreign correspondent of the *Independent Evening Post* of Taipei that I must first of all read thoroughly two ancient Chinese books.

"The first is a work of fiction," he said, "but you must digest this in order to capture the flavour and the subtleties of the Chinese mind and how it nearly always works on the plane of espionage. It is called *San Kuo,* or *The Romance of the Three Kingdoms,* what you would describe as an historical novel written by Lo Kuan-chung of the Yuan dynasty (1260–1341).

"The second and more categoric book, in effect a text-book on espionage and the arts of war, is by Sun Tzu. Unless you are able to absorb in detail the content of these two books you will—to use an American-ism—never get to first base in writing your history. You will not only not understand all that has happened since, but find all that is happening now is meaningless."

Indeed my informant went further than this. He declined absolutely to give me any other information until I had satisfied him that I had read, understood and remembered these two books.

I will return to the subject of *San Kuo* later. In the meantime it is important to understand just how advanced a thinker Sun Tzu was.

One must bear in mind that China was already a civilised group of states some few centuries before the birth of Christ. According to legend there was a Golden Age as far back as 2300 B.C. when scholars flourished and when it was recorded that one powerful prince "rose up ten times during a meal to give audience and thrice while he was having a bath tied up his hair that he might listen to the complaints of his subjects."[2]

As early as 600–500 B.C. Lao Tzu was propounding his own philosophy of life, while Confucius and Sun Tzu were contemporaries—in some of the translations and amendments to Sun Tzu's work there are references to Confucius. The latter was born in 551 B.C. and died in 479 B.C., greatly regretting that nobody seemed to have taken any notice of his teaching. This is perhaps not surprising in that he never wrote a book; and all that is remembered of his sayings, as with those of Jesus Christ, is what has been handed down by the relatively small number of students whom he taught. Yet more than a thousand years after his death a Chinese emperor was to declare that "Confucius is to the Chinese people what water is to fishes: without him they cannot live properly."

Many Chinese scholars and some who were generals rather than scholars revised and amended the works of Sun Tzu. Fortunately so many of them did this that, by comparison of one with another, it is possible to get a very clear idea of his theories. The first translation of his works made available to the Western World was the French version by a Jesuit priest, Father Joseph Amiot, in 1782. It was called *Les Treizes Articles de Sun-tse*. However, as Lionel Giles declared in his own translation of Sun Tzu into English in 1910, this work was "little better than an imposture. It contains a great deal that Sun Tzu did not write and very little indeed of what he did."

Curiously enough, throughout the nineteenth century, except for some Japanese experimenters, no translator attempted to work on Sun Tzu even though it was then known that he was regarded in China as the author of the oldest and best compendium of military science and the arts of espionage. In 1905 Captain E. F. Calthrop, of the Royal Engineers, brought out the first English translation under the title of *Sonshi,* the Japanese translation of Sun Tzu's name. But he made it clear that he had depended on the help he had had from two Japanese and this again marred the translation, resulting in many vital omissions and some inaccurate interpretations.

Then in 1910 Lionel Giles, an assistant in the Department of Oriental Printed Books and MSS in the British Museum, London, produced what is unquestionably the best, the most scholarly and the most honest of all translations of Sun Tzu's work, though even this has been the subject of some carping criticisms from pedants. However, I have tried to make the best of all worlds by concentrating on the espionage section of Sun Tzu's work, carefully studying the various shades of meaning which Giles so painstakingly offers, dwelling also on the imaginative interpretations provided by the skilled and subtle Jesuit mind of Father Amiot and not least on an even more recent simplified and summarised translation published in 1943. For those who wish to read a concise summary of Sun Tzu I can do no better than recommend them to read *The Principles of War,* by Sun Tzu, published during World War II by Welfare Publications, sponsored by the Royal Air Force in Ceylon.

This last booklet contains a foreword by Air Vice-Marshal Alan Lees, which states: "One of the main purposes of Welfare being to comfort the mind and strengthen the spirit of all ranks, the publication of the present work requires no apology—for there is nothing more comfortable to the mind or fortifying to the spirit than that knowledge of our enemy whereby the art of his destruction shall be made perfect.

"The time is not yet ripe for a full relation of our recent campaigns to the basic doctrines set forth by Sun Tzu, but those with experience of the Japanese in Malaya and elsewhere will find their understanding deepened by a study of his book, and will find themselves the better able to guide those who have yet to meet this subtle and dangerous enemy."

What prompted the publication of Sun Tzu in this encapsulated form at that time was the knowledge that the Japanese had based their World War II tactics on his teachings. Nor is this merely gossip that has been bruited about. Captain Malcolm D. Kennedy, who was attached to the Japanese Army as a British liaison officer in the late 'twenties and early 'thirties, writes that "the espionage methods described by those two warriors, Sun Tzu and Wu Tzu, and the principles laid down by them were still being studied by the Japanese Army in the days when I was attached to it."

Captain Kennedy mentions Wu Tzu as well as Sun Tzu. There is still some confusion about Wu Tzu. It is not even certain whether Sun Tzu and Wu Tzu are not one and the same person and that the confusion arose because Sun Tzu was in the service of the state of Wu and became known as Sun Tzu of Wu. On the other hand there is this record in the *Shih Chi* (Book of History) which appears to refer to both men as contemporaries: ". . . in the ninth year [506 B.C.] King Ho Lu of Wu addressed Wu Tzu-hsu and Sun Wu, saying: 'Formerly, you declared that it was not yet possible for us to enter Ying. Is the time now ripe?'."

Whereas in the rest of the world at this period the only records handed down to us are mainly a combination of legends passed by word of mouth and certain tablet writings, China was then as now perhaps the most historically conscious nation on Earth. This whole vast area might be divided up into separate kingdoms, but they all shared a common language and script. In the Shang era, as long ago as 1500 B.C., the post of Historian was a Government office and eventually was extended into a ministry with a permanent staff of historians. Thus the career of Sun Tzu is briefly but lucidly described in the *Shih Chi* of Ssu-ma Ch'ien.[3]

According to Ssu-ma Ch'ien, Sun Tzu was a native of the state of Ch'i at the mouth of the Yellow River, but he spent most of his life in the service of the neighbouring state of Wu. He is referred to as "Sun Tzu of Wu".

Ssu-ma Ch'ien is generally considered to be the most detailed biographer of Sun Tzu, though what he says about his hero is often anecdotal. In one such story he tells how Sun Tzu's *Art of War* brought him to the notice of Ho Lu, who was King of the state from 514–496 B.C.

"I have perused your thirteen chapters," the King told Sun Tzu. "May I submit your theory of managing soldiers to a slight test?"

"Certainly," replied Sun Tzu.

"May the test be applied to women?"

Sun Tzu promptly agreed and arrangements were made to bring a hundred and eighty women out of the palace. He divided them into two companies and placed two of the King's favourite concubines as leaders of each company. Spears were then given to each woman.

Sun Tzu then asked the assembly if they knew the difference between front and back and left hand and right hand. They assured him that they did and, on the basis of this, he explained elementary drill details to them.

The women indicated that they understood what he meant, but when Sun Tzu gave the order "Right turn", they made no movement, but burst into fits of giggling.

Sun Tzu then said: "If words of command are not clear and distinct, if orders are not thoroughly understood, then the general is to blame." So he started to explain the drill again and then gave the order "Left turn". Once again there was no movement, only a gust of laughter.

"If a general's orders are clear and soldiers disobey, then it is the fault of their officers," said Sun Tzu, who thereupon ordered the leaders of the two companies to be beheaded.

The King of Wu protested and begged that his two favourite concubines should not be executed. He assured Sun Tzu that he was quite satisfied with his ability to handle troops without his taking any such drastic measure.

Sun Tzu, however, did not relent. "Having received Your Majesty's commission to be general of his forces, there are certain commands of Your Majesty which, acting in that capacity, I am unable to accept," he informed the King.

He saw that the executions were carried out and replaced the two women with two other leaders. Then he gave his drill orders again and everything was carried out exactly as he decreed without a single mistake. Sun Tzu then reported to the King that his soldiers were properly drilled and disciplined and ready for his inspection. "They are now ready to do anything you desire, Sir, and you may bid them to go through fire and water and they will not disobey."

Whatever the King of Wu felt about the fate of his favourite concubines he seems to have accepted the wisdom of Sun Tzu as he thereupon appointed him general of all his troops. Ssu-ma Ch'ien reported that

6

Sun Tzu defeated the Ch'u state in the west and forced his way into Ying, the capital, while in the north he "put fear into the states of Ch'i and Chin and spread his fame abroad among the feudal princes. And Sun Tzu shared in the might of the King."

It will be noted that Ssu-ma Ch'ien refers to Sun Tzu's "thirteen chapters". It is even suggested by some translators of the Chinese original text that these chapters were specially written for the King, to whom Sun Tzu was said to have been recommended by Wu Tzu-hsu. Yet in the bibliographical section of the *Han Shu* there is a passage which states that "the works of Sun Tzu of Wu" are in "82 *p'ien* [chapters], with diagrams in 9 *chuan*". This would suggest that Sun Tzu wrote considerably more than the thirteen chapters mentioned by Ssu-ma Ch'ien. Another source, Chang Shou-chieh, refers to an edition of Sun Tzu, of which the "thirteen chapters formed the first *chuan*" and indicating that there were two other *chuan* as well.

It seems probable that the "thirteen chapters" were written first and contained the basic premises of Sun Tzu, but that he added to his work from time to time, probably to the extent of some hundreds of thousands of words. Possibly he developed further themes of his own. More likely he received various queries from the King on points raised in conversation between them and he replied to these in writing. One must remember that the works of Sun Tzu were studied by all the leading soldiers of China down the centuries, with the probable exception of Han Kao Tsu, founder of the Han dynasty (206 B.C. to A.D. 221), who was certainly no scholar. But many of these generals were scholars and had individual ideas. They may well have added commentaries of their own to the works of Sun Tzu and some may have even edited versions of them.

This digression on Sun Tzu will illustrate the enormous task and challenge which the writing of a history of the Chinese Secret Service presents. It covers a period of more than two thousand five hundred years and, inevitably, there must be some gaps in a narrative spanning so long a period.

Fortunately a great deal of this ancient history is well documented and gradually a pattern emerges. It is a pattern totally different in many respects from that of any other major Secret Service in the world. "Intelligence" to the Chinese mind has a much more catholic meaning than to those who use this word in its narrow Secret Service context in the Western world. In many respects—and this is even truer today than in earlier centuries—intelligence gathering to the Chinese could be termed "self-education". It covers quite an astonishing field.

The modern Secret Service of the Chinese People's Republic has in an unostentatious, plodding manner achieved some quite astonishing successes in its relatively short history. It has been able to avoid many of the errors into which the Soviet Union fell in their early efforts to build up an Intelligence organisation. It has kept its secrets more efficiently than most, and, while a great many books and articles have been written about the American, British, German and Russian Secret Services, very little has been published about the Chinese Intelligence organisation and its extensive ramifications.

That so little is known about the modern Chinese Secret Service is due very largely to the fact that its agents are very rarely captured and it has very few defectors. Having embarked on this history after having written histories of the British and Russian Secret Services, I quickly found that to get at the facts I had to create my own mini-intelligence organisation!

Therefore I must put on record my deep appreciation of what my team of spies and researchers achieved over the past few years. There were no fewer than twenty-three of them covering all areas of the world, slowly building up a picture of what the Chinese Intelligence Service has been doing in each territory where it operates. The operation had the code-name of "Jackdaw".

Often it was a case of referring a report from Taiwan to a source in Hongkong for checking, or tracking the answer to a clue found in Seoul to a college in Cambridge. To the best of my knowledge no one member of the team knew any of the others, so there was

8

no opportunity for collusion. Sometimes reports came by post, sometimes by hand; occasionally there were cryptic cables, including one which said that "the jackdaw is a voracious bird"! Some valuable information has been obtained by analysing messages picked up by ham radio fans, two of whom picked up some remarkable scoops in this manner.

I hope this will seem an objective work. Though the setting up of a personal espionage system to obtain most of the data could be construed as a "hostile act", I like to feel that the end result is to show some admiration and much sympathy and understanding of many, if not all, of the things which the Chinese People's Republic are trying to do.

2

The Five Varieties of Spying
550-450 BC

The end and aim of spying in all its five varieties is knowledge of the enemy.

Sun Tzu

WHILE I am not here concerned with the purely military and strategic side of Sun Tzu's *Principles of War*, it should be mentioned that the bulk of his dissertation deals with these. "War," he states in his preliminary considerations, "is a great affair of state, the realm of life and death, the road to safety or ruin, a thing to be studied with extreme diligence."

In philosophic mood he goes on to say there are "five threads to the warp of its texture"—the Ethic, Heaven, Earth, Leadership and Material. "Ethic it is which makes the people at one with their rulers": Chairman Mao would hardly disagree with this sentiment. Heaven, he explains in rather subtler fashion, must be interpreted in the sense of divination, divining the right moment to act, the right moment from the point of view of the seasons and elements and the right moment tactically. In referring to Earth he means knowledge of the terrain, ability to assess distances and the time taken to cover them. Leadership is self-explanatory, but by "Material" he made it clear that this covered morale of officers, drill and discipline of the men and supplies given to them.

There is perhaps nothing remarkably sagacious in this summing up of established facts, but it is worth noting that more than two thousand years later Kuropatkin, when reporting to the Czar upon the Russo-Japanese War, said: "Today more than ever the moral strength of an army is governed by public opinion. Therefore in order to be successful, a war must be popular, the whole people must strive for success in harmony with the Government. But the aims that we pursued in the Far East were understood neither by our soldiers nor their officers."

That great military genius, Ts'ao Ts'ao (third century A.D.), actually worked on Sun Tzu's text and is said to have "drastically cut out all redundancies and reduced the work to thirteen chapters". E. Machell-Cox, in the introduction to the R.A.F. edition of Sun Tzu, states that "the great and baleful Ts'ao Ts'ao had left a pregnant, if somewhat gnomic commentary on it" (the works of Sun Tzu).

Whatever the full truth, it seems indisputable that the thirteen chapters existed in Ssu-ma Ch'ien's time more or less in the form that we have them today. They convey in a remarkable fashion the direct, lucid mind of the soldier, the keen and accurate observer and something both of the philosopher and strategist. The simplicity of Sun Tzu's statements is such that he may often seem to the sophisticated modern Westerner to be tritely turning what is self-evident into original thought. For those who may feel this I can only say that he was setting down for the very first time axioms of military strategy and espionage tactics which have over the centuries become too obvious. But, as Mr Machell-Cox wisely comments: "Sun Tzu

10

is fundamental and, read with insight, lays bare the mental mechanism of our enemy. Study him and study him again. Do not be misled by his simplicity."

Today Sun Tzu would probably be what we call a "back-room general". The outline of his career is sketchy and one cannot be sure that he was the leading general in the field in the campaigns of his era. He was undoubtedly the adviser on military matters to the King Ho Lu, yet he does not seem to have been the all-conquering campaigner such as Wu Yuan, Po P'ei and Fu Kai, all of whom are mentioned as leading generals of Ho Lu. But that he was the planner behind their victories does not seem in doubt.

In his *Impartial Judgements in the Garden of Literature* Cheng Hou has this to say about Sun Tzu: "His thirteen chapters are not only the staple and base of all military men's training, but also compel the most careful attention of scholars and men of letters. His sayings are terse, yet elegant, simple yet profound, perspicuous and eminently practical. Such works as the *Lun Yu*, the *I Ching* and the *Tso Chuan* all fall below the level of Sun Tzu."

Sun Tzu ranged over the essential qualifications for generalship and command, the evils of political control (meaning the interference of a King or prince with his general), military intelligence, the economics of war, how war could be waged at the enemy's expense in forage, the handling of forces, tactics, field lore, psychological signs and portents and a whole host of subsidiary questions.

But it is when he deals with "the use of spies" that Sun Tzu most reveals his far-reaching grasp of the essentials of national security. For one who would seem to be obsessed with the need for spying he certainly did not reveal any weakness for exploring the time-wasting bypaths of espionage. The first point he makes is that from which the quotation at the beginning of Chapter One of this book is taken. Expounding the theory that a properly organised spy system can save money rather than waste it, he says:

"Raising a host of a hundred thousand men and marching them great distances entails heavy loss on the people and a drain on the resources of the State.

11

The daily expenditure will amount to a thousand ounces of silver. There will be commotion at home and abroad and men will drop down exhausted on the highways.

"Hostile armies may face each other for years, striving for the victory which is decided in a single day. This being so, to remain in ignorance of the enemy's condition simply because one grudges the outlay of a hundred ounces of silver in honours and emoluments for spies is the height of inhumanity. One who acts thus is no leader of men, no present help to his sovereign, no master of victory." [1]

The word "spy", for which there is a single character in the Chinese language, may at first seem obscure, for in ancient times this character was said to denote "a chink", or sometimes "a crack" or "crevice". But from any of these meanings we can derive the sense of a peep-hole, so it would seem that the original Chinese conception of a spy is one who peeps through a crack.

Sun Tzu's arguments of the economics of war and their link with the need for efficient espionage can be appreciated in their true context when one bears in mind that in the China of this period it was customary for a state to be divided into blocks of about fifteen acres. Nine such blocks formed a unit. The tenants of eight such blocks cultivated the ninth for the state. In wartime one of the families had to serve in the army, while the other seven contributed to its support. A levy of a hundred thousand men would affect the economy of seven hundred thousand families besides their own.

Thus Sun Tzu developed the theory that to wage war economically and to defend the state against war there should be a permanent espionage service aiming at gaining knowledge of both neighbours and enemies. "Foreknowledge cannot be got from demons, nor of experience (which becomes out of date)—it must be got out of men—spies." [2]

There should be five varieties of spying and five different types of spy. He named these spies as "the local spy", "the internal spy", "the converted spy", "the condemned spy" and "the ordinary spy". "When

12

these five kinds of spy are all at work, none can discover the secret system." Sun Tzu called that system "the divine manipulation of the threads, the most precious treasure of any prince of men".

Local spies meant employing the services of the inhabitants of a district and the point was made that "in the enemy's country, one should win over people by kind treatment and so enrol them as spies". There is no hint that they should be threatened or blackmailed: recruitment was to be based on showing good will.

Internal spies were defined generally as enemy officers or civil or military personnel, winning them over and using them as sources of intelligence. Some guidance was given as to the type of person who might usefully be sought to serve in this capacity: "worthy men who have been degraded from office, criminals who have undergone punishments, favourite concubines who are greedy for gold, men who are aggrieved at being in subordinate positions, or who have been passed over in the distribution of posts, others who are anxious that their side might be defeated, fickle turncoats who like to have a foot in each camp".

Such people should be approached secretly and whenever possible won over by means of presents: the emphasis was much more on the "rich present" than the blunt bribe. "In this way you will be able to find out the state of affairs of the enemy's country, ascertain the plans that are being formed against you, and moreover disturb the harmony and create a breach between the sovereign and his ministers."

Sun Tzu went further than merely recruiting spies in enemy territory in this way. His aim was also to convert the enemy's spies into his own service and, he added, "by bribes . . . to induce them to carry back false information as well as to spy on their own countrymen".

From subsequent commentaries on Sun Tzu over the ages it appears that some Chinese generals took the view that a wiser course was not to try openly to convert an enemy spy, but to pretend he had not been detected and then to contrive to let him take away a false impression of what was going on. But this was not Sun Tzu's view. He believed that such tactics, far from being cautious, actually involved grave risks, as one could never be sure that the enemy spy had not realised what was happening. Instead he insisted on treating the converted spy generously and ensuring his allegiance.

The tactics of the "condemned spy" was something rather more devious and, in a literal translation from Sun Tzu, may even seem obscure. Indeed, it is possible to interpret the purposes of the "condemned spy" in a variety of ways. Lionel Giles, who translates "condemned spies" as "doomed spies", defines this tactic as "doing certain things openly for purposes of deception and allowing our own spies to know of them and report them to the enemy".[3]

In the R.A.F. translation "having spies condemned is doing something to deceive abroad, and having our agents declare it and remain with the enemy". Again, a somewhat vague interpretation, but this is supplemented by a footnote which explains that such tactics cover the activities of the Japanese envoy, Kurusu, who totally misled the United States on Japanese intentions prior to the attack on Pearl Harbour.

Lionel Giles, after citing various authorities on Sun Tzu, states that such a tactic would mean that the condemned spies "would be those of the enemy, to whom our own spies had conveyed false information". He adds that this is "unnecessarily complicated. Tu Yu gives the best exposition of the meaning:

" 'We ostentatiously do things calculated to deceive our own spies, who must be led to believe that they have been unwittingly disclosed. Then, when these spies are captured in the enemy's lines, they will make an entirely false report, and the enemy will take measures accordingly, only to find that we do something quite different. The spies will thereupon be put to death.' "

All of which shows that, though he might sometimes adopt an attitude of benevolence and cajolery, Sun Tzu could also be devastatingly ruthless in his use of spies. In the *Ch'ien Han Shu* Li I-chi is described as playing the role of a condemned spy in 203 B.C. when sent by the King of Han to open peaceful negotiations with Ch'i. Subsequently the King of Ch'i was attacked without warning by Han Hsin and, angered by the treachery of Li I-chi, he ordered the latter to be boiled alive.

On the subject of "ordinary spies" (some translators call them "surviving spies") Sun Tzu had this to say: "This is the ordinary class of spies, properly so called, forming a regular part of the army—those who bring back news from the enemy's camp." Such a spy should be a man of keen intellect, in outward appearance a fool; of shabby exterior, but with a will of iron: "He must be active, robust, endowed with physical strength and courage; thoroughly accustomed to all sorts of dirty work, able to endure hunger and cold and to put up with shame and ignominy."

Again one must stress that in this period the vast subcontinent of China was to the Chinese all that was known of the world. And it was a world in which, though divided into several states hostile to one another, all people spoke the same language. To this extent the duties of an ordinary spy were somewhat simplified. Deception was that much easier: the man of one state could easily pass for the citizen of another.

In a commentary on Sun Tsu's ideal "ordinary spy" Ho Shih told how the Emperor T'ai Tsu sent Wu Ta-hsi to spy upon the enemy: "He was accompanied by two other men. All three were on horseback and wore the enemy's uniform. When it was dark they dismounted a few hundred feet away from the enemy's camp and stealthily crept up to listen until they succeeded in catching the passwords used by the army. Then they got on their horses again and rode boldly through the enemy camp under the guise of night-watchmen. More than once, happening to come across a soldier who was committing some breach of discipline, they actually stopped to give the culprit a sound cudgelling! Thus they managed to return with the fullest possible information about the enemy's dispositions, and received warm commendation from the Emperor, who, in consequence of their report, was able to inflict a severe defeat on his adversary."

Sun Tzu was so adamant about the absolute necessity of espionage always being successful that he insisted on designating the "ordinary spy" as the "surviving spy". The implication was clear: any spy who did not survive did not deserve to be a spy.

He also urged that "with none in the whole army are more intimate relations to be maintained than with spies". The spy was to be privileged even to enter the general's private sleeping-tent: he should have direct access to his leader at all times. And ruthless though he could be in his attitude to "condemned spies" and to the King's favourite concubines, he laid down that "in connection with the armies spies should be treated with the greatest kindness".

So, in Sun Tzu's conception, the good spy was a superior being, a great hero and one to be honoured. It was a concept that has too often been ignored by later military leaders, especially in some Western countries, where Army leaders have frequently been, and still sometimes are, contemptuous of spies, even those of their own side.

All communications with spies should be conducted by "mouth to mouth", so it would seem that Sun Tzu did not favour written reports. By implication he would also seem to have taken the view that a written report could be coloured or inexact, lacking spontaneity, whereas a verbal report could be checked by instant questioning so that the spy would not have a chance to change his story as he might do if he wrote it down. In any case most of the spies of that day would be unable to write reports of real value.

But, though warning that in dealing with spies one must be sure as to their integrity of character, experience and skill, Sun Tzu was emphatic that they could only be managed with "benevolence and straightforwardness" and that "when you have attracted them by substantial offers, you must treat them with absolute sincerity, then they will work for you with all their might".

With Sun Tzu it was a case of the iron hand in the velvet glove, an exceptionally subtle blending of the liberal and the authoritarian. Thus, "if a piece of secret news is divulged by a spy before the time is ripe,

16

he must be put to death together with the man to whom the secret was told".

He also laid down as a function of intelligence that "whenever you shall desire to crush an army, to assault a city, or to slay a single man, you must first have knowledge of that army's defensive dispositions, its leader, his staff and confidants; of the city's gates; of the individual's household. Our spies must be instructed to seek knowledge of these things."[4]

The enemy's spies who "came to spy on us" must be sought out and "tempted with bribes, led away and comfortably housed". In this way they would become "converted spies", available for service. Sun Tzu's axiom was that it was through the information brought by the converted spy that it was possible to acquire and employ local and inward spies: "We must tempt the converted spy into our service, because it is he who knows which of the local inhabitants are greedy of gain, and which of the officials are open to corruption. It is owing to his information, again, that we can cause the condemned spy to carry false tidings to the enemy."

"A truly enlightened prince and the truly wise general take only the wisest for their intelligence which is of vital import in war and is the means whereby your armies should move." Sun Tzu gave examples of this from past history, referring to the "god-like wisdom of Ch'eng T'ang and Wu Wang", which led them to employ I Lin and Lu Shang—and this again suggests that espionage was effectively practised even before the fourth century B.C.[5]

Nevertheless it was Sun Tzu who spelt these things out concisely and in text-book form. What he preached and wrote formed the basis for Chinese espionage over many centuries, being constantly revised and adapted and the source of most new ideas in its field.

3

Mutual Espionage 450-50 BC

The beast called the dragon can be tamed and trained to the point where you may ride on its back, but on the underside of its throat it has scales a foot across that curl back from the body and anyone who brushes against them is sure to die.

Han Fei (the Legalist philosopher)

Sun Tzu put espionage into perspective, analysed its implications and moulded it into a system, governed by rules, which has stood the test of centuries. But, as one would suspect from his findings, he was already able to build on the foundations of an internal code of espionage which had been adopted by certain of the various Chinese kingdoms for a long time.

There has been a curious tendency among some Westerners to equate the tightly knit internal security system of Mao's China with that of other Western communist states. A parallel there may be, but it goes no further than that. Mao, with that sense of history which is the hall-mark of political wisdom, has been most careful not to borrow his theories from the West, but to expand into a contemporary, egalitarian philosophy many of the teachings of the past. No one has been so careful to concede that China has a great heritage on which the wise can usefully build and adapt. This is in part at least a measure of his success.

In the fifth century B.C. the philosopher Mo Tzu advocated a system of "reporting good and evil to superiors", under which groups of families would be mutually responsible for each other and obliged to denounce each other's crimes and weaknesses under pain of dire collective punishment. This system was adopted in some kingdoms. It was not so much a system of tyrannical law and order as an attempt to civilise a whole community, to enforce good behaviour.

From Mo Tzu to Mao Tse-tung is a long step and yet, as will be seen, the philosophical link is there. What Mao has done is to take the materialism out of Marx and, in a subtle and almost romantic way, to try to breathe into Marxism an idealism which the Western communists have missed. What Mao says in effect is that Chinese communism is what life was really like in the golden age of China before there were slaves and when communal freedom was enhanced by the teachings of the early philosophers.

One must remember that the oldest written records of Chinese history were contained in the inscriptions on bones dug up by farmers near the city of Anyang at the end of the nineteenth century. The writings on those bones differed very little from modern Chinese and they revealed that a literate, civilised society existed in China as long ago as 1300 B.C. Scholars were honoured even at this early date, and when Confucius went to school about 540 B.C. he not only learned to write the difficult Chinese language, but to study history and mathematics. He, too, belonged to the state of Lu, where he started his career as a Collector of Grain Tithes. It was his teachings, concerned almost entirely with the art of living and codes of conduct, which influenced both Mo Tzu and Sun Tzu to some extent, though each was much more authoritarian in approach than Confucius would ever have been.

In the fourth century B.C. the numerous small states and kingdoms of China had, by partial amalgamation, been reduced to seven. One of the most powerful of these was Ch'in, where feudalism was absolished, men were conscripted for the army, villages were grouped into larger units and Mo Tzu's system of internal espionage was introduced. In effect this meant that every household in each group of villages was responsible for the behaviour of every other household.

In the following century this not immoderate system

19

of "mutual espionage" was welded into something much more of a tyranny by the first Ch'in Emperor, Ch'in Shih Huang Ti (259–210 B.C.). He was ambitious, ruthless and desirous of conquest. Not for him the moderation and humanism of Confucius, but the code of the Legalist Philosophers who declared that men were not naturally good, that it was impossible to trust them or depend on their sense of good will: only by an iron hand could they be curbed and tamed.

Ch'in Shih Huang Ti tightened up internal security by repressive measures. He ordered the burning of Chinese literature, condemning it as something totally subversive: and any man who was found with as much as a tiny fragment of Confucian teachings in his possession was put to death. Ch'in Shih took as his personal philosopher the legalistic Han Fei; though there is some irony in this because Han Fei had cunningly interpolated into his works advice on how a minister might exploit his ruler: "Don't waste wisdom on him until you have fully insinuated yourself into his confidence, adapt your arguments to his state of mind, never try to prove him wrong, give him credit for every success even when the idea was yours and he had opposed it." Li Ssu, Ch'in's chief minister, took care that his master never read this part of Han Fei's works. As a result he remained the power behind the throne of a dictator who acquired the largest empire in China, built the Great Wall to keep out the barbarian hordes to the north and extended his realm to the far south and the sea, including in it the states of Wei, Chao, Yen, Han, Ch'i and Ch'u.[1]

Scholarship was discouraged except for that which was strictly practical and uncontroversial. Hundreds of scholars were tortured and executed, but many of these managed to hide their books, bricking them up inside walls or in the roofs of houses, even in the tombs of their ancestors. A Board of Censors was set up to check the activities of the mandarinate itself in much the same way as the Control Commission of the Chinese Communist Party checks its officials and cadres today.

Li Ssu was, however, sufficiently flexible to feel

there was some advantage to be gained by having a few scholars as his tame allies. He therefore advised the Emperor to announce that seventy selected scholars were to live permanently at court "to advise the ruler". There is little indication that their advice was sought and one doubts if they ever risked giving it unasked.

One wonders if Li Ssu was haunted by that passage in Han Fei's works which he suppressed from his master; because after the Emperor died Li Ssu arrested Han Fei and forced him to commit suicide. Retribution swiftly overtook him, for after he had quarrelled with various Legalist philosophers he lost his office and eventually died under torture.

An empire had been established and, through dictatorship, the unification of a number of states achieved, but Ch'in Shih Huang Ti had left behind him an unhappy legacy. Learning has always been deeply respected by all classes in China and the resentment against the burning of books lingered for centuries. Because of Ch'in Shih Huang Ti's glorification of war a reaction set in. As Chinese literature re-established itself so war came to be denounced as evil and alien to the spirit of the people.

It was not until the Han dynasty came into being that a form of Civil Service was created in China and paved the way ultimately for a more hierarchical Secret Service than that advocated by Mo Tzu. But though it became a branch of the state it was almost certainly not as effective as Mo Tzu's "mutual espionage" among households, depending largely on the Confucian theory of its holding "the mandate of Heaven". This was a bureaucratic but benevolent Secret Service on the whole, so unconcerned with the normal affairs of espionage that it was more judicial in its functions than anything else, yet curiously without any legal powers. It was, like the rest of the Civil Service, intensely inward-looking, and existed to preserve the *status quo*. Even the precepts of Sun Tzu were temporarily forgotten.

In the meantime, though the emphasis was on a centralised security system, the people themselves had little but contempt for it and many of them tended for both their personal needs and their political ambitions to form secret societies. The Chinese have shown over the ages a positive genius for organising themselves into secret societies. The importance of some of these societies to anyone tracing the eventual development of a national Secret Service cannot be underestimated. Down the centuries they helped both to destroy any effective centralised Intelligence body, rendering it insignificant, and, at other times, to contribute towards new concepts of intelligence. There is no doubt at all that the modern Chinese Secret Service has been since the latter part of the nineteenth century influenced, moulded and developed through the many secret societies that have sprung up throughout its history. These societies have worked like a series of rocket-boosters to periodically propel Chinese espionage into a system that is unique in the world.

This is not to assert that the secret societies have been miniature secret services, though in some instances they have acted as the intelligence organisation of a sect or body of people. Whatever motives may have given them birth, they need to be studied before one can begin to understand the contradictions and complexities of Chinese espionage.

One of the commonest types of these early secret societies was that of a money-lending fraternity; another was a mutual defensive organisation against bandits. Some societies would start because a few people wanted to build up reserves of money as a mutual protection fund against the misfortunes of life. Each would contribute a sum, loans would be made to the less fortunate among members and meetings would be held to decide who should replenish the funds and who borrow from them. Even in these early ages such societies were extremely efficient and, above all, kept their dealings secret. From similar societies today among exiles all over the world Chinese espionage is effectively and silently financed in the most economical fashion.

Inevitably, as these ancient societies grew, they became rather more political in their aims. A money-lending society could develop into a protection society against bandits and that in turn would evolve into a secret sect for plotting the overthrow of a rival society or even a government. Mo Tzu himself had founded a secret society whose aim was to defend the poor and the weak, though it demanded from its members the kind of discipline and obedience that would ensure that "the faithful would walk through fire or on sword blades" if so ordered.

During the Han dynasty (203 B.C. to A.D. 220) there was a Red Eyebrows Society and a Yellow Turban Society. The former was a group of rebellious farmers, who caused a great deal of trouble to the dynasty, while the latter comprised peasants led by an itinerant magician who trained his members in military tactics and organised them into communes. The Yellow Turbans eventually grew into a huge organisation which revolted against the régime. Something of their size can be gauged from the fact that in one insurrection they lost more than half a million members in battle.

Some secret societies were religious organisations linked to Taoism and Buddhism. There was even one secret society organised by wives who employed as members men who spied on the women's husbands. There were also other societies that were mainly criminal in their activities, but on the whole they professed good even if they practised it in a devious and somewhat contradictory manner.

Such societies admittedly scarcely seem like the foundations or even the offshoots of a Secret Service in the modern sense and a purist would say that they are irrelevant to the main purpose of this book. Nevertheless they were basically societies engaged in forms of intelligence—local, professional, occupational or even matrimonial—and to omit mentioning them would be to miss the intensely esoteric and catholic flavour of the Chinese intelligence system, which is so frequently concerned in matters with which any other Secret Service would never trouble itself. These were the early forerunners of later, more sophisticated and certainly more terrible secret societies which became

23

appendages of the espionage organisations of the emperors of China.

One of the most difficult things to pin-point in Chinese intelligence today as much as yesterday is where it begins and where it ends. It is exceedingly hard for any Westerner to draw exact borders within which to confine this subject. This is perhaps due in no small measure to the fact that when the early mandarins of the Civil Service first attempted to seek intelligence and to analyse it they relied greatly on that extraordinary work *I Ching,* or *The Book of Changes.* And, as C. J. Jung wrote about this work, "the Chinese mind, as I see it at work in the *I Ching,* seems to be exclusively preoccupied with the chance aspect of events. What we call coincidence seems to be the chief concern of this peculiar mind, and what we worship as causality passes almost unnoticed. We must admit there is something to be said for the immense importance of chance. . . . While the Western mind carefully sifts, weighs, selects, classifies, isolates, the Chinese picture of the moment encompasses everything down to the minutest nonsensical detail, because all of the ingredients make up the observed moment."[2]

We will look at *I Ching* again later, along with other works that have affected the development of Chinese espionage. For the moment it is as well to remember that when the Civil Service was first organised in China it was of a calibre unknown in and vastly superior to anything found in Europe. Entry was by competitive examination, the civil servants themselves were all scholars and so, in the first century B.C., it evolved out of the mandarinate. The Secret Service was not named as such: there was no word for it. A rigid historian would deny perhaps that anything approaching such an organisation existed. But it was there, like a pale, flickering light, living anonymously in the realm of the Reminders, a hierarchy of senior civil servants who were part administrators, part ombudsmen, part advisers and collectors, guardians and interpreters of intelligence.

As a security service it may have lacked the cohesion and precision of its predecessors and it was certainly

24

not as oppressive or as ruthlessly effective as they had been. There was no single service devoted solely to intelligence: the Reminders had many tasks to fulfill and intelligence-gathering was only one of them. They had no powers of punishment or arrest: they were simply and solely advisers. But their advice was based on a widespread internal intelligence system and it was heeded more often than not.

It is within the scope of this intelligence system that one must look to discover some of the original genius of the Chinese interpretation of the functions of an Intelligence Service. Much of the information which the Reminders sought was extraordinarily enough for the purpose of making the life of the people happier. To find a parallel to this one must imagine the American C.I.A. being detailed to travel around Alabama to find out what makes the Negroes there so wretched, what individuals were contributing to this and how blatant extravagance by the whites could cause racial tensions.

The basis of administration and the code of ethics of the Reminders was Confucianism, which had now come back into favour. The department which dealt with intelligence reports and advised on them was known as the Censorate. It was the duty of a Reminder, for example, to advise an Emperor to curtail extravagant spending, if this was known to be having a bad effect on public opinion. He could also inquire into individual cases of exploitation and intimidation as well as conditions in prisons. It all sounds more like a society of benevolent ombudsmen rather than an espionage service, yet espionage for the benefit of the people it undoubtedly was.

Occasionally, but this was rare, an Emperor would resent the advice of a Reminder and punish him. Yet the proof of the efficacy of the system was that it lasted for so many years that in A.D. 1600 a visiting European wrote that "the Reminders are both revered and feared and regarded as the equal of princes".[3]

4

An Occult Approach to Intelligence 50 BC-AD 265

In it are included the forms and the scope of everything in the heavens and on earth, so that nothing
escapes it. In it all things everywhere are completed,
so that none is missing. Therefore by means of it we
can penetrate the tao of day and night, and so understand it. Therefore the spirit is bound to no one place,
nor the Book of Changes to any one form.

(trans. of *I Ching* by Cary F. Baines)

CONSULTATION of *I Ching*, or *The Book of Changes*,
by the early sifters and analysers of Chinese intelligence continued for centuries and no doubt some of
its precepts and certainly the training it provided have
subconsciously influenced even contemporary assess-
ments of all intelligence gained. For, while the teachings of *I Ching* may seem like cabbalistic mumbo-
jumbo to a Westerner, one must remember that it
provided philosophy and mental stimulus as well as
occult practices. Nor does it behove the Westerner to
sneer at the use of astrology and mysticism when one
recalls that espionage and occultism have been inextricably mixed in the leading Secret Services of the
Western World down the ages. Even in World War
II both the German and British Secret Services actually engaged astrologers and one of them, Louis
de Wohl, was made an Army captain, given a room
in the War Office and commissioned to make horo-
scopes of Hitler to forecast his future moves. There
was, of course, a sound practical reason for this in
that Hitler was known to consult astrologers and

frequently to act upon their advice. All de Wohl had to do was to make use of his knowledge of the methods of Hitler's astrologers and to work out the same kind of forecasts that they would come up with.

Richard Wilhelm has declared that *I Ching* is "unquestionably one of the most important books in the world's literature . . . and it has occupied the attention of the most eminent scholars of China down to the present day. Nearly all that is greatest and most significant in the three thousand years of Chinese cultural history has either taken its inspiration from this book, or has exerted an influence on the interpretation of its text."[1]

This is a sweeping assertion and yet it is not easy to find any evidence to contradict it. The origin of *I Ching* dates back into what can only be described as mythical antiquity. Both Confucianism and Taoism, not to mention the works of Lao-tse and such modern scholars as Lin Yutang, have their roots in the *Book of Changes*. Some indication of the power and influence of *I Ching* can be gleaned from the fact that it was the only book which was not condemned to be burnt by the Emperor Ch'in Shih Huang Ti. It was honoured and consulted by statesmen and scientists.

Of course the *Book of Changes* has been distorted and even exploited dishonestly by scholars, cranks and charlatans of other nations; and again, as Richard Wilhelm writes, "hair-splitting cabbalistic speculations came to envelop it in a cloud of mystery".[2] But under both the Ch'in and Han dynasties its teachings emerged as a formalised philosophical system and an almost compulsory source for consultation.

It could be argued that the Chinese depended too much on *I Ching* as a kind of mystical computer that would always provide the right answers, and that this hindered their progress in the spheres in which the Western World started to draw ahead of China. Certainly this is true to a very great degree, though it cannot all be blamed on *I Ching*. But in the context of intelligence or, more accurately, the interpretation of intelligence, to dismiss *I Ching* as irrelevant would be to ignore fundamentals.

Nobody can say for certain when the first text of *I*

Ching appeared, but it was probably between 1200 and 1100 B.C. In the following centuries it became a work that was consulted not only by all scholars who wished to establish the true answer to some abstruse question, but also to solve many purely simple domestic problems as well. Its inspiration was sought by fathers wanting to know to whom and when they should marry off their daughters, by generals seeking guidance on how to win battles and by spies seeking information they could not gather by conventional methods. Even the language of Sun Tzu's textbook on espionage suggests that he was influenced by its general principles: his similes and metaphors were in substance those of *I Ching*. More important still, the psychological teachings of *I Ching*, though not in any esoteric or cabbalistic form, can be traced in the methods employed by the Chinese Secret Service today. Mao Tse-tung himself has turned *I Ching* to his advantage in the same way that he has turned Marxism and communism into the totally different Maoism.

All this needs to be said before explaining, how exactly the *Book of Changes* has been, or is, used. But before going into these details it should be made quite clear that it is the philosophy and teachings of *I Ching* that have lasted and that the practice of consulting it is certainly not encouraged in China today. This may seem like a contradiction of what has already been written, but then the Chinese genius has survived because of and not in spite of its contradictions. Or, to cite one of my anonymous informants: "In China we live and think in balanced extremes. If you take humility and gentleness and add to it arrogance and militancy the result is moderation. When the Chinese genius expresses itself moderation is the result. Of course, at all times and all moments it does not work this way. But as the sub-conscious aim is always in this direction overall it works."

When the ancient Chinese had an intelligence problem—that is to say, one they could not solve by normal processes—they would turn to the *Book of Changes*. They would place the book on a table which faced south. Then they would take fifty yarrow stalks (although it could just as well have been matchsticks), put one aside and, holding the remaining forty-nine in the hand, let them trickle onto the table. With quick movements of the right hand the fallen yarrow stalks would be divided into two sections; these would be further divided so that the final result was three sections of stalks, representing one line of a hexagram. I will not go into minute details of how the numbers of stalks in each section indicated a continuous *Yang* or a broken *Yin,* because for this to make sense the *Book of Changes* would have to be studied in depth: I might add that it has baffled many Western scholars, including those who are also Sinologists. But ultimately the whole system would be repeated twelve times until two hexagrams were established, at which point the *Book of Changes* would be consulted to find the meaning of each hexagram.

When the confrontation between China and India occurred in the mid-sixties I am told that certain members of Chiang Kai-Shek's Secret Service in Taiwan turned to the *Book of Changes* for an answer as to whether or not Mao would succeed in his objectives. The first answer that came was:

Six at the beginning means:
When ribbon grass is pulled up, the
      sod comes with it.
Each according to his kind.
Perseverance brings good fortune and success.

It then seemed even to his opponents in Taiwan that Mao was right. They next put the question: "India has been confronted and she seems tactically to have been defeated. What happens now?" The answer came:

Nine in the fifth place means:
Standstill is giving way.
Good fortune for the great man.
What if it should fail, what if it should
      fail? In this way he ties it to a cluster
      of mulberry shoots.

The interpretation of this by the Taiwanese—and one must assume that Peking would have arrived at the same conclusion—was that the right man, able to restore order, had arrived. The issue of the frontiers was clear and it was in China's favour. But in such a period of good fortune it was unwise to press success too far: success was only assured with the greatest caution. Therefore this was the moment to halt and consolidate. Or, as Confucius might have put it, "Danger arises only when a man feels secure in his position. Therefore the superior man does not forget danger in his security, nor ruin when he is well established, nor confusion when his affairs are in order. In this way he gains personal safety and is able to protect the empire."

The paradox of the Chinese is that, though a nation of gamblers, the very thought of the risks they take imbues them subconsciously with a great sense of the need for caution. Perhaps they have gambled so much and so often that they always bear in mind the possibility of failure. Individually gambling may work disastrously; collectively it seems to be leavened with an instinctive quest for the antidote to failure.

"To explain in modern terms just how the *Book of Changes* was used for so many centuries by those dealing in matters of espionage is not easy," my Taiwanese informant explained. "Espionage deals in facts, but you must remember that very often the facts do not fit into a pattern; they cannot easily be explained; they may even contradict one another. It is then necessary to interpret them, to discover the missing link that would explain all.

"In the West you would do this by a laborious process of checking and double-checking, of spending a long time trying to discover more facts. You might arrive at the right answer when it was too late, or you might never find it at all. Or you would use what you call intuition. Your spy chief would say, 'I feel it is really like this—I can't tell you why, but I have a hunch.'

"Well, we Chinese would somehow think along other lines. We would not be so arrogant as to go on our hunches and we would be impatient for an answer and would not want a prolonged search for something we might never find. We should also have enough gambling instinct to turn to the *Book of Changes*. But it would still mean something more than all this. You in the West might turn to prayer for inspiration. We would turn to the *Book of Changes* not merely to seek inspiration and guidance, but also to let its inherent wisdom seep into our minds. We should get an answer from the *Book*, perhaps not the one we sought, or wanted to hear, but we should act on what it told us.

"You must try and understand that the *Book of Changes* is not the sort of thing you look up and get one simple answer. You don't ask a question such as 'who are the spies in our midst?' and get a name or names in response. What you get is guidance, something that hints who they might be, or where they might be found. Curiously enough, I can recall one example of this question actually being posed.

"It was in Macao when I was on a mission there. My companion and I had good reason to believe that there was a spy in our midst. Certain information was coming back to us that could only have come from a spy.

"But we had no inkling of who he might be. He could have been one of three people. I said, 'Let's consult *I Ching*' and we did. The answer that came up was:

"Six in the fifth place means:
Remorse disappears.
The companion bites his way through the
    wrappings
If one goes to him,
How could it be a mistake?"

I indicated to my informant that if I had been given such an answer I should have been totally baffled. He giggled. "Well, yes, even a Chinese could be puzzled at first," he replied. "So were we. Then we pondered the inner meaning. What it really meant was that in some way we had what you English so delightfully call 'barked up the wrong tree'. There was a man among our three suspects who was not what he might seem. He was an ally of ours and at the right moment

31

he would reveal himself and then we should trust him and work with him.

"We waited a while and sure enough one of those three men turned out to be not a spy, but a double-agent who had been posing as an enemy agent."

My friend, however, admitted that not every spy master among the Chinese, whether of Taiwan or Peking, consulted *I Ching*. "It would be regarded as superstitious to play with yarrow stalks today whether in Peking or Taiwan, but this does not mean that the *Book of Changes* is not respected. I am reliably informed that Mao Tse-tung has always been fascinated by the book and has reaped great benefit from it. But this does not mean he consults it. I am an exception, if you like. But it is a mere coincidence that I am a believer in *I Ching* and an intelligence officer. You must not think that I consult the book *because* I am an intelligence officer."

There was one further question I put to my friend: "What about the failures of *I Ching*? How often did it fail?"

"It is not the book which fails. What you learn from it can only be wrong in the sense that you do not understand it, or misinterpret it. If you are attuned to *I Ching,* you should not misinterpret it. But even when you interpret it correctly, it is true that you may not find the correct answer. Therefore it follows that if you do not find the right answer, the fault may be one's own. If you pray to God and he does not answer your prayer, you do not blame God, or you shouldn't. Nor should you blame *I Ching*."

Whether Mao Tse-tung is fascinated by the distilled wisdom of the *Book of Changes* I do not know. I have heard from two sources that he has occasionally made reference to it in conversations. What is certain is that a great source of inspiration to him, especially in his early days, was the *San Kuo* (*The Romance of the Three Kingdoms*) referred to in the first chapter.[3]

"One reason why the *San Kuo* should be just as compulsory a book for students of espionage in China today as is *The Art of War* is that Mao Tse-tung has based many of his tactical moves on what he has learned from that work," was what the foreign correspondent of the *Independent Evening Post* of Taipeh told me.

The Romance of the Three Kingdoms is an extremely long historical novel written by Lo Kuanchung of the Yuan dynasty A.D. 1260–1341), its plot being based on events covering the period from A.D. 168–265. It opens with the threatened decline of the Han dynasty in the reign of Ling Ti and the insurrection of the Yellow Turbans. At this time Liu Pei, a descendant of the Imperial Family, entered into a solemn compact with Kuan Yu, now the deified God of War, Kuan Ti, and Chang Fei to help each other to uphold the tottering dynasty. Liu Pei later assumed royal power and became known as Chao-Lieh Ti, and the empire was divided into three states, Wei, Shu and Wu. Tyranny and bloodshed mark the narrative for nearly a century until the usurper Ts'ao Mao of the Wei is deposed by his Minister, Ssu-ma Ch'ao, whose son became the consolidator of the empire and founder of the Tsin dynasty, being the Wu Ti of history.

This work clearly shows how the *Book of Changes* was consulted by directors of spies of the period, notably by Kuan Yu, and its pages are filled with ingenious spy plots, espionage techniques, and examples of the teachings of Sun Tzu put into practice.

It relates how when K'ung-Ming proposed to renew the attack on Wei, Chiang-Wei defeated the army by means of a forged letter. A spy was captured and he insisted that he was "not really a spy in the bad sense. I was bringing a secret communication for you, but I was taken by one of the parties in ambush."

He added that he was a confidant of Chiang Wei who had given him the secret letter for Ts'ao Chen. The letter stated:

"I, Chiang Wei, your guilty captain, make a hundred protestations to the great leader, Ts'ao, now in the field. I have never forgotten that I was in the employ of Wei and disgraced myself: having enjoyed favours, I never repaid them. Lately I have been an unhappy victim of Chuko Liang's wiles and so fell into the depths. But I never forgot my old allegiance. How could I forget? Now happily the army has gone west and Chuko Liang trusts me. I rely upon your leading an army this way. If resistance be met, then you may simulate defeat and retire, but I shall be behind and will make a blaze as a signal. Then I shall set fire to their stores, whereupon you will face about and attack. Chuko Liang ought to fall into your hands. If it be that I cannot render service and repay my debt to the state, then punish me for my former crime. If this should be deemed worthy of your attention, then without delay communicate your commands."[4]

Ts'ao Chen was pleased by the letter and rewarded the spy, telling him to return and say the plan was accepted. Ts'ao Chen was nonetheless advised not to fall into the trap.

The book contains many examples of the kind of deadlock that often ensued as a result of warring espionage groups being keenly matched in the battle of wits. It explains a good deal of the intricacies of the Chinese character, not least in the words it puts into the mouth of Ts'ao, who killed the entire family of his host on one occasion simply because he believed —quite wrongly—that they were plotting against him: "I would rather betray the whole world than let the world betray me."

Thus the villain of the *Three Kingdoms* is really its hero, about whom a poet composed this epitaph when he died in A.D. 210:

> *The thoughts of heroes are not ours*
> *to judge,*
> *Nor are their actions for our eyes*
> *to see.*
> *A man may stand the first in merit; then*
> *His crimes may brand him chief of*
> *criminals.*
> *And so his reputation's fair and foul.*
> *In all things great, his genius masters*
> *him.*

Dennis Bloodworth wrote in *The Chinese Looking Glass* that "American military analysts now pay serious attention to *The Romance of the Three Kingdoms,* for it has gradually dawned on the West that the inspired trickery practised by that legendary third-century slyboots of a strategist, Chuko Liang, remains as subtly influential among the Chinese as an early mother's knee-sermon. Recognised as a worthy preceptor by Mao, carefully studied by the Vietcong guerrillas in South Vietnam, Chuko Liang was a 'Sleeping Dragon', a sage in retreat who never wielded a sword, for the essence of the great Chinese military tradition has always been that brains baffles brawn."

It is not generally appreciated that the Chinese were advanced seamen long before any European nation. Not only did they invent the sternpost rudder more than a thousand years before Christ, but they used craft in a semblance of naval warfare in the first and second centuries A.D. When Wang Chun's spies returned with news that the enemy had laid chains across the river and erected giant hammers as obstructions to ward off any naval assault, he ordered his men to make numerous rafts and to fix to them straw effigies of men garbed in armour. The rafts were then sent down the river with the current. When the enemy saw them approaching they immediately believed they were being confronted by a large force, panicked and fled.

Then Wang Chun sent a small number of manned rafts down the river. The crews lifted the giant hammers out of the water without meeting any opposition. Armed with torches soaked in linseed oil, they lit these when they came against the chains across the river and held them against the links until they melted and broke. Thus, according to *The Romance of the Three Kingdoms,* "a spy ruse saved the day and rafts went downstream, conquering wherever they came".

5

Empress Wu's Bronze Urn and Wang An-shih's Family Spy System AD 48-1076

We should be apprehensive and careful
As if we were on the brink of a deep gulf,
As if we were treading on thin ice.
The Book of Odes

CHINA'S attitude to women has always been ambivalent. On the one hand there is the old Chinese saying that "among those who cannot be trained or taught are women and eunuchs", while on the other there is the precept laid down in *The Book of Filial Piety* (second century B.C.) that "an Emperor first sets an example to his subjects by showing a dear love to his mother".

Yet down the centuries China has produced some remarkable women both as rulers and as scholars, and the first female historian was Chinese—Pan Chao (A.D. 48–110). Her diligent scholarship over the years resulted in the *Han Shu,* which she started with her brother and which ran into ten volumes. But even she was sufficiently aware of the low esteem in which women generally were held that in one of her books she wrote: "I am a humble person, but with a monkey's wit."

Pan Chao had another brother, Pan Ch'ao, who was not only a soldier but one of the first of the Chinese leaders to attempt systematically to obtain intelligence from outside China. He not only crossed over to the western borders of China, but made excursions deep into the heart of Central Asia to visit some of the tribal kingdoms. His sister, however, played a considerable part in all this, both in advising him how to set about his mission and in helping to compile his intelligence reports on his return when he was received as a great hero and given the title of *Ting Yuan,* or "Pacifier of Distant Lands".

It was no easy task for a young and relatively inexperienced man who was literally going into the unknown. He had been on the Commander-in-chief's staff, but never before had he been given such an important assignment. But there seems to be abundant evidence that what he lacked in experience was compensated for by the lessons of history imparted by his sister. Pan Chao had recorded in great detail the fate of a much earlier traveller, Chang Ch'ien, who also had ventured into this terrain and who had been captured by the Hun and kept prisoner for ten years. Sister Pan Chao had given her brother all the information which Chang Ch'ien had brought back with him on his escape from imprisonment. She warned her brother that he must set out with only a very small party so that it would be clear to the tribesmen that he had not come prepared to attack anyone. By this means he might win allies. His brief was to observe what went on, to make an assessment of the tribes he visited and to find among them allies who would help to defend China from the raids of the Hun.

Pan Ch'ao had some of the lively gifts of observation and originality of a Sir Richard Burton and much of the panache of a Commando leader, allied to undoubted talents as a wise and enterprising spy. But to his sister he still owed an immense debt for her advice and suggestions.[1]

It was in A.D. 73 that Pan Ch'ao arrived in what is now known as Turkestan with a mission of only thirty-six men. He very soon discovered that the first tribal king he visited was secretly receiving a Hun delegation at the same time. Pan Ch'ao also sensed that the Hun was making a more favourable impression on the king than he was. Thereupon he detailed his party to find out as discreetly as possible where the Hun delegation was being lodged. They discovered the native official who had been given the task of looking after the Hun delegation, locked him up and then set out at night to surround the Hun quarters.

Remembering no doubt Sun Tzu's teachings on the value of the use of fire to draw out an adversary, Pan Ch'ao ordered fires to be started and then, when the Huns came out of their quarters, his party set upon them and killed all the Huns who escaped from being burned to death in their tents. Pan Ch'ao took the head of the leader of the Hun delegation and presented it to the tribal king.

It was an astonishing risk to take because the tribal king could easily have disarmed the small party of Pan Ch'ao and ordered their arrest, or even their execution; but Pan Ch'ao felt that psychologically he had impressed the king who had previously believed that the Huns were unconquerable. His judgement— or could it have been the judgement of his sister?— was right, for the tribal king immediately agreed to make a treaty of alliance with China and to offer his son as a hostage as an assurance that he would keep to his pledge.

Pan Ch'ao made alliances with other native kingdoms, again following the precepts of Sun Tzu that spies and allies should be won with "gifts and kindness". It was the policy of "containing the barbarians", which became known as *i yi chih yi,* and was to be the fixed method by which China dealt with aggressive neighbours over the next thousand years. He travelled far into the Gobi Desert, won to his side one tribe after another, engaged the best of the tribesmen as spies and in due course won authority over a vast area of Central Asia, almost to the thresholds of Europe. Altogether he spent the best part of thirty years in Central Asia, having won the allegiance of something like fifty tiny tribal kingdoms. He was only recalled to China after his sister had made a special petition to the Emperor, asking that he might be allowed to retire: "He is hard pressed by old age and like a horse or a dog that has long served his master, he has lost his teeth." Shortly after his return he died.

Pan Ch'ao was thus the first man to establish an external espionage system for the Chinese empire and in this connection it is worth noting again that as far as the Chinese people were concerned the only world that mattered was China itself, so that this probing into the outer world was not a result of aggressive policies, but of a desire to live at peace with her neighbours.

A few centuries later (A.D. 625–705) another remarkable woman wielded power in China. As a tiny chit of a girl, aged twelve, she came from obscurity to the Imperial Palace of T'ai Tsung of the T'ang dynasty to become one of the Emperor's concubines.

This arrival of a dominant, highly successful female monarch was not altogether unforeseen. Astrologers pointed out towards the end of the reign of T'ai Tsung, founder of the T'ang dynasty, that the star Venus was in the ascendant and visible in daylight for several days in succession. This, they declared, meant that a female would be all powerful in China in the near future. They were even prepared to go further than this and to assert positively that a female named Wu Wang (the Martial Prince) would come to power.

She eventually arrived and her name was Wu Chao.[2] She was beautiful, intelligent and apparently astonishingly far-sighted and full of initiative at a very early age, making full use of the concubinate to learn the arts of diplomacy and intrigue. Realising that the Emperor had not many years to live she surreptitiously turned her attention to the Crown Prince. When the Emperor died, with a great display of dignity, she made a studied, pious gesture by entering a cloistered retreat.

Wu Chao's departure was quickly noticed by the Crown Prince, who became the new Emperor, and he promptly brought her back to the Court and reinstated her in the concubinate. Eventually he divorced his wife and installed Wu Chao in her place. One can imagine that such upheavals in the hierarchy caused problems for the secret police of the day and they foolishly split up into rival factions, some supporting the new Emperor, others backing Wu Chao. But it did not take long for Wu Chao's strong character to influence a somewhat reluctant monarch and she began to assume many of his powers. She used this influence mainly to eliminate all likely successors to the monarchy: when her husband died, Wu became Empress in her own right with full powers to rule.

It had been announced that a stone had been found in the Lo River bearing a mystic inscription which read: "The Holy Mother has come among men to rule with perpetual prosperity." This was presented to the Empress as a symbol of her overlordship.

Her methods were as ruthless as those of any man. She had brought about the divorce of the previous Emperor's wife by implementing her in a bogus plot to poison the Emperor, involving another favourite of the concubinate as well. Wu Chao is also said to have poisoned one of her own sons and to have murdered several other princes. She established spies among the women of the concubinate and created her own personal force of secret police.

Indeed, she was the first ruler of China to set up a Sovereign-controlled Secret Service which in authority and effectiveness was practically omnipotent, though it took some years before she completely eliminated other branches of secret police not under her control. The main task of her personal secret police in the earliest days—long before she became Empress—was to keep her informed of all possible rivals, either among the women of the concubinate or males likely to succeed the Emperor. By the time Wu Chao became Empress she knew exactly who her enemies were and she proceeded to have them murdered, publicly executed or sent into exile, not merely according to her whim, but to her careful consideration of the effects of each sentence on public opinion. Rarely was such a despot so acutely conscious of the value of understanding the feelings of the people: it was Wu Chao's saving grace.

To ensure that none of her late husband's family would challenge her supremacy she stamped out any revolt by eliminating brothers, cousins, nephews and uncles one by one. Not even the Empress's son-in-law, Hsueh Shao, husband of her favourite daughter, escaped this ruthless purge. He was not actually killed, but merely allowed to starve to death in prison. Slowly, too, those secret police who were considered either hostile to the Empress, or thought to be conniving with her enemies, were also liquidated.

Prior to her coming to the throne the head of police and torturer-in-chief had been Lai Chun-ch'en. During the years 689-690 he, aided by his confederate, Chou Hsing, had denounced and executed a number of people who were regarded as opposing the new regime. But the Empress, who so shrewdly informed herself of the motives which actuated her henchmen, soon realised that in many instances Lai Chun-ch'en and his secret police were pursuing private vendettas of their own. Matters came to a head when these two secret police chiefs attempted to stage a Watergate-style scandal around the figure of the revered and honest Hsu Yu-kung. The latter had tried to secure the acquittal of a provincial governor who had been framed by Lai Chun-ch'en: the secret police then sought to prove that Hsu Yu-kung was plotting to release criminals from jail.

The Empress decided that whatever uses Lai Chun-ch'en may have had in the past, he was now over-reaching himself and playing a personal power game. When the secret police chief demanded the execution of Hsu Yu-kung, she refused his request, though agreeing to dismiss him from office. This was a ploy on her part to play for time, for she trusted Hsu Yu-kung absolutely, but wanted to prevent Lai Chun-ch'en from suspecting her true motives. The Empress was sure that the honest Hsu Yu-kung would sooner or later reveal his own doubts about the chicaneries of the secret police.

And so it proved to be. When sometime later Wu Chao promoted Hsu to the office of Censor, thus recalling him to favour, he sought an audience and declined the appointment, saying: "I have heard that a deer on the hills and in the forests is hunted constantly for its flesh. Your Majesty wishes to make me an officer of the law, but I would not dare to connive at the perversion of Your Majesty's laws, thus I will certainly be done to death."[3]

Wu Chao fully understood now what he was hinting at and realised that many of the executions and persecutions carried out in her name by the secret police

were not to safeguard her own position but to increase
the powers of Lai Chun-ch'en and Chou Hsing. She
insisted that Hsu Yu-kung should take up his office
as Censor and from then on the ascendancy of the
two secret police chiefs began to wane. The Empress
decided that the best method of trapping this pair of
rogues was to set one against the other.

Chou Hsing had been accused of having been in
touch with a recently executed general, so the Empress
summoned Lai Chun-ch'en and asked him to investigate the case against his principal aide. It was a risk,
but Wu Chao felt sure that Lai Chun-ch'en would not
hesitate to hide the purpose of his investigation from
his closest associate. This proved to be the case. Lai
invited his colleague to dinner and then asked Chou
Hsing to think up some new method of forcing accused persons to make confessions, subtly hinting that
in many instances what was wanted was a false confession from an innocent victim.

Chou Hsing, who had a ready answer for most
queries of this nature, did not hesitate for a moment.

"That is quite simple," he said. "You just have a
cauldron of boiling water, bring in the accused and
say to him, 'Unless you confess at once, you will be
thrown into the cauldron.' What else can he do but
confess, if he wishes to escape death?"

Lai Chun-ch'en then had a cauldron of boiling water brought into the room in which they were dining.
Pointing to it, he said to his colleague: "My friend,
we have ample evidence against you, so, unless you
heed my advice, you had better jump into the cauldron."

Chou Hsing, of course, confessed all, and to eliminate the first of the secret police leaders, the Empress
ordered his immediate banishment to Kuangtung. But
whether by some hint dropped by the Empress to
her own personal secret agents, or as vengeance for
one of the persons he had unjustly executed, Chou
Hsing was murdered on his way to exile.

Lai Chun-ch'en was for the time being allowed to
carry on in his office in the belief that he had the full
confidence of the Empress, but from that day his every move was watched by Wu Chao's own agents.

Having begun her reign in such a despotic and blood-thirsty manner, the Empress then ruled with a surprising benevolence which, by oriental if not occidental standards, could be interpreted as aiming for the greatest good for the greatest number. In some ways she could be compared with the Russian Empress, Catherine the Great. Certainly she had the same sexual appetite, taking lovers until she was well into her seventies.

Her secret police were maintained as efficiently as ever and they gradually acquired supremacy over the official Secret Service of Lai Chun-ch'en. If her courtiers lived in terror of them, their effect was to instil honesty and loyalty into the Empress's advisers. But Wu Chao genuinely wanted to have an independent source of intelligence; she was wise enough to realise that the instrument she had created could, if not made to understand that she had other sources of information, become a monster which in the end would hold her in its grip.

Wu Chao then created what became known as the Bronze Information Urn. The Empress ordered this urn to be set up outside the Imperial Palace so that any citizen, however humble, could put into it any note, petition or letter, or (if he could not write) get some professional letter writer to do the job for him. The object of this urn was to provide the Empress with intelligence, to keep her in close touch with what the ordinary people were thinking. It is perhaps worth comparing it with the Yellow Box which, nearly 1,200 years later, the Czar set outside the Winter Palace in St Petersburg.

As I wrote in *A History of the Russian Secret Service*, "A Czar who wanted to know what his people thought and felt and to learn what they observed might have gleaned much from the Yellow Box. But Paul merely allowed these reports to develop phobias in his own mind so that on the strength of hearing that an officer wore his hat at the wrong angle he had him sent to Siberia."

Wu Chao, the ex-concubine, was much wiser. She realised that much of the information she could receive would be worthless, but, as she told her advisers, "to find a perfect gem one may have to travel for years across the length and breadth of one's kingdom. It is simpler and quicker to let others travel and bring what they believe to be gems to me." To test the intelligence of the people who would drop items of information into her urn, she decided to give it four slots. Into one slot citizens could put petitions, in another they could place evidence of maladministration, treachery or complaints against the regime (including, of course, the Secret Police!); in the third slot they could include demands for setting wrongs right, including suggestions for the promotion of worthy people; in the fourth slot (and in some respects this proved to be the most useful of all) were to be placed "prophecies".

It was in the sphere of prophecy that the Bronze Urn produced a remarkable amount of diverse information and not just speculative forecasts. Whereas in Russia, even in the eighteenth century, such a request would have brought forth a mass of superstitious mumbo-jumbo and the cranky gibberings of itinerant monks and members of strange sects, in China in the seventh century it stimulated not only many wise forecasts based on genuine evidence, but a wealth of factual intelligence. Perhaps some of the donors of such intelligence had consulted *I Ching,* but whatever the source of their prophecies, they invariably supported them by convincing facts.[4]

Thus the Empress Wu benefitted from the Bronze Urn where Czar Paul was to fail lamentably with his Yellow Box. She listened to criticism and, if she thought the critics had something useful to offer, she gave them office. Through the information that trickled into the Urn she was able to dismiss incompetent officials, check corruption and set right many wrongs. Indeed, the Urn proved so useful that in the long run, towards the end of her reign, Empress Wu was actually able to dismiss her secret police.

C. F. Fitzgerald writes of the problems confronting the Empress prior to the introduction of the Bronze Urn, saying that officials had not always sent informers to the capital and that though there were "informers in all parts of the Empire . . . people held their

44

tongues and did not dare to hold discussions", adding that later the Empress used her own system not only to discover "lurking nests of opposition, but also to promote useful men who were brought to her notice as informers. The Empress remained very suspicious of the higher ranks of the official world and was determined to have men whom she could trust about her. This aim soon converted the intelligence system into a veritable secret police which gradually assumed more and more power, and used it more and more cruelly. . . . The rapidity of action and efficiency of the new secret police was surprising to an age when such methods were largely unknown, and certainly more unfamiliar than they are to our own."[5]

It is perfectly true that in the early years of her reign Empress Wu made full use of the official secret police, under Lai Chun-ch'en, who were as brutal as any in history. They devised the most frightful and ingenious tortures by which to exact confessions and actually started a School of Torture which had its own text-book setting out the subtlest of methods by which these barbarities were to be practised. All one can say in favour of their system was that in its diabolical cunning and sophistication it achieved far greater results than those so unimaginatively practised centuries later by Himmler and Beria. There was even an attempt to lure the victims of persecution into believing they were just being called in for a friendly chat over a cup of fragrant tea by inscribing over the entrance to the Secret Police headquarters, torture chambers and prison the words *Li Ching Men,* meaning the "Gate of the Exquisite View"!

Opinions among Chinese scholars today differ somewhat on the subject of the Bronze Urn. There seems to be no doubt that it was given the Empress's full blessing and therefore set up in the Hall of Audience. However, some authorities suggest that the actual idea for the urn came from the son of one of the Censors. But I rather think this assertion may be merely a part of the legends of the times, as it has also been said that an enemy of this same alleged inventor of the Urn deposited incriminating evidence against him into the Urn with the result that the originator of the Bronze Urn lost his head.

One of Empress Wu's most illustrious advisers and sifters of intelligence from the Bronze Urn was her personal Head of Intelligence, the mandarin Ti Jen-chieh, who was not only Secret Service chief, but a judge and detective as well. It was the exploits of Ti Jen-chieh that inspired the eighteenth century detective stories which were created around his name, known as the *Dee Goong An*, later to be adapted and fictionalised by the Dutch diplomat, Dr R. H. Van Gulik, in his series of books known as the "Judge Dee Stories", since popularised on television and cinema screens.

Many of the Judge Dee stories are pure fiction, though based on the life of the period, but some of them are undoubtedly partially factual. It would, however, be rash to cite any of them as evidence. Yet they do reveal something of the sophistication of this loyal and honest servant of the Empress and his uncanny knack of sniffing out plots against her, solving crimes which baffled the secret police and generally protecting his ruler—who is reported to have wept bitterly at his death.

Ti Jen-chieh was something of a philosopher who looked on the sifting of intelligence rather like solving a crossword puzzle or reading fortunes by cards. As far as the Bronze Urn was concerned, what interested him most was the slot in the Urn which faced north, entitled "Penetration of the Abstruse" and into which were supposed to be submitted the prophecies, forecasts based on factual evidence and all "plans for secret military strategy". But Ti Jen-chieh only came to power after a lengthy battle of wits with Lai Chun-ch'en who at one time managed to have his adversary arrested.

Lai Chun-ch'en always varied his modes of obtaining confessions according to the people he interrogated. On this occasion he had asked the Empress in advance to decree that all those who confessed their guilt would have their lives spared. Ti, as wily as he was loyal to his Empress, without any prevarication or delay, straight away told his interrogators that it was true

46

there had been a conspiracy, but that it was against the old officials of the T'ang.

Having confessed, Ti was allowed a measure of freedom, though still kept under close watch by his guards with whom he soon made friends. He complained to them that the weather was so hot that his coat was unsuitable: would they kindly return it to his home and ask his son carefully to remove the thick woollen lining. Unsuspecting, the guards agreed to do this, not realising that inside this lining Ti had hidden a letter to his son. This letter ordered his son to seek an immediate audience with the Empress at which he was to explain the false plot that had been launched against him by Lai Chun-ch'en.

Empress Wu was shown the letter which had been hidden in the lining of Ti's coat. Immediately she sent for Lai Chun-ch'en and demanded an explanation. The secret police chief, who was always a resourceful thinker on the spur of the moment, replied that as no clothes had been taken away from the prisoners it was quite impossible that such a letter had been smuggled out. Therefore it must be false. To try to settle the matter quickly he produced a faked confession from Ti, at the end of which the latter asked for a death sentence as punishment.

At this point the situation for Ti looked bleak indeed, but his life was saved by an unexpected intervention. A 10-year-old nephew of one of the secret police's victims also secured an audience with the Empress and when asked why he had come, the boy replied: "My father is dead and my family ruined, but this is due to the fact that Lai Chun-ch'en and his men have perverted Your Majesty's laws. If Your Majesty does not believe it, ask any of your Ministers, whom Your Majesty knows to be loyal and pure, and in whom Your Majesty puts trust. The conspiracy is the work of Lai Chun-ch'en himself."[6]

After that the Empress sent for Ti Jen-chieh who was able not only to gain his own freedom, but to obtain from the Empress the release of the other men arrested with him.

The fate of Lai Chun-ch'en was a difficult one for the Empress to arrange satisfactorily without considerable loss of face. It was true (and she knew it would always remain a stain on her character) that for many years, to ensure her position and eliminate her enemies, she had depended heavily on Lai Chunch'en: to order his death now might raise the question in the minds of her advisers as to whether she would ever defend any of her Ministers. So Lai Chunch'en was demoted to a relatively insignificant appointment in one of the other provinces: it drastically reduced his status and re-assured his enemies by clipping the previously uncontrolled powers of the secret police.

Ti Jen-chieh from then on became the Empress's most trusted adviser and one who inevitably seemed to anticipate the slightest threat of danger to her person, and whose judicial interpretation of intelligence reports made him renowned as the wise man of the Court.

Early in the tenth century A.D. China had a foretaste of the communist doctrines which were to be introduced to the nation with the coming of Mao Tsetung. The name of this purveyor of a primitive form of communism was Wang An-shih, a brilliant and studious young man, who, at the age of twenty-one, passed the state examinations for a doctorate.

A scholar he may have been, but he certainly was no aesthete: "how can poetry prepare the mind for an administrative post?" was his carping query. It was not an original criticism even in those days. Chinese philosophers had nearly always kept their feet firmly planted on the ground and Confucius himself had suggested that the memorising of the three hundred odes was pointless if someone who knew them was given an assignment and did not know how to act.

Wang An-shih probably regarded much of the learning of his day as being what the modern Chinese would call "deviationism", in the sense that any philosophy, ideas or learning which detracted from the urgent tasks in hand tended to make people deviate from reality. He was born into an age of intellectual turmoil when the Sung dynasty was weak and when many long-established beliefs were being questioned. At the age of thirty-six he submitted to the Emperor a thesis advocating a number of reforms, which became known as the *Ten-Thousand Word Memorial*. It is a classic model for posterity on which, no doubt, Mao Tse-tung has based much of his thinking. His aim was to carry out drastic land reforms in favour of the peasants, to cut Government expenditure *and* to increase Government revenue. One proposal was to set up a state credit bank for farmers, loans being given in the spring and paid back after the autumn harvests. He preferred taxing citizens to conscripting them, and to use the taxes to pay for work on state projects. Pawnshops were to be nationalised and interest rates reduced.

Wang was swiftly promoted, first to the Treasury, then to the Chancellery and, finally, to a post specially created for him and to which, in modern parlance, one can only give the name of Minister of Economic Planning. When his mother died, he went into mourning and retirement for three years, after which he was made Governor of Nanking. Finally he was made a Privy Councillor by which time his planning ministry had as many as 1,080 rooms for his staff and files.

It was at this time that he tackled the question of espionage. The country was in an unsettled state, suffering from banditry and lawlessness, and Wang decided that a comprehensive spy system was required to combat all this. His system owed much to the Legalist philosophers and to the teachings of Mo Tzu about "reporting good and evil to superiors". Always let it be noted, in considering *any* Chinese system of espionage, that the emphasis was as much on reporting good as on reporting evil. Therein lies the subtle difference of their system from that of the rest of the world.

Apart from organising communes and families on an economic basis, Wang An-shih also introduced a tithing system whereby families were organised into units of ten, fifty, and five hundred. All members of these units were responsible not only for the crimes of any single member, but for those committed by any strangers, relatives or guests who were staying with them. There was also a proviso that they should report on good deeds as well, so the system maintained a

49

certain balance and did not degenerate into a means of persecution.

Confucianism had made the family into a very strong unit, but one that tended until then to be inward-looking, to protect itself and have little care for the national interest. Wang's plan was to make each citizen and family feel that they were an important and integral part of the nation. The carrot which he dangled in front of them was that of protection by the state, in return for which the family kept the state informed of what was happening. Peasant farmers were freed from the racket of tax collection, but requested to collect their own taxes; instead of being conscripted into the army, they were hired to do work for the state; and the looting by soldiers of peasants' crops and possessions was effectively checked by Wang's army reforms.

The spy system he instituted became a model for future generations. It was lost sight of in some centuries, but it was revived both by the Manchu dynasty and the Kuomintang, while Mao Tse-tung has himself brought his espionage system of today far closer to that devised by Wang An-shih than any other in history. But the main point today is that the emphasis is on the fact that the Wang An-shih methods are regarded as good education and, under Chinese communism as much as any other system, good education is looked upon as the key to people's hearts and minds. It can hardly be said that this is true of western communism with its emphasis on conserving strength through brute force.

Wang himself was devoted to improvements in the educational system of China and, to quote one of his sayings, "the more the soaring bird sees below, the better he can be emulated by those he observes" is a typical oblique reference to his appreciation of how education could improve the quality of espionage. He re-organised the National University and insisted on greater care being taken in the selection of students. He was an egalitarian with a keen realisation of the need for an élite. He instituted studies in medicine and military science.[7]

It was the power of Wang's mind, his ultra-efficient,

down-to-earth practicality which enabled him to get his own way. In many respects he was an unattractive personality—quarrelsome, doctrinaire and, by all reports, dirty in his personal habits: it is said that he had to be forced into a bath by his servants. He was honest to the point of being almost super-human and this may have been one reason for his survival in an age when such a virtue was rare, yet he was described as being "dressed like a barbarian and eating the food of pigs and dogs". Yet he continued to enjoy the support of his Emperor even despite the criticisms of the powerful Reminders. His power lasted until the year 1076 when the Emperor dismissed him, though giving him the title of Duke, and his reforms lasted for many more years until they were gradually eroded. Nevertheless his influence has lasted down to the present day as that of an idealist who sought to improve the lot of his countrymen.

6

Challenge of the Mongols 1076-1692

In Xanadu did Kublai Khan
A stately pleasure-dome decree,
Where Alph, the sacred river, ran
Through caverns measureless to man
Down to a sunless sea.
Samuel Taylor Coleridge

GRADUALLY the system and order which Wang An-shih had brought to China were eroded away. The army was neglected and starved of horses for its cavalry and so the nation became wide open to the depredations of the barbarians to the north and west.

Barbarians they may have been in comparison with the Chinese, but their achievements were formidable, their successes of a kind that makes the deeds of Alexander the Great and Napoleon seem like minor military campaigns.

It was in 1222 that Genghis Khan returned to his native Mongolia after his devastating conquests of large areas of Western Asia, much of Russia, some of Eastern Europe, including Poland and lands up to the Baltic Sea. But still he was not content: there were other horizons to conquer and of these China was by far the most attractive. Perhaps he had a premonition that he would eventually die in action for he always insisted that "my children may one day dwell in walled cities and make their homes in stone houses, but I shall always live in a tent, a nomad's life".[1]

Yet in his last years this uncultured Mongol genius revealed a passionate desire to learn something of Chinese thought and teachings, to which end he had a Chinese philosopher brought to stay in his camp. Meanwhile he bided his time for a Chinese campaign. When the Golden Emperor of Cathay unwisely asked for Mongol aid in his continual war upon the ancient dynasty of Sung in South China, the Mongols sent Chepe Noyon with a cavalry force to fight beside the Cathayans, using them as spies to prepare the way for a surprise attack. Subutai, Genghis's foremost general, went to study the situation in North China and sent back various reports for suggested action, but Genghis still hesitated about attacking a civilised power. He never realised his dream of conquering the whole of China because five years after his return to Mongolia he was killed in battle.

Genghis's sons carried on their father's campaigns and within six years of his death they had secured Korea, whose total submission was won by Subutai, and a great part of northern China. However southern China remained free and was still being firmly ruled by an Emperor of the Sung dynasty when, in 1260, Kublai Khan inherited the whole of the Mongol empire.

In these early years of Mongol threats China was out-manoeuvred by the superior external espionage system of the enemy. Cathay had been cleverly infiltrated and Mongol spies were ordered to bring back

Chinese informers. Whenever the Mongol armies advanced they took with them interpreters, who were used to administer the captured areas, and merchants whom they employed as spies.

The Chinese may have been slow to react to the Mongol spy threat, but on a much smaller scale they, too, did some effective infiltration, though of a somewhat oblique kind. It is quite possible that the Chinese philosopher who went to stay in Genghis Khan's camp had been a secret agent. Certainly Ye Liu Chutsai, one of the leading officials of the Kin empire that was overrun by the Mongols, was acting on the principle that infiltration pays when he accepted Genghis Khan's invitation to assist in governing this new acquisition to the Mongol empire.

Ye Liu Chutsai was able to ensure that the Kin empire was not totally Mongolised, that it retained an essentially Chinese form of administration and he was enabled to do this by convincing the Mongols that peace and security depended upon keeping the people content. Harold Lamb, in his biography of Genghis Khan, wrote that "Prince Ye Liu Chutsai laboured with heroic fortitude to consolidate the empire of the Mongols, while seeking to restrain them from further annihilation of human beings. . . ."

The Chinese were always sure that in the long term the Mongolian invasion of their lands would fail. Their attempts to obtain intelligence about the outside world and the Mongol empire were only made in desultory and haphazard fashion because they were not interested in extending their own territories, but only in containing the invader. And it could be said that one of their wisest coups had been to persuade Genghis Khan to provide a Chinese tutor, Yao Shih, for Kublai Khan. Yao Shih was always close to Kublai Khan, following him on his campaigns, whispering advice at his elbow; and it was partly due to his influence that the conquest of the Sung empire took so long and was relatively bloodless.

Yao Shih, like Ye Liu Chutsai, was in effect a powerful one-man Secret Service, aiming at curbing the excesses of the invader and maintaining the Chinese way of life. Though each man appeared to serve the enemy, neither was what in modern terms would be called a Quisling; both worked secretly for the good of their respective empires and in the course of time their people benefitted from it.

The subtlety of Yao Shih and indeed of the whole Chinese people in adversity is well illustrated by an anecdote handed down to posterity. On an occasion when Kublai Khan's forces were camping outside a walled Chinese city, poised for attack the following day, Yao Shih told his former pupil of the story of a Chinese general who took a city without killing a single inhabitant and without closing down a single business. "This was the highest kind of generalship," he told Kublai Khan.[2]

The message sunk home. Kublai Khan also wished to earn the accolade of supreme generalship from his former tutor. That night he ordered his soldiers to make banners on which were scrawled the message: "Do not kill on pain of death." Next day the banners were carried into the city and placed at key points in the market place and on street corners. The inhabitants surrendered peacefully and all were spared, including the soldiers forming the garrison.

When Kublai Khan became the first foreign ruler of China he preserved most of the ancient customs and laws, retaining Yao Shih as his adviser. The latter suggested Kublai Khan should retain the Chinese mandarins as administrators and this he did. He also persuaded the new ruler to defend Chinese culture and to set up a new centre for scholars in Peking. Then outside Peking at Xandu, the same place which Coleridge in his poem called "Xanadu", Kublai Khan built a splendid palace and created a royal park.

In effect it was the Chinese who retained their influence throughout Kublai Khan's reign, and when his successors revealed none of his virtues or enlightenment it was only a matter of time before once again the Chinese acquired mastery of their own lands. Kublai Khan was anxious to learn from the Chinese; those who followed him were ignorant and, in many cases, did not even wish to learn to read or write. Eventually the Chinese revolted and overthrew the barbarians, destroyed the palace at Xandu and established the first Ming Emperor as ruler of China.

From that moment for many centuries to come China turned her back completely on the outside world, closed the ports which Kublai Khan had opened to international trade, restricted foreign immigration drastically, ended all external intelligence and discontinued cultural relations with other peoples.

China sought only to preserve her own heritage, to keep it uncontaminated from outside influences; in short, to shut her eyes to the outside world and to believe that by doing so she could somehow avoid another catastrophe like that of the Mongol invasion. Over the centuries she managed, however, to enlarge her empire, adding on Mongolia, Sinkiang and Tibet to the main Chinese empire without in any way opening herself out to the rest of the world. The main aim of the "Secret System" of this period was to prevent the Chinese from having any close contact with Westerners. Indeed, to have attempted to bring in any information on the outside world in this era would have been almost an act of treason.

Internally espionage was less well organised than in earlier centuries. It was much more haphazard and, partly as a result of this, there sprang up a new form of Secret Service—the "Secret System" of the eunuchs. In the early stages there was nothing organised about the eunuchs' power game. They were castrated male servants of the women of the court and their numbers varied from one generation to another. Sometimes they totalled a few hundreds, at others they could be counted in thousands. Not surprisingly, in view of their numbers, some of them were exceedingly able men. They had close contact with the Emperors and court officials and thus either overheard or learned a great many state secrets. By reason of this they were able to form powerful groups of espionage, sometimes in the service of an Emperor, sometimes of a Minister or, quite often, in their own interests.[3]

One of the ablest of the eunuchs was Cheng Ho, a tall man with an air of authority, who was Head Eunuch of the Inner Court. The Emperor Yung-Lo made him an Admiral of the Fleet and he set about resolutely building up China's naval strength.

Cheng Ho in the fourteenth century was powerful enough to break to a limited extent the ban on contact with the outside world. Prior to his day most of the records of Chinese travellers to the west were those of Buddhist pilgrims. Cheng Ho determined to make annual expeditions by sea in quest of knowledge of the outside world, but even he was cautious in this respect, and it was clearly laid down that he should not attempt to conquer any other country he visited, or build up trade overseas. The object of the expeditions was to show the flag and reveal the might of the Ming dynasty.[4]

However, there were occasions when Cheng Ho went beyond the terms of his brief. When he visited Ceylon he captured the King and brought him back to China to pay tribute to the Emperor. The countries he visited included India, Borneo, Ceylon, Aden, Mecca (he was a Chinese Moslem) and parts of Africa.

There is some evidence that Cheng Ho amassed considerable intelligence on the countries he visited and that he wished to use this to impress the Emperor. But during his absence the other leading eunuchs had banded together and formed a powerful group whose main purpose seemed to be concocting false evidence to bring charges against their rivals. They not only opposed Cheng Ho's voyages on the grounds that they were needlessly extravagant, but ordered his logs and many of his reports to be destroyed.

Cheng Ho's reports could have been of immense value as a source of intelligence for future generations. When an Emperor asked to see them, it is recorded in the court archives that "the Minister Liu Ta-hsia extracted the Cheng files and burned them because he imagined that the contents were so bizarre and filled with exaggerations as to be incredible". On the other hand the policy of China still remained basically opposed to contact with the outside world and even when the emperors extended their empire it was not so much acquisitive as defensive, the aim being to

56

create a number of small buffer states between the empire and the barbarians.

On the whole this policy succeeded remarkably well within the limitations laid down, but one marked failure was the Vietnamese War of 1418–28. Vietnam had been dominated by the Ming dynasty for some years. True to their policy of winning over the leading men of any country they conquered, the Chinese had offered a position of honour and great wealth to one Le Loi, a Lord of the fief of Lam Son in Vietnam. He not only rejected their offers, but in 1418 proclaimed an armed revolt against the Ming, adopting the title of Binh Dinh Vuong ("The Pacification King").

For the next few years Le Loi steadily improved his position, gaining authority over wide areas of Vietnam and inflicting several defeats on the Chinese. By the end of 1427 86,000 Chinese troops had withdrawn from Vietnam and the country was completely liberated. It is perhaps not without historical significance that Le Loi made Hanoi the new capital.

It was a measure of the effective decline of Chinese espionage in this period that, in the words of one historian, a relatively unknown Jesuit missionary named Lafarge, "the failure of the Chinese to procure accurate intelligence in an area they knew so well [Vietnam] was such that they might almost never have occupied that land."

There were a few tentative attempts to correct this deficiency and to warn of its consequences. One such was the creation of the sixteenth century Chinese novel, *Chin P'ing Mei* (*The Golden Lotus*), a work that was for centuries regarded as so pornographic by Western translators that even as recently as 1939 Colonel Clement Egerton's version in English rendered all the naughtier parts in Latin.[5] In fact the novel is Rabelaisian rather than pornographic, erotic rather than salacious. It is said that the author of *Chin P'ing Mei* impregnated the corners of his manuscript with poison and sent it to the Prime Minister, an enemy of his, in the hope that the latter, licking his fingers to turn the pages, would meet with a fairly swift death.

So it may well have been, but there is little doubt

57

that, though the novel may have been intended to deal out death, it was a warning against corruption and faulty security. *Chin P'ing Mei* told the story of a prosperous family of Hsi-men Ch'ing and its ruination through corruption, bribery, promiscuity, the cult of the more bizarre forms of sexual activity, worldly ambition and indifference to the outside world. But the dire warning was wrapped up in a work of fanciful and erotic fiction that reads like a Chinese version of *Fanny Hill*—some of the sexual practices are so acrobatic that they cause the concubine Plum Blossom to say: "You mustn't do this again. It is simply not fun. My head and eyes swim so that I hardly know where I am."[6]

It may be that the legends which have grown around *Chin P'ing Mei* are purely symbolic. It could well be that the author sought first to arrest attention to his work by making it especially erotic, but that he warned the Prime Minister that if he licked his fingers avidly to turn the pages the more quickly he would be as surely poisoned as his own corruption and indifference was poisoning his country.

The decline in the quality of Chinese intelligence in this period, and indeed in some instances its almost total lack, paved the way to the Manchu conquest in the seventeenth century. In 1644 the Manchus occupied the imperial capital of Peking and set up the Ch'ing dynasty.

The Manchus, like the Mongols before them, were barbarians in comparison with the Chinese and because of this, and also because they were without any qualifications for administering a civilised country, they were forced to learn Chinese and to employ Chinese civil servants to enable them to govern. The result was once again that the Chinese culture predominated and it was the invaded who assimilated the conquerors rather than the other way round. Eventually the Manchu language fell into disuse and the Manchu regime became almost indistinguishable from a typical Chinese administration.

The Chinese empire expanded and, thanks to the military organisation of the Manchus, became easier to hold. And expansion of the empire once again brought China into contact with the Western World. Of all the Western visitors to China in the early part of the seventeenth century the Catholic missionaries made the greatest impression, especially the Jesuits, who were respected by the Chinese for their mathematical knowledge. Some of them were employed by the Government for making astronomical calculations and for regulating the calendar.

One of the foremost of these Jesuit priests was Adam Schall who, while in Peking in 1644, sent a petition to the Emperor requesting him to "test publicly the accuracy of the prediction of the solar eclipse at a proper time."[7] As a result of this Schall was made Director of the Bureau of Astronomy in Peking.

Schall's long-term aim was not so much to impress the Chinese with his learning as to use his influence to convert the Chinese to the Roman Catholic faith. Prior to this the Jesuits had been out of favour at the court and many of them had been expelled from China. Schall regarded the efforts of the earlier Catholic missionaries as crude and brash and inevitably inviting hostility, and he was quite content to bide his time and increase his influence before attempting any conversions. His regard for the wisdom and knowledge of the Chinese was much greater than that of his predecessors. His unostentatious methods paid off. In due course he made some thousands of converts, including fifty women in the Emperor's palace, some forty eunuchs and more than a hundred of the members of the Court.

Adam Schall effected a measure of infiltration into Chinese life far greater than that of any other previous Westerner. But he was faced with opposition on two fronts: first by jealous and hostile missionaries of other Catholic orders who criticised his methods— "the Jesuits would be shamed and confounded," they said[8]—and by the anti-Christian campaign of the rival Chinese astronomers.

Yang Kuang-hsien was the chief spokesman for the latter and in 1664 he denounced Schall in these terms in a petition to the Court:

"The Westerner Adam Schall was a posthumous follower of Jesus, who had been the ringleader of the treacherous bandits of the Kingdom of Judea. In the Ming dynasty he came to Peking secretly and posed as a calendar-maker in order to carry on the propagation of heresy. He engaged in spying out the secrets of our court. If the Westerners do not have intrigues within and without China, why do they establish Catholic churches both in the capital and in strategic places in the provinces? During the last twenty years they have won over one million disciples who have spread throughout the Empire. What is their purpose? Evidently they have long prepared for rebellion. If we do not eradicate them soon, then we ourselves rear a tiger that will lead us to future disaster."[9]

Though jealousy was the root cause of this Maoist-style denunciation of Adam Schall, anti-foreign feeling was running high and the Chinese counter-espionage team who had allied themselves with the compatriot astronomers genuinely feared that Schall aimed at usurping power at the Court. In the long term this was undoubtedly what he did seek, though it was power spiritual rather than power temporal. A full investigation of the charges against him was carried out and, by the standards of those days, Schall had a fair trial and remarkably humane treatment—far more so than he would have received at, say, the hands of Cromwell's judges.

He was acquitted of having perpetrated any astronomical errors, but was found guilty of plotting and encouraging heresy. The original sentence was "death by dismemberment", but on account of his age this was commuted to banishment. In fact he was allowed to remain in his Peking residence under house arrest. There he died in 1666 at the age of seventy-five. Meanwhile the Emperor's security forces set about preventing a recurrence of Jesuit intrigues. Catholicism was prohibited in China, missionaries were banished from the capital and churches were closed. Nevertheless Chinese respect for learning ensured that the valuable mathematical and astronomical work of Schall was not forgotten, especially as the investigation had upheld him in this. Two years after Schall's death the Emperor Shun-chih died and was succeeded by his 14-year-old son, K'ang-hsi, who with the questioning arrogance of youth began to doubt the accuracy of his own Chinese astronomers' calculations, thus indirectly causing events once again to veer in favour of the Catholics. Father Ferdinand Verbiest, who had assisted Schall in his work, had escaped persecution and he boldly decided to push ahead from where Schall had left off: he issued a challenge that the Chinese astronomers should verify their calculations which, he claimed, were wrong.

The Chinese astronomers made excuses to the Emperor, but he insisted on a thorough inquiry. The outcome of this was that the two chief Chinese astronomers, Yang Kuang-hsien and Wu Ming-hsuan, were arrested and Verbiest was made chief of the Astronomical Bureau. Soon Verbiest became one of the closest of the Emperor's advisers and almost certainly an unofficial personal Intelligence Officer to the young K'ang-hsi. He acted as interpreter for foreigners visiting the Court and received by the Emperor, learned Manchu and wrote a Manchu grammar, while spending much time in creating and inventing things to surprise and delight the Emperor—such as pulleys, sundials, water-clocks and miniature peep-shows. He set about reforming the calendar and soon found that his work at Court precluded him from many of his religious duties so that he had to write to the Father Superior asking for a dispensation, hoping that in time his efforts would be rewarded by converting the Emperor to Catholicism.

Curiously, this time it was the Catholics themselves and the Jesuits in particular who were most hostile to and suspicious of Verbiest. When he wrote to friends in Europe for funds to assist him in his work for building up the Imperial Observatory and paying the inevitable bribes, he used Flemish so that other Jesuits who might intercept his letters would not be able to read them. But there was almost certainly another reason for this subterfuge: some of Verbiest's letters contained requests for intelligence on the Emperor's behalf. He was especially asked to obtain information on the armaments of other nations. "It is recorded that in 1674," wrote Father Mation Ripa, that Verbiest was ordered to obtain details of and to ensure the delivery of "light but effective cannons, convenient for transportation" for use in putting down insurrection in South China.[10]

In 1682 Verbiest was made Assistant Director of the Board of Works because of his work in finding and producing armaments. By this time he was a key figure in the Chinese hierarchy. He was also chosen by the Emperor to accompany him on a visit to Manchuria and even during this trip he was pressed to continue his astronomical findings. It cannot be overstressed that to the Chinese mind in this period the top priority, in intelligence matters, was astronomical and mathematical calculation and knowledge of the stars and the heavens. For such information the Chinese would use bribery, espionage, theft and, if necessary, threats of death or imprisonment. This fact is important in assessing much of their contemporary attitude to all knowledge on space exploration.

Verbiest described in his diary how one night when the sky was clear the Emperor asked him the Chinese and European names for the stars appearing on the horizon: "he [the Emperor] himself named first those that he had already learned. Then, taking a little celestial map that I had given him some years before, he began to calculate from the stars what hour of night it was, taking great pleasure in showing those around him how much skill he had acquired in science."[11]

K'ang-hsi ordered Verbiest to prepare astronomical tables for 2,000 years into the future and to compose records of the latitudes of cities in Manchuria which were to be added on to all future Chinese maps. Over the years Verbiest's influence, due no less to his tact than his ability, steadily increased. He might have proved to be the ablest Intelligence chief China had for many years but for his untimely death in 1687 at the age of sixty-four when he was thrown from a horse. But he had already provided something China had previously lacked—a steady stream of intelligence from Russia, in which country he had acquired many valuable contacts almost entirely through his diligence as a correspondent.

The Emperor gave him a state funeral and for some few years after this the Catholic Church's position in China seemed much more secure. Indeed to some extent the Jesuits, who had criticised Verbiest, carried on his work as unofficial intelligence officers and it was largely due to their efforts that the Treaty of Nerchinsk in 1689 was drawn up between China and Russia. An edict of "toleration" of the Catholic Church was pronounced in 1692 and the Jesuits were permitted to build a church in Peking as well as to carry out a cartographical survey of the empire. But none of the Jesuits possessed Verbiest's tact or skill in negotiating with the Chinese and some of the later missionaries displayed the same brashness and crudeness of approach of their earlier predecessors. Slowly the Chinese critics of Catholic influence gained the upper hand, but the final blow was the abolition of the Jesuit Order in Europe by Papal decree.

Ho Shen:
Banker, Pawnbroker
and Spy Chief
1692-1797

I wake up in the morning and seem to hear someone
in the house sighing and saying that last night someone died. I immediately ask to find out who it is, and
learn that it is the sharpest, most calculating fellow in
town. Ah, is this not happiness?
—*Chin Shengt'an* (impressionistic critic of the seventeenth century)

BY the middle of the eighteenth century China already
had a population of some two hundred millions compared with Britain's seven millions. This fact needs to
be appreciated to understand how the Chinese, with
the largest population in the world and the most ancient of cultures, were able to view with downright
complacency if not controlled disdain the brash efforts of a tiny nation like Britain to spread its diplomatic tentacles in the Far East.

To the educated young buck of mid-eighteenth
century England the "grand tour" of Europe, taking
in mainly Italy and sometimes Greece and Turkey, was
the sum total of extending his cultural experience. It
was not until European travellers to the Far East became more numerous in the long reign of the Manchu
King, Chien Lung (1716-1796), that their reports
of the exotic beauties of China, the mysteries of its
"Forbidden City", created the romantic cult for
Chinoiserie. Then in France and England craftsmen

began to copy and adapt Chinese works of art, imitating the lacquered cabinets, painted porcelain, even the parasol; and reproducing pagodas and pavilions such as the one which the Prince Regent had built at Brighton.

The Forbidden City of Peking began to have a special allure for the more adventurous European traveller. It was still perhaps the most security-minded city in the world, this tight, compact, closely guarded walled city, set in the centre of the Imperial city. It was dubbed the Forbidden City because no one could pass through its gates except on official business. Inside its territory were the Emperor's Palace and many handsome residences. Nobody was allowed to leave this inner city without permission and this was very rarely granted.[1]

The Secret Service or "Secret System", as it was usually designated, which controlled the Forbidden City and protected the Emperor was a curiously balanced organisation depending almost equally on the mandarinate or upper bureaucracy and the eunuchs. Occasionally an Emperor might himself take closer control over the "Secret System", but more usually he depended on the intelligence he received from mandarins and eunuchs equally. But by the mid-eighteenth century the power of the eunuchs, or at least of some eunuchs, was probably greater than that of the mandarins where security was concerned.

Under Chien Lung the Summer Palace had been enlarged and some sixty thousand acres of gardens had been created to give an impression of great natural landscapes of exceptional beauty with hillocks and tiny valleys, lakes and waterfalls, rocks and caves, with some two hundred pavilions scattered around the grounds. The Emperor himself was both a scholar and a dreamer. He had ordered the building of seven large libraries in different regions of China, with instructions that each was to contain an encyclopaedia of 36,000 volumes which had been compiled from all that was best in Chinese history, philosophy, literature and science. But it was the dreamer in Chien Lung which caused him to compose a poem which began:

Over the moat by a bridge
To the library encircled by hills.
Under the green shade of the Wu-tun trees
I feel as happy as can be.
And when the rain-drops fall
Their music fills me with poetic ecstasy.

Chien Lung was only half-Manchu, his mother, an actress whom his father had made a royal concubine, having been pure Chinese. Probably from his mother he inherited his aestheticism and fondness for poetry and not least that strong romantic streak which was eventually to turn into a major liability. When he came to the throne he was twenty-five years old, handsome and athletic, a skilled archer and horseman as well as a scholar.

As a young man Chien Lung had, fallen in love with one of his Emperor-father's youngest concubines. Court protocol demanded that he should pay no attention whatsoever to any of the Emperor's concubines and keep his head averted. But the romantic young prince defied protocol: one day he crept into the apartment of the concubine, Ma Chia, and coming up behind her as she brushed her hair, placed his hands over her eyes. Startled, the young girl raised her hand in defence and accidentally struck Chien Lung in the face with her comb.

The wound on the prince's face did not escape the notice of his mother who inquired what had happened and, being a dominating and purposeful woman, she soon got the truth of the incident from her son. Secretly she gave instructions to one of the eunuchs to have Ma Chia strangled, whether out of jealousy or simply to end a possible intrigue is not clear. Another eunuch warned Chien Lung what was about to happen, but the warning came too late. Dashing to her apartment, he found the girl already dying.

"The religion of the Manchus was the Tibetan form of Buddhism," writes Bernard Martin, "so he [Chien Lung] believed in reincarnation. In desperate grief he bit a finger and slashed a drop of his blood on the dying girl's neck, swearing that by this blood-

66

stain he would know her again in whatever form her spirit returned to earth."[2]

Chien Lung had numerous other wildly romantic love affairs and most of them ended unhappily. One of these affairs so upset his young empress that she committed suicide. All this may seem somewhat remote from the subject of secret service, but it was through the bloodstain which Chien Lung allowed to drop on to the neck of the dying Ma Chia that Chien gained one of the most despotic—and certainly the most powerful—of Secret Service chiefs of the eighteenth century. He was indubitably more powerful than Napoléon's master-spy chief, Joseph Fouché.

Some years after Chien Lung came to the throne his attention was drawn to a young palace guard named Ho Shen. For on the neck of this guard was a mark like a bloodstain which Chien Lung claimed was identical with that on the neck of the dying Ma Chia. He was certain that the bloodstain was genuine and permanent, but to prove to his own satisfaction that this was not a mere cut which would disappear after a few days or weeks he bided his time. The mark like a bloodstain—presumably a red birthmark—proved to be permanent and Emperor Chien Lung was thereby convinced that Ho Shen was the reincarnation of Ma Chia: his wish had been granted.

From that day Ho Shen was given rapid promotion. first to chief of the palace guard and then to appointments within the Chinese bureaucracy. The exact relationship between the two men must remain a mystery. There is no doubt that the Emperor believed that the lovely Ma Chia had come back to him in the shape of the young guardsman and there may have been a homosexual association. But it is clear that Ho Shen could do no wrong in Chien Lung's eyes, that he trusted him completely and eventually made him Grand Chancellor and head of his Secret Intelligence. Ho Shen was given full powers to sift and analyse all information which mandarins, eunuchs and spies passed into the palace.

The story of Ho Shen has so far not been fully investigated by Western scholars, possibly because they felt the reincarnation legend was far-fetched, possibly because his character and personality did not appeal to them. But Ho Shen is nevertheless important because no one did more than he not only to bring about the decline of the Christian influence in China, but to thwart efforts by Europeans to gain a foothold in trading posts or diplomatic representation in Peking. Nobody did more to curb the power of the eunuchs, who had become far too numerous at the court. Chien Lung's grandfather and father had drastically cut down the number of eunuchs by some thousands, but early in the reign their numbers had increased to more than five thousand.

Ho Shen's tasks as Intelligence Chief were threefold; first, to keep the Emperor and himself informed on the disturbances among minorities which began to occur in various regions of China; second, to control Western merchants and reduce the influence of the missionaries; and, finally, to stamp out the intrigues of the eunuchs who in the past had so often been allowed to operate their own intelligence systems.

Chien Lung himself was, of course, a remarkably able exponent of Chinese achievements to Europeans. While the missionaries returning to Europe from China told of increasing difficulties and even persecution, other travellers spoke with admiration of the "philosopher-Emperor", as Chien Lung became known. The libraries he had set up were praised as examples of the breadth of Chinese culture; Montesquieu in his *L'ésprit des lois* in 1748 urged that China beyond all other countries in the world deserved close study by Western scholars, while that clear-minded cynic Voltaire gave a boost to Sinophilism by his eulogies of Chien Lung and his somewhat overdrawn picture of Chinese tolerance and the Peking bureaucracy as the benevolent guardians of the people.

Much of this praise and enthusiasm for *Chinoiserie* in both the fields of the arts and of philosophy was the product of minds overheated by romanticism, for the idea of a benevolent bureaucracy was held by neither Chien Lung nor Ho Shen. The Emperor himself once deliberately composed a bitingly satirical song entitled "The Emperor in quest of an honest official". This he sang to his retinue at court, while playing his own accompaniment on the drum, and no doubt he intended that the message should not merely be indelibly inscribed in the minds of those present, but that they would pass it on. As for Ho Shen, he certainly served his master loyally, while helping himself at the same time. He was the first to complain about the dishonesty of court officials and eunuchs and made no secret of the fact that he preferred not to have keen-witted, clever people around him. Often he would quote to his master the words of Chin Shengt'an given at the beginning of this chapter.

History has to some extent maligned Ho Shen. Undoubtedly he enriched himself on a scale which puts him among the greedier of Secret Service chiefs: he was the antithesis of England's Walsingham, who almost ruined himself by spending his own money on espionage. On the other hand he was not so very different from the European spy chiefs of the eighteenth century when, in Britain, France and Russia, bribery was rife among such officials on a huge scale. The hypocrisy of Western diplomats in condemning Ho Shen, as so often they did in dispatches to their respective governments, is somewhat ridiculous when one considers that the European diplomats were the most blatant bribers of all. Sir Robert Murray Keith, the English Minister in Russia, in this same age admitted that he was provided by his Government with £100,000 for spying and bribery and for "such gratifications as I may judge necessary to make from time to time to particular persons".

Many of these Western diplomats gave bribes to obtain intelligence and gladly accepted bribes from other governments, for which they sold information. Admittedly sometimes the "other governments" were allies, though this was not always the case. But treachery to China, or even the sharing of China's secrets with a seemingly friendly power, was something the Chinese did not and still do not practise. Ho Shen was loyal to his Emperor and his country, but he understood what many Western spy chiefs have never understood—that bribery alone is a crude method of obtaining intelligence and that the spy chief to whom all information flows is often the man who not only holds on to his money, but controls the source and supply of money—in short, the man who can impress on the person wishing to sell information that whatever other transaction he might make could not be kept secret.

The combination of Chien Lung and Ho Shen was an admirable one. The Emperor, possibly because of his actress mother, possessed the common touch to a remarkable degree, though this was always subtly controlled. He had the Manchu gift of dignity and authority combined with a Chinese talent for mixing easily with the people, and he could enter into plebian frivolities without losing his authority. As a public relations officer for Chinese philosophy, art, architecture, products, poetry and way of life he was incomparable. Ho Shen, who shared his Emperor's mistrust of the eunuchs and realisation of the dangers of "eunuch power", knew exactly how to obtain the maximum amount of information from Western visitors without giving much in exchange. Yet he was always able to use his Intelligence Service to ensnare these Europeans and bemuse them with the glamour of the high life in Peking, the exquisite manners of the court and the fact—as Lin Yutang put it—that China has a "lyrical philosophy".[3]

The result of all this was a tremendous boom in exports of Chinese products to Europe—tea, porcelain, carved ivories, lacquered furniture and other goods, silks and many works of art. For such goods the Chinese were paid in gold and silver, and the revenue swelled the Peking Treasury to the extent that the *Peking Gazette* was able to announce that so much money had accumulated that all tax payments could be cancelled. This is something which would hardly be likely to happen in any modern Treasury and, bearing in mind that Ho Shen was Grand Chancellor, it does not suggest that he was altogether unmindful of the people.

Indeed he increased his wealth to a large extent to increase his power, knowing full well that even a Grand Chancellor to whom his ruler was devoted would be at a disadvantage without some degree of independence. Ho Shen was Grand Chancellor and chief of intelligence for twenty years and he enriched himself and ensured the support of those under him by insisting that each government post, every spy, every promotion in the army and all contracts for services and sales of goods with foreign countries were negotiated directly through him. Ho Shen decided who was chosen and what were the terms of any agreement, and he exacted his own price for any such decision.

It has been suggested that Ho Shen added to his wealth by blackmail and extortions and, say Bernard Martin and Shui Chien-tung, "by revealing some state secrets and concealing others".[4] This latter may well have been true, but then such tactics are invariably even today part and parcel of the strategy of any Secret Service chief, even in a democracy. But never did Ho Shen forget that his duty was to China. Much of his wealth he owed to the devotion of the Emperor, who regarded him as a spiritual bond with his long dead love; and gifts were freely given to him in the form of expensive works of art, palaces and estates in various parts of China. It is true that Ho Shen kept a tight control over all financial transactions, that he owned forty-two banks and a tenth of the pawnshops in Peking. But it was through the knowledge of financial transactions he acquired by his ownership of the banks and the tit-bits of intelligence he gleaned from people patronising the pawn-brokers he controlled that he was able to be such an efficient Chief of Intelligence.

The pawnshop is, perhaps, as natural and perhaps even more effective an instrument of espionage as the brothel, yet it is a measure of Chinese perspicacity that they alone among the nations of the world have from time to time utilised the pawnshop in the national interest.

Ho Shen was foremost among those who sought to contain and where necessary curtail the interest of foreigners in China: generally speaking, he contained the trade and encouraged it wherever and whenever it was one-way—that is, from China to Europe—but rigorously restricted the influence of the missionaries, keeping a secret watch on all their moves. Thus the missionaries were driven out of Peking and persecuted and harried in the provinces. Some Jesuits in Nanking the Dominicans in Fukien were executed in 1747 after Ho Shen claimed to have details of missionary plots against the regime. Under the Emperor K'ang-hsi there had been probably as many as three hundred thousand active Catholic converts in China, though nothing like the totals claimed by some missionaries. Ho Shen was determined to see that this number was drastically reduced so that it could never become a powerful minority; on the other hand he was sufficient of a realist to know that some of the Jesuits had much to contribute in the fields of learning, astronomy and medicine.

He played an ambivalent rôle in his relations with Christian missionaries, welcoming but always watching them at the court, luring them away from their religious duties by flattery and offers of work as interpreters, astronomers, cartographers, painters, engravers, architects, mechanics and engineers. The ablest of these missionaries came to preach the gospel, to win converts and establish churches, but they ended up by becoming court officials strictly under Ho Shen's control. In a sense he subjected these missionaries to a kind of spiritual castration, isolating them from their orders and their normal religious routines by getting them to design buildings, to make Western-style clocks and to paint the Emperor's concubines. Adam Schall and Verbiest had never lost sight of their main purpose—to win converts—but both Ho Shen and to a lesser extent Chien Lung were subtle enough to reduce many of these missionaries to mere pampered puppets of the court, subtly brain-washed by the tolerance of Chinese philosophy, the epicureanism of Li Liweng, the hedonism of Yuan Tsets'ai and the gay, macabre jokes of Chin Shengt'an, who had something of the Jesuit in his make-up.

But, while making use of Europeans in this way, China never imbibed Western ideas and the fact that Christian infiltration into the country had been remarkably successful on a small scale in the previous century made Ho Shen determined to organise an underground campaign against the itinerant priests. His agents travelled the length and breadth of the empire spreading stories against the missionaries: they were accused of being sodomites, of bewitching women and children, of practising not medicine but witchcraft and, worst of all, of combining to form a secret society to ensnare the Chinese people. The agents' stories were sufficient to produce a good deal of persecution and the cause of Christianity was hardly helped when the missionaries themselves went underground and travelled around in disguise. This soon reached the ears of Ho Shen who gave orders for their arrest and execution. But, doubtless to assuage the consciences of the missionaries employed at the court, Ho Shen was more tolerant to those Catholics, especially the priests, who actually lived in Peking.

Jonathan Spence in *The China Helpers* writes that "population pressures had pushed the Chinese peasants to the very margin of subsistence, that in the late eighteenth century the appalling corruption of the Chien Lung Emperor's favourite, Ho Shen, had driven the regime to the verge of bankruptcy, weakened Imperial authority and demoralised the bureaucracy, that the Ch'ing armies had proved almost incapable of putting down the increasingly frequent peasant revolts, and that foreign governments were growing impatient with their 'vassal' status".[5] This is a somewhat jaundiced view of a regime which achieved the extraordinary feat of making the West enthusiastic about China while keeping Western influence politely but firmly at arm's length. This modern view of the Chien Lung era certainly does not bear out the contemporary reports either of Jesuits returning to Europe, or of other European observers of the Chinese scene. Indeed it can be said that in the more advanced radical minds China was held up as a model, a glimpse of utopia, to Europe until the French Revolution caused the continent once again to become inward-looking, a trend which inevitably seems to follow left-wing revolts.

Ho Shen, it is true, had to face many peasant revolts, but most of these he detected in time and swiftly and efficiently crushed. The agrarian problem, which was linked with that of the population dilemma, could hardly be blamed on Ho Shen or his Emperor. China had always been a nation of peasant farmers and as the population grew so there was less and less land to divide between the sons of each farmer who died. Such small patches of land as were inherited barely provided subsistence, with the result that the farmers sold the land to grasping, eighteenth-century speculators, who then rented the land back to them at unduly high rents. It was in the short term a recipe for poverty, in the long term a certain guarantee of a communist revolt stemming from the peasants.

Short of organised birth control (then unknown and even today with all possible techniques available still extremely difficult to implement in remote parts of the world where prejudice and superstition defy science), there was little the ruling classes could have done about the agrarian-population problem short of returning to the primitive communist precepts of Wang An-shih. That was far less practical in the eighteenth century than it had been in the era of Wang An-shih. As an aside it might also be mentioned that Ho Shen's highly personal and certainly exclusive system of espionage was not as all-embracing as that of Wang An-shih's family spy system. Nonetheless China achieved some success in containing, if not solving, this problem by cancelling all tax payments on no less than four occasions on account of the wealth received from sales of products to the West.

Over the Western traders Ho Shen kept a tight control. This was regarded as a sphere which was very much a matter of national security. To sell to the foreigner was beneficial; to allow him to get even the slenderest of footholds on Chinese territory was a retrograde step. This was the thinking which dominated the whole subject of East-West trade. Under Ho Shen's direction, merchant firms were appointed to be licensed brokers for the conduct of the trade. One group of "security merchants," as they became known, controlled the "junk" trade along the Chinese coast northwards, a second dealt with the trade with South East Asia and a third (and the most important from the intelligence-gathering point of view) looked after trade with the Europeans.

This last-named group was formed into what the European traders knew as the Cohong (more accurately the *Kung-hang,* or "officially appointed merchants"). This guild, or organisation under Ho Shen's close supervision, held a monopoly which controlled all trade with the West. In effect each ship entering Canton port would be safeguarded or "guaranteed" by one of the Cohong merchants acting as "security officer". This system was not quite so bureaucratic as it might at first seem in an era when trade was mainly free and a matter of individual bartering. It was intended primarily as a front line security defence against Western infiltration of China and to keep a close watch on all attempts at private deals or efforts to set up agents inside China. But to a large extent these defensive rather than purely bureaucratic measures were forced on the Chinese as a countermeasure to the British East India Company, which had sought to dominate and bulldoze its way into China as it had bullied, harried, cajoled, blackmailed and waged war on traders in other parts of the Orient.

There was in fact in the reign of Chien Lung a parallel with the nuclear stalemate today between Soviet Russia and the West: what began with aggressive intentions on the part of the buccaneer traders of Britain was answered by the formation of the "security merchants". The latter counteracted the aggressive drive of the East India Company: to take the heat out of the situation, in modern parlance, the East India Company set up a Canton Committee to accept responsibility for all British ships, traders and personnel. This acceptance of Chinese control gave the British East India Company a distinct advantage over other European rivals in trade. But, as in the civilised though equally bogus S.A.L.T. talks between East and West on nuclear matters today, the bargaining and counter-bargaining was tough and each side gave away as little as possible. But as long as Ho Shen was in charge China on the whole had by far the better part of the bargain.

Merchants entering the country were subject to

drastic regulations. Ho Shen mistrusted women and one of his sayings was that "women and eunuchs were the head and tail of the demon dragon". Thus he forbade any trader to bring his wife, or even his mistress, into China. To ensure that he could keep them under closer supervision he would not allow them to ride in sedan chairs: he had seen too many disappearing tricks practised through use of this mode of transport, not to mention the unseen slipping of messages through curtained doors. No merchant was allowed into the gates of the Forbidden City and even in Canton they were confined to an area outside the city itself known as the "Thirteen Factories". At one time he made it a rule that they should spend a certain period of the year in Macao which then, as now, was regarded as the perfect place for easily keeping foreigners under observation.

No special privileges were conceded to the traders: they were subject to Chinese law which included arbitrary imprisonment and sometimes torture. But the demand for Chinese goods from the West ensured that on the whole the traders kept to the rules and a polite, if uneasy, relationship was maintained between the two sides, despite an occasional rogue elephant on the British side.

One enterprising young Englishman, James Flint, tried to break the Canton monopoly in the middle of the eighteenth century and daringly sailed up to Tientsin in 1759 to present a petition to the Emperor. He naïvely believed that if the Emperor knew of the extortions of money that were exacted at Canton he would cancel them and give him greater freedom of trade. All this was done through an interpreter—naturally an interpreter of Ho Shen's choosing—and the immediate result was not merely that James Flint was imprisoned in Macao for three years and then expelled, but that the Chinese interpreter who had full knowledge of all these goings-on was himself summarily executed.

Eventually in 1793 a mission, headed by Lord Macartney, was sent to China from England. It was a most carefully chosen mission, for by now the British had had sufficient experience of Chinese methods and attitudes to be anxious to avoid both the over-eager brashness of some of the missionaries and the impolite arrogance of the traders. They decided that the right approach to the Emperor was to be a combined effort of aristocrats on the one hand, artists, musicians and painters on the other, a few surgeons, some naval and military officers and a landscape gardener. The object of this quite costly operation was to try to persuade the Chinese to correct the unfair balance of trade which at the time was solely from China to Britain and not at all from Britain to China.

There had been several attempts by other countries to bring about some trading treaty with China which included diplomatic representation, but they had nearly all been rebuffed out of hand. However, rebuffs seemed only to stimulate the urge to establish normal diplomatic relations, as statistics show. Between 1662 and 1762 there had been 216 missions overseas to Peking, while between 1762 and 1860 there were 254.

Lord Macartney, who headed the British mission, had been an envoy to Russia and a Governor of Madras. His main object was to seek permission for trade at Ningpo and Tientsin and to request that no dues or fees be paid except those authorised by the Emperor. In other words the British wanted to cut out the middle men and to be in a better position for dictating trade terms. It was made clear to Macartney by the Chinese officials that he must perform *kotow,* the traditional Chinese protocol for total obeisance before the Emperor, when he presented his credentials. Macartney refused absolutely to do this, claiming that he would do no more than he did to his own King—make obeisance on one knee.

Many gifts were brought by the British mission, including a planetarium, flying balloons, specimens of the latest field artillery and—rather inadvisedly—a gigantic burning glass. Each gift was carefully inspected by either Ho Shen or his agents and the Intelligence Chief was quick to implant in his master's ear the idea that the burning-glass was a particularly sinister gift as it had no real use: fire was so easy to obtain anyhow. It is reported that on Ho Shen's orders the burning-glass was taken away and buried.

The mission remained in China for seven months, always courteously treated, but always closely watched by Ho Shen's spies and subjected to many irritating restrictions. One edict actually stated that "the foreign barbarians may visit the flower gardens and a Buddhist temple on the 8th, 18th and 28th days of the moon, but not in parties of more than ten at a time and only with a Chinese official as escort".

It all came to nought. The Emperor received Macartney with quiet dignity and ignored his refusal to *kotow,* but in replying commended "King George III for his respectful spirit of submission" and then gave the mission the *coup de grâce* with these words: "Your sincere humility and obedience can clearly be seen. As to what you have requested in your message, O King, namely to be allowed to send one of your subjects to reside in the Celestial Empire to look after your country's trade . . . this definitely cannot be done.

"He could neither behave like a Western Ocean man who comes to the capital to enter our service [an obvious reference to such men as Schall and Verbiest], remaining at the capital and not returning to his native country, nor could he be allowed to go in and out and to have regular correspondence [in short, he could not be permitted to spy] . . . his speech would not be understood, his dress would be different in style and habit and we should have no place to provide him with a residence [meaning quite clearly that he would not be allowed to live in Peking].

"We have never wished to force on others what is difficult for them to achieve or to abide by. . . ."

The sum total of the very long edict was to say in the politest way possible that not only was it impossible for a British embassy to be set up in Peking, but that this applied to all Westerners. Perhaps the punch line in the whole message was contained in the following passage: "The virtue and power of the Celestial Dynasty has penetrated afar to the myriad kingdoms, which have come to render homage and so all kinds of precious things from over mountain and sea have been collected here . . . Nevertheless we have never valued such articles, however ingenious, nor do we have the slightest need of your country's products and manufactures."[6]

Lord Macartney's comment privately on the disastrous mission was that "The Empire of China is an old, crazy, first-rate Man of War. . . . She may, perhaps, not sink outright; she may drift some time as a wreck, and will then be dashed to pieces on the shore, but she can never be rebuilt on the old bottom."[7]

There he was half right and half wrong. China could not indefinitely live in isolation from the rest of the world: the longer she did so the harder her fate. On the other hand Macartney failed to foresee that it was still on the ancient culture and philosophies of China that the nation was to be rebuilt in the mid-twentieth century.

Within two years of Macartney's visit the Emperor Chien Lung died. It was his fifth son who succeeded him and Ho Shen had consistently underestimated the threat this young man posed. For years he had detested Ho Shen, but kept his thoughts to himself. He never trusted anyone prior to his coming to the throne. Then he struck immediately: his first order was to have Ho Shen arrested. An investigation into his affairs was conducted and under torture the Grand Chancellor confessed that a vast sum of gold, silver and other monies was to be found hidden in secret chambers built into the walls of his palace. It was estimated that his total wealth was the equivalent of ten years' revenue to the Chinese Empire.

Yet even then he was respected to the extent that he was allowed to carry out his own death sentence by hanging himself with a silken cord.

8

The Secret Police of the Green Standard 1797-1840

Land troops could neither ride nor shoot and the water troops could not sail or fire a cannon. The officers could only keep accounts.

Tso Tsung-t'ang, Governor of Chekiang, 1860

WHEREAS in culture and respect for learning the Chinese could well be said to be the "French of the Orient", in their Secret Service activities over the centuries they can perhaps only be compared with the British. Having made this statement, it needs some qualifications, amplification and explanation for risking what is at best an enigmatic personal opinion.

First of all, it cannot be overstressed that China's leadership over the centuries as the chief cultural and philosophical influence in the Far East can only be compared to the position which France held in the West for so many centuries. This is recognised by so shrewd an observer of the international scene as Lin Yutang who writes: "I regard the Chinese as most closely allied to the French in their sense of humour and sensitivity, as is quite evident from the way the French write their books and eat their food, while the more volatile character of the French comes from their greater idealism, which takes the form of love of abstract ideas. . . ."[1]

It should be noted that Verbiest, a Frenchman, was one of the most trusted of advisers to the Chinese in the early days and that during the period when the People's Republic of Mao Tse-tung cut themselves off completely from the rest of the world, they retained close links with the French. The affinity extends at least to the fringes of secret understandings, if not to the secret service.

Up to this point in time—the beginning of the nineteenth century—this history of the Chinese Secret Service must give the impression of being written by an author who attempts a strip-tease act, only to start putting on his clothes again every few centuries before repeating the performance, and never making the final revelation. We started with the incredible wisdom and text-book genius of Sun Tzu in the fourth century. Soon much of what he so carefully taught was forgotten or abandoned; and we had the family espionage system of Wang An-shih only to see the Chinese turn in upon themselves, isolate themselves from the rest of the world and allow such a secret service as they had to degenerate into eunuch power.

True, in the last chapter we saw something of how Ho Shen created an intelligence system that served its purpose as long as China's aim was to ignore the rest of the world. But to date the overall picture is one of flashes of genius that suggest consummate skill and originality in secret service, dismally and disappointingly leading to no single system that would gradually evolve into a comprehensive Secret Service. It is in this respect that the Chinese Secret Service can be compared with the British. Each has had its men of genius, its original ploys, its ability to make use of such bizarre subjects as astrology and even mythology in espionage and counter-espionage. But each, too, has had appalling failures, periods of disintegration in Secret Service, and squandered opportunities. There is, however, one important difference: the spectacular coups of the British Secret Service down the centuries have been so well publicised that its reputation has tended to be over-estimated; the activities of the Chinese in the field of intelligence have never been fully analysed and are, even today, very much *under*-estimated.

Following the end of Chien Lung's reign and the death of Ho Shen, national security in China rapidly disintegrated until by the early eighteen-thirties it was of so little account that China could no longer withstand the pressures of the Europeans to establish firmer relations in its territories.

The system by which intelligence reports reached Peking was in itself hopelessly outdated and clumsy. The Emperor and his advisers depended almost entirely on local officials for what intelligence they received from far-flung parts of the empire: such officials were not always well versed in the basic requirements of their jobs and were sometimes reluctant to report ill-tidings which they thought would displease Peking. Things were not so well organised as under the regime of Ho Shen, as most intelligence was sent in the form of "memorials" to the Emperor rather than to an Intelligence Chief. Thus the *taotai,* local bureaucrats in class 4A of the Civil Service, who were the lowest authorities permitted to send reports direct to the Emperor, often felt inhibited about what information they should pass on.

Apart from this disadvantage communications were both cumbersome and slow; there were fifteen thousand post-stations in the empire and communications between these and Peking were maintained almost entirely by couriers on foot, who passed their reports from post to post (usually between three and ten miles apart) in a relay system in which the handing over was not always speedily negotiated. Thus a dispatch from, say, Nanking to Peking, a distance of 766 miles, could, if the utmost speed was ensured and no accidents befell the messenger, take twenty-four days or more to reach the capital. From other centres of the empire the time taken might be anything up to sixty days. Though it was never officially admitted—indeed delays were usually concealed from the Peking authorities by the officials concerned—sometimes such messages took three months to arrive at the capital.

Not surprisingly, secret societies flourished in this period and many of them were a direct threat to the state. There was the White Lotus rebellion between 1796 and 1804 which started in the mountainous area around Szechwan, Shensi and Pupei. This was a revolt against the tax collectors launched by a band of men who revived the ancient White Lotus Society, which had originally been a religious cult. It was an anti-Manchu rebellion and, though never organised into anything more effective than roving, raiding bands, gained an advantage from the mountainous, largely inaccessible terrain from which it operated.[2]

China was also threatened from the sea, not by the Europeans whose challenge was mainly commercial, but by pirates on the south-east coasts. The Chinese navy, such as it then was (in effect, little more than a coastal police force), failed to check the raids of the pirates who had bases in Vietnam and even on remoter stretches of the China coast itself. The marauders had bigger and faster ships than the Chinese navy possessed and were more adept in seamanship. Some idea of their dominance can be gleaned from the fact that in 1806 they attacked Taiwan with more than a hundred ships and ten thousand men.

Other secret societies which grew in influence in this period were the Triads, the Eight Trigram Society and the Heavenly Reason Society. The last-named was perhaps the most impudent of all, even if one of the least powerful, for it not only organised rebellions in Chihli, Honan and Shantung in 1813, but established contact with some of the eunuchs at the court with the object of capturing the Forbidden City. True, their plot was foiled and this premature revolt was swiftly put down, but it was a measure of the growing contempt for authority and the laxness of security that such an attack was even considered.

The Triad Society was by far the greater menace on account not only of its huge membership, but its tighter organisation, its disciplines, codes of secrecy and, perhaps even more important, the extent to which it was able to operate among Chinese exiles outside the boundaries of China. In Chapter Three reference has been made to the Chinese genius down the centuries for organising themselves into secret societies, how these have both helped to destroy any effective centralised Intelligence Service on occasions though yet in the long run able to contribute effectively to new and more sophisticated concepts of a secret service.

No other nation has had this experience to anything like the same extent. The closest examples are Italy, where the *Mafia* has some parallels with the Triad Society, and pre-revolutionary Russia where there was a whole range of revolutionary secret societies from anarchists and communists to eccentric religious sects such as the Chlysty. But none of these societies contributed so much to the essential know-how for the creation of an overseas and foreign espionage service, which China had previously lacked, as did the Triads. In the early part of the nineteenth century it could be said that the Triad Society was an independent secret service both inside China and outside its borders, though totally aloof from the Establishment. Certainly it was more powerful and better informed than the scant, barely perceptible and attenuated bureaucratic Intelligence Service in Peking.

In its early days the Triad Society had many aliases, which used to confuse the authorities. In one area it was known as the Heaven and Earth Society, in another as the Hung League. There are some Chinese scholars today who insist that it dates back to pre-Christian times, though there appears to be no firm evidence of this. It was Buddhist in origin and certainly existed in some form or other as early as the late seventeenth century where it was organised from a monastery near Foochow. Over the ages it had been more Chinese than the Sinolised Manchu establishment and had as its motto "Down with the Ch'ing and Back with the Ming"; its prime object being to overthrow Manchu rule.

For years it had remained dormant, using oaths of absolute loyalty on pain of death to ensure secrecy, and it had perhaps succeeded in stifling any premature revolts by turning itself into a mutual aid society for its membership. In its use of secret signs, esoteric rites and passwords it could be compared with the Masonic movement in Europe. And, like the Masonic movement, it has retained its strength over the centuries. It was of special value to travellers, those who found it useful to be helped and guided by fellow members when they moved to strange places; and in time the Triad Society, which was strongest in the south of China, extended its influence to other South-East Asian countries where there were Chinese inhabitants. Once it had established this dominance over Chinese in other lands the power of the Triad Society became much greater and its intelligence service second to none, for reports were always being brought back by smugglers, pirates, seamen and merchants who had joined its ranks.

The word Triad in the sense in which it is employed by this secret society refers to its symbol of a triangle, the sides of which represent Heaven, Earth and Man living in harmony or communion with one another. There is a secret cipher, based on multiples of three, which, in its ratings, perhaps displays the delicious Chinese sense of humour at its best—108 for Man, 72 for Earth and a mere 36 for Heaven! No doubt to a Westerner a Chinese would deny any significance in this; privately I have known them to chuckle over the subject with great glee. Even entrance fees are paid in a rate of multiples of three according to the means of the new members.

The Triad Society lacks the pomposity and more ridiculous aspects of Masonry and avoids the more blatant examples of Mafia gangster ritual, while preserving a certain impish freshness in its esoteric functions. One could say that with the Triads Puck leaps through the window, waves a wand and dispels pretentiousness, retaining only the sheer fun of belonging to a secret society. While the Masons have their somewhat sombre, satire-inviting modes of recognition, the Triads turn identification signals into a kind of gay adventure with such enchanting varieties of sign language as arranging cigarettes or matches on a table, or tattoo marks, a particular way of holding chopsticks and even the use of a certain number of fingers to grasp a glass during a drinking bout.

This last method, I am reliably told, is almost impossible for anyone other than a Chinese to grasp, if indeed anyone can remain sober during its performance. Of course, one is always conscious that the friendliest, most honest and most highly intelligent of Chinese (even those one has known for years) are not above pulling one's leg. But I gather that in one such drinking game one has not only to remember how many fingers one may place around a glass on a particular round of drinking, but that this number may vary according to one's rank in the hierarchy, one's turn to get the drinks or propose the toast, and whether it is before or after the twentieth of the month (Chinese calendar).

Little was done to check the growth of the Triad Society in the early part of the nineteenth century, though under Chia-ch'ing (1796–1820) persecution of the Christians and a close watch by the secret police on all missionaries were not only maintained, but stepped up. Those missionaries who were not arrested and expelled were forced to keep on the move. Because some of them foolishly adopted disguises and even posed as beggars or mendicants when visiting homes to give communion to converts they were not surprisingly regarded as a secret society themselves, though of course a foreign one trying to subvert the Chinese people. In one single year more than eight hundred Christians were arrested in Szechwan alone (1815), two of the leaders being sentenced to death by strangulation and eleven others made to wear the *cangue,* a wide, square wooden board round the neck, for the rest of their lives.

Incredibly, there was no attempt to try to understand Christianity, to learn how it was practised in Europe, or even to ascertain how other countries survived without being subverted by it. The lack of intelligence of the outside world at this period in China was parallelled only by their appalling geographical ignorance. This was exemplified in a Kwantung gazetteer produced in Canton, then regarded as the chief city to have contacts with the West and by far the best informed in China. Those who compiled this work were so ignorant of the outside world that they placed the Philippines just below Southern India, stated that England was another name for Holland, of which it was a dependency, and that France was originally a Buddhist country, but had become converted to Catholicism because Christianity was an idea that had been developed by the later Buddhists.

There were a few merchants who were much better informed, but, realising how little credence would be attached to their views, they kept such information to themselves. Later on, these same merchants were to help provide the background for a more extensive Secret Service. One of the most notable of these was Yang Ping-nan, who compiled his own work, *Hai Lu*, a secret and unpublished edition of which provided a complete map of London and all the bridges over the Thames together with such details as the supply of water to the city, how its shipping trade was organised and the number of prostitutes and how they were classified. One interesting comment was that "the prostitutes of London do not seem to be employed as spies as in China: it is doubtful if they are intelligent enough for such duties".[3]

Gradually, the isolation which China had imposed on itself in relation to the outside world was eroded, first by trade, then by pressure from the two main competitors for the Canton markets, the British and Americans. Other Western governments began to follow, though sometimes they adopted the device of employing an Englishman who knew the intricacies of bargaining with the Chinese and actually lived in Canton as a consul.

Britain continued to press her demand for diplomatic equality and commercial opportunities—in short, the demand for two-way trade. Both Britain and the U.S.A. began to insist that they could not submit to the barbarities and indignities of Chinese law and arbitrary arrest. Early in the nineteenth century a degree of extra-territorial rights came to be enjoyed in practice equally by Britain and the U.S.A., if not actually with the formal permission of the Chinese Government.

In the sabre-rattling, swashbuckling era of Lord Palmerston's Foreign Secretaryship, Britain decided on a show of force against China. When Lord Napier went to Canton in 1834, meeting with Chinese recalcitrance and the usual curbs on trade, he was able to show up the feeble state of internal security by distributing specially printed Chinese handbills which informed the Chinese of how the Ch'ing officials, by refusing Britain trade concessions, were actually robbing the Chinese people of the benefits of reciprocal prosperity. Many of these handbills circulated far and wide and made a distinct impression on Chinese traders, or would-be traders, but officialdom's only reply was to stop all supplies reaching the British factory at Canton. Napier sent two frigates up the river and ordered them to fire on the Chinese forts.

There was now a confrontation between the British and Chinese governments. Napier had made a foolish move, for he had inflicted a defiant and insulting gesture on a proud nation somewhat unnecessarily, while in fact all that was needed was to have allowed the handbills to do their work, and to have then left the British free traders and the Cohong merchants to work out a compromise. At this level nobody wanted confrontation, but only a process of bargaining.

Chinese Security no longer controlled the trade with the West; the Canton system had broken up and the Cohong had ceased to dominate the Chinese side of the trade. It was generally realised that a one-way system of trade was doing no good to China and that many Chinese merchants were not only anxious to trade freely with the West, but in some cases were doing so surreptitiously.

British diplomatic, military and naval pressure increased, often quite ridiculously, with further expeditionary forces by the Royal Navy which rarely succeeded in establishing more than a temporary advantage, though leaving behind them lasting ill-will. Such flag-wagging, jingoistic bravado was quite unnecessary in the case of China as a security-minded, powerful, isolated entity was falling apart: bribery alone would have sufficed without using gun-boats to step up trade.

The Chinese army was badly disciplined, its morale was low and its leadership corrupt. There was no adequate intelligence system within the Army itself. Indeed, not only were military administration and intelligence almost totally lacking, but the Ch'ing dynasty now relied almost entirely on the Chinese Constabulary for secret service work. It was better known as the Army of the Green Standard, totalling about half a million men—even this estimate is dubious for it is known that in a number of cases wages were claimed for members who did not exist. It was also claimed that the Army of the Green Standard covered the whole empire: this again was an exaggerated claim for in some provinces it was barely represented at all.

The truth was that discipline both in the Army and the Civil Service had become so slack that there was little difference between an Army officer and a merchant (often the former gave more time to performing the functions of the latter), between a Secret Service Green Standard officer and a middle-man trader or import-exporter, while the rank and file often existed only on paper. Sometimes names would be added to the strength of the Green Standard which merely represented so much extra cash going into the pockets of the officer who had faked them.

In *A History of East Asian Civilisation* it is recorded that "The Malpractices of this Chinese Army [the Green Standard] became a byword. Officers would fail to report vacancies, keep non-existent persons on the rolls in order to get their rations, and hire temporary substitutes at times of inspection. They even enrolled their cooks and servants as troops so as to receive their rations also—the rolls might be full, but the ranks empty. . . . Its training stressed form without content . . . like play-acting."[4]

The era of the Western penetration of China through pious religious motives was ended: in no other part of the world did Western Imperialism appear at its worst than in China during the early part of the nineteenth century. The blustering, blackmail, crude threats, contempt and downright cruelty on the part of the Western nations, and especially the British, was unparalleled in other parts of the world. British imperialism in China was far, far worse than in Africa or any of the British colonies. Perhaps it was that deep down in the heart and mind of the British adventurer, diplomat, merchant, general or admiral who ventured into these parts was a feeling of inferiority, subconscious perhaps, but conditioned by the sense that the people they faced were by tradition, philosophy and in the arts of graceful living, down to a peasant level, so much better equipped to know what life was all about and how it should be enjoyed.

9

The Opium Wars
1840-1864

Though not making use of opium oneself, to venture
nevertheless to manufacture and sell it, and with it to
seduce the simple folk of this land, is to seek one's
own livelihood by exposing others to death . . . Sup-
pose there were people from another country who carried opium for sale to England and seduced your people into buying and smoking it, this would arouse deep
hatred.

    Lin Tse-Hsu (in a letter addressed to Queen Victoria)

DISINTEGRATION of the machinery of both national
and local government, the rise of pirate-power along
all the Chinese coasts and the refusal of the Western
powers to take no for an answer in their demands for
reciprocal trade marked a steady whittling away of the
power and influence of the Emperor from the end of
the eighteenth to about the middle of the nineteenth
century.

The British were by far the most determined, the
shrewdest and the most ruthless of all the Western
nations trading, or trying to trade, with China in this
period. The British East India Company was the dominant force in putting into practice British Government
policy. It had, of course, a great advantage in having
already acquired vast business experience in the Far
East through its dealings in Madras, Bombay and Calcutta over two hundred years. After defeating its rival,
the French East India Company, the British company
had in some areas established direct rule for itself.
The fact that it was nominally under the control of the
British crown did not deter it from pursuing its own

sometimes blatantly piratical and at others maleficent policy.

Privilege and patronage played their part in the company's methods of doing business and, despite its quasi-official status, it was manipulated for private rather than public profit, for the interests of the few rather than that of the nation in the long term.

The directors of the British East India Company evolved a plan by which they could break down the one-way monopoly of Sino-British trade: this was, quite simply, by the export of opium, grown in British India, to China where up to this date it was unknown. Soon this trade was to be worth millions of pounds a year to Britain. It grew to such an extent that the revenues of British India gradually became dependent on the opium trade with China.

By this time it was not difficult to break the bans on two-way trade imposed by the Emperor. The Chinese pirates had themselves contributed to the weakness of the Emperor's case. Even as early as 1797 the pirate squadrons of the China seas actually had shareholders and formed a combine under a certain self-styled Admiral Ching. He not only plundered the coasts but forced the coastal villagers and fishermen to retreat into the interior.

As a bribe to stop his piratical adventures Ching was offered the post of Master of the Royal Stables, but, as soon as they heard he was considering acceptance, his shareholders arranged for him to be poisoned. However, his widow summoned the pirate crews and explained to them what had happened and urged them both to turn down the Emperor's offer and to deal out vengeance to the shareholders. Thus Madame Ching became chief of the pirates, directing them so successfully that she not only often defeated the Emperor's forces, but inflicted a code of harsh discipline on her crews.

This indomitable widow commanded some six hundred war junks and forty thousand victorious pirates, sailing up the Sikiang and burning and looting villages. She was a serious threat to the whole conception of Imperial China at this period.

On the occasion of a second challenge to the pirates

by the Imperial forces, the Emperor's Secret Service devised a bizarre plan for thwarting the forthright, dominant and seemingly indestructible Widow Ching. As the Imperial ships closed in on the pirate squadrons in the Sikiang River they sent out on the wind scores of rice-and-reed-paper kites which the wind bore down to the pirates.

The Widow Ching studied these strange floating messages and noted that they told the fable of a dragon which had always given protection to a fox even though the fox remained ungrateful. The message, repeated so often in kites and streamers, became more disturbing: to this forthright female pirate it was more morale-destroying than any direct war, as had been intended by the Secret Service.

In the end the allegorical messages of the Secret Service bore fruit. The Widow Ching ordered herself to be rowed to the Imperial flagship and, as she clambered aboard, she made the laconic comment: "The fox seeks the dragon's wings."[1]

In this manner the Secret Service won the day: the campaign of the pirates was called off and the Widow Ching not only received her pardon, but for the remainder of her life concentrated entirely on the opium trade. But it was a hollow defeat in the long-term for the Secret Service in that the opium trade paved the way to the domination of China by the Western powers in general and by Britain in particular. Not that this was apparent at the time, for a contemporary Chinese historical chronicler wrote that: "Ships began to pass and repass in tranquility. All became quiet on the rivers and tranquil on the four seas. Men sold their weapons and bought oxen to plough their fields. They buried sacrifices, said prayers on the tops of fields and rejoiced themselves by singing behind screens during the day-time."

The opium trade was not confined wholly to the British: the Americans also participated, though not to the same extent. By the early 1830s the deliberate and insidious export of opium into China by Britain and America was beginning to balance trade. Just how cynically this vicious trade was being pursued—and let there be no doubt that it was done as much to

92

demoralise the Chinese as to counteract the one-way trade taboo—can be summed up by this quotation culled from the log book of the British opium smuggler, Captain Innes: "Employed delivering briskly. No time to read my Bible or to keep my journal."[2]

In 1800 the Emperor Chia Ching had banned opium from China. By this time it was belatedly realised what moral havoc it was playing with the Chinese people as well as the way it was making inroads into Chinese currency. But the demand for opium became so great that corruption and smuggling nullified the ban.

By 1829 the British were exporting more than twenty-one million dollars' worth of opium annually from India into China, while the Americans acquired about four million dollars' worth of trade. The damage done to the people by the opium trade was only slowly realised, as also was the fact that the Chinese were paying out vast sums of silver for the opium. It must be admitted that the Imperial Secret Service was the last to realise the implications to the morale of their own people and the drain on the Treasury.

The events which ultimately led to the Opium Wars were speeded up in 1834 when the old East India Company monopoly of trade was broken and independent merchants began to attempt to build up their own trade with China. Then it began to penetrate the minds of the Government in Peking that opium, grown in India, was the secret and vital commodity of exchange for the silks and teas which the Western World bought from China. Thus, as the Chinese demand for opium grew under the seductiveness of the drug, so the balance of trade became as unfavourable to China in the 1840s as it had been to Britain fifty years previously.

The British had deliberately stepped up the production of opium in India so that it could be sold at lower prices in China, but with still greater overall profit. The opium poppy as the basis for a drug had been known in China for many years, but the smoking of opium on a large scale only developed in that country after the British-inspired trade drive. Once the trade was launched the increase in the demand for the drug was at a phenomenal rate: the number of chests of opium exported or smuggled into China in 1800, when the Emperor officially banned it, was only about four thousand, yet, despite the ban, this had risen by 1821 to about forty thousand.

Opium-smoking became prevalent in the Chinese Army, in the lower echelons of the Civil Service and even among the entourage of the Emperor himself. It was because the smoking habit cut right across the class structure that it did so much harm, lowering the living standards of the poorer classes because it cost them so much, and creating corruption and demoralisation in the highest classes.

At length the Emperor appointed Lin Tse-hsu as his Special Commissioner to Canton charged with the task of stamping out the evils of opium smuggling and with full powers to organise a special secret service for this purpose.

This was the first occasion in the nineteenth century when China's Secret Service was forced into action against a foreign power. It called for a man of exceptional character with great organising ability and one who would have to fight on two fronts at once, against the British smugglers and merchants on the one hand, and the Chinese intermediaries in the traffic on the other.

Lin Tse-hsu has been characterised in Britain as brutal and obstinate and, of course, as the foremost enemy of Britain in China. In fact he was a reasonable and gentle man, a scholar whose journals are full of shafts of wisdom, with a talent for poetry. He was widely read and fully understood the virtues and strengths as well as the vices and weaknesses of the Western World. He had a gift for summing up situations in neat phrases as when he declared: "It would seem that the Jesus-religion preached by Matteo Ricci was Catholicism, whereas the Jesus-religion preached afterwards by Verbiest was Christianity. The two terms 'Catholic' and 'Christian' must depict some such difference of emphasis."[3]

It was, of course, solely because the East India Company had not wanted to pay for Chinese goods entirely in silver that it had decided to make opium the equivalent of a hard currency. Thus the cultivation of the poppy not only came under a strict monopoly, but was made compulsory; a contemporary observer in India at that time wrote: ". . . the cultivation of the poppy, the preparation of the drug and the traffic in it until it is sold at auction for exploration are under a strict monopoly. . . . Vast tracts of the very best land in Benares, Behar and elsewhere in the northern and central parts of India are now covered with poppies; and the other plants used for food or clothing, grown from time immemorial, have nearly been driven out."[4]

China was now facing a heavy loss of silver through the opium traffic, but it had not been until 1825 that the Censors detected that the inflow of opium was its cause. Even Lin Tse-hsu set about his task in somewhat leisurely fashion at first. Born in 1785, he was well into his fifties when allotted the post of Anti-Opium Commissioner. He had had thirty-five years' experience of administration in various branches of the Civil Service and the reputation of being a moderate reformer, an honest executive and extremely conscious of the moral threat which opium-smoking posed to the Chinese people.

Yet, so slow was travel in the Imperial China of this era, that, on taking up his appointment, his journey from Peking to Canton, where he arrived on 10 March 1839, covered a period of more than two months, averaging a mere twenty miles per day. But once in Canton he set about organising his intelligence service with vigour, stressing that one absolute necessity of this service was for it to have several interpreters and translators, as he insisted on obtaining copies of all Western books and newspapers and having them combed for any small clue or item of information which might throw light on the opium traffic.

This emphasis on first studying the subject under investigation through the media of books and newspapers, technical magazines and even commercial house organs, is a permanent feature of Chinese Intelligence work. One comes across it again and again, just as much, if not more so, in the 1970s as in earlier centuries. It may seem a slow and third-hand method of setting about inquiries which call for direct fact-gathering, but it gives the sifters of intelligence the supreme advantage of knowing the background to their subject thoroughly so that they cannot be fooled or fobbed off by inaccurate information from their agents in the field. It also means that much intelligence can be more cheaply and accurately obtained in this manner than by risking valuable agents who may be caught.

Lin Tse-hsu appointed as his chief translator a man who had been taught Latin by Catholic missionaries and had learned his English from Church of England missionaries in Malacca. "The influence of Protestantism will counteract the Catholicism and the fact that the Catholics have already seen this has required some imagination on their part," declared Lin Tse-hsu.

On the strength of the intelligence that he gathered Lin Tse-hsu sent letters to Queen Victoria, pointing out the evils of the opium trade and hoping that by this direct appeal he might achieve more than by direct action against the merchants. It is a passage from this letter which is quoted at the beginning of this chapter.[5]

As far as his agents inside China were concerned Lin swiftly tracked down all the middle men of his own race who imported and distributed the opium. This was his main aim and he believed—mistakenly as it proved—that if he could destroy this network and at the same time make a great crusading appeal to Queen Victoria over the heads of the diplomats, politicians and merchants, he could solve the problem. Certainly his policy was worth trying, but he soon found that the British merchants and organisers of the traffic could not so easily be forced to give up. They intended to hold on to their stockpile of opium until new networks for distributing it could be built up inside China.

It was then that Lin made a series of miscalculations. First of all he blockaded the section of Canton where the British and American merchants had been allowed to set up establishments, ordering the confinement of some three hundred and fifty men, including Queen Victoria's representative, Captain Elliot, in what were known as the Thirteen Factories. This move was supported by the great mass of the

Cantonese people, among whom propaganda against the merchants had been carefully worked up by Lin's agents. And Lin scored one quick, spectacular success: he forced the merchants to deliver up their opium stocks and on 3 June 1839, had the whole lot publicly destroyed, a total of twenty thousand chests of the drug.

But the merchants, far from regarding this as a defeat, took the view that Lin had overreached himself and by his action directly challenged the power of the British Crown. The merchants were released after they had surrendered their stocks and they quickly made representations to the British Government that such treatment could not be tolerated and that a show of force should be made against China.

A series of incidents inflamed the situation. In July 1839, some drunken British sailors killed a Chinese peasant and the Chinese authorities demanded that the criminals be handed over to their jurisdiction. Captain Elliot refused this request and—one suspects with deliberate intent to affront China—carried out his own inquiry and then blandly announced that he had been unable to identify the killers.

Lin was in many respects a wise man and a scholar, but like many scholars he cherished certain odd items of information which, though recorded as fact in some journals, were unable to be checked against the most advanced Western technical knowledge. He believed that a ban on the export of Chinese tea and rhubarb would ruin the health of the Westerners. Indeed he sincerely believed that if Britons were deprived of rhubarb they would all die of constipation. He was also badly misinformed by the military and naval section of his espionage service, having been told that any British warships venturing up Chinese rivers could easily be destroyed by archers at strategic points and by fireships.

Thus once again a section of Chinese Intelligence had done an excellent job inside its own territory, but sadly failed in getting all the right information from outside it. Because of this the potential military power of the British was hidden from Lin and the result was the First Opium War.

It was one of the blackest chapters in British commercial imperialism. From 1839 to 1842 British troops were landed on the Chinese coast, occupying Canton, Amoy, Shanghai and Ningpo and cutting off the Grand Imperial Canal, the main trade route between North and South China. Prior to this Lin had attempted to fight a rearguard action by forcing the British community to retreat from Canton to Macao and later to Hongkong, an island which was then largely uninhabited, but soon to become the chief European port of the Far East.

But it must not be thought that Lin Tse-hsu was altogether the victim of false intelligence and ignorance of Western science. Inevitably even so astute a Chinese scholar as Lin would have been at a disadvantage in assessing Western technology and scientific progress, not to mention medical knowledge. What cannot be stressed too much is that all the time he was attempting to learn from the West, to absorb and analyse the information that flowed in to him and, even when relations with the Western World were at their worst, he still retained a few trusted Western advisers, of whom probably the closest was Dr Peter Parker, an American missionary and writer who had gone out to China in 1834.

Parker was frequently consulted by Lin Tse-hsu. It may seem strange that he was not asked the truth about the rhubarb folk tale, especially as Parker was invited by Lin to treat him for hernia trouble as well as to work out a plan for curing opium addicts. The American on his part was anxious to see the opium traffic ended and to work for peace between China and the Western powers.

Even when the majority of Westerners were forced to leave Canton, Parker remained there, carrying on not only his medical work, but doing translations for Lin.[6]

From 1840 onwards there was little Lin Tse-hsu could do to check the Western powers either through the use of his intelligence service, or by his secret diplomacy. He tried to cut off supplies to Hongkong, but failed. When the British expeditionary force seized

Chusan Island, south of Shanghai, in the summer of 1840 it was clear that his days in office were numbered. By the autumn he had been recalled by the Emperor and dismissed from his post. By this time the British were within a hundred miles of Peking and Lin was blamed for causing the war.

The British expedition was not merely an attempt to protect their nationals: it was punitive and brutal aggression. As the forces advanced they looted indiscriminately, killed civilians and humiliated the Chinese in every possible way. The superior modern weapons of the British were too powerful for the Chinese, whose government belatedly began to seek negotiations.

There was considerable opposition to the Opium War in England, but this of course was not reflected by the conduct of the war in China, though the British Inspector of Trade at Canton wrote privately of the "disgrace and sin of this [opium] traffic forced on China".

A harsh treaty was imposed on the Chinese when the British finally won the war. China was compelled to legalise the opium trade and pay an indemnity for the stocks which had been captured and destroyed by Lin. The treaty of Nanking in 1842 also provided for the surrender of Hongkong to the British and the opening of five major ports in China to British trade. In addition British nationals were exempt from Chinese law and given extra-territorial rights. Further than this China had to give an undertaking not to charge more than 5 per cent import duty on foreign goods, thus in effect preventing the development of her own industry.

Once the British had shown what they could impose on China the other Western powers followed suit. Caleb Cushing, of the United States, bluntly demanded a similar treaty with the Chinese and to add insult to injury rounded off his note with the comment that refusal to negotiate would be regarded "as an act of national insult and a just cause for war". The Treaty of Wanghsia in 1844 was a direct result of this demand by the U.S.A. and, while obtaining extra-territorial rights, in some respects it obtained even greater advantages for America than Britain had acquired. The French followed suit shortly afterwards, taking care to benefit from the experience of both British and Americans.

What left such an unpleasant odour to the aftermath of the Opium War was that the Christian missionaries had in some cases sided with the opium merchants and actually taken money from them for acting as intermediaries for negotiating with the Chinese, while the British were blatantly hypocritical in pretending, not least to their own people, that the war had nothing to do with the opium traffic, but was merely to bring the blessings of modern civilisation to China and to ensure free and fair trade. And when the Chinese negotiators challenged Sir Henry Pottinger, the British envoy, to help prohibit the growth of the opium poppy, he admitted to them privately that "it is not a very pleasant trade", but made the astonishing, irrelevant and untrue statement that to stop it would be "inconsistent with our constitutional system".

Thus the legal importing of opium into China, causing misery and poverty and wrecking human lives, continued until 1917 and extra-territorial rights for foreign nationals were not legally ended until the middle of World War II when the aid of China was needed in the war against Japan. The opium trade grew enormously and by the middle 1850s it had reached eighty thousand chests a year, almost four times as much as before the Opium War. To make matters worse, China, who had previously exported textiles to the West, now imported cotton—to the great detriment of her economy.

What is abundantly clear is that, after the disastrous defeat which was suffered diplomatically by Lin Tse-hsu, China ceased to have any effective Secret Service which could combat her Western enemies for many years to come. For this the decaying, reactionary and still feudal court of the Manchus was mainly responsible.

The Manchus, it is true, faced trouble on every front, internally as well as externally. There was the remarkable success achieved by the Taiping revolution, launched as a passionate crusade by Hung Hsiu-chuan, who formulated a strange new creed that was partly his own adaptation of Christianity, partly political, anti-feudal, borrowing not a little from the earlier ideas of Wang An-shih, demanding that "all land under heaven should be cultivated by all the people under heaven"—which, in effect, meant equalitarian agrarianism.

Western missionaries at first were tempted to be well disposed to Hung Hsiu-chuan because he based his faith on Christianity, but when Hung's armies swept across China, destroying their enemies, they began to back the Manchus, if only to see law and order restored. Yet Henry Meadows, the British Consul at Shanghai, in a dispatch to Lord John Russell, the British Foreign Secretary, on 19 February 1861, wrote that in territory occupied by the Taipings through which he had passed "there must be greater security of life and property than in those occupied by the Manchus".

The Manchus' now impotent Secret Service failed totally to check Hung's revolution and for fourteen years the Imperial Government was engaged in checking the Taipings' ravages while the Europeans, both merchants and diplomats, took every advantage of this situation in strengthening their foothold in China and setting up new spheres of influence there.

It is clear from contemporary reports that the European Secret Services were active in China and that they amassed a great deal of information about the Taipings' military strength and their policies. Indeed there had been some advice from both the British and French Secret Services that their respective governments should make a deal with the Taipings, secretly arming them to defeat the Manchus and then, having used them to gain control of China, manipulate them as the main instrument of Western policy.

Such advice was discarded. Neither the British nor the French merchants liked Hung and his revolutionary talk, but at the same time they were happy that he should weaken the authority of the Manchus. But as the Taiping campaign continued the Western powers became alarmed that China might sink into an uncontrollable situation of chaotic government incapable of taking decisions or of doing any trade at all. In this the Western powers made just as false a reading of the situation as the Chinese had in the latter part of the eighteenth century, for the Taipings, given Western backing, might have helped build a new and more modern China and in the long run been a better proposition for the West. On the other hand they equally mistrusted the Western powers and suspected that there was some kind of a plot to exploit them against the Manchus, so they consistently refused all foreign aid.

It is therefore apparent that the Western Secret Services were not all that much superior to the Chinese in this period. Many of their spy-masters completely misread the turbulent situation inside China without having any of those excuses, such as the lack of technical knowledge from which the Chinese Secret Service undoubtedly suffered.

It is difficult, writing in the latter part of the twentieth century, to be objective about Western policy at this time. To write in accordance with contemporary *mores* and the acknowledged humanistic creeds of the 1970s is to underline the statements of Chairman Mao and to admit the errors of the worst forms of irresponsible and selfish capitalist government. It is true that the Western powers in China in the middle of the nineteenth century were grasping, greedy, cruel, racially-prejudiced and had double standards of morality, exemplified in the fact that they did not care which side they supported just as long as they succeeded in dominating China and squeezing the last ounce of trade advantage from that country. On the other hand, bearing in mind the fact that the Western powers—and this included some of the more enlightened Radicals among them—regarded themselves as the torch-bearers of civilisation, that they were determined to win for their own peoples every possible advantage in the world, they were at least resolute, courageous and determined defenders of the prosperity of their own people.

The awful tragedy of the nineteenth century attitude may in the long run lie not so much in the harm

it wrought among backward peoples and colonial de-
pendents, but in the psychological back-lash of
stricken consciences which has caused the Western
governments increasingly in the twentieth century to
lose not only their nerve, but their fundamental beliefs in their own people and, worse still, in their
duties to their own people. This clash between conscience and will to govern has resulted in many of
these Western Governments falling easy prey not
merely to the governments of former underdeveloped
countries, but to the Secret Services of the latter as well.

The Western Powers turned the screw on the Manchus, trying to expand their influence in China. They
wanted an excuse for, if not launching another war,
at least further naked aggression. This came in 1856
when the Chinese Government captured a Chinese
opium junk which was flying the British flag. Using
this as a pretext, the French and the British declared
war on China—the Second Opium War. In 1857
Canton was bombarded by the combined Anglo-
French forces and the latter also landed troops at
Tientsin, only eighty miles from the Chinese capital.

Again the Manchus were forced to concede terms
to obtain peace. In 1858 they paid indemnity for the
war, conceded the right for foreigners to live in Peking,
strengthened and extended the legislation both of the
opium traffic and the rights of missionaries and opened
new ports to settlements by foreign administrations.
Russia, who had not taken part in this war, and the
United States, who had not declared war but had taken
part in hostilities, gained considerably from the Anglo-
French Treaties in managing to make similar treaties
with China on the basis of the "most favoured nation
clause".

The Manchus, not unnaturally, according to their
own leisurely approach to life, delayed in ratifying
these treaties. The response of the Western powers
was almost as appalling as that of Attila the Hun.
The Anglo-French forces fought their way into the
capital and destroyed the Yuan Ming Yuan Summer
Palace, which contained one of the world's greatest
art collections. Victor Hugo, writing in 1861 in complaint against this senseless destruction, said that "the

governments are sometimes robbers, the people never. I hope, one day, when France is liberated, these 'prizes' will be given back to China."

In these negotiations with the Manchus one small reservation had been won by the Chinese from the West: it was that the concession allowing British ships to navigate the Yangtse River would become operative only as soon as peace was restored in Taiping territory. From then on it was only a matter of time before the Taipings, hitherto sometimes silently supported by the West, were totally defeated by the Sino-Anglo-French manoeuvre. Soon the British and the French were fighting alongside the Manchus against the Taipings.

This in effect put the Manchus further under Western control, as the British sent gun-boats up the Yangtse River, supplied the most modern rifles to the Manchus and provided Army officers as advisers to the Imperial Court.

Hung died at Nanking in 1864 and six weeks later the Manchus captured that city. Thus the Western powers in their pursuit of so-called progress backed the corrupt and recalcitrant Manchus and finally helped to destroy the Taipings whose aim was to ensure that all should be well fed, that opium smoking should be punished and corruption stamped out.

10

Empress Tzu-hsi and the Secret Service of Li Lien-ying 1852-1870

Even in your secret chamber you are watched;
See you do nothing to blush for,
Though only the ceiling looks down upon you.
The Book of Odes

BY the middle of the nineteenth century everything pointed towards the ultimate breaking-up of the Chinese empire and the seizure of power, if not the total control of territories, by the Western powers. The Emperor Hsien Feng was so lacking in adequate sources of intelligence that he had only the vaguest ideas about what was going on in the country he ruled. Added to this was the fact that there was no male heir to the throne, a portent which filled courtiers and people alike with grave misgivings.

In consequence of this, one day in 1852, some seventeen beautiful maidens, each of them seventeen years old, were summoned to appear before the Emperor and Empress so that Hsien Feng could choose a consort in the hope that one of them would provide him with a son. Among those so favoured was a girl named Lan Kei, the daughter of a minor Manchu official. She had been engaged to marry a young Manchu guardsman, named Jung Lu, but, being both ambitious and flattered by the command to appear before the Emperor, she was determined to make the most of this opportunity. She was helped and coached on the points of etiquette and behaviour by a senior Court eunuch named Li Lien-ying, who had undertaken the mission of interviewing the girls to be presented to the Emperor.

It is said that Li Lien-ying, impressed by her purposeful character and bearing, instinctively saw in Lan Kei (the name meant "Orchid") a future ally at court and that he was equally determined to further her ambitions and ensure that she would be chosen. He advised her not to wear any make-up because "your personal beauty is sufficient" and to wear a lavender dress which he was sure would meet with the Emperor's approval.

At the presentation Lan Kei showed such self-possession and composure and concentrated her whole attention on the Emperor in such an adroit yet un-ostentatious manner that, while she felt she had immediately won his approval, she was sure she had incurred the Empress's dislike. A few days later Li Lien-ying called at her house with a sedan chair and informed her that it was the Emperor's wish she should join his harem and become his favourite concubine, but making it clear that to win the permanent affection of the Emperor she must present him with a son and heir.

So Lan Kei became Emperor Hsien Feng's favourite and at the same time she formed a close alliance with the eunuch Li Lien-ying, who aspired to be the chief intelligence agent at the court. Four years later she presented Hsien Feng with the male heir he wanted, an event which was celebrated in the Forbidden City with a public holiday, firework displays, theatricals and widespread rejoicing. So great was the joy at the birth of a son that prisoners were given amnesty, caged birds were set free, fish that were being kept alive in water awaiting their transfer to the market were instead thrown back into lakes and ponds, and decorations were put up everywhere.

However, in some circles, especially those that were close to the Empress Tzu-an, the news of the birth of a son was greeted with suspicion and even with whispers of a palace plot. It was known that Li Lien-ying was Lan Kei's closest ally at Court and rumours suggested that the male baby was not hers at all, but that the eunuch Li had obtained one from a poor woman whom he had had murdered so that her secret should never be known.

Most probably these rumours were false: certainly there is no proof of them. But it is certain that Lan Kei heard all about them and that made her all the more determined to confound her enemies in due course. She suspected, probably rightly, that her chief enemy was the Empress Tzu-an.

In honour of her giving birth to a male heir Lan Kei was henceforth given a new name and title—Tzu-hsi, which means "Auspicious and Motherly", the former designation being apt, the latter to prove somewhat inaccurate. For with Tzu-hsi, as henceforth she was always known, devotion to a son was of much less importance than personal ambition.

Then in the year 1861 Tzu-hsi's son became the Emperor on the death of his father and Tzu-hsi was not only exalted to the title of Dowager Empress (shared with Tzu-an), but occupied the post of co-Regent in the Government. As she was given a palace of her own on the western side of the Forbidden City she became known as the "Western Empress". She was well prepared for her new rôle, for not only had she used her influence with Li Lien-ying, but in the lifetime of the Emperor Hsien Feng she had persuaded him to let her study affairs of state, to see petitions presented to the Court and even to be in a position to advise on certain appointments.

In this manner she quickly learned that the Emperor was not obtaining adequate intelligence on what was going on in his domains, and she was determined to remedy this in her own way and to her own advantage. Romantic historians have painted Tzu-hsi as a great beauty: it would be fairer to say, in the light of some not altogether flattering portraits, that her looks were not her fortune, but that her personality, strong character, charm and intelligence set her out above men and women of her age.

Probably because of her youth, possibly because she thought the conservative elements in the Government were her natural enemies, Tzu-hsi in her early days sided with their opponents, who, if far from radical, were at least opposed to Hsien Feng having fled from Peking in the face of the Western invaders. Indeed, it was this strategy on her part which had deeply impressed the men at the Court: they saw that a female was more of a fighter than the Emperor himself.

Tzu-hsi had urged the Emperor to remain in Peking. He had declined her advice and made the feeble excuse that he was going to Jehol on "an autumn tour of inspection", this city (now Chengteh) being the site of the Manchus' north-east palace. But Tzu-hsi remained in the capital and to some extent became the mouthpiece of the absent and frightened Emperor.

She was only twenty-five years old when she witnessed the invasion of Peking by the Western powers and the destruction of the Summer Palace by the British forces, ordered by Lord Elgin on the slim pretext that some European envoys had been harshly treated. "Its deliberate destruction, for no military purpose, roused intense indignation throughout China," wrote Bernard Martin and Shui Chien-tung. "The charred ruins were left untouched as a monument to European barbarity."[1]

The Emperor inevitably lost face by fleeing from the capital, whereas Tzu-hsi enhanced her status by remaining and in some respects acting on behalf of the then feeble Hsien Feng. But there seems little doubt that the ambitious concubine used this situation to her own advantage, by staying behind in Peking and winning allies in her determination to see her son as the legitimate successor to Hsien Feng.

The true story of the fate of Hsien Feng, like that of the birth of his son, despite much probing by modern historians, remains even now a matter for some speculation. Both events may to some extent have been controlled by the Secret Service which, as in the reigns of previous weak Emperors, had grown up and even improved—probably because of the ineptness of the Emperor rather than despite it.

It is therefore possible that whether or not the son of Tzu-hsi was that of Hsien Feng, the Secret Service had a plan ready to produce a substitute son if the Emperor proved incapable of producing a son himself. Indeed it could be that Tzu-hsi was herself incapable of producing children and that this discovery could have produced a close bond between her and Li Lien-ying. Similarly with Hsien Feng, the Secret Service—and at this period as for many years to come this in effect meant the intelligence service of Li Lien-ying—may have made provisional plans to dispose of him even if he died a natural death.

Tzu-hsi had managed to install in the Summer Palace at Peking as commander of the Imperial Guard Jung Lu, the Manchu guardsman to whom she had formerly been engaged. Gossips said that he was now her lover and also one of her chief sources of intelligence, though not to the extent that Li Lien-ying was. Another close ally at this time was Prince Kung, who, while the British and French troops were skirmishing in the outskirts of Peking, was given the task of negotiating with them, while Tzu-hsi with all the Grand Councillors and the Imperial eunuchs set out for Jehol.

Some sources state that the Emperor, "weakened by the turmoil around him, fell ill and died in Jehol".[2] But Bernard Martin and Shui Chien-tung make the blunt allegation that Tzu-hsi "did not wait on events, events must happen at her bidding. She ordered her faithful Li to poison the Emperor and steal the great seal, used on all important documents. When this murder was accomplished her spies reported that the Grand Secretary intended to make himself Regent."[3]

Whatever the truth it is indisputable that Tzu-hsi acted swiftly, ruthlessly and from a position of great strength. This was almost entirely because she was the only person in the Imperial Court with an intelligence service that was effective. "A small woman with a strong chin, Tzu-hsi rapidly developed a taste for power with an outstanding ability to hold on to it," writes Marina Warner.[4] "Obstinate, capricious and inquisitive, she manipulated the Throne's advisers by posing as a helpless female at the head of a vast empire, by staging sudden violent rages, or by adeptly picking the exact Confucian maxim or hallowed historical precedent to confound her ministers. . . . Tzu-hsi's tyranny was effective."

The battle for power after the death of the Emperor was certainly not made easy for Tzu-hsi. The Grand Secretary anticipated that she would contest his own claims to the Regency, though he did not know that she had the Imperial seal safely hidden in her luggage. Tzu-hsi had carefully studied Chinese protocol and she knew that without this seal all edicts on the transfer of power were invalid. Thus any attempt by the Grand Secretary to take over the Regency would have been illegal.

The funeral procession from Jehol to Peking followed its traditionally deliberate slow pace and Tzu-hsi took advantage of this by going ahead of the others to Peking while the Grand Secretary and his allies were plotting to have both her and the Dowager Empress assassinated. It was Jung Lu, now certainly Tzu-hsi's lover, who learned about this plot and was able to warn both the royal ladies about the Grand Secretary's intentions. Thus by the time the funeral procession reached Peking, Tzu-hsi was in full control of the situation and not merely ready to deal with the plotters, but fully conversant with all the legal processes essential for her next step to power—a share in the Regency.

Tzu-hsi never allowed her prejudices to blind her to reality. In this instance she acted with perfect logic: the lives of both herself and the Dowager Empress were threatened; therefore, however much they may have been enemies in the past, this was the moment to make a pact and to share the Regency. Giving Jung Lu full powers, she ordered him to arrest the Grand Secretary, who was immediately charged with treason. Producing the official seal she had herself and the Dowager Empress proclaimed joint-Regents during the minority of the new boy-Emperor, her son.

From this time onwards she decided, as a precautionary measure, to divide the control of her Secret Service into two sections, one under Li Lien-ying, the other under Jung Lu, who for a brief time had the nominal title of Chief of Intelligence. Tzu-hsi must have been an extremely clever psychologist: she judged that this would keep Li Lien-ying on his mettle and ensure that he made even greater efforts to prove his loyalty. With others it might have had an exactly contrary effect: with the eunuch, conscious of the influence of the lover-guardsman, it made him even more determined to prove his devotion to the concubine whose cause he had for so long supported.

Ultimately it was Li Lien-ying who became the senior and indeed the most influential chief of intelligence, for his leverage was that as a eunuch he was always personally closer to the Empress than any lover could hope to be. It was on his advice that the personal property of the Grand Secretary was confiscated and made over to Tzu-hsi so that she could take her first step towards building up her own personal fortune. From that period she gradually created for herself an impregnable position. The Dowager Empress was ageing and in poor health and not really interested in affairs of state so there was little competition from that quarter. Both Jung Lu and Li Yien-ling ensured that Tzu-hsi had an excellent intelligence service that provided her with daily reports on what was going on; and they marginally improved the quality of information concerning what the Western powers were doing in China itself.

The boy Emperor was controlled by his mother (with the constant admonitions of Li Yien-ling and Jung Lu) in much the same manner as a ventriloquist's doll. He was taken out of his nursery chambers and installed on the throne only when Tzu-hsi decreed it. Even then he was subjected to the pantomime of his mother being hidden behind curtains at the back of his throne, whispering to him what he was to say and listening to every word he uttered. As one contemporary scribe put it: "The boy Emperor Tungchih ruled with his mother whispering behind the curtain."[5]

It was a period of great difficulty in the task of governing China, trying to prevent her from disintegrating into minor kingdoms with whole areas being given over to agrarian experiments or banditry. If there was a ruler to meet the needs of the hour it was Tzu-hsi and, like Empress Wu before her, she showed an intelligence, courage and ruthlessness the equal of, if not greater than, the same qualities in any previous Emperor. She was in fact a highly intelligent tyrant devoted to defending the now seriously threatened Empire.

Nor did China's problems lie solely with the Western powers. The Chinese were on the worst possible terms with the Japanese, who had been backed by the Americans, while even the British had begun to see advantages in having Japan as an ally not merely to turn the screw still harder on the oppressed Chinese, but also as a potential ally against Czarist Russia. Japan, in the eyes of the Western powers, was a relatively tiny land mass, whereas China was a vast continent-sized nation which was ripe for plucking and sharing out among themselves.

Tzu-hsi's Secret Service was effective not only in putting down the remnants of the Taiping revolutionaries, but in establishing intelligence links with Russia. She ordered Jung Lu to have his agents infiltrate the ranks of Consular servants and to carry out their work of sabotaging the Taipings from this seemingly inauspicious vantage point. Perhaps nobody but Tzu-hsi would have considered such a ploy workable. But her agents carried out their tasks efficiently. When the Taipings were driven out of Ningpo in 1862 it was reported that: "One of the principal murderers and torturers . . . was one A-fook, the British Consul's boy, or personal attendant . . . who was dressed up in silks and who, stuck upon a pony, paraded the city with attendants, ordering them to execute the unfortunates and issuing orders (which were actually obeyed) to the English soldiers."[6]

Tsu-hsi was a realist. She hated the Western powers and with good reason: she had seen the destruction they had wrought in her country. But she had the good sense to know that they could not be ignored, that a *modus vivendi* must be created. Similarly, while she was absolutely ruthless in crushing the remaining members of the Taiping revolution, she appreciated the need for reforms in the empire.

Her son, the Emperor, not being allowed to behave other than as a puppet, spoiled by the women of the court and (deliberately, one suspects, on Tzu-hsi's orders) corrupted by the eunuchs, most of whom were her secret agents, he became a dissolute young man with no conception of his imperial rôle and caring even less about it.

Tzu-hsi knew exactly where she was going. She never had the least intention of handing over power to her son, for she was convinced that she alone had the gifts which would save the Empire. The truth is that she did manage to postpone the breaking-up of the empire for many years and was its last really competent ruler. If her two Secret Service chiefs had been as competent as she was herself, less corrupt and less insular, she might well have saved the empire for another generation.

But her Secret Service was, in these early years of her assumption of power, too closely concerned with domestic details. Both Li Yien-ling and Jung Lu became so involved in competing for the Empress's favours and in furthering her cause domestically that they had little time for building up really efficient intelligence outside China, though what they achieved was vastly superior to anything appertaining to the previous Emperor's reign and they at least established tenuous links with Russia for the first time for many years.

One question remains unanswered and perhaps only a close look at Tzu-hsi's largely personal Secret Service could answer it. This is the debatable point as to whether the Emperor Tung-chih died a natural death, or whether, like his father, he may have been killed by the Secret Service. One must remember that Tzu-hsi was a diligent student not merely of Chinese law and protocol, but of Chinese classical history, and she had been known to express her great admiration for the talents of the Empress Wu, who, as we have seen, was never reluctant to have her enemies murdered.

When Tzu-hsi was thirty-seven, her son came of age and she was by law obliged to hand over power to him. It could be argued that as she had dominated him as a child, so she could continue to influence him as Emperor. To Tzu-hsi's legalistic mind, however, this was not the same thing as actually possessing the full and valid powers of a ruler.

Reports on what happened at this time differ. Some

113

say that Tzu-hsi chose a wife for her son and that she strongly disapproved of his excursions to the brothels of the poorer quarters of Peking outside the walls of the Forbidden City. Others assert that, though Tzu-hsi kept a close watch on affairs of state after her son achieved full powers, "the Emperor and the young Empress did not wish to refer everything to the former Regent, and their independence offended Tzu-hsi. She had no intention of allowing an unruly son and a mere daughter-in-law to settle matters as they pleased." [7] These reports do not altogether ring true. If Tzu-hsi chose a wife for her son, one can be sure she would have selected either an ally or one who was compliant to her wishes. Then again, knowing the stern authority which the Regent wielded over her son, it is hard to accept the story that he would defy her wishes by going to the lowest type of brothel outside the Palace precincts in the poorest quarter of the city and, what is more, to be conducted there by the eunuchs who were her own agents, or at least under the control of Li Yien-ling. "These excursions may have cost him his life," writes J. Dean Barrett. "He died, perhaps from smallpox, perhaps from venereal disease, after two brief years as, nominally, a real ruler." [8]

As to how he died one cannot be sure, but much evidence points to the fact that the end was engineered by his mother in such a manner that death appeared to Court officials to have been from natural causes. Dispatches from the British Consul, although they are merely a summary of reports brought to him, suggest that "the progress to perdition, if not to actual death, of the young Emperor had been organised over a long period by Li Lien-ying who not only encouraged, but arranged for him to be smuggled out of the Summer Palace to the kind of bordellos which are normally frequented by the very lowliest of the Chinese people." [9]

It is probable that the Emperor Tung-chih died from venereal disease: he had no son and was said, because of a disease he had contracted, to be incapable of producing children. On the other hand Bernard Martin and Shui Chien-tung assert that while the

114

young Emperor was suffering from smallpox, Tzu-hsi learned that "the Empress was pregnant. This was not at all what she wanted . . . if the child were a boy, he would be heir to the throne and his young mother would become Regent."[10]

Whatever the Emperor was suffering from, it is clear from all the evidence that for a while he seemed to be recovering and then had a mysterious relapse. Within a few hours he was dead. He may have been poisoned: that is impossible to prove. But it is almost certain that he was slowly dying and that venereal disease dating back to the earliest days of puberty was the cause of this, and not smallpox as has been suggested.

An American missionary of the period, Jonas Rotblat, a close associate of that great American adventurer, Frederick Townsend Ward, who was one of the principal intriguers among the Westerners in China in this era, stated long afterwards that he had been consulted over a period of years on the subject of venereal disease by Li Yien-ling. "I was asked to supply a great deal of information to which, at that time, there were no easy answers. One of them was the effect of the disease on the mind, the other was the length of time it took to kill a person and the third was to what extent it rendered the victim incapable of bearing children."[11] It could therefore be that the eunuchs, ordered by Li, or even Jung Lu, if not by Tzu-hsi herself, were responsible for luring the young Emperor to the brothels and ensuring that he contracted venereal disease. On the other hand this disease can be a slow killer and it may be that in the end the young Emperor was simply poisoned, possibly at the very moment when he was recovering from smallpox.

Sinisterly melodramatic as such devious and complicated plots may seem, what happened afterwards shows that Tzu-hsi was capable of such infamy. When the Emperor died she called a Council of Ministers and urged that her sister's baby son should be proclaimed Emperor with herself and Tzu-an as joint Regents again. At the same time, having heard the rumour that the Empress was pregnant (whether by her supposedly impotent husband, or another man, is not clear), she took her on one side and suggested that traditionally the truly noble and loyal wife followed her husband to the grave—in other words, committed suicide.

The foolish young wife killed herself and so all was neatly arranged for Tzu-hsi to put her plan into action. Once again she was Regent and the 4-year-old son of her sister, Kuang-hsu, was declared Emperor. Despite the secrecy with which Tzu-hsi set to work to achieve her objectives, these events did not prevent whispers of scandal and there were many courtiers who suspected a diabolical plot.

This scandal came out into the open when one mandarin committed suicide at the tomb of Tung-chih in protest against his mother's chicanery in having her rivals removed and thereby ensuring her retention of the power behind the throne.

But Tzu-hsi was in such a strong position and her Intelligence Service, which now really deserved capital letters to make it official, was so efficient an instrument in safeguarding her powers that she overcame all obstacles. The combination of Li Yien-ling and Jung Lu, the former with his total control of the eunuchs and servants inside the Court and his close watch on the mandarinate, the latter with his agents among his guardsmen and his relations with some of the Europeans, made Tzu-hsi's position absolutely secure as far as internal threats were posed.

11

Secret Funds Diverted from the Vital Needs of Empire 1864-1885

> The Chinese have always accepted implicitly the belief
> that . . . in judging calligraphy and painting, the highest
> criterion is not whether the artist shows good tech-
> nique but whether he has or has not a high personality.
> *Lin Yutang*

CALLIGRAPHY and espionage may seem peculiar subjects to link together, even if in modern times some
would-be-trendy executives of Western business have
insisted on having the handwriting of prospective employees analysed before making a decision on their
applications. But in China right down the ages calligraphy has been regarded not merely as a fine art
in itself, the equivalent of painting, or of music, classical dancing or architecture, but a key to underlying
truths, an essential key to character, personality and
reliability.

For these reasons over the centuries the finest
known specimens of calligraphy have been regarded
with the same awe and reverence that in the West
have been reserved for the works of Michaelangelo or
the paintings of Rembrandt, for the glories of Versailles and the sonatas of Beethoven.

From the earliest times in China, Emperors and
mandarins have reflected this reverence by considering it one of the prime duties of the Secret Service
to recover lost works of art, whether they have just
disappeared or been stolen. It is not putting too fine
a point on the history of the Chinese Secret Service up
to the latter part of the nineteenth century to say that
possibly one of the reasons why it so often seemed

ineffective by normal standards, and certainly why it was so lacking in overseas intelligence, was because the recovery of art treasures and especially highly valued specimens of calligraphy was regarded as one of its principal functions.

It is necessary to digress for a moment back to the fourth century when the great poet of the age was one Wang Hsi-chih, distinguished for his artistry as a Chinese calligraphist. He composed a celebrated essay known as *The Orchid Pavilion,* composed at a pavilion bearing this name in the Shanyin of Kweich'i for the Water Festival. I will not quote from this essay in any detail, but it is important to give this translation of the latter part of it: "Alas! as we of the present look upon those of the past, so will posterity look upon our present selves. Therefore have I put down a sketch of these contemporaries and their sayings at this feast, and although time and circumstances may change, the way they will evoke our moods of happiness and regret will remain the same. What will future readers feel when they cast their eyes upon this writing."[1]

Wang's verse—twenty-eight sentimental lines with 324 calligraphic characters—aroused delight and praise because of the incomparable beauty of his writing. It was this quality which to the Chinese mind lent greatness to his essay even more than the substance of the essay itself, because in Chinese eyes the beauty of the writing was indivisible from the greatness of the thoughts. It is said that Wang's calligraphy on this occasion rose to great heights because he wrote his essay-poem while somewhat inebriated and that, though he tried in later years to emulate the original masterpiece, he failed to acquire the same flowing grace or rhythms of writing.

Nevertheless the reputation of Wang Hsi-chih went down in history as the greatest calligrapher of all time. Though his works were lost, or, as some alleged, bequeathed to his family who hid them away, for centuries they became collectors' pieces. The best known, of course, was that of *The Orchid Pavilion.* Indeed this story has been standard literary fare for Chinese schoolchildren even up to the present day.

The last, seventh-generation survivor of Wang's

family became a monk and resisted attempts by the Emperor T'ai-tsung of the Tang dynasty to make him surrender the manuscript of *The Orchid Pavilion*. Then the Emperor gave his Secret Service orders that their entire efforts were to be devoted to the recovery of this manuscript and that no other task was to be allowed to divert them from this single mission.

By the seventh century, after long periods of civil war, Wang's manuscript was missing, as were many other works of art. Some had been destroyed; others were kept carefully hidden. When order was restored at the start of the Tang dynasty (618–907) the Emperor sent out his secret agents to recover all works of art for the Imperial Palace. Sometimes he paid for what was found, sometimes not. One of the major problems in collecting works of art at the time was that many counterfeits were offered. It must be remembered that the recovery of art treasures in general, and the finest calligraphical manuscripts above all, was rated as much in the interests of the Empire as would have been worthwhile espionage in the Western World.

After the Emperor had found that he had on occasions paid out money for fakes he set up a Secret Service Board of Experts to authenticate works of art, the first such aesthetic tribunal known in history and one which was an integral part of the Secret Service.

Among the many treasures the Emperor Tai Tsung acquired were some genuine examples of the art of Wang Hsi-chih, but not the most famous of them all, *The Orchid Pavilion,* or as some have named it, *The Story of the Picnic.* The Emperor offered members of his Secret Service a large reward for it and finally one agent, Liao Tchien, succeeded in finding out that a descendant of Wang was abbot of a small Buddhist monastery in a remote and mountainous part of China. It was also indicated that the abbot himself was a calligrapher.

Liao was convinced that the abbot, if he had any inkling of what was required of him, would either refuse outright, or, being a calligrapher, at best offer some counterfeit version of the real manuscript. However, he agreed to take some genuine and some counterfeit manuscripts with which to test out the abbot, and set off in a palanquin with an armed guard.

When he arrived at the monastery the gate-man refused to let him in.

"Tell your master," said the wily Liao, "that I have brought some reputed examples of Wang Hsi-chih's calligraphy, handed down in my family. I want him to look at them and tell me if they are genuine."

After a long wait the gate swung open and Liao and his retinue marched in. Once they were inside the monastery they were sure of being able to stay for several days, since the rules of hospitality required that a guest in such remote places be given time to rest before leaving.

Liao showed his manuscripts to the abbot, but first of all revealed only the fakes. They were swiftly dismissed as counterfeit by the abbot. Finally he examined the authentic manuscripts and after looking them over carefully declared: "At least they are not obvious forgeries."

"How can we be sure?" asked Liao.

"The only way," said the abbot, "is to compare them closely with a Wang manuscript known to be genuine."

"Where can I find such a manuscript?"

After a pause the abbot said: "Wait until all the monks have gone to sleep."

Late that night he took Liao into the monastery library, climbed a ladder to the top of the shelves, reached into a recess just under the roof and drew out several scrolls. He brought them down and spread them out on a table.

All were works of Wang and one of them was *The Orchid Pavilion.*

After careful comparison the abbot told Liao: "Your manuscripts are genuine." Then he climbed the ladder and put his own manuscripts back in their hiding place.

Next day the abbot had to leave the monastery to attend ceremonies that would keep him overnight in a distant town. Late that night Liao went into the library, climbed the ladder and removed *The Orchid Pavilion.* In its place, among the abbot's other scrolls, he left a note saying: "The missing manuscript was taken by order of the Emperor. If you have any objection, you may come and present it at court."

Having done this Liao announced that he was leaving, expressing great regret that he could not wait to thank the abbot personally for his hospitality.

What happened after this is somewhat of a mystery which still intrigues the China of today. It is said that the Wang scroll was carefully copied and that Liao retained the original for himself, while giving the copy to the Emperor. This is plausible, knowing how revered this work of Wang was. Indeed possibly no other manuscript in the whole of history has been coveted by so many people.

Argument today within the Chinese Politburo is being waged as to the authenticity of the extant manuscript of *The Orchid Pavilion*. Kuo Mo-jo, President of Peking's Academia Sinica, who has survived in the Communist Party's hierarchy by penitently admitting "cultural revisionism" in the past, claims that the manuscript is not genuine. But other Chinese scholars insist that it is. Some argument hinges on whether Wang's masterpiece, allegedly written when he was, if not drunk, at least partially intoxicated, must obviously differ from his calligraphy when sober. Whatever the outcome of this prolonged intellectual debate, the fact is that the Chinese officials of today have organised the distribution of copies of the alleged manuscript for the masses to study. Not even the Cultural Revolution has changed the attitude to calligraphy of the seventh century.[2]

This present-day veneration for the calligraphy of Wang Hsi-chih and of *The Orchid Pavilion* in particular is not confined simply to Communist China. It is just as much a cult of the Chinese in Taiwan, or in the United States, or in Singapore, or wherever else they are to be found in large communities. Lin Yutang, writing of this poem essay in 1937, made the point that "the manuscript of this essay, or rather its early rubbings, are today the most highly valued of Chinese calligraphy, because the writer and author, Wang Hsi-chih, is the acknowledged Prince of Calligraphy. For three times he failed to improve upon his original handwriting, and so today the script is preserved to us in rubbings, with all the deletions and additions as they stood in the first draft."[3]

This is but one example of how much time was occupied and what considerable sums of money diverted from secret funds, and therefore from the Secret Service, by the policy of Emperors down the ages using their Intelligence Services to recover great works of art and manuscripts. In the earlier centuries this may culturally have been a good thing, but by the nineteenth century, when there was a real need for a Secret Service to concentrate on what China's growing numbers of enemies were plotting, the use of secret agents as art collectors rapidly became an irrelevance and even a fatuity. Today again this ancient practice of using the Chinese Secret Service to acquire works of art has taken on a new and much more relevant meaning: for works of art substitute the words "learning and knowledge, with special reference to the latest technological knowledge" and one has a fairly clear picture of the modernisation of an ancient technique. But that is a story which rightly belongs to a future chapter.

The Empress Tzu-hsi certainly utilised her Secret Service for adding to her personal wealth in the shape of works of art, though this was always secondary to its main function which was to maintain her as the power behind the throne and always one or two steps ahead of her enemies. But she was determined to rebuild from the ruins left by the British and French in their vandalism directed at the Summer Palace and other buildings in 1860-61, and she not only indulged in reckless expenditure in re-creating a Summer Palace, the I Ho Yuan, or Garden of Harmonious Old Age, but robbed the Chinese Navy of funds from which to do this; and she also ordered Li Lien-ying to scour the country for works of art with which to fill her palaces. The cost of running her household amounted to the enormous sum for that era of £6,-500,000 a year, and it is not without significance that the controller of the household was also Li Lien-ying.

Tzu-hsi believed that the best method of maintaining her prestige and impressing the foreigners who now came to China in greater numbers was by not merely preserving, but enhancing the splendour of the Imperial Court, by building up the image of a picturesque and mystical Empress surrounded by pomp and ritual. Out of the ruins left behind by the Anglo-French vandalism she created not merely new palaces, but bridges across artificial streams and bizarre monuments. Her gardens were planned to create the illusion of a remote countryside with huge boulders of rockery to represent miniature hills and cliffs. During the winter months she was carried in her sedan chair across the Forbidden City to the Sea Palaces, built on three artificial lakes and given the exotic names of the Hall of Sparkling Brightness, the Peak with the Wonderful Cloud Wreath and the Hall of Sweet Dew. There was also a pavilion called Delay of Southern Fragrance and shaped like a fan, which lay spread out alongside another lake. It was in these surroundings that Tzu-hsi indulged her great passion for painting, which she took very seriously indeed.

Mainly through the influence of Li Lien-ying, she had the absolute loyalty of all the Court's eunuchs, and Li himself accompanied her on many of her forays from palace to palace. He has been described as an ugly man, with a wrinkled face, but tall and with "beautiful manners. . . . He had become a eunuch after puberty, and his nickname Pi-hsiao Li ("Cobbler's Wax" Li) referred to a boyhood apprenticeship to a shoemaker. It was rumoured that, tempted by the riches and favours of the Imperial Court, Li had castrated himself with his cobbler's knife."[4]

Like Ho Shen before him, Li enriched himself through having control of the household and Secret Service funds and through the bribes he took. He lived until 1911 and was said to be one of the richest men in China, with a fortune running into at least two million sterling, much of it obtained from property and pawnshops, which, again like Ho Shen, he ran on a huge scale as part of his intelligence network.

Tzu-hsi regarded him as highly as she did her lover, Jung Lu, and throughout her life depended on him almost absolutely, showing her esteem by decorating him with the peacock's feather and the ruby button of the second rank, a favour never before conferred on a eunuch.

Under previous reigns when eunuch power was utilised as the basis of a Secret Service it had always been confined to intelligence gained inside the Forbidden City. The eunuchs had been forbidden to leave the Forbidden City on pain of death so they were unable to obtain any first-hand information from other parts of the country, which was one of several reasons for China's lack of intelligence from the outside world. However, Tzu-hsi took the view that those eunuchs who could be trusted should be given greater scope to obtain information, even if this meant their leaving the Palace precincts.

She gave greater powers and more freedom to the eunuchs and this greatly annoyed one of her leading courtiers, Prince Kung. An Te-hai was her eunuch tribute-collector and, despite the law which banned eunuchs from leaving the Court, Tzu-hsi sent An Te-hai to Shantung in 1869 ostensibly to gather tribute, but much more likely for the specific purpose of gleaning intelligence. The arrival of An Te-hai in Shantung was reported back to Prince Kung in Peking and the latter promptly had the eunuch executed, an act for which Tsu-hsi never forgave him.

It was at this stage that Li Lien-ying acquired even more power, taking on some of the confidential work that hitherto had been conducted by Prince Kung. He flattered Tzu-hsi outrageously, bestowing on her the title of "Old Buddha", a gesture which from anyone else might have resulted in instant decapitation on Tzu-hsi's command, but which was tolerated from this loyal, if wicked, adviser. The story goes that once during an acute drought Tzu-hsi prayed for three days for rain and on the third day rain came. "You see how great Your Majesty is," Li told her. "See how Buddha answers your prayers. It is almost as though you were Buddha himself."

Li suggested that it might enhance Tzu-hsi's reputation if the nickname he had given her were allowed to leak out to the populace, as she would then be believed to have occult powers. Tzu-hsi agreed and so "Old Buddha" came to be a name known and used not only among the Chinese people outside the Forbidden City, but by foreigners as well.

This is a typical example of the superstitious, insular outlook of this period at the Manchu Court. The situation has been aptly summed up by John K. Fairbank, Edwin O. Reischauer and Albert N. Craig when they wrote: "China's antiforeignism was expressed in negative policies of noncooperation and avoidance of Western contact for almost two decades after the Opium War. Since this period saw the opening of Japan and the rapid advance of technology and national power in the West, China's lethargy in responding to the Western challenge in these years was disastrous. But the empire was not only too self-contained, but also too much absorbed in domestic difficulties to make a vigorous response in these middle decades of the century."[5]

Yet it need not have been. In the context of the theme taken as the mainspring of this chapter—the Chinese quest for knowledge and academic studies as the basis for all worthwhile intelligence—the one man who had revised this precept in a modern sense during the nineteenth century in China was the chief of intelligence who had been recalled in disgrace—Lin Tse-hsu. He had systematically reorganised intelligence on the basis of gaining factual, written knowledge of new Western techniques and sciences and even to some extent in the field of the arts. Though this was done primarily with the aim of stamping out the opium traffic, Lin Tse-hsu was much bigger a man intellectually than his one single failure may have suggested. He was really attempting to reorganise and revolutionise the Chinese Secret Service because he fully appreciated how lacking it was in the most elementary conceptions of what the Western world was achieving. His recall to Peking in disgrace was the sole cause of this reorganisation not being continued and it was a grave error by both the Emperor and the mandarinate.

His greatest contribution to the task of gathering intelligence had been the corps of translators he had set up to deal with all the works of Western countries. Much of this work he salvaged in that he turned it over to a close colleague, Wei Yuan, who in 1844 produced his *Illustrated Gazetteer of the Countries Overseas (Hai-kuo t'u-chih)*, a work which was perhaps hampered by its being a somewhat rough and ready study of the material so swiftly collected, but, which also contained some recommendations on how to tackle relations with "the barbarians" (i.e. the Westerners). But Wei Yuan missed his chance by merely using the knowledge he had gained to confirm his hostility to the West, and this showed itself in his eagerness to learn about and accept their weapons, while underrating their real achievements in peaceful development and technology.

12

The Rise of the "Boxers" 1871-1898

Unwittingly to himself, perhaps, he [Hung Hsiu-chuan] will teach us where to introduce the wedge, where to rest the lever; and it will not be many years ere we find European influence, hitherto so powerless in the high exclusive walls of the palace of Peking, operating with wonderful force at the courts of a score of kingdoms, petty in comparison with the great aggregate of which they once formed a part.

Tyler Dennett in an article on *Americans in Eastern Asia* in the *North American Review*, July, 1854

THE quotation above was an over-optimistic assessment of the effectiveness of Hung Hsiu-chuan and his Taiping rebellion, for it soon became clear that the Taipings had no intention of becoming the instruments of foreign intervention in the affairs of China.

And yet here at least was one striking contrast to the mentality of the average European diplomat or statesman—a recognition that there was a great deal to learn from China. In the long-term, of course, Tyler Dennett was right: the memory of the Taipings and their short-term achievements lived on and inspired many other revolutionaries in the latter part of the nineteenth century just as some of their ideas have found an honoured niche in the China of today. Even Tzu-hsi's autocratic and in many cases brutal rule helped by its stark contrast to preserve the memory of the experiment of Hung Hsiu-chuan in a new conception of living. The Taipings, despite their refusal to become the tools of the Europeans, had absorbed many Western ideas and adopted those, including vaccination, which seemed to indicate genuine progress. But the Europeans, instead of realising that they could achieve a worthwhile exchange of ideas with the revolutionary forces, merely sought for some opportunity to exploit these ideas for aggressive purposes of their own. The result was the slow build-up of many new secret societies, some dedicated to the overthrow of the Manchus, but most devoted more than anything else to the destruction of the "foreign devils", as the Western people were known.

After the destruction of the Taipings the Manchu dynasty slowly acquired a modest amount of Western weapons, though not of the most sophisticated kind, nor enough to permit them to embark on foreign adventures, but ample to put down most of the anti-Manchu revolts which sprang up from time to time. In one of these, in 1868, the Manchus had been helped by the French to quell a revolt in Hopei and Shantung. Four years later there was a mutiny of the Miao in Kewichow province and in 1873 a rising by the Moslems in the north-western provinces had to be put down.

Some, but not all of these revolts, were supported by the Westerners, occasionally by the British to off-set French influence—and *vice versa,* though on the whole the French remained loyal to the Manchu dynasty. There was, however, a realisation in Peking that China needed to win Russia as an ally, partly to counter-balance Japanese acquisitiveness, but also to safeguard her own borders in the west while having to cope with the Western nations' infiltration in the east. It was a policy that might have made sense if Russia had been a more stable nation, but it reflected China's disregard for and lack of foreign intelligence that she should ally herself with the one great power nominally belonging to the West, though spread out deep into the east, who was itself besotted with internal revolts and the growth of revolutionary ideas. The Manchus saw some vague comparisons between their own conception of imperial power centred in the Emperor and his court with that of Russia and Czarism. Without doubt, even with their extremely slender intelligence system inside Russia, they also saw how the Czar was faced with the same kind of internal revolt that they faced with the Taipings.[1]

In fact the Taiping revolutionary war, limited though it may have appeared, was sufficiently fierce to cause as much loss of life as the total number of people who died in the Napoleonic, Crimean, American Civil War and Franco-Prussian conflicts. The casualties were not so well publicised: that was the only difference. But the defeat of the Taipings was not in vain: it gave rise to great hopes for the future among the few; not least among them Sun Yat-sen, who was born in 1866, and who learned from the cradle the message which the Taipings had to hand on to future generations.

But the Manchu Government simply did not learn anything at all except in order to prolong their own power for some fifty years. It is a measure of their refusal to face realities that in 1867 they actually sent a diplomatic mission abroad *under the leadership of an alien,* the American Anson Burlingame.[2] The British started to steal territory from China by annexing the Kashgar region (Chinese territory) and using it as a buffer state for their Indian empire. As for the Russians, despite the attempt by China to win them as allies, they sent troops into the Ili region to extend their own territory in the east.

In assessing the stances taken by the Government of China today one must bear in mind the fact that armed expeditions into Korea and Indo-China were undertaken by the Western powers in the nineteenth century and that, with the sole exception of

General de Gaulle, the lessons of these acts of political piracy were not learned in the twentieth century by the West.

In both 1867 and 1871 the Americans sent troops into Korea, China's neighbouring state in the northeast, while in 1871 the U.S.A. encouraged the Japanese to occupy the then Chinese-occupied Liu Chiu Islands, now Okinawa. At the same time the United States Embassy in Tokyo backed a Japanese attack on Taiwan, where American landings had been made in the period between 1850 and 1867.

Then in the mid-1880s the British seized Burma and the French took Vietnam, in both cases acquiring territory which posed a barely disguised threat to the Chinese empire and which in some instances was used as such. Meanwhile Japan modernised herself on a western pattern, while the Russians, despite tentatively friendly approaches through the Chinese diplomatic and Secret Services, managed to manipulate the somewhat unexpected gestures of Chinese goodwill to their own advantage.

In November, 1860, five days after the British and French negotiators left Peking, the Russians achieved a considerable diplomatic triumph by persuading the Chinese to concur in the cession of the east coast of Manchuria. The Chinese should have been able to have foreseen this Russian intervention in their own sphere of influence as, since the seventeenth century, the Chinese had had to contend with Russian pressure for expansion in the east. But the Russian Secret Service had gained rather more ground than the extremely limited Chinese Secret Service in this period, and they had used an ecclesiastical mission to probe Chinese intentions.

Corruption and bribery prevented the always greedy chiefs of Chinese intelligence in this era from safeguarding their country's interests adequately, and it was a simple matter for a concession for a railway in Manchuria to be secured by Russia with a million-ruble bribe to Li Hung-chang, who was then conducting foreign affairs for the Manchu dynasty. The money to finance this railway was obtained by the Czar from French financiers, and all Russia had to do, mainly through its allegedly friendly links with the Chinese Secret Service, was to grease the palms of Chinese agents and obtain promises from China that such developments would be protected.

It is equally true that China was driven into a position of opposition to Japan by the Western powers, as the United States encouraged Japan to modernise without attempting to obtain special privileges from her, and Britain also supported Japan against China as a counter-balance against Russia.

After the death of Frederick Townsend Ward, the buccaneering American adventurer who stamped his personality on the Western incursions into China, Major Charles George Gordon (later to be known as General Gordon of Khartoum) was loaned from the British Army to the Western Powers' command in China. Such a title might be disputed on technical grounds by some historians, but this in effect is what it was.

Gordon was an extraordinary mixture of Puritanism, piratical imperialism, fanatical devotion to Christianity in a somewhat vulgar evangelistic sense and a sublimated, controlled, but nevertheless homosexual urge towards the pursuit of youths, all of which qualities were inextricably woven into a certain intricate, if devious, thread of golden idealism. If one wanted an easy symbol of Victorian hypocrisy in its worst form Gordon undoubtedly supplied it, yet there were inspired moments when he saw the truth and bravely stood for it in a manner unknown to any of his contemporaries. Only his death at the hands of the Mahdi's men in Khartoum, in a carefully dramatised, probably suicidal impulse, in the Sudan led to the myth of this most improbable of all heroes of the British Empire.

Bible-basher, evangelist, a soldier who claimed almost a personal relationship with Jesus Christ, Gordon was in some esoteric way the praying Mantis of British imperialism, one who, despite all his religious upbringing, could describe the destruction of some hundreds of buildings in China, saying that he and his men: ". . . went out, and, after pillaging it, burned the whole place, destroying in a Vandal-like manner most valuable property which would not be replaced for four millions. We got upwards of £48 a-piece prize money before we went out here, and although I have not as much as many, I have done well. The people are civil, but I think the grandees must hate us, as they must after what we did for the Palace. You can scarcely imagine the beauty and magnificence of the places we burnt. . . . Everybody was wild for plunder."[3]

Yet "Chinese" Gordon, bearing in mind these sentiments expressed in a letter to his mother from this sanctimonious, military humbug, had a touch of genius and his compassion could on occasions rise far above those of his fellow men and set him apart from them. He was not unconscious of the wrongs of British imperialism when he paused for prayer or thought (neither gifts given to the average British military commander of the time) and he not only received recognition from the Chinese military forces, but, like Ward before him, was given Chinese military rank under Governor Li Hung-chang.

Gordon, as is clear in his correspondence, was able to travel in China to an extent almost unknown to any other Westerner, especially in the north. No doubt it was one method by which the Secret Service mandarinate in Peking kept themselves informed, but at what cost: any intelligence that they were given was entirely at the discretion of a foreign government; for there can be no doubt that Gordon regarded himself as representing Britain first and China a very bad second.

As to the extent of Chinese control over such Western military entrepreneurs, this can be summed up by Gordon's comment in a letter to his sister: "I shall go to the Great Wall if I can in a short time, and thence send you a description and eventually a brick from that fabric." Apart from which he dispatched to his family quantities of loot, sables, jades, vases and enamels with concise instructions as to how they were to be divided up between "the tribe of Gordons".[4]

In 1884-5 the French launched war on China in retaliation for the aid which the Chinese "Black Flag" volunteers gave to the Vietnamese. A year later China, having suffered some thousands of men killed, surrendered all rights in Vietnam, while Japan took advantage of this to send her troops into Korea.

Externally disaster followed disaster for China. Whereas in the fifteenth century Muscovite Russia and Ming China had been 2,000 miles apart at the nearest point, separated by deserts, mountains and steppes, by the 1880s the moving frontiers of Czarist and Manchu expansion had met, dividing the intermediate lands into Russian and Chinese Turkestan. By the Treaty of Peking in 1860 the Chinese were compelled to accept the completion of the Czar's Far Eastern provinces and, in 1864, a rising under Yakub Beg against the Manchus resulted in the setting up of a separate state. Thus the Russians obtained a foothold in Sinkiang on the Ili River midway between the Pamir junction and the Mongolian frontiers in the Altai.

Again in 1864 in the Treaty of Chuguchak Russia further advanced her frontiers and gained some three hundred and fifty thousand square miles of Chinese territory. So much for Chinese Intelligence's links with Russia, so much for Chinese diplomacy. After this the authorities in Peking ceased to rely on direct relations with the Russians, but set up their own team of agents inside Russia to keep them informed. And once more the resilience of the Chinese, the effectiveness of their intelligence when properly directed and given full rein, proved themselves. The recovery was sensational: in 1881 Yakub Beg was killed and the Chinese recovered the Ili salient under the Treaty of Ili, sometimes also referred to as the Treaty of St Petersburg.

Tzu-hsi maintained her influence, which was still paramount in the Chinese empire, despite the accession of her baby nephew, Kuang Hsu, to the throne. Though he had been singled out for the succession by Tzu-hsi, he disliked his benefactor and sided with the Dowager Empress Tzu-an. The secret bond between Kuang Hsu and Tzu-an was, of course, reported to Tzu-hsi by Li Lien-ying, who was now not only chief eunuch and chief of intelligence, but consulted on all vital matters of state by Tzu-hsi before any other member of the Chinese Government.

Tzu-an greatly detested the arrogance and impudent behaviour of the chief eunuch and demanded of Tzu-hsi that she should control her favourite. The occasion for this protest was said to be a result of Tzu-an learning of the *tête-à-tête* picnics which Tzu-hsi and Li had together on the palace lakes, dressed in fancy costumes, but with Li being permitted to wear the imperial yellow robes, said to be exclusive to the Imperial family. Soon afterwards Tzu-an died, having, so it is said, eaten some cakes sent to her by Tzu-hsi. There were rumours that Li Lien-ying had had her poisoned and that he had decreed she should be buried swiftly without her relatives seeing her body in case they caught her disease.

Whatever the Secret Service achieved or did not achieve in this period, one thing is certain: it managed to cover up all traces of its main activities, for neither its successes nor its failures can positively be attributed to Li Lien-ying with the exception of a few coups. In matters of security he seemed able to preserve absolute secrecy, though it is certain that success in preserving power internally was often at enormous cost in failure to check the advances of China's aggressive neighbours and the machinations of the Westerners.

In 1887 Kuang-hsu attained his seventeenth year and Tzu-hsi, then fifty-five, had to surrender her powers of regency, though in effect she was still the dominant influence at the Court. Even then she insisted on choosing his wife, though he protested against her selection. The young Emperor, while he disliked her, yet feared her: he also knew that Li Lien-ying had a total monopoly of intelligence and that he could not make a single move without Tzu-hsi learning about it. Kuang Hsu was ruler in title, but Tzu-hsi held the reins of power through the Secret Service.

However, the young Emperor did attempt to put through some reforms, though he was always careful to mention these to Tzu-hsi first. Among the reformers were those who wished to see an end to eunuch power as exemplified by Li Lien-ying. These reformers recalled how another eunuch, Ho Shen, had similarly usurped the functions of government, bypassing the mandarinate and using his personal influence with the ruler to control both policy and the Secret Service. One reform that was favoured by many, possibly as a means of strengthening the Government's sources of information, was the abolition of the examination system in the advancement of Civil Servants.

Then in 1894 came war with Japan. Prior to this date Japan had been regarded as an inferior power, a negligible satellite of China, despite the fact that she had learned the very lessons from the West which China had neglected—the modernisation of the nation and the creation of an efficient army and navy. Japan had her spies inside China, one of them being Sidney Reilly, already a double-agent working for the British,[5] but China had not even deigned to consider spying on Japan.

Sidney Reilly was at this time working for Britain and Japan. A Middle European whose real name was Sigmund Georgievich Rosenblum, Reilly (the name he adopted eventually) was engaged by the British Secret Service to spy in Russia, but he included China in his territory and it was from here that he started making overtures to the Japanese.

Such was the contempt in which Japan was so foolishly held that the reaction of Tzu-hsi to the war with Japan was that it interrupted the celebrations for her sixtieth birthday, in token of which every senior official was expected to donate to her twenty-five per cent of his annual salary. The war to some extent interfered with the collection of these "tokens" but, as the man responsible for obtaining them was Li Lien-ying, it was all gathered in eventually.

Within a year Japan inflicted a humiliating defeat on China and the Western powers followed this up by falling over one another in their efforts to grab further concessions from the dying Manchu empire. Russia, anxious to check Japan, forced China to lease her the naval base of Port Arthur; Germany, utilising the excuse that two of her missionaries had been killed, took over the port of Tsingtao and actually obtained a "leasehold" of the eastern Shantung peninsula for 99 years, while France captured the bay of Kwangchow Wan in South China. The Yangtse valley was more or less claimed by Britain, while Russia exploited Manchuria and Mongolia.

Criticism of the Manchu regime began to grow. Not even Li Lien-ying could silence the growing realisation that China had been subjected to intolerable humiliations and that her fate was at the mercy of other powers. Tzu-hsi was fully cognisant of what the foreigners were doing to her country and her hatred of them grew daily. She now knew that the pomp and ritual with which she surrounded herself and the Intelligence Service she depended upon were insufficient either to impress or deter the Westerners from further predatory acts. She turned her attention instead to those subversive forces inside her empire which were most xenophobic. These included the Boxers, a secret society which was both anti-foreigner and anti-Christian and also hostile to the Manchu dynasty, and a revival of the Triads, whose aims were similar to those of the Boxers, but more sophisticated and backed by considerable intelligence from the Chinese overseas.

In effect both the Boxers and the Triads were trying to acquire the kind of detailed intelligence on the Westerners which the Chinese Secret Service had so lamentably failed to provide. In the beginning no doubt this was a subconscious urge whipped up by hatred of the "foreign devils", but it was out of the revolutionary if sometimes unsophisticated techniques of these secret societies that China's modern Secret Service eventually emerged.

The Boxer movement itself was a form of revived Triad Society under the name of *I-ho-ch'uan,* evolving from the Eight Trigrams Society of the eighteenth century, another anti-Establishment organisation. The Boxers were regarded as subversive by the Court from the very beginning on account of their historical links. Though they were officially suppressed in the early years of their movement, they went underground and became particularly powerful in Chihli and Shantung.

The name "Boxer" was, of course, a European nickname for the movement's Chinese name, *I-ho-ch'uan,* which is not easy to translate accurately into English, at least not in a few words. Simplified, the name means "Righteous and well-trained Fists", for which the British substituted the word "Boxer". The full meaning of the title is much more subtle than this: the nearest a Westerner can get to defining it is that it was a society dedicated to setting things right inside its own country and in order to achieve this practising the ancient Chinese art of boxing ("to harmonise the fists") and the calisthenic military art, a form of strengthening and beautifying exercises intended to harmonise both mind and body in preparation for battle. It had something in common with the "Strength through Joy" movements which sprang up in Europe in the mid-thirties of the twentieth century.

The Boxers, however, were a thoroughly reactionary organisation, possessing none of the progressive ideas of the Taipings, and their xenophobia showed itself in a belief in magical arts, Taoist sorcery and incantations which were supposed to give them supernatural powers. They saw themselves as the ultimate saviours of their country and believed that only their organisation could provide China with the kind of Secret Service it needed, meaning by this a Secret Service which would enable them to drive out the "foreign devils". Some inkling of this firm belief of theirs regarding a Secret Service may be gleaned from the fact that they made study of *The Romance of the Three Kingdoms* compulsory reading and that the figure of Kuan Yu in that book was declared their "God of War".

The revival of the Triads, on the other hand, was something much more paralogistic, though in a lower key, less reactionary and altogether more outward-looking. As has been seen from earlier chapters, the Chinese Triads were originally pledged to self-protection and devoted to certain moral ideals and even semi-religious principles, much closer to Freemasonry than to any sinister secret society. They had links in the early days with the Taipings, in whose philosophy they saw some common ground. Indeed the Taipings copied some of the ideas and secret signs of the Triads, while many Triads joined the Taipings. Later there was some dissension between the Triads and the Taipings as the former believed that the latter did not always give full backing to their own local revolts in such places as Amoy and Shanghai. But the very nature of the Triads' philosophy and the fascination of their Hung Mun ritual have led them to be courted and used by various political parties and by Secret Services and private armies throughout history.

Their great asset was, of course, that they had access to foreign intelligence through Chinese communities overseas, and that hence in most respects they were far better informed about the outside world than was the official Secret Service in Peking. It is a curious commentary on the insularity of that Secret Service that it did not seek to harness the Triads to its own organisation.

But Dr Sun Yat Sen, the father of modern China, and his followers certainly saw the great advantages to be obtained from establishing links with the Triads and this he and his followers did about 1890. They went much further than this: they organised the Chung Wo Tong Triad Society in Hongkong in 1890 to form an external base for a political struggle to overcome the Manchu dynasty. It was an astute move, it provided Sun Yat Sen and his followers with the essential intelligence which they needed for their own development as a real political force.

However it was the Boxers to which Tzu-hsi secretly leaned, for not unnaturally one so dictatorially-minded as this Dowager Empress would instinctively see more possibility in turning their reactionary ideas to her own advantage than in seeking allies among the progressive forces. She also secretly encouraged their anti-Christian campaign and declined to take action against them. Yet the Boxers were not merely anti-foreigner, they were anti-Manchu and devoted to the restoration of pre-Manchu China.

On the other hand the young Emperor, after the defeat by Japan, leaned strongly towards the reformists led by K'ang Yu-wei and by Yuan Shih-kai, a warlord who was later to become China's first Republican President. Yuan Shih-kai had been a commander of troops in the disastrous war against Japan, and he was in fact as much responsible for the defeat as any other commander. But, sensing that defeat could spell loss of power for him with Tzu-hsi, he tried to play it both ways by making secret overtures to the Emperor, while using the knowledge he gained from these to keep Tzu-hsi informed and so to regain favour with her.

Word went out both to Li Lien-ying and to Jung Lu that the closest watch was to be kept on the Emperor's intentions, for the truth was that the Secret Service took little notice of the Emperor, but still considered itself bound to Tzu-hsi. They did not have to seek far for a reliable informant. Once Yuan Shih-kai was consulted by the Emperor he was privy to the latter's plans for backing the sweeping reforms proposed by K'ang Yu-wei. He listened to all that was suggested and nodded in approval. He also assured the Emperor that his troops were at the disposal of his ruler and that they would not allow Tzu-hsi to leave the Summer Palace before the reforms were carried out.

K'ang was a dreaming, impractical idealist who stood no chance against the wiles of Yuan Shih-kai. Had he been less of a philosopher and more of a statesman it is doubtful if the Emperor would have consulted Yuan Shih-kai. But K'ang's ideas for reform took some bizarre forms: he dreamed of world government, dominated of course by China, of the ending of family life (perhaps the most revolutionary idea of all in Chinese eyes) and a scheme by which marriages would last only a year, after which new partners would be obtained and all children would be brought up by the State outside their homes in communal schools.

The Emperor must have known that most of these revolutionary changes would be opposed by his aunt, Tzu-hsi, and he should have realised that they were too extreme even for the most ardent of the moderate reformists. But, like Napoleon before him and Harold Wilson after him, Emperor Kuang-hsu was devoted to the conception of "a hundred days of reform", to the extent that the very catch-phrase became an obsession with him; and in June 1898 he issued edicts under this very title.

Some of these reforms might have been achieved if the Emperor had had the Secret Service on his side, or even had some backing among one or other of the European powers. But not only did Tzu-hsi have the Secret Service almost entirely under her personal control, but she and not the Emperor had the only direct diplomatic links with China's powerful neighbour, Czarist Russia. Israel Epstein wrote: "Tzu-hsi's clique was at that time inclined to lean on Czarist Russia, with the result that the Emperor and the reformers were favoured by Britain, America and Japan."[6]

"Favoured" they may have been in theory, but there was no positive backing for the Emperor from any of these three nations. Yuan Shih-kai proceeded to double-cross the Emperor, going to Tientsin to tell Jung Lu, then a provincial governor, what was planned. He did more than this: he told Jung Lu that the Emperor's plans included a plot to assassinate Tzu-hsi, which was totally untrue.

Jung Lu immediately informed Tzu-hsi and she received confirmation of what was afoot from Li Lien-ying. The "Hundred Days of Reform" were doomed before they began, despite the fact that between 11 June and 11 September 1898 the Emperor issued a whole series of decrees and edicts drafted for him by K'ang Yu-wei. Many of these were moderate and sensible—the abolition of the antiquated Confucian tests for Civil Servants, educational improvements, the setting up of a university and plans to organise committees to improve and control agriculture, transport and mining, and universal military training. The last-named was deliberately planned to put an end to the corruption and decadence of the Manchu army.

Tzu-hsi's first reaction was that the Emperor must be killed. She is said by some to have broken into his bedroom and ordered his instant death. But for once her Secret Service had obtained some vital intelligence on the intentions of foreign powers. Her Russian allies through the Secret Service made it abundantly clear that the murder or execution of the Emperor would not be tolerated: this would only open the way to widespread chaos in the empire and increasing revolts in the provinces. The European Secret Services operating in China had no illusions about Tzu-hsi: they were fully informed of her secret flirtations with the Boxers and knew that eventually there must be a show-down with her. They, too, made it clear that the death of the Emperor would cause them to intervene directly in the affairs of the Chinese empire.

Tzu-hsi was not, however, deterred from acting against the Emperor and re-establishing her own rule. At the age of sixty-three she staged a *coup d'état* with the aid of Li Lien-ying and Jung Lu. The Emperor was not killed, but he was forced to abdicate and was kept in confinement on Ying Tai, a small island in the lake of the Winter Palace.

The seemingly indestructible Tzu-hsi was once again firmly in control of the situation. She knew that the reforms proposed by the Emperor would have slowly destroyed Manchu power and made this clear to all her courtiers, rescinding almost every decree of the young Emperor (who, incidentally, remained under arrest until his death in 1908). As for the rebels, Tzu-hsi ordered "execution on the spot" for all ringleaders who were caught. K'ang Yu-wei and some of the other reformists escaped, but those who were caught were summarily dispatched by being cut in half at the waist.

From that moment the Empress was determined to use the Boxers as her allies in whipping up hatred against the foreigners and eventually, or so she foolishly hoped, to drive them out of China. It was, of course, easy enough to capitalise the anti-foreign feeling in China: the Europeans were blamed for the defeat of China by Japan; the Germans were especially hated for their brutality in Shantung where they had not only plundered the land, but burned down whole villages to "punish the people for their unfriendliness". There was also wide-spread resentment of the way in which extra-territorial rights were exploited by the Europeans to the disadvantage of the Chinese people.

Thus came about the gradual alliance, built up through careful negotiations by the Secret Service, between Tzu-hsi and the Boxers, who were in fact anti-Manchu. It was an astonishing metamorphosis on both sides. In their early years the Boxers had not disguised their dislike of the Manchus, while Tzu-hsi for years refused to have anything to do with them. One day a Boxer leader was secretly brought to the palace to meet the Empress and from that day she lent her backing to a secret society of thugs who had already become notorious for their kidnapping and subsequent torturing of Chinese Christians and the murder of foreigners. And for years Boxer propaganda had actually been critical of the Manchu Court in pamphlets such as this:

"China has been celebrated for its sacred teaching. . . . All this has been changed. Scholars are not made use of by the government. Official positions can be bought. Mandarins must be bribed. The court indulges blindly in mere amusement, repenting of nothing, learning nothing. . . . Foreign devils come with their teaching of Christianity. Their churches are without human relations and being most cunning have attracted the greedy and covetous."

Tzu-hsi was clever enough to realise that the Boxers had no positive political aims, unlike the reformists, with whom they had no links at all. Their one aim was to drive out the foreigner and, if this was achieved by allying herself with them, Tzu-hsi felt quite sure she could herself deal effectively with this fanatical rabble if indeed they were successful.

So she called off her own soldiers who had been sent to suppress the Boxers in some provinces, informed the Boxers through intermediaries that they had just complaints but that all China's troubles were due to the "foreign devils". If the Boxers really wished to drive these people out of China, why then she would support them and they would then see that China would quickly be restored to her former glories.

Li Lien-ying was in favour of a machiavellian deal with the Boxers, but Jung Lu warned the Empress that she was taking a grave risk in supporting them and that if a Boxer rebellion was unleashed and there was widespread bloodshed among the European colonies, then China might well see all the great powers ganging up against her. Advice in the Secret Service was divided and there is no doubt that Jung Lu was right whereas Li Lien-ying not only tried to flatter Tzu-hsi by commending her idea, but played on her superstitions by suggesting the Boxers were invincible and that not even European bullets could kill them.

The end of the Chinese empire was drawing near, but it was still to dwindle on for a few years more, recovering from almost total devastation by a miraculous deal with the Europeans, but only at enormous cost in blood and wealth.

13

The Kidnapping of Sun Yat-sen 1894-1900

If my honourable elder brother read that a man's voice could be heard from Canton to Amoy, he would marvel at the power of his lungs: yet a feeble old man could be heard with an instrument connected with the iron electric serpent. . . . There is no end to these wonders. . . . These are the doings of men we have in our conceit called *barbarians,* and have pictured in our country as monsters, having ears reaching down to the ground, and short legs and long arms like monkeys!
Extract from a letter from a Chinese emigrant to Australia in the 1890s

SUCH sentiments as these might have been understandable in the sixteenth century, yet it is a measure of how far China had allowed herself to slip back into the past, into self-deceit and misrepresentation, under the latter-day Manchus that such a letter could have been written in the 1890s by one who had left China and discovered the truth.[1] This is not to assert that the behaviour of the Westerners had not been barbaric, for it is still undeniable that in many respects it was more horrific, sadistic and downright cruel towards the Chinese than to any other people in the world in this period. Nevertheless, the Chinese had so far forgotten their heritage of learning and improving on their own wisdom as to blind themselves to the good things which the West had to offer.

Sun Yat-sen was one of the exceptions. Perhaps this is best illustrated by a few quotations from Westerners who knew him. James Cantlie, a young and rising surgeon in Hongkong, who became closely associated with Sun Yat-sen in a number of activities, wrote: "I have never known anyone like Sun Yat-sen. If I were asked to name the most perfect character I ever knew, I would unhesitatingly name Sun Yat-sen."[2] Arnold Toynbee, the British historian, said of him that he was one of "the most eminent figures on the stage of modern world history".

In this chapter, which mainly concerns the rise of Sun Yat-sen, it is necessary to step back in history for a few years. Having already taken a peep into the last years of the nineteenth century during which the Manchu empire was merely prolonging its death rattle and, as a dying man will, attempting to rise from that death bed in one last struggle for survival, the story of Sun Yat-sen needs less explanation.

Sun Yat-sen was fortunate in that he was brought up in a village near Canton where there happened to be a good school—a rarity in China in that time. For the most part such education as the children received was on the classical pattern, and to some extent at least consisted in learning and reciting what they did not understand. It is recorded that young Sun Yat-sen questioned the wisdom of this and was promptly caned for his insolence.

His family grew crops on the small plot of land for which they paid a high rent and taxes; they lived modestly and knew what poverty was like. It was because they were poor that Sun's eldest brother emigrated to Hawaii and when Sun Yat-sen was twelve his brother suggested he should join him. It was then that Sun, like the Chinese emigrant whose letter is quoted at the beginning of this chapter, began to see that there was another world where one could learn things one could understand, so that he, too, could write home that the English ship in which he had travelled was "just a beam of iron which reached through one side of the ship to the other to strengthen it. How could men move such a colossal affair?"

He went to a boarding school run by the British Bishop of Honolulu and from that time became a Christian, though never in any sense a practising member of any Church. Towards the end of his life he declared: "I am a Christian, but I do not belong to the Christianity of the churches, but to the Christianity of Jesus who was a revolutionary." How many revolutions have been started in the name of Christ's principles?

Returning to China, Sun Yat-sen took with him some of the precepts of Christianity allied to a keen appreciation that the West had something to offer China, while proudly believing that China had much to offer the West. His family were horrified at the manner in which he had embraced Christianity, but Sun defied them and when back in his own country established close links with missionaries.

This was regarded as outrageous defiance of family principles and young Sun Yat-sen was banished from his village. He had no money and he had to walk to Canton from whence he secured a passage to Hongkong, where he was helped by an American missionary. In this colony he felt free to talk and criticise the Chinese Government with fellow students and he learned a great deal more of Western ways. Having completed his education with the aid of the missionaries he became first a hospital attendant and then a student in the Alice Memorial Hospital in Hongkong, eventually at the age of twenty-six acquiring an English medical degree.

Sun Yat-sen first practised surgery in the Portuguese colony of Macao, but he was resented by the local doctors and returned to the mainland. Gradually he was drawn into politics, becoming rapidly convinced that there was no future for China under the Manchus. He was appalled not only by the poverty and misery he saw in all the parts of China he visited, but by the corruption and cruelty. He determined to switch from medicine and surgery to a revolutionary career.

As early as 1894 he organised a political association—the Hsing Chung Hui, or "revive China" Society. His aims were Westernised and modernised, though some of his inspiration he took from the Taipings and much more from the Non-conformist and more radical of the missionaries. But he was convinced that to take her proper place among the nations of the world on terms of equality China needed a republic after the American pattern and a Western-style bureaucracy. To achieve these things was a task of such magnitude that it required an organisation with its own intelligence service that could outwit and match that of the Manchus.

Young Sun Yat-sen was intelligent enough to appreciate that the Manchu Secret Service was only really effective inside China and that in the long run what would turn the tide against the Manchus would be the weight of republican sentiment not merely in the homeland, but among the millions of Chinese exiles in various parts of the world. He was determined that these exiles should form the hard core of his own intelligence service.

For this reason he utilised the Triads and helped in the formation of the Chung Wo Tong Triad Society in Hongkong as a base for his intelligence operations. There was nothing starry-eyed about this young man's aims, or his methods of setting about them. He was a radical in the sense that he was anti-Manchu and wanted to see China become a democratic republic, but he was also closely allied with the new Chinese capitalists and merchants who desired freer trade with the West and who, particularly in South China, wanted to see their cotton trade boosted.

As far as China's ever-changing Secret Service was concerned two factors at this time were of paramount importance. The first was Sun Yat-sen's far-sighted plan for utilising the Chinese abroad as a great intelligence network for combining to overcome the Manchus. The second was the belated, but then determined, reaction of the Manchu Secret Service to start operating overseas so that they could counteract the Triads' network. The end result was that Sun Yat-sen's policy was to form the basis of a new conception of secret

145

service in the early part of the twentieth century, while the Manchus through concentrating on hunting Sun Yat-sen round the world ultimately failed to make any impression at all overseas.

During and after the Taiping revolution there had been an enormous increase in the number of emigrants from China. Then in the 1860s the Manchus had permitted the Western powers to recruit "coolie" labour in China under the Tientsin Treaties and many poor peasants were shipped to Manila, Hawaii, Malaya, the United States, and the West Indies, rather fewer then to Australia.

Sun Yat-sen realised that these exiles from China wanted protection from their own Government and that they did not get it. Therefore he had a ready-made propaganda weapon in his political campaign to win adherents among the overseas Chinese by promising that a republic would provide such protection. Such promises appealed as much to the relatively few, though sometimes quite powerful, Chinese merchants who had established themselves abroad as they did to the "coolies".

"To keep the masses in ignorance is the constant endeavour of Chinese rule," wrote Sun Yat-sen. "In this way it happened that during the last Japanese incursion [the war of 1894–5] absolutely nothing was known of the war by the masses of China, in parts other than those where the campaign was actually waged."[3]

It was in direct consequence of the defeat by the Japanese that Sun Yat-sen made his first and abortive attempt with other "Young China" revolutionaries to capture Canton and depose the authorities. The plans for this coup were made in the "Young China" headquarters in Shanghai, the aim being to take the Cantonese authorities by surprise without bloodshed, but by using the threat of an overwhelming force.

"It was arranged," wrote Sun Yat-sen, "that on a certain day in October 1895, these men should march across country, one body from the south-west, the other from the north-east, towards Canton. All proceeded satisfactorily and they commenced their advance. Frequent meetings of the Committee of Reformers were held, and arms, ammunition and dynamite were accumulated at the headquarters. . . . The soldiers advancing across the country were to be still further strengthened by a contingent of four hundred men from Hongkong. . . . Whilst the conspirators sat within their hall a telegram was received to the effect that the advancing soldiers had been stayed in their progress and the reform movement forthwith became disconcerted. . . . A general stampede followed: papers were burnt, arms hidden and telegrams dispatched to Hongkong to stop the contingent from that place."[4]

The rebellion had been made possible as a result of funds supplied from Chinese exiles in Honolulu, Singapore, Australia and elsewhere. But the money did not altogether match the quality of the rebellion's leaders, always excepting Sun Yat-sen. Arms were still not available in sufficient quantities to ensure success, so wiser counsels prevailed and the attack on Canton was delayed.

Men were drafted to Hongkong to be prepared for an attack on it and arms and ammunition were smuggled in cement casks. Money was subscribed lavishly and foreign advisers obtained. There were even attempts to secure the co-operation of the Japanese Government, but without any tangible result. Sun Yat-sen does not tell us what codes, if any, were used in the telegrams. It seems probable that the Manchu Intelligence Service suspected something from the telegraphic traffic and that they had agents in Shanghai to tip them off. On this occasion the Manchu Secret Service proved too strong for the revolutionaries. Several of the leaders of the "Young China" movement were arrested and some executed, but Sun managed to escape. A prominent Hongkong merchant who had established links with the "Young China" movement gave them away to the Manchu Government. He had been involved in syndicates for mining and railway concessions and, because of his tip-off, the cement casks were examined and the arms cache discovered. Sun Yat-sen, realising that the *coup d'état* had no chance at all, went into hiding for two or three weeks in the impenetrable pirate haunts of the Kwang-tung

Delta and in the labyrinth canals where their craft sheltered.

"After several hairbreadth escapes," he wrote, describing his escape, he got "on board a steam launch in which I sailed to Macao. Remaining there for twenty-four hours only, I proceeded to Hongkong, where, after calling on some friends, I sought my old teacher and friend, Mr James Cantlie. Having informed him that I was in trouble through having offended the Cantonese authorities, and, fearing that I should be arrested and sent to Canton for execution, he advised me to consult a lawyer."[5]

The Manchu Government were now well aware who was the ringleader of the "Young China" movement and they realised that in dealing with Sun Yat-sen they had on their hands a highly intelligent and dangerous enemy of the regime. He was put on their list of "wanted criminals" for shipping barrels of revolvers into Canton in 1895 and a price of £100,000 was put on his head.

Luckily he now had an extensive network of Chinese exiles in many parts of the world. In his own account of how he escaped from Canton he tersely refers above to "several hair-breadth escapes". In fact he got away from the city by being lowered over the walls in a basket.

From Hongkong Sun escaped to Japan and in Kobe he dressed as a Japanese and grew hair on his upper lip in the fashion of the males of that country. From Kobe he went to Yokohama and then to Hawaii where he was given refuge by his Chinese friends.

Tzu-hsi was furious at the audacity of Sun Yat-sen's plans to capture Canton and at the ease with which he had escaped. It was only gradually that it dawned on her that the Secret Service had no roots among the Chinese in exile whereas Sun Yat-sen had. It now transpired that the doctor was organising branches of his movement all round the world, bringing in restaurant proprietors, laundrymen, shopkeepers and merchants from whom he gained not only moral support, but funds as well.

It was clear that the Manchu Intelligence was impotent outside its own domains and for once Tzu-hsi bypassed her Intelligence chiefs and ordered her Minister in Washington to arrange for Sun Yat-sen to be kidnapped. This was the first occasion on which a Chinese diplomat overseas had been used for espionage work.

The Minister in Washington must have been severely shocked by the instructions given to him and he seems to have delayed in taking any action. Sun Yat-sen had by this time (June 1896) left Hawaii for San Francisco where he stayed for a month before going to the east coast. The Chinese Minister in Washington then learned that the doctor planned to go to Britain, so he passed on Tzu-hsi's instructions to the Chinese Legation in London.

Sun Yat-sen stated that "in New York I was advised to beware the Chinese Minister to the United States, as he is a Manchurian, and has but little sympathy with Chinese generally and a reformer in particular." He arrived in Liverpool and in October 1896 went straight to London where he stayed at a hotel in the Strand.

The Chinese Legation in London acted much more swiftly than their opposite numbers in Washington. They sent spies to Liverpool to watch the arrival of Sun Yat-sen's ship. He had been followed to London and watched all the way to his hotel. However, circumstances had helped the Manchu officials in London for they had realised that one of Sun Yat-sen's chief friends, his former teacher, Mr Cantlie (later Sir James Cantlie), was living close to the Chinese Legation in Portland Place. It was therefore quite simple for Legation servants to keep a discreet watch on the Cantlie household, knowing almost for certain that sooner or later Sun Yat-sen would be sure to call on his old friend. Nor did they have long to wait. The day after he moved into the hotel in the Strand Sun called on the Cantlies, who gave him a warm welcome and found him lodgings at 8 Gray's Inn Place, Gray's Inn, Holborn.

For this operation of keeping a watch on Sun Yat-sen the Chinese Legation in London had been given the assistance of two secret agents of Jung Lu, whose aid had been particularly sought by Tzu-hsi. She suspected that the American Minister in Washington had been dragging his feet over apprehending Sun and was determined that the same thing should not occur in London.

Peking's orders to their representatives in London were that their own agents should undertake the kidnapping of Sun with the wholehearted assistance of the Chinese Legation, but that the secret agents were themselves to be responsible for shipping him back to China "as a lunatic". It was essential, the Manchus pointed out, that Sun should be brought back alive so that he could be tortured to make him reveal the names of all the leaders among the Chinese exiles of his movement in the U.S.A., Britain, Hawaii, Hongkong and elsewhere.

The Chinese were quickly made aware that Sun was organising the London end of his network and that he intended to raise funds for the "Young China" movement in the British capital. What worried both the Chinese Minister in London and the two agents who had been sent over to organise the kidnapping was that at this period of Chinese history there was so much unrest internally and so many groups of Chinese were trying to plot against the Manchu empire that in Chinese diplomatic missions overseas the personnel often included paid foreigners who were considered more trustworthy than the Chinese! This is a state of affairs which had never before and has almost certainly never since occurred in Chinese diplomacy.

Sun Yat-sen was not difficult to shadow as his daily routine included regular visits to the Cantlie home in the study of which he spent most of his time. From his own account it does not seem that Sun had the slightest suspicion that he was being shadowed, or that the Chinese Legation in London had any intention of kidnapping him. He mentioned that reference was made in the Cantlie household to the Chinese Legation being in the neighbourhood and that Mr Cantlie "jokingly suggested I might go round and call there; whereat his wife remarked, 'You had better not. Don't go near it; they'll catch you and ship you off to China.' We all enjoyed a good laugh, little knowing how true the womanly instinct was, and how soon we were to experience the reality."

Indeed, Sun Yat-sen admitted that he did not even trouble to find out exactly where the Legation was. One Sunday morning, 11 October 1896, at 10:30 a.m., Sun was walking towards Devonshire Street, which was very near to the Chinese Legation, intending to join the Cantlies at a church service, when a Chinaman approached him from behind and asked him if he was Chinese or Japanese. Sun replied that he was Chinese and that he came from Canton. The man replied: "We are countrymen and speak the same language; I am from Canton."

"It should be observed," wrote Sun Yat-sen, "that English or 'Pidgin', that is 'business' English, is the common language between Chinamen from different localities. A Swatow and a Cantonese merchant, although their towns are but 180 miles apart may be entirely ignorant of each other's spoken language. The written language is the same all over China, but the written and spoken languages are totally different and the spoken languages are many. My would-be Chinese friend, therefore, addressed me in English until he found my dialect. We then conversed in the Cantonese dialect."[6]

While the two men were talking they were joined by a second Chinaman and together they urged Sun to come with them to their lodgings to have "a smoke and chat". Sun declined politely, and then a third Chinaman appeared and the man who had first approached him left.

"The two who remained further pressed me to accompany them, and I was gradually, and in a seemingly friendly manner, led to the upper edge of the pavement when the door of an adjacent house suddenly opened and I was half-jokingly and half-persistently compelled to enter by my companions, one on either side, who reinforced their entreaties by a quasi-friendly push.

"Suspecting nothing, for I knew not what house I was entering, I only hesitated because of my desire to get to Mr Cantlie's in time for church, and I felt I should be too late did I delay. However, in good faith

151

I entered, and was not a little surprised when the front door was somewhat hurriedly closed and barred behind me. All at once it flashed upon me that the house must be the Chinese Legation."[7]

It might appear that Sun Yat-sen was somewhat lacking in awareness that he was a hunted man in that he did not suspect anything until it was too late. True, he had been warned in the U.S.A. but nothing had happened to him, which may have made him careless. But one must remember that at this time Sun was anxious to win recruits from overseas and therefore would not wish to offend potential allies by refusing their offers of hospitality; that London was considered by any fugitive from overseas as the safest city in the world at that period; and, finally, two points which seemed totally to rule out any plot so sensational as his kidnapping: first that Sun Yat-sen was aware that the Manchus Secret Service had never hitherto extended itself beyond the fringes of Asiatic Russia, and second, as what seemed a guarantee of civilised behaviour, the Counsellor at the Chinese Legation in London was a trusted Englishman, Sir Halliday Macartney.

It was quickly evident that he had been kidnapped and was being held by force in the Chinese Legation. After being taken from one room to another it soon became obvious that there was some disagreement as to which was the safest place in which to incarcerate him, which rather suggested that the plans for his kidnapping were somewhat casual. Eventually he was taken to a room on the third floor with a barred window looking out to the back of the house. Here he was confronted by "an old gentleman with white hair and beard" who turned out to be none other than Sir Halliday Macartney, the bumptious and fatuous tool of the Manchus.

"Here is China for you," said Sir Halliday. "You are now in China [meaning, of course, that the Legation was Chinese territory legally]. Your name is Sun Wen and we have a telegram from the Chinese Minister in America informing us that you were a passenger to this country by the S.S. *Majestic,* and the Minister asks me to arrest you."

Sun Yat-sen asked the reason for this.

"You are detained here until we learn what the Emperor wishes to do with you."

Sun asked if he could let Mr Cantlie know where he was. This request was refused, but he was told he could write to his lodgings for his luggage to be sent to him. He then asked to write to another friend, a Dr Manson, and was given pen and paper to do this. In his letter he told Manson that he was confined in the Chinese Legation and asked him to tell Mr Cantlie to get his luggage for him. Sir Halliday, however, objected to the use of the word "confined" and insisted on the message reading: "I am in the Chinese Legation. Please tell Mr Cantlie to send my luggage here."

"It was very evident my interrogator was playing a crafty game to get hold of my effects, and more especially my papers, in the hope of finding correspondence whereby to ascertain who my Chinese accomplices or correspondents were," stated Sun Yat-sen.[8] However, he gave the letter to Sir Halliday, believing that an Englishman's word was his bond and that it would be delivered. If this seems naïve on the part of a Chinese, one must remember that Sun was a Christian and cherished the belief that all Christians maintained Christian standards.

In fact Sir Halliday Macartney, now an ageing and foolish bureaucrat, was being used by the Chinese as a cover for their operations, had long been in the service of the Manchus and had a record of cynical disregard for human life. It is perhaps worth recording that even General Gordon had been shocked by his complacency in the face of oriental barbarities.

When the execution of the Taiping chiefs had been ordered in 1863, Gordon believed that as a British officer he had guaranteed the safety of those Taipings who had honourably surrendered and insisted that the executions should not take place, or he would "forthwith proceed to attack the Imperialists and to retake from them all the places captured". [9]

The Manchu official who had given the order for

the executions was Li Hung-chang, whose Western Secretary was Halliday Macartney. When Macartney called on General Gordon he found him "sobbing and before a word was exchanged, Gordon stooped down and taking something from under the bed, held it up in the air, exclaiming: 'Do you see that? . . . It is the head of the Lar Wang, foully murdered'."[10]

Macartney took the whole situation quite calmly and in total contrast to Gordon, who immediately withdrew to Kunshan and refused to take part in any further campaigns against the Taipings.

Sun Yat-sen was then kept under lock and key at the Chinese Legation in London and, on the instructions of Sir Halliday Macartney, an additional lock was put on the door of his room. Outside a guard of two was constantly maintained, and, as a precaution against there being a spy among the Manchu ranks, one was always a Chinese and one a European, presumably a Briton.

Some hours later a guard came into Sun's room and said that Sir Halliday had given orders for him to be searched. The guard took Sun's keys, pencil and knife, but, recorded Sun later, "did not find my pocket in which I had a few bank notes". He was given some milk, and two English servants lit a fire in his room.

Sun had written a note to Cantlie before his pencil was taken from him and he tried to persuade the English servants to have this delivered. However, by the following Tuesday, having received no further information, he suspected that the note had not been dispatched.

On the fourth day of his captivity Tang, who was one of his kidnappers, came to see him and asked that he should confess everything: "You are well known in China. The Emperor and the Tsung-Li-Yamen are well acquainted with your history."

Sun pointed out that this was England and not China and that if the Chinese wished to have him extradited, they must inform the British Government, and he did not think the latter would allow him to be surrendered. He was then told that they had no intention of asking for legal extradition, but that a steamer was ready to take him, that he would be bound and gagged and placed on board and taken to Canton for trial and execution. Tang added finally: "The steamboat company are friends of Sir Halliday Macartney and will do what they are told."

On the Thursday Tang again came to see Sun and hinted that there was some hope of his saving his life, but that Sun must "do what I tell you". This was to write to Sir Halliday Macartney in English, denying that he had anything to do with the Canton plot, declaring he had been wrongly accused by the mandarins and that he came to the Legation to ask for redress.

"I wrote to his dictation a long letter to this effect in Tang's presence. . . . I handed it to Tang, who went off with it . . . and I never saw the intriguer again. This was no doubt a very stupid thing to have done, as I thereby furnished my enemies with documentary evidence that I had come voluntarily to the Legation. But, as a dying man will clutch at anything, so I, in my strait, was easily imposed upon," was Sun's comment on this incident.

Slowly Sun realised that his position was becoming desperate and that he had been made to fall into a trap by writing this confession, no doubt at the behest of the cunning and unscrupulous Sir Halliday Macartney. It was clear by this time that it was Sir Halliday rather than the Chinese Minister who was the real power in the Legation, at least as far as this Secret Service operation was concerned.

Sun tried writing messages appealing for help, weighting them with coins he had secreted on his person and throwing them out of the window in the hope that somebody might find them and pass them on to the authorities. But they were all retrieved by the Chinese Legation guards and it is not true, as has often been reported, that Sun was rescued through a passer-by finding one of these missives.

There was, however, one English servant whose conscience seems to have been touched by the fact that Sun was a political refugee. He was obviously frightened to do anything which might lose him his job, or result in his being locked up by the Chinese, but Sun talked with him, convinced him he was being confined illegally and, to try to clinch the issue, gave him twenty pounds in notes which he had managed to hide.

The servant, whose name was Cole, must have gone home to discuss the matter with his wife and it seems to have been her influence which finally clinched things in Sun's favour. For Cole returned to the room and, according to Sun, declared: "I will try to take a letter to your friend. You must not write it at the table, as you can be seen through the keyhole, and the guards outside watch you constantly. You must write it on your bed."

Paper and pencil had been placed by the coal scuttle in Sun's room. He then lay down on his bed and scrawled a hasty note to Cantlie on a visiting card. At noon Cole returned and Sun pointed to where the note had been hidden.

In fact everything worked out better than Sun could have wished. Cole's instinct was to have the card posted anonymously to Cantlie, but his wife, who seems to have been the conscience-stricken conspirator giving courage to her panicking husband, pointed out that speed was all important and that a letter written on a Saturday would not reach Cantlie until the following day (there were Sunday posts at this time) and then he would be able to do little before the Monday.

So Cole went round to Cantlie's house with the message together with another note which read: "There is a friend of yours imprisoned in the Chinese Legation here since last Sunday. They intend sending him out to China where it is certain they will hang him. It is very sad for the poor man and unless something is done at once, he will be taken away and no one will know it. I dare not sign my name, but this is the truth, so believe what I say. Whatever you do must be done at once, or it will be too late. His name is, I believe, Lin Yen-sen."

Cantlie had been surprised that Sun Yat-sen had not called on him and it at once dawned on him that his friend must have been kidnapped. It was 11 p.m. on Saturday 17 October when Cantlie received this note and the Foreign Office was closed for the weekend. He informed the police, who referred him to Scotland Yard. The latter showed no interest whatsoever (there was no Special Branch in those days) and merely referred Cantlie to the Foreign Office.

Fortunately Cantlie realised the need for speedy action and, despite these rebuffs, consulted a judge and various officials, thus obtaining some slight elucidation on what could be done, but with no real offer of aid. Nevertheless he managed to smuggle in a reply to Sun through the servant Cole which said: "Cheer up! The Government is working on your behalf and you will be free in a few days."

It was a cheerful message, but it certainly did not represent Cantlie's feelings of frustration and foreboding. The only individual who seems completely to have retained commonsense and the right intuitions during this period is Mrs Cantlie, who had anticipated the dangers which the proximity of the Chinese Legation posed for Sun and who, on her own responsibility, had gone round to Sun's lodgings, collected all his papers and correspondence and had, as soon as she heard of his kidnapping, had the papers destroyed. In this whole affair of bungling on both sides—Chinese and British—it was the amateur Mrs Cantlie who behaved most like a professional secret agent.

Sun Yat-sen later commented on her rôle, which undoubtedly prevented the Chinese Government and their Secret Service from stamping out Sun's organisation: "If some of my friends in various parts of the world have had no reply to their letters, they must blame this considerate lady for her wise and prompt action and forgive my not having answered them, as I am minus their addresses and in many cases do not even know their names. Should the Chinese authorities again entrap me, they will find no papers whereby my associates can be made known to them."[11]

Cantlie tried without success to contact Sir Halliday Macartney during the weekend. Eventually he tracked down Cole, who, trembling with fear, agreed to disclose the secret of Sun's imprisonment. Cole was then asked where Sir Halliday could be found, Cantlie assuming, quite wrongly, that if only Sir Halliday could be found all would be well, not realising that in effect this extraordinary Briton was acting as an agent of the Chinese Secret Service.

It was then that Cole made it clear that Sir Halliday was in London, but merely lying low, that he went to the Legation every day and that it was he who had locked Sun in his room. From Cole came the proof that the Legation authorities had been reinforced by Secret Service agents from China. He informed Cantlie that Sun Yat-sen was to be declared a lunatic and removed to China in two days' time. He did not know by what line of ships Sun was to be sent, but "a man of the name of McGregor in the City had something to do with it". Cole also confirmed that two or three men, dressed as Chinese sailors, had been to the Legation during the week and Cole had no doubt they had something to do with Sun's kidnapping.

Dr Manson, Sun's other friend in London, called at the Chinese Legation and through an interpreter was confronted with the man Tang. Manson said he wished to see Sun Yat-sen; Tang denied there was any person of that name in the Legation. Manson then replied that he was quite sure he was there and that the Foreign Office and Scotland Yard had been informed of this.

Apparently Tang put up such an impressive performance in denying the story that even Manson began to doubt it. Sun's remarks on this are not without interest when considering the intricate subject of Chinese espionage: "Thus can my countrymen lie: Tang even shook the belief of a man like Dr Manson, who had lived in China twenty-two years, who spoke the Amoy dialect fluently, and was thereby more intimately acquainted with the Chinese and their ways than nine-tenths of the people who visit the Far East."

Cantlie then engaged a private detective to have the Legation watched. But he still felt that time was against him and that desperate measures were required. By a brilliant inspiration he decided to give the newspapers his story. In the end it was the press which saved Sun Yat-sen.

Taking a cab late on Sunday night, Cantlie went to *The Times* office. He gave them his remarkable story and then returned to Portland Place to keep his own watch on the Legation until the following day, when the private detectives started their day-and-night watch.

But it was the *Globe* rather than the sedate *Times,* always timorous of the Establishment, which really splashed the story and thereby raised the wrath of the radicals who saw this as a *cause celèbre* with which to belabour the Tory Government of the day.

"STARTLING STORY! CONSPIRATOR KIDNAPPED IN LONDON! IMPRISONMENT AT THE CHINESE LEGATION" ran the *Globe*'s headlines. Once the story had been ventilated in the press it was almost a matter of hours until a reluctant Government could be pressured into action.

The Foreign Office still back-pedalled and tried to avoid having to take action themselves, not wishing to create international repercussions by becoming involved in the incident. It was only when proof was produced that a passage had been requested at the Glen Line offices that the Government became convinced there was a substantial case for intervention.

On October 22 a writ of *habeas corpus* was made out against the Legation and Sir Halliday Macartney in person, but the judge declined to agree to this. It would seem that the judge allowed himself to be blinded with prejudice because a Briton happened to be the Counsellor at the Chinese Legation. *The Times* was slow in taking up the case, but the *Globe* and the *Daily Mail* both pursued it to the fullest extent. Each sent reporters to the Chinese Legation, but they were met by the lying Tang, who merely laughed off the whole affair as a huge imposition.

It was not until noon on the Monday that Cantlie submitted his statement in writing to the Foreign Office. They still took the view that the proofs of his detention were inconclusive and mere hearsay, but six detectives were detailed for duty outside the Chinese Legation. It was the *Globe* which really aroused widespread interest in the affair and thus influenced the authorities, though it is not clear who gave the *Globe* the story. One knows that Cantlie gave it to *The Times* and he himself says that later he was questioned by the *Globe,* but, in his own words, he told them he "felt bound to let *The Times* make it public first".

But the *Globe* did not wait and one must therefore assume that they obtained the story from another source. This could only have been from Cole (which seems highly unlikely), or Mrs Cole (rather more likely), from another sympathiser with Sun inside the Chinese Legation (rather less likely), or from one of the missives, weighted by coins, that he had tossed through the window (improbably because this window was at the back of the building).

Sir Halliday Macartney was finally discovered at an address which suggested he had been deliberately keeping in hiding—the Midland Hotel—and he eventually told the press that "the man will be released, but this will be done strictly without prejudice to the rights of the Legation involved". He also denied that Sun Yat-sen was the true name of the man they had in detention, obviously an attempt to minimise the issue. He added: "We have no doubt of his real identity, and have been from time to time fully informed of all his movements since he set foot in England. He came of his own free will to the Legation and was certainly not kidnapped or forced or inveigled into the premises. . . . There appears to be some ground for suspecting that this peculiar visitor, believing himself unknown, came with some idea of spying on us and getting some information."[12] Sir Halliday also stressed that the man was a Chinese subject and on Chinese territory in the Legation and therefore subject to Chinese jurisdiction.

An interesting aside on all this is the statement of Sun Yat-sen that Tang "expressed the position pretty exactly when he told me that the 'Minister is but a figure-head here, Macartney is the ruler' ".

Sun's friends trusted neither the British Foreign Office nor the police, and made their own plans for rescuing Sun if all else failed. This was that Sun should be aided by having the window of his room broken, bars removed so that he could climb out on to the roof and walk across to the nearby residence of Lord Powerscourt. In case Sun was able to make an escape by this means a cab was kept waiting nearby to take him to the home of a friend.

Cole had apparently sent a message to Cantlie that he would have "a good opportunity to let Mr Sun out on to the roof of the next house in Portland Place to-night. . . . If I am to do it, find means to let me know."

Cantlie showed this letter to Scotland Yard, but, probably fearing Foreign Office disapproval, they said they thought this was "an undignified procedure" and persuaded Cantlie that the attempt should not be made.

Then on 23 October Sun was taken from his room by his Chinese guards and told that Macartney wanted to see him downstairs. He was told to put on his coat, hat and boots. "I descended the stairs," he said later, "and as it was to the basement I was being conducted, I believed I was to be hidden in a cellar whilst the house was being searched by the command of the British Government."

But Sun's fears were not realised and soon he was confronted with Cantlie, an Inspector from Scotland Yard and a messenger from the Foreign Office. It was then that Sir Halliday Macartney appeared and handed over the various belongings he had taken from Sun, who was told he was now a free man. The party was then let out by the back door of the Legation.

Sun Yat-sen never had any doubt that it was Macartney who was the principal figure behind these machinations in London: he never once saw the Chinese Minister.

One final point should be made in fairness to the English servant at the Chinese Legation, the man Cole. When Sun gave him the twenty pounds in notes he had in desperation intended it as a bribe, but Sun had this to add on the subject: "He [Cole] did not understand that I gave him the money by way of fee at all; he believed I gave it him to keep for me; he told Mr Cantlie he had the £20 the day he got it, and offered to give it to him for safe keeping. When I came out Cole handed the money back to me, but it was the least I could do to urge him to keep it."

It was Lord Salisbury, who had become Prime Minister the previous year, who personally intervened for the release of Sun Yat-sen, and whose terse note to Sir Halliday Macartney gave the latter no choice but to obey his instructions. Belatedly *The Times* commented in a leading article that "we cannot conceal our surprise that Sir Halliday Macartney, himself an Englishman, should have taken any part in a transaction manifestly doomed to failure, and the success of which would have been ruinous to all engaged in it".

14

The End of the Manchu Secret Service 1898-1903

After we lost Canton, our old files on barbarian affairs in Yeh Ming-ch'en's office were looted by the English barbarians, and the traditional methods have all been seen through. Our techniques of control are lost, and our intelligence and courage exhausted.
Report to the Emperor of China by his advisers, 11 June 1858

WHEN Horatio Nelson Lay, the Englishman who became Inspector-General of the Chinese Customs, conducted talks with Ch'i-ying and other advisers to the Emperor in June 1858, he shocked them by producing a memorial which Ch'i-ying had written to the Emperor in 1844 and which the British had captured with other papers at Canton some 13 years later.

This memorial threw some light on Chinese dealings with Westerners and showed how the methods of intelligence techniques governed their diplomacy: "There are times when it is possible to have them [the Europeans] follow our directions but not let them understand the reasons. Sometimes we expose everything so that they will not be suspicious, whereupon we can dissipate their rebellious restlessness. Sometimes we have given them receptions and entertainment, after which they have had a feeling of appreciation. . . . With this type of people from outside the bounds of civilisation, who are blind and unawakened to styles of address and forms of ceremony, if we adhered to the proper forms in official documents and let them be weighed according to the status of superior and inferior . . . they could not avoid closing their ears and acting as if deaf."[1]

If this was the position in 1858, one does not require much imagination, in the light of what we have seen of the decline of the Manchu empire, to visualise how much more the quotation at the title heading of this chapter applied at the end of the century. If there were a few unscrupulous Englishmen such as Macartney who were prepared to act as lackeys of the Manchu Secret Service and to bend the rules to suit Imperial chicanery, there were many others, already fully implemented into advisory posts with the Chinese establishment, who put Britain to the fore and China very much to the rear. Horatio Nelson Lay, whose first names no doubt encouraged his belief in the myth of British superiority, was one example of the latter.

One of the points to be remembered in connection with this Chinese dependence in some spheres on Western advisers is that so many groups inside China were trying to overthrow the Manchu empire, that foreign missions were often headed by paid foreigners who were considered more trustworthy than the Chinese. This factor in Manchu thinking has been mentioned before, but it is important that it should be borne in mind because, despite Tzu-hsi's fanatical hatred of the "barbarians" and her almost self-destructive urge secretly to back the Boxers, she and her advisers still heavily relied on what Jonathan Spence calls "the Western helpers".

Tzu-hsi was growing old and perhaps a little bewildered at the pace at which the West was gaining control of the situation inside China. If she felt resentment and hatred, then the Boxers certainly gave her cause for clinging to the idea of a Boxer rebellion as providing the last possible chance for driving out the "barbarians". But those, like Jung Lu, who took a realistic view of the extent to which the West's indirect control of China had progressed warned her she was gambling recklessly.

Israel Epstein wrote: "The Manchu rulers in Peking, seeing the movement [the Boxers] was spreading like lightning, were fearful of being swept away by it. They therefore pretended to put themselves at its head, issued eloquent, patriotic-sounding proclamations and, under popular pressure, actually 'declared war' on the imperialist powers. But even as fighting was going on inside Peking itself, they sent a slavish circular appeal to the same powers which sank to the depth of saying that 'your noble country . . . has never exhibited any covetous desire for territory'. They begged the foreign governments not to be taken in by appearances and make the mistake of suspecting the dynasty of 'favouring the common folk'. Finally they stated that 'China is at her wit's end to raise funds for armies . . . and in order to get out of this difficult tangle, she can but have recourse to the assistance of your noble country'."[2]

Thus the totally decadent Manchus were trying to play it both ways in a singularly inept manner, totally lacking either in any belief in their own Intelligence Service, or in any genuine conviction as to which policy they ought to follow. The result was an ambivalent and perfidious attitude to the Boxer rebellion in 1900, the Manchu court being quite incapable of knowing what to do.

The Boxers attacked the Legations Quarter in Peking and it was soon apparent that their zest for bloodshed was such that it would not be likely to stop short of the Court itself. Thus there was the tragic-comical paradox of the Manchus appealing to the hated "barbarians" for help against the rebels whom they had secretly backed. The Boxers were double-crossed to such an extent that Tzu-hsi sent in food supplies to the Legations Quarter at the very moment when it was being attacked both by the Boxers and her own troops!

The empire was absolutely divided in its counsels; many provincial governors, except in North China,

where the Boxers were dominant, sided with the Europeans and ignored the calls to war. Meanwhile a combined force of Americans, British, French, Germans,
Italians, Japanese and Russians marched on Peking,
halting the Boxers' advance and seeking every excuse
to give the final kick to the dying Manchu empire.

The massacres in Peking in this year were as bad
as anything that had happened earlier in the century.
B. L. Putman Weale describes how the "barbarians"
behaved: "A curious young man from one of the
Legations . . . volunteered to play the part of executioner. . . . This man had done it always with a shot-
gun and he seemed to gloat over it . . . as soon as
he saw me he made a long broken speech . . . 'The wells
near the Eastern Gates, have you seen them, where
all the women and girls have been jumping in? They
were afraid of the troops.' Then he came up to me and
whispered how soldiers were behaving after they had
outraged women. . . . He said that our own inhuman
soldiery had invited him to stay and see."[3]

Thus Manchus and Westerners, each for their own
ends, came together, but only for a brief spell. This
time the "Westerners" came in for the kill, to impose
their will totally on what remained of the Chinese empire. But the uneasy relationship was not to blossom
into any sudden friendship. The Westerners were well
aware that Tzu-hsi would have used the Boxers to
drive them out if she had retained her confidence in
controlling the situation. But, having been saved from
the Boxers, in the end, it was Tzu-hsi herself who had
to flee from Peking, allegedly in the disguise of a
commoner's clothes.

The Peace Treaty ending the Boxer rebellion was
signed at Peking on 22 December 1900. Its effect
was to preserve the crumbling façade of the Manchu
empire for a few years longer, but effectively to put
the whole of China under Western domination. Two
years later Tzu-hsi returned by train from Shensi to
Peking, the first Chinese ruler ever to travel by this
means.

Her court had been in exile for two years, yet during
this time she had been as ruthless as ever. She had
taken into exile with her both the abdicated Emperor

165

and his favourite concubine Pearl. Tzu-hsi ordered her eunuchs to hurl the concubine down a well, while forcing the Emperor to watch this "execution".

But on returning to the capital Tzu-hsi refused to accept absolute defeat: she maintained all her court exactly as before, she behaved as the same supreme ruler, but she set out to woo the Westerners she despised. Though now in her seventies, the Empress took the greatest care with her appearance and, though widows were not allowed to use make-up, she "first sprayed her face with a mixture of glycerine and honeysuckle of her own concoction, and then, as her dark complexion was not admired in China, wore a pinkish powder and rouged her bottom lip and cheeks to disguise it; she scented herself generously with musk; she sweetened her breath with betelnuts . . . she now had the grey streaks in her once raven hair blotted out with black dye."[4]

And it is to the credit of this ageing tyrant that she managed to charm Westerners who saw her in these last years of her life. It is said that even then her voice was like "rhythmic poetry, fresh and silvery". Though loathing all foreigners deep down in her heart, she invited the wives of foreign diplomats to her parties, even persuading them in conversation that she believed in reform and proposed to abolish corporal punishment. Indeed she introduced an edict which appeared to do just this, but within a few weeks of its promulgation she had a Reformist flogged to death. For behind her all the time was Jung Lu, now and until his death in 1903 much more the chief adviser than was Li Lien-ying.

It is said that Tzi-hsi died from eating a surfeit of crab-apples with clotted cream shortly after her seventy-third birthday. Asked when dying if she had any words of wisdom to pass on to her successors, she is alleged to have said: "Never again allow any woman to hold the supreme power in the State and never again allow eunuchs to meddle in government matters." It was the wisest advice any of the Manchu rulers ever gave to his successors and it not only marked the end of eunuch rule inside the palace, but the outdated conception of a Secret Service dominated by leading eunuchs.

In 1894 Sir Robert Hart, another leading Western adviser to Imperial China and one who had been appointed Inspector-General of the Imperial Customs Service at the age of thirty-four, predicted that "Chinese blood has been well cooled by the training its brain has had the last twenty centuries, but I think it quite possible that one of these days despair may well find expression in the wildest rage and that one day we foreigners, one and all, will be wiped out in Peking".[5]

Only six years later this predicted "wildest rage" manifested itself prematurely in the Boxer revolt. But Sir Robert Hart by no means regarded the putting down of that rebellion by twelve Western nations' combined expeditionary force as conclusive: "Twenty millions or more of Boxers, armed, drilled, disciplined and animated by patriotic motives will make residence in China impossible for foreigners, will take back from foreigners everything foreigners have taken from China. In fifty years' time there will be millions of Boxers at the call of a Chinese Government. There is not the slightest doubt of that."[6]

It was in August 1900 that Sir Robert made that further prediction. Exactly fifty years later China was actively aiding North Korea against the United Nations forces and, in January 1950, Britain had already recognised the Communist Government of China.

Tzu-hsi lived on until 1908 and she preserved all the outward trappings of the Manchu government, which, though dependent on the Western powers, preserved many of its privileges. But ten Western powers had the right to maintain their own troops in Peking itself to guard their Legations and to house them in a section of the city in which, by an agreed concession, "Chinese people shall not have the right to reside". The Westerners even had their own parks in some areas in which notices were put up at the entrance stating that "Chinese and Dogs" were "not admitted".

The Manchu Secret Service was now to all intents and purposes as near non-existent as mattered. Internal security was left entirely to the police who kept a vigilant watch for dangerous Reformists and characters like Sun Yat-sen. But the Chinese instinct for survival and an almost subconsciously patient urge slowly to rebuild an Intelligence Service which would one day replace that of the Manchus revealed itself in the growth of secret societies in the early part of the twentieth century. These societies served many purposes, mainly for the protection of Chinese nationals at home and overseas, but not least for the most intellectual and progressive of the leaders as a basis for a new Secret Service for the Republic of China, which the Reformists felt could not be long delayed.

Sun Yat-sen, now a figure of considerable stature on account of his world-wide travels, his adventure in London and the organisation he had so carefully built up, had behind him an Intelligence organisation which the Manchus could not hope to match. It cast its net right across the Pacific and Atlantic Oceans. And in 1902 there was established in Shanghai the Chiao-yu-hui, a secret society concerned with developing a new type of education and which purported to use schools as a secret revolutionary combine. This society aimed at compiling new and improved school textbooks in its early stages, but it was a short step from this to turn it into a revolutionary agency.

One of its leading members, Ts'ai Yuan-p'ei, not only laid emphasis on the importance of using schools and teachers as revolutionary agents, but went much further, urging not only the teaching of the history of popular national uprisings in China, but physical training, the rudiments of military discipline and bomb technology. "Do not be afraid to die or to kill," was one of the precepts he insisted on having introduced into these schools' curriculum, and to some extent the society borrowed some ideas from the Russian anarchists, though in many respects its discipline was superior and its long-term aims more coherent.

Later in 1902 the Chiao-yu-hui supported the founding of the Ai-kuo Academy for boys and girls, providing it with staff and textbooks. This school, set up in November 1902, was ostensibly to provide places for some hundred pupils who had walked out of the Nanyang College in Shanghai, following a revolt against an autocratic and unpopular teacher. The walkout was symptomatic of the rebellious, if sullen and controlled, mentality of students after the Boxer rising had been crushed.

While the European powers and the United States increased their stranglehold on the Chinese economy, wresting every advantage from control of the railways to making harsh trading restrictions which favoured themselves, the Reformists were by no means inactive. They were among the first to realise the implications of the alliance signed between Britain and Japan in 1902. In its general terms this alliance claimed to pave the way to a state of "peace in the Far East" and to "ensure the territorial integrity of China". In effect it was designed by the British to curb the Russians not so much in China as in any intentions they might have (greatly exaggerated in the British mind) towards the north-west frontiers of India, while secretly agreeing that Britain should have the right of armed intervention in China and that Japan be entitled to similar rights in Korea.

Sun Yat-sen was closely informed on the secret manoeuvres which were going on behind the scenes in connection with the Anglo-Japanese alliance partly through Britons who supported his cause, while for his internal intelligence he relied increasingly on a peasant society known as the Ko Lao Hui or "Elder Brothers".

"The cream of China's educated youth were forming secret societies, founding underground newspapers and undertaking anti-dynastic actions of various kinds," wrote Israel Epstein.[7] "Sun Yat-sen from his exile was organising with indefatigable energy. He travelled to all parts of the world where there were Chinese communities and young Chinese men and women were studying, gathering funds, hammering out a programme, setting up clubs and newspapers, buying and shipping arms."

Sun had not forgotten the lesson of his kidnapping in London and he determined that never again would he allow himself to be so foolishly trapped. He created a set of rules for himself for safeguarding his movements, which he memorised and adhered to rigidly.

All the time he kept travelling around the world, organising cells among Chinese exiles wherever there was a Chinese community of any size.

There were few countries he did not visit in Europe, the Americas and the Pacific. The sole exception was Russia, where he knew there existed a police state and a battle between a monarchist regime decaying like the Manchus and underground revolutionaries. But he had also been warned that in Russia the tattered remnants of the Manchu Secret Service still had a few spies. Knowing that there was an uneasy, tenuous and suspicious relationship between the Czarists and the Manchus, with a good deal of bribery on both sides, Sun suspected that the Russians might betray him to the Manchu spies.

He need not have worried. The Russians, who were at this time spending more money on their Secret Service than any other power in the world, had somewhat exaggerated ideas about the presence of Manchu spies in their midst. The truth was, as Sun learned years afterwards, that the farcical situation of Chinese spies in Russia was that the Manchus did not know they existed (at least in 1902-3), while the spies themselves did not know that the Manchus were no longer all powerful. Nor did they appreciate that any information they sent to the Manchus never reached them, but was relayed either to the British or the Russians.

Sun never made it absolutely clear why he avoided visiting Russia, but the implication was that he feared the Russians would betray him to the Manchus. He had carefully studied the espionage lessons of the Boxer rebellion. One of the first to learn of the dispatch of American troops from Manila to China to help quell this rising, he also realised to his horror that at that time, inside China itself, the Westerners had organised their own corps of spies on the Boxers' strength and movements from native converts to Christianity and the "rice Christians of the mission schools". Sun had many friends among Western missionaries, but he was desperately anxious that these should not employ their converts against their country in future.

On several occasions Sun entered China in disguise, always closely taking the political temperature and assessing his chances for a successful coup. Despite all the careful precautions he took and his avoidance of arrest, he tended to be misled by his Western friends and to trust them too much. This was understandable: it was Westerners who had helped him as a youth and he felt he owed them much, while it was his English friends who rescued him from the kidnapping in London. Perhaps, too, his conversion to Christian ideas made him rate his Western friends too highly —and in later life caused him to be too charitable towards his enemies. For, as will later be seen, Sun's virtues in the long run caused him to commit many errors.

Meanwhile, at the end of 1902, Sidney Reilly was reporting back to the British Secret Service that "the Manchus are finished. It is only a matter of time before China becomes the playground of the great powers. Their intelligence service, such as it is, for all practical purposes simply does not exist. But I should warn you that in this vacuum which is left a new and much more dangerous Secret Service will eventually spring up. Today it is like the sperm inside the womb. Tomorrow? Perhaps a fully fledged child."[8]

At this time Reilly was playing a very strange game and working as a double, if not a treble, agent. He was certainly working for the British (he might, though this is less probable, also have been working for the Russians) and he had begun to spy for the Japanese. As I wrote in my *History of the British Secret Service,* "He certainly sold information to the Japanese as well as the British. No doubt both benefited equally well and Reilly could, of course, salve his conscience by the fact that an Anglo-Japanese alliance had been concluded in 1902. Yet at the very time he was supplying information to the Japanese he informed his chief in London that he wanted leave of absence because he did not want to be embroiled against Russia in the Russo-Japanese War that was even then imminent, and that he was afraid any information he gave London might be passed to the Japanese. Then he disappeared for several months into China, living in a lamaserie in the province of Shen-si and becoming a Buddhist."

Curiously Reilly was given permission to have this leave of absence, but the question which has not yet been answered is for whom he was spying in China. An efficient agent, he never seems to have been suspected by any of the Chinese. There is little doubt that he was supplying Britain with information on the underground movements in China and that much of this intelligence may later have been used to trick Sun Yat-sen.

15

The Su-pao Sedition Case 1902-1904

If reforms cannot be realised, there should be revolution; if reforms can be carried out there should also be revolution.
Chang Ping-lin cited in Hsin-hai ko-ming, source materials on Chinese revolutionary movements, edited by the *Chungkuo Shih-hsueh-hui,* June 1903

THERE were many occasions between 1902 and 1911 when the Reformists seemed to be on the point of seizing power. Sun Yat-sen was more than once about to arrange a *coup* only to find himself thwarted by the tenuous liaison between Western Intelligence Services and the Manchus. It is incredible how blind were the Western Secret Services to the substantial advantages for them in backing Sun Yat-sen forthrightly.

Then in 1903 came substantial evidence of what the Western powers were missing. Like people who have deteriorated from one coronary thrombosis to another the Western powers in China were shattered and bewildered by the *Su-pao* sedition case in Shanghai which revealed the growing presence of the Chinese Reformists' underground intelligence.

Su-pao was a small reformist newspaper in Shanghai, then the journalistic centre of China, which contained articles by young Radicals. This brought to the attention of the Westerners, no less than to that of the decaying empire, the existence of yet another secret society which spied upon the foreigner and urged revolution.

The *Su-pao* case was tried in the Shanghai Settlement in 1903 and was almost the last sustained act by the Manchu Government against the Reformists in their futile, but still determined attempts to check the growth of revolutionary zeal. But the trial, which might have been a supreme show-down between the old regime and the new, to the total defeat of the latter, was hampered by the Manchus' weakness in relation to the Western powers. The latter were still pursuing their feeble and unintelligent policy of making gestures in favour of the Manchus' regime, while not discouraging any outside interference with it.

The Russians had posed a threat to the Manchu regime after the return of the Empress Tzu-hsi in 1902 by refusing to move from the positions they had occupied in the north-east provinces of China. They were intent on gaining Manchuria. Meanwhile, under pressure from the Reformists, Tzu-hsi had agreed to a programme of moderate reforms.

The reforms, however, were of a kind that might well have been accepted as admirable ten or fifteen years previously, but were now regarded as unmeaningful concessions of a very minor kind. The whole question of educational and examination reforms for admittance to the Civil Service was left unsatisfactorily vague.

New divisions in the Reformist groups emerged, but from the point of view of the development of a shadow Secret Service the key man was Chang Ping-lin, who was a fanatical radical, determined to mould future generations of students in the cause of republicanism. In many respects Chang Ping-lin was more suited to the work of re-organising a national intelligence service than was Sun Yat-sen himself. Chang Ping-lin was unencumbered by any respect for or dependence on Western missionaries or sympathisers: he was in contrast to Sun Yat-sen almost xenophobic.

Chang also established close links with the Japanese, though he found the organisation of such allies limited to a very few intellectuals. In this respect he anticipated Sun Yat-sen, who, in August 1905, brought about a merger of the "Revive China" Society with other revolutionary groups in Tokyo, linking them up with the Tung Meng Hui (Revolutionary League).[1]

In this period Tokyo and Shanghai were the main action points for Radical opinion and where they were most easily brought into coherent organisation. But though Shanghai was a centre of intense revolutionary acitivity it was also a major sphere of British influence and the British had a majority in the Municipal Council, which was the governing body of the area. Thus British legal practice was the main influence in Shanghai.

Shanghai's Legal Council was to a very large extent treated as though it were an appendage of the Western powers and to some extent controlled by the Diplomatic Corps. In the *Su-pao* case the Shanghai Council wanted to unseal the office of the newspaper only a few days after the sealing since no charges had been heard in court. There was during the entire hearing of this case a constant power struggle between China and the West. At the same time both the Chinese authorities and the Western powers each equally claimed to be acting in "the best interests of China".

The newspaper *Su-pao* was started up in Shanghai in 1896 and eventually purchased by Ch'en Fan, a supporter of the Reformists. Ch'en Fan increased the circulation of the paper by making it of special appeal to students to about a thousand in June 1903, a modest rise by modern standards, but quite impressive in the Shanghai of that era. Ch'en Fan had gone out of his way to invite young Radicals of proved ability not merely to contribute to the paper, but to help him coordinate revolutionary propaganda.

Su-pao became increasingly radical and revolutionary in its tone and Westerners at least, eagerly reading the paper, expected that sooner or later the authorities would be forced to take action against it. The final

174

blow came when Chang Shih-chao became editor in June 1903, and proceeded to publish a whole series of ultra-Radical articles.

On 30 June 1903, six journalists, alleged to be on the staff of *Su-pao,* were arrested at the request of the Chinese authorities charged with discussing "the abolition of the Imperial prerogative and other forbidden questions". A request was made for the accused to be handed over to the Chinese authorities for immediate execution. This demand was over-ruled and it was agreed that the full charges must be heard and dealt with by the courts.

The full charge was that the accused did "maliciously print and publish, or cause to be printed or published, certain treasonable seditious libels in a Chinese newspaper called *Su-pao,* in order to incite treason, discontent and create disturbance and to bring His Majesty the Emperor and His Government into hatred and contempt".

The fact that "His Majesty" was still under detention and to some extent held in contempt by the Court and the Empress Tzu-hsi, gave the affair even more of an Alice-in-Wonderland touch. The trial was not held until the following December, mainly due to a tremendous effort by the Chinese authorities to force the total surrender of the accused without a trial. There was no doubt at all that the Chinese Government looked upon Shanghai as the focal point of the revolutionary movement and therefore had been determined to make this a major issue.

But the trial dragged on, despite efforts of the Manchus to thwart justice being done and to get a quick decision. The whole affair of the *Su-pao* inevitably built up into something like an international issue, as the case became linked with the much larger subject of the status of Shanghai itself and in this respect the Westerners were at least as alive as the Chinese officials themselves to the points of dispute. The Westerners realised that they dared not concede one iota of legalistic advantage to the Manchus, even if revolutionaries might gain any advantage thereby.

There had been several plots about this time, all differing in their degrees of radicalism and revolutionary fervour, but almost all devoted to overthrowing, or at least clipping, Manchu power. Sun Yat-sen and his own followers and some other small groups separate to him, but generally supporting his aims, were for the abolition of the monarchy and the formation of a republic. There was also the K'ang-Liang Party, reformist in essence, but wishing to oust Tzu-hsi with British aid and to establish the exiled Emperor Kuang-hsu as a constitutional monarch.

Student magazines sprang up overnight in various parts of China, all urging reforms of various kinds. But, without question, *Su-pao* was the most influential and the spearhead of the underground intelligence movement upon which all the reform parties based their strength. The revolutionary movements were, of course, particularly aided in having Shanghai as a base because the International Settlement there was outside Chinese jurisdiction and because as an international zone inside China it lent itself to espionage and the gathering of intelligence. Shanghai as an international settlement in the early 1900s became a major spy city just as Tangier did in World War II and for the same reasons: its international regime guaranteed its neutrality and to some extent protected the spies who came in and out.

There was, of course, a good deal of bargaining between the Western powers and the Chinese Government, but one of the vital points about the International Settlement of Shanghai was this neutrality, which was jealously and vigorously guarded by the Westerners, and which gave to Chinese Radicals inside the Settlement the freedom denied to them in the empire itself. The compromise arrived at on this point was that while the Western powers guaranteed that the Settlement would not be used as a base for revolutionaries to plot the overthrow of the empire, radicals had a greater freedom from arrest here than in China proper. Hence the origin of the phrase "to be shanghaied", which arose when radicals were kidnapped in Shanghai and dragged over the border to be dealt with in Imperial China territory. There were several attempts to kidnap radicals and as a result a sentry was posted in front of the Mixed Court in Shanghai to prevent any Chinese from being "shanghaied" into the interior.

The real issue behind the *Su-pao* case was the threat posed by the Chiao-yu-hui Secret Society, more especially as this society had prompted a number of student strikes in 1902–3. This was why every effort was made by the Chinese Government to get the accused surrendered to them so that they could be dealt with inside the empire.

The Ai-kuo Academy in Shanghai was also a continuous threat to the Chinese Government as it was continually exploited as a key centre of the revolutionaries' espionage organisation. Late in 1902 the Academy's funds began to dwindle and to put this right it was decided that a rota of members had in their turn to provide articles and information to the *Su-pao* in exchange for which payments were made to the Academy. Perhaps this arrangement more than any other pin-pointed the subversive and espionage activities surrounding *Su-pao* and its links with the secret service of the revolutionaries.

Just how good the Chiao-yu-hui intelligence was—and, though this was then only a secret society, it is important to remember that it formed in part, along with Sun Yat-sen's organisation, the nucleus for the Chinese official Secret Service of a decade later—can be gathered from the fact that they obtained full details of Russian moves in Manchuria as well as unmasking many scandals involving bribery from Westerners which had led Imperial officials to make concessions.

Protests were made by the Chinese authorities. The Treaty Commissioner, Lu Hai-huan, wrote to En-shou, Governor of Kiangsu that "in the International Settlement of Shanghai there are a number of so-called enthusiasts who have held meetings in the Chang Garden to discuss affairs. Their pretext is that they are resisting the French and Russians, but they are really planning revolt. You are requested to arrest and deal with them."[2]

As a result instructions were given to the Shanghai Taotai, Yuan Shu-hsun, to have the suspects arrested. By this time they had compiled a list of known Radical activists, but the Municipal Council stood out against any wholesale arrests and the *Shanghai Times* lent full support to the Council's decision.

In June 1903 *Su-pao* had not merely maintained its radical line, it had gone much further, Chang Shih-chao, its new editor, stating that "the revolutionary party is the only answer for China". Later Chang Ping-lin made it clear that the policy was "no compromise or cooperation with the Manchus or with the K'ang-Liang Party. . . . If reforms cannot be carried out, there should be revolution; if reforms are undertaken, there should also be revolution."[3]

Tokyo was a natural base for the Chinese radicals at this time, partly because Western ideas were stimulating thought and being adopted in Japan, but also because the Japanese loathed the Manchu regime. Indeed some of the Chinese radicals, especially those of the student generation, borrowed ideas from Japanese radicals. In the forefront of these was a 19-year-old student agent named Tsou Jung, who became one of the ablest intelligence men in the revolutionary ranks. It was he who brought with him from Japan the document known as the *Ko-ming chun* ("The Revolutionary Army") from Tokyo and had it published in China, where it became one of the most highly prized of secret underground text-books.

It became clear to the more enlightened Westerners that it would be a grave error to antagonise the radicals and that, with the inevitable decay of the Manchu Empire, the radicals might well be needed as future allies. This was particularly true of the British Liberals, even though as a party they were in opposition at the time.

So it was not surprising that the only leading radicals arrested were Chang Ping-lin, the most outspoken of them all, Tsou Jung and Lung Chih-chih—and in fact the first two each offered themselves up to the authorities in order to publicise the points at issue so that the affair could not be hushed up, greatly embarrassing the Westerners by their action.

On the other hand the radical forces were also acutely embarrassed by a dispute among them between Wu Chih-hui and Chang Ping-lin. This arose over the behaviour of students at the Ai-kuo Academy, Chang Ping-lin wishing to discipline the cadets, but Wu Chih-hui siding with them. This resulted in a break between the Chiao-yu-hui secret society and the Academy.

Western sympathisers undoubtedly aided the accused in the *Su-pao* trial, who also received funds from Japan. It may well have been that some Western money went to pay counsel for the accused, as some of the defendants dismayed the Chinese authorities by engaging Western counsel. A great deal of manoeuvring for advantage went on, sometimes even by the radicals with friends inside Manchu China. As J. Lust sums it up: "Many of the reformers and revolutionaries were related to high officials or gentry or connected with them by ties of patronage. . . . Chang Chih-chao is nowhere mentioned in official documents, apparently because at the time he was a cadet at the Nanking Military Academy. . . . Perhaps this gentry solidarity was also at the bottom of the strange case of Wu Chih-hui. . . . Statements were furious and obscure on Chang's part and evasive or contradictory on Wu's, but the following appears to be the course of events behind the scenes at the end of June. A secret meeting between Wu and Yu Ming-chen (or his brother) had been arranged by Wu's son just before the raid on the *Su-pao* office. During the interview Yu treated the affair as a comedy, but he advised Wu to leave China. Before sailing, Wu visited Chang Ping-lin and Tsou Jung who were then in prison. Chang accused him of collusion with Yu over the *Su-pao* in return for his freedom. They were in prison; he was not. Wu displayed an uneasy conscience and the dispute led to a lifelong feud between the two. Wu had been accused of acting as a spy. There is no direct evidence for this in the documents."[4]

It was then alleged that Yu Ming-chen deliberately arranged for the arrests to be made in a leisurely fashion, with secret prior warning to the suspects, so that the remaining members of the *Su-pao* group could escape before being detained. Devious as such a procedure might sound, from Yu's point of view it would avoid exacerbating Western opinion and still keep a kind of peace with the Chinese Government.

The Westerners themselves were no less devious in their attitude to this trial. The Municipal Council in Shanghai had asked for the addresses of the accused and sent them a questionnaire—deliberately framed, it is said, as a broad hint for them to go underground. It was fairly obvious that up to the last moment they wished to stop the trial taking place without seeming to be implicated in any such desire.

What had undoubtedly angered the Westerners who helped to run Shanghai was that the Imperial Government had sent a large number of secret agents into the International Settlement to build up evidence against the accused and to use blackmail and other threats against supporters of the radicals.

Nobody on either side—the Chinese Government or the Westerners—was really sure how the trial would develop, or what surprise the other side would spring on it, and this was why it dragged on inconclusively for so long and with so many excuses for delays and requests for time to collect further evidence. The truth was that the Imperial Government had only the slenderest evidence upon which to proceed in an International Court. Because of this they made prolonged attempts through diplomatic channels to persuade the Shanghai International authorities to extradite the accused.

For a time there was a slender majority inside the Diplomatic Corps in favour of extraditing the men, the Russians taking this view very strongly and to a large extent the French and Germans concurring with them, but the British and Italians strongly opposed extradition.

Eventually the much-postponed trial was held, from 3 to 6 December 1903, and not until there had been all manner of thoroughly undemocratic and in some instances downright farcical negotiations and plots behind the scenes as to how the case was to be settled. One suggested compromise was that the accused deserved to be executed, but that in view of the forthcoming birthday celebrations of the Empress such a sentence should be reduced to imprisonment, with the understanding that after four months in prison they would be freed.

Even during the trial the behaviour of the Chinese Magistrate, the British Assessor and others in the judiciary involved in the case was somewhat bizarre, with the Chinese Magistrate prematurely circulating his own verdict and the British Assessor putting this on one side and giving out *his* opinion. The British Assessor's view was that sentences of three years for Chang and two years for Tsou were sufficient.

In the end, after much further wrangling, the Chinese had to accept the Assessor's sentences and, as he had laid down that the sentences were to date from the beginning of the trial, they were in effect still further reduced.

For those in the underground the result of the trial was a barely disguised triumph: in defeat they had gained in prestige and influence with the Western Powers almost as much as they had lost. From then on there was a speeding-up of the Reformist Underground. In spite of arrests and even executions inside China, Sun Yat-sen managed to organise his espionage corps of students and others to infiltrate the Chinese Army and to report back on every move from within.

In 1904 revolutionaries led by Huang Hsing felt themselves strong enough to launch a peasant revolt in Hunan province and the Chinese merchant and middle-class in that same year planned a successful boycott of American goods as a protest against the "brutal racial discrimination against Chinese" in San Francisco and Los Angeles. That this was not just a pretext for anti-foreign feeling but was based on factual evidence may be understood from an impartial observer, the American professor, Harley F. Mc-Nair, who enumerated massacres, beatings, arrests and deportations as well as legislation against "Mongolians", citing the suicide in 1903 of a Chinese military attaché in San Francisco who had been subjected to gross ill treatment by the American police.[5]

16

The Phantom Secret Service 1904-1916

My faith in human dignity consists in the belief that man is the greatest scamp on earth. Human dignity must be associated with the idea of a scamp and not with that of an obedient, disciplined and regimented soldier. The scamp is probably the most glorious type of human being.

Lin Yutang

LIN YUTANG, as he has himself admitted, is "spiritually a child of the East and the West", and therefore his views have the virtue of being sufficiently objective to be covered by an appreciation of the Chinese and the Westerner. But, being also essentially Chinese, such a sweeping statement as this must be taken rather more seriously than if it came from a Western mind, in which case it would probably be written off as an epigram.

There is a clue in this philosophising by Lin Yutang to something of the seemingly esoteric, but in many ways merely practical and indeed almost casual characteristics which go to make up the basis of modern China's intelligence system. Yet here again the paradox of so much that is Chinese rears its head snakelike with a hiss as much as to say, "A scamp, yes, but do not be misled by apparent artlessness: underneath this casual attitude is a deadly sting."

Lin Yutang went on to say that "this scamp that the Creator has produced is undoubtedly a brilliant chap. He is still a very unruly and awkward adolescent, thinking himself greater and wiser than he really is, still full of mischief and naughtiness and love of a free-for-all."[1]

182

While the Manchus had become slaves to their own dead ritual and unscamplike philosophy of life, the Chinese scholars had never, except for those corrupted by the Court, allowed themselves to become professional academicians, as had (and as indeed have still today) so many Western scholars. They always allowed for that spark of madness and nonconformity, that element of the scamp which is in so many Chinese students.

Chinese intellectuals have always tended to escape from the Establishment, to pursue an independent line and to regard even a "scamp-like" deviation from tradition as being rewarding for its own sake. One cannot compare this with Western deviation from the Establishment, or the contempt of Western students with the existing order of things, for the truth is that the Western intellectual or student lacks the subtlety of Chinese humour and sensitivity. Where the Westerner is not a likeable scamp, but a humourless, disgruntled mumbler of hackneyed revolutionary phrases, the Chinese counterpart of his is conscious of his own effortless superiority, therefore able to behave like a scamp and to proceed on a perhaps more tortuous, but undoubtedly more dedicated and surer path. The former can shout slogans but does not know where to go from there: at heart he is still a conformist; the Chinese appears to shout slogans rather more loudly, but under the mask of being a scamp is possessed of greater dedication, integrity and knowledge of where he is going.

This may seem a roundabout way of explaining how every defeat China has suffered has led to an improvement in her Secret Service, but unquestionably the "brilliant scamp" to whom Lin Yutang refers is the clue to how after each defeat of a regime there has emerged, *while in exile, while harried, hunted and without any official status,* a Secret Service better than any that went before, as efficient in its unofficial status as many Secret Services have been when backed by their own Governments. No other race in the world has produced such an effective Secret Service as has China on a number of occasions from an organisation built up in exile. The nearest approach to it in the

Western World was that of the French Resistance movement in World War II and even then that was achieved with outside aid.

Throughout the first decade of the twentieth century the Secret Service of the China that was to come—Republican China—developed through several channels, most of them in the end to be welded into a single force. William Martin, the American Consul-General in Hankow said on March 7 1906 of Hunan province, then a hotbed of revolutionary espionage: "Everything may be as peaceful as a summer landscape and in half an hour, like a moving tornado, the trouble comes upon you, the numbers growing every moment."

The Reformists and revolutionaries who had created their own intelligence services had, perhaps more than any other revolutionaries of their period, imbibed deeply from the experience of travelling overseas and from the advantages of Western education, as well as learning from the Japanese, previously regarded as an inferior oriental satellite of China. But the Chinese Imperial Civil Service, even though the old examination system had at last been abolished and a Western rather than a Chinese classical education became essential to joining its ranks, was in a state of confusion. The mandarinate, mainly totally lacking in any contact with the West, was committed to a system it barely understood.

Then, in October 1911, the garrison troops mutinied and the Reformists who had long ago infiltrated the Imperial Army proclaimed a Republic. Soon units in other provinces joined them and the Regent for the last Manchu Emperor, who was then still a child, signed an edict of abdication. It is important to note that the mutiny, when it came, was planned, organised and headed by secret agents of the Tung Meng Hui, that society which had as long ago as 1905 achieved the amalgamation of the "Revive China" Society with other revolutionary groups in secret meetings sponsored by Sun Yat-sen in Tokyo.

This secret society selected Hankow as its first target because it was the industrial and commercial centre of Central China and nearby was China's largest arms store in Hanyang. The Tung Meng Hui organised revolutionary workers to storm and capture this arsenal.

The Imperial Navy had been ordered to sail up the Yangtse River to check the rising, but, while anchored off Hankow, the crews, supported by some officers, refused to fire on the revolutionaries. With Tzu-hsi and the Emperor Kuang-hsu dead and the child Pu Yi on the throne, the perplexed Imperial Government had no answer to the well organised revolt.

The Manchu rule was over and Imperial China was dead for ever. In its place was the nucleus of a promisingly progressive and intelligent Republican Government. But a curious situation had developed, a pattern totally different from that of any other revolution of the twentieth century. Whereas in Russia it was the extremists who possessed and eventually totally controlled the Intelligence Service and the moderates, the Mensheviks and the Liberals who were liquidated as a result, in China it was the Liberals and moderates who possessed and controlled what Secret Service there was and the minority hard-liners who seized power. It was one of the few instances in history where the forces possessing the best intelligence organisation failed to win complete control.

However it should not be thought that the designation "hardliners" refers to left-wingers. Rather were they the right-wing, right-about-turn opportunists. And, tragically enough, those who brought these unscrupulous political manipulators to power were the Western nations themselves who, fearful lest the Reformists should eventually seek to clip their wings, sought for allies who would check republicanism from spreading too far.

The man who thus came to power as President of the Republic was that oriental Vicar of Bray, Yuan Shih-kai, the crafty and ambitious general who had first sided with the Reformists in 1898 and then betrayed them into the hands of the Empress Tzu-hsi.

Had Sun Yat-sen imbibed fewer of the virtues of Christianity and been less trusting of his fellow men, he should undoubtedly have made the imprisonment of

Yuan Shih-kai one of the prime tasks of the Republicans. Yet the man who had created a brilliant intelligence service, who had gone to Japan to recruit and organise Chinese students at colleges and military academies in that country into a League of Sworn Brothers—vowing to spread revolutionary propaganda when they returned to China—lamentably failed to eliminate his chief enemy.

Yuan Shih-kai had control of North China and his army was able to cope with any hint of insurrection there. From this position of strength he started negotiations with the Reformists in the south and at the same time established communications with the Western powers. The latter, welcoming a "strong man", lent Yuan £25 millions and persuaded the merchant class among the Reformists that a settlement with Yuan was better than civil war and a peasant revolt.

The aims of the two sides were totally different: the Reformists wanted Western style democracy, whereas Yuan simply represented himself, and all he desired was to set up a dictatorship which would ultimately give him sufficient power to restore the monarchy with himself as Emperor.

Prior to the coming to power of Yuan, Sun Yat-sen had been acknowledged as Provisional President of the Chinese Republic on 1 January 1912. He had achieved his main aim: he had destroyed the Manchu regime. But he paused too long before consolidating his position, turning instead to seeing that the economic life of the country progressed smoothly and using all the knowledge and experience he had acquired in the West to make plans for the re-development of agriculture, transport, shipping and banking.

So that he could concentrate on these matters, which he considered vital for the future of China, he voluntarily handed over the Presidency to Yuan Shih-kai. It was a grave error of judgment. His second mistake was to fail to win over the peasants by introducing at once what had been one of the vital points in the Tung Meng Hui programme—the equalisation of land ownership. This meant that Sun lacked a broad base for support and gave the cunning Yuan every effort to divide and rule.

For the Chinese empire had crumbled into a territorial shambles, with Mongolia and Tibet declaring
themselves independent and other spheres of influence
divided up between supporters of Sun, minions of
Yuan and various warlords. Israel Epstein makes these
apt comments on the sad transition from Manchu rule
to the Republic: "the constitution . . . contained property qualifications for the vote which deprived the
majority of the people of the suffrage. And by the
summer of the same year [1912] the peasants, who
had expected a better life from the revolution, were
being shot down by Yuan's troops. Though under the
Republican flag, these troops enforced the collection
of feudal rents and exorbitant taxes no less savagely
than when they had flown the dragon of the Manchus. . . . It taught them, once and for all, that a
revolution is not won by merely changing the form of
government."[2]

In the end Sun's experience and especially his Secret Service triumphed. Reports came in to him of
the reversion to Manchu-style government being perpetrated under the guise of the revolution. Despite
the errors he had made he had one tremendous advantage: the Tung Meng Hui secret society which he
had helped to launch and which was the basis of
his Secret Service became the Kuomintang. The Kuomintang was for a time almost the chief opposition
party in Parliament and, of course, highly critical of
Yuan Shih-kai. And when Sun Yat-sen realised his
mistake in trusting Yuan he created a small, élite
organisation within the Kuomintang which he named
the Tung Meng Hui Club, but which in effect was a
kind of phantom Secret Service.

There was, in fact, a phantom Secret Service and also
a phantom government, for the Kuomintang Party
set up their own government at Canton in the extreme
south of China under Sun's leadership. This was a
democratic, reformist party, but in many respects conservative rather than revolutionary, depending mainly
on the commercial middle classes and the Chinese
overseas. It was because the Kuomintang Secret Service, though a phantom, minority organisation, had
such strong links overseas that it was so vastly supe-

rior to anything Yuan could produce. The latter believed intelligence was a waste of time and that the threat of force was sufficient to maintain government.

Thus the President had an army and all the trappings and instruments of authority, but no Intelligence Service worth the name, while the Kuomintang had no army of its own, but relied almost entirely on its espionage system. It was an extraordinary situation and a fascinating and bizarre portrait of a struggle for power. Yuan went further in the direction of establishing military dictatorship and, when he failed to get his way, ordered whoever stood in his path to be secretly assassinated. The Kuomintang combatted his power by sending out their secret agents to make pacts with the war lords, the provincial military governors who sought to strengthen their own position by establishing separate spheres of self-government.

Some Western nations continued cynically to back Yuan solely because they believed he would ensure their own commercial interests in China even after he had ordered the assassination of Chiao-jen, the Kuomintang's candidate for Premier, when the Kuomintang had gained a majority of seats in the first Parliament (a fact which Yuan chose to ignore). But the United States had by now ended its brief period of imperialist filibustering and President Wilson stopped American bankers from lending any money to Yuan, saying that "these loans seem to touch the independence of China itself".

In 1913 Sun Yat-sen launched his second revolution, aimed at overthrowing Yuan, but this again failed owing to Sun Yat-sen's lack of support from the peasants and agricultural community. So Sun Yat-sen was forced back into exile, but not before he had been tipped off by the Kuomintang Secret Service that he was the next on Yuan's "elimination list": for a while he and his closest supporters fled to Japan. Here he founded a new and more authoritarian political organisation called the Chunghua Kemintang (Chinese Revolutionary Party), which had one single aim—to defeat Yuan.

While Sun Yat-sen was in exile the secret agents who stayed behind formulated a brilliantly clever scheme for undermining Yuan Shih-kai. They went around tea-houses and other places where people gathered and told jokes against him, their artists drew cartoons showing him as a figure of fun and these were passed around in the streets. It was all very subtly done, but in China a joke against somebody or a cartoon lampooning an individual can have a far more devastating effect than it would in the West. To understand this one must only think of the mid-'thirties when similar jokes and cartoons made Hitler and the Nazis figures of grotesque folly.

It is worth pin-pointing this exquisite sense of lampoonery which the Chinese possess and which they utilise in their intelligence work. In 1936 a sketch in a London revue was banned by the Lord Chamberlain because it made blatant fun of Hitler. The producer happened to mention his dismay at the loss of a good laugh to a Chinese diplomat in London who had seen the revue.

"You have quite a simple remedy," replied the Chinese diplomat smilingly, "and you will find it makes a much more subtle joke and one much more damning to Herr Hitler. You must make the wife in this scene say very innocently to her husband, 'Oh, darling, what was that thing you were told not to do?' He need not reply, nobody need mention Hitler or the Nazis, but he just takes a black comb from his pocket and holds it perpendicularly to his lip just under his nose. To the audience it will just look like a Hitler moustache. They will understand all right what is meant."

Thus, though Yuan outlawed the Kuomintang throughout China after Sun Yat-sen had gone into exile in Japan, his authority was slowly undermined. Tzu-hsi, despite every conceivable obstacle, had retained power for so many years because she was the type one cannot lampoon. But Yuan was a much less impregnable character than Tzu-hsi and the subtle campaign left him dispirited.

Meanwhile in Japan Sun Yat-sen received regular reports from his agents inside China. By this time he had learned the absolute importance of a strong Secret

Service and the need for tempering democratic ideals with a disciplined party dictatorship. This he argued, and his Secret Service bore him out, was the only way in which China could be re-unified and her broken remnants put together in one piece.

When World War I broke out in August 1914, the Japanese were on the side of the Allies, though their only land battle with the Germans was in China where, in Shantung province, they forced the capitulation of the German garrison and naval forces. The fact that Japan had actually sent troops onto Chinese soil was perhaps fatal to Chinese interests: it sowed the seeds of imperialist aggression twenty years later. Japan, who had sympathised with the Chinese Reformists, now saw a chance to make China part of her sphere of influence. Indeed there are some reasons for believing that this was one of the reasons why Japan entered the war against Germany.

The Kuomintang Intelligence Service warned that Japan had designs on China as early as 1915. Their agents in Japan, well established over a number of years, had penetrated the intricacies of Japanese secret societies, leading them to discover that in 1915 the Japanese militarist Black Dragon Society had made these plans for the future: "When the European war is terminated . . . in anticipation of the future expansion of European influence in the continents of Europe and Asia the Imperial Japanese Government should not hesitate to employ force to check the movement before this occurrence. Now is the most opportune time for Japan to solve the Chinese question. Such an opportunity will not occur again for hundreds of years."[3]

Sun Yat-sen was convinced of Japanese perfidy shortly afterwards when there came dramatic confirmation of this warning from his Secret Service, one member of whom had actually infiltrated the Black Dragon Society, perhaps the only Chinese ever to do so. For the Japanese Ambassador in China demanded of Yuan Shih-kai that the Chinese Government should agree to all Japanese acquisitions in Shantung province, to have special railway rights, to possess the former Russian leasehold of Dairen and Port Arthur and the South Manchuria railway captured by her in the Russo-Japanese war of 1904-5 and also to have control over other Manchurian railways, as well as mining rights in Inner Mongolia, and, perhaps the most impertinent of all demands, that China's largest industrial enterprise, the Hanyehping Iron and Steel Works on the Yangtse River should be made a Sino-Japanese combine, with, as a final touch, the proposal that China should neither open new mines without Japanese consent, nor lease any port or island along her coast to any power other than Japan.

There were, however, secret clauses in the formal proposals and these were obtained by Sun's agents and will explain more than anything else how China came to mistrust and break with Japan rather than seek the kind of working relationship between two oriental nations which had seemed perfectly natural only a few years before. The secret clauses provided that China should employ financial, military and political advisers and, even more incredibly, that the police departments of China should be jointly administered by the Chinese and Japanese. They also decreed that China should buy half her munitions from Japan and that Japan should be given certain railway rights in Chinese territory.

Yuan Shih-kai, who had come to power as the strong man of Chinese politics, abjectly capitulated to these quite extraordinary terms which would have been humiliating for an enemy to have extracted from a vanquished nation let alone demanded from an ally. Perhaps Yuan Shih-kai sought by agreeing to this deal to put an end to the co-operation which had existed between Japanese radicals and the forces of Sun Yat-sen.

Armed with details of the secret clauses in Yuan's agreement with the Japanese, Sun Yat-sen was able gradually to swing opinion to his own side. His allies existed in strength in far-off regions and what ultimately restored Sun's influence was the strength of his agents in exile, not least among the Vietnamese, for in 1908 he had set up in Hanoi armed Tung Meng Hui groups who penetrated into China from Vietnam.

Believing that Japan was a close ally, despite the ignominious concessions he had made to that country, Yuan made his bid to re-establish the monarchy. He aimed to have himself proclaimed as Emperor on 1 January 1916, but the Sun Yat-sen Secret Service swiftly plotted a diversion. This was the staging of a rebellion of senior Army officers in Yunnan province which was intended to focus attention on the general revulsion for the restoration of the monarchy. It forced Yuan to postpone his claim to the throne and in June 1916 he died.

But, despite Sun's control of the only effective Secret Service in the whole of China, power did not automatically shift to him. There was still a "phantom government" and a "phantom Secret Service": China did not become unified after Yuan's death, it split up into warring factions, Sun having control only over a part of the country, while the warlords and provincial governors controlled the rest. Some of Yuan's followers established their own localised rule, notably the Anhwei province which was backed by and supported Japan, the Hopei province, supported by the British and Americans, and in Manchuria the Fengtien government which was again pro-Japanese.

This was the beginning of the demoralising system of the two Chinas which was to continue for more than half a century: in the World War I period it was something equivalent to the battle for regional power of the barons against the King in medieval England. It certainly put the clock back for China at the very moment when it needed to be extensively put forward. Thus the pro-Japanese Anhwei clique first gained control of the Peking Government, headed by Tuan Chih-jui.

From the point of view of the Allied powers, representing a majority of the Western nations, the Tuan Chih-jui faction was admirable. They wanted China to join in the war against Germany, to provide coolie labour for the Western front and, in return, promised to restore to China her "lost territories". This latter promise was always extremely vague: to the most optimistic of the Chinese it meant all territories they had lost since the decline of the Manchu empire. But to the more cynical of the Allies all it meant was that China should be given full rights over those areas in her territory over which Germany had previously had control.

Sun Yat-sen had been adamant against China joining in the war; he had argued, with a great deal of commonsense, that just as China could not afford to be embroiled in a civil war, so she could not risk the meagre gains which involvement in a far-off war of no concern to her might bring. In fact Sun was convinced that China's first task was re-unification and that she needed her workers at home, not overseas.

But the Chinese Government decided to send a labour corps to France and Sun's advice was disregarded. Just how far-seeing Sun had been can be seen from the fact that the two hundred thousand peasants who were drafted into the Chinese Labour Corps, under British command, were used in the most menial of tasks, being sent into the major combat areas in France without arms, but with instructions merely to dig trenches and bury corpses. They were treated as fifth-rate citizens.

Worse than this, it was soon apparent that the Allies had little intention of giving China any reward for providing them with troops. The biggest offenders were Britain and France and the most dishonourable of all the politicians trafficking in Chinese lives was David Lloyd George himself, the British Prime Minister, the man who had hypocritically helped to win the 1906 landslide Liberal election on the cry of "Chinese slave labour" allegedly used by the Tory Government. Lloyd George used his Chinese "slaves" in World War I and then secretly promised Japan the very ex-German colonies already pledged to be returned to China.

But perhaps the most disastrous result of all this double-crossing was that it developed a deep mistrust between Britain and the United States. Up to the beginning of World War I Britain had been the dominant power in China, but as that war progressed so she increasingly came under pressure from both the United States and Japan, each of whom sought to gain advantages in China after victory had been won, though to be fair the United States largely recognised Japan's special interests in China only under Japanese threats of barely concealed blackmail about continuing the war.

Sun Yat-sen had foreseen that the world war would bring out the worst in the Western powers and disorientate their conceptions of political morality: he also saw much further than this, describing World War I as the "second industrial revolution" and begging the Western powers to see that disaster and a slump of appalling dimensions lay ahead unless the artificially developed war munitions factories in Europe and America were not converted to producing machinery and machine-tool products for China and other under-developed countries when victory was won. He prophesied rightly that unless this was done, mass unemployment would be the result.

His warnings were neglected: all he forecast came true and Sun, relying on the reports he had from his Secret Service, began to believe that he must look for allies among the very people he had previously despised—not merely the extremist radicals, but the newly developed Communist Party of China.

17

General Ma, or "Two-Gun" Cohen 1905-1923

> I came to realise that every civil war in China proceeds simultaneously on two fronts, military and political, and of these the political is the more important. While two groups of armies were fighting—not very hard—the two sets of leaders were constantly trying to come to terms with some faction on the other side. If they succeeded, they'd join forces and turn on the ones who'd been left out of the deal.
>
> *General Morris Abraham Cohen*

MORRIS (MOISHE) ABRAHAM COHEN was born in Stepney in London's East End on 3 August 1889, the eldest son of immigrant Jews from Poland. At the age of ten he was classified as a juvenile delinquent and, as a result, was one of fifteen boys enrolled in the new Hayes Industrial School in 1901.

Not an auspicious start to life, but Morris was a bright, quick-witted lad and, when he left the training school in 1905, he was immediately sent out to Canada to join family friends who had settled in Saskatchewan. For a year he worked as a farmhand, but the sharp Cockney Jew, with his love of the big cities, was not really happy in this environment and he soon headed back to the bright lights of the larger Canadian towns.

Travelling from one town to another, he undertook a variety of jobs in quick succession—salesman, cheap jewelry dealer, circus spieler, entertainer and professional gambler. A chance encounter brought him unexpectedly in touch with the Chinese Secret Service in Edmonton, the capital of Alberta, hardly the kind of place one would expect to find Chinese, let alone a branch of their intelligence.

Morris Cohen befriended a man who was being robbed and through this single good deed quickly became on good terms with the Chinese community in Edmonton. There was in this community a branch of Tsing Chunghui, another secret society devoted to the cause of Sun Yat-sen's intelligence network, at that time dedicated to the overthrow of the Manchu empire. Shrewdly, the leading member of Tsing Chunghui in Edmonton summed up Morris Cohen as a useful ally and an uncommitted "young man of the world, a Jew whose family had been glad to get away from Poland and who had himself been in trouble in England". Here, they felt, was a brother exile, and a friendly and clever one at that.

There undoubtedly exists between some Chinese and certain types of Jew a mutual understanding and respect that goes much deeper than an ordinary, well-founded relationship between people of different races and creeds. One would be unwise to generalise about this because there are probably more exceptions to this trend than there are examples of it. But when it happens it results in a relationship which can be truly remarkable and lasting. Cohen provides one striking example of this special, if relatively rare, relationship between Chinese and Jew, but it is particularly true of the Chinese Secret Service, certainly over the past eighty years, that there have been a few, but nevertheless highly rewarding, instances of secret Chinese-Jewish co-operation in various parts of the world.

It would appear that Cohen was tested out for about two years before he was eventually made an honourary member of Tsing Chunghui, which was in itself a remarkable achievement for a foreigner. But though a swashbuckler and possessing that sense of drama and flamboyance which is characteristic of some Jews, Morris Cohen was essentially discreet. Throughout his life he was a legendary character and as many myths grew around his name as those which surrounded Lawrence of Arabia. But, unlike Lawrence, Cohen did not himself subscribe to the legends; indeed, in many instances he openly denied the best of them, especially those of which he might justly have been proud. It was this quality about Cohen which endeared him to the Chinese he served.

For example, by his own admission, despite more than twenty years' residence in China, Cohen was not fluent in speaking Chinese and often needed to use an interpreter. When the story was put out that Cohen had saved Sun Yat-sen's life in London when he was captured by Chinese seamen, Cohen was the first to deny it.

In 1910 Cohen was still in Edmonton where he had by this time made a considerable amount of money in real estate. He continued to advise his Chinese friends on a wide range of subjects as well as to attend meetings of the Tsing Chunghui and to help raise funds for the revolutionary cause. When he made a profitable deal he would give a percentage of the money received to the cause, sometimes fifty, sometimes a hundred dollars.

Cohen urged the Tsing Chunghui that an attempt should be made to give a smattering of military training to some of the young Chinese in exile. "One day a few thousands of amateur soldiers in Canada, the United States and Manila may make all the difference to the success of your revolution," he urged.

About this time Sun Yat-sen, who had been travelling around the world on one of his periodic tours of Chinese communities, met Cohen for the first time, probably in 1910. Sun was extremely impressed by Cohen's ideas and asked him to come as his bodyguard on a two-month tour of Canada and the United States.

This marked the beginning of a long association between Sun Yat-sen and the young man from London's East End and there is abundant evidence that Cohen was trusted as much as any Chinese secret agent and that he undertook not only many important intelligence tasks, but that he was both a military adviser and an arms supplier for the Chinese.

At the end of Sun's tour of Canada and the United States the revolutionary leader asked Cohen to purchase arms and ammunition for shipment to China and gave him permission to raise his cadet corps among the Chinese community.

Sun left for Japan and Cohen returned to the Chinese community in Edmonton and his real estate business. The fact that he was highly regarded by Sun greatly enhanced his prestige among the Edmonton Chinese. Nobody seems to be quite sure when he acquired the nickname of "Two-Gun" Cohen, but it was probably about this period when he began training his boy soldiers and eventually established a cadet corps of four hundred and fifty Chinese boys: "every man Jack of them all future colonels," he once said, more in jest than in boasting. The origin of the nickname is said to be that Cohen often carried an automatic in his shoulder holster and a Smith and Weston on his hip. Even in these early days as corps trainer he was known to the Chinese as "General Ma", or *Mah Kun*.

In 1911, while the Manchus were in the process of being finally overthrown, Cohen made various trips to Europe, ostensibly in connection with a new business project which involved the development by Belgians of land in British Columbia, but this would appear to have been a useful cover for some of his arms purchases for Sun Yat-sen, all of which he masterminded most skilfully in an entirely secret manner.

The following year saw Cohen back in Canada, not only actively campaigning for the Kuomintang, but also taking part in Canadian politics and concerning himself especially with the naturalisation and registration of potential Chinese voters.

Sun Yat-sen invited Cohen to join him in China in 1913, but Sun's subsequent exile to Japan when Yuan Shih-kai seized power and the advent of World War I interfered with this plan, which might well have altered the course of Chinese politics in some respects. For Cohen's counsels at this stage might have influenced Sun had the former actually been with him. Though Sun, as we have seen, was against China being dragged into the world war, Morris Cohen believed that there were practical advantages to be gained from doing this. He had warned Sun of the growing threat of Japan to China and he foresaw the Japanese winning concessions from the Allies inside Chinese territory if China remained aloof.

When war broke out Cohen offered his young amateur soldiers, now totalling seven hundred and fifty Chinese, as a complete unit to serve alongside the Canadian Army overseas, but this suggestion was politely rejected by the Canadian Government. Two years later the irrepressible Morris Cohen, impatient at Sun's continued exile (by this time he had been exiled to Hongkong following a brief take-over of the government in Canton), joined the Irish Guards and eventually went to France in 1917. Here he received a message from Sun, asking him to join his staff when the war was over.

In 1918 Cohen was seconded to the Chinese Labours Corps for a short time, after which he returned to his own unit, was wounded and invalided back to England. At the end of the war it was soon clear that he had lost none of his zest for the Chinese cause. When he returned to Canada in 1919 one of his first acts was to organise a strike among Chinese workers at a packing plant because unemployed veterans were demanding their jobs.

Sun now earnestly begged for Cohen's aid. He realised how far-sighted Cohen had been in stressing the perfidy of Japan, for it was now only too clear that this relatively small country with its large population had her sights firmly fixed on expansion not merely to Manchuria, but to the Chinese mainland generally. It was Japan rather than the Western powers who was now China's main enemy.

Fortunately the United States had also seen these dangers, though to a lesser degree, and she had encouraged China to stand firm and reject some of Japan's demands. But both Britain and France had pressured China into reluctant acquiescence in the transfer to Japan of the German-leased territory of Kiaochow in Shantung which had been captured by the Japanese shortly after war began. Anglo-French backing for Japan against China at this period was the sequel to secret deals made during the war for Japanese naval aid against German submarines.

The effect of the backing given by two of the leading victorious European powers to Japan against China was to create widespread resentment among the younger Chinese against the Western powers generally, driving some to sympathise strongly with vanquished Germany and others to turn with interest to the Russian experiment. After the 1917 Revolution in Russia news filtered through to China about the Communist Government and a little later a small but remarkably efficient Chinese Communist Party came into being.

Eventually this party formed an alliance with Sun Yat-sen, but that is a long and complicated story. That some of the leading radicals swung over so swiftly to the extreme left was not surprising: the direct cause was the betrayal of the democratic revolution of Sun Yat-sen and his allies by the military dictatorship of Yuan Shih-kai. These young Radical students saw peasants shot down in front of their eyes by Yuan's troops, who exacted the same feudal rents with all the brutality of the Manchu regime. For them communism was not merely a new creed: it was the only safeguard against dictatorship by an individual.

Three names among the original leaders of the Chinese Communist Party should be noted. The ablest at that time and the one whose prestige was highest was Chu Teh, an officer in the Chinese Army who had led the revolt against the Manchus in Yunnan province. It was he who became Commander-in-chief of the People's Liberation Army which defeated the armies of Chiang Kai-shek after World War II. The second in importance at the time was Tung Pi-wu, a revolutionary from Hankow, who quickly came to the fore in the Communist Party. The third, the least important at the time, but ultimately to be the greatest of them all, was a young student from Hunan province, the 24-year-old Mao Tse-tung.

Sun had grave problems to cope with when eventually he returned to China and took power once again; the warlords were still troublesome and in control in some provinces; the Chinese economy had not advanced anything like that of the neighbouring Japanese and there was a growing awareness among the Chinese working class that in one form or another their exploitation continued as much under the new Republic as it had under the old monarchy.

On the cultural side there was also a revolt, just as there had been in Russia. Lu Hsun became known as the Chinese Gorky and a writer of fiction named Mao Tun not only developed what was called "revolutionary-democratic literature", but eventually became Minister of Cultural Affairs years afterwards in the People's Republic of China. A great awakening in cultural circles and study circles, especially among students, occurred all over the country. The youthful Mao Tse-tung sponsored one such movement with a People's Study Group in Hunan province, while in Tientsing there was founded the "Awakening Society" by a fastidious but dedicated young man named Chou En-lai.

Not surprisingly, at the Versailles Peace Conference China made demands for the abolition of all foreign spheres of influence, an end to extra-territorial rights, the return of all leased concessions, the withdrawal of all foreign troops from China, and, finally, the cancellation of the Japanese "Twenty-one Demands" of 1915.[1] China was treated like a pariah at Versailles; all her claims were rejected and Japan was so blatantly favoured that all Germany's former rights in railways, stations, property and mines were handed over to Japan.

From that day ultimate revolution in China was only a matter of time. Fortunately for China it came later and more surely rather than suddenly and haphazardly.

Sun Yat-sen was always apprehensive about the Russian experiment and doubted whether it could be applied to China as conditions in the two countries were so different. But he was still sympathetic to the Russian revolution and extended a hand of friendship to the Chinese Communists. Indeed the alliance between Sun Yat-sen and the Communists, though loose, was warm if, on Sun's side, cautious in approach. Both Mao Tse-tung and Chou En-lai held junior posts in Sun's Nationalist Government. He summed up his own attitude in this manner: "The Republic is my child . . . I am trying to keep it afloat . . . I call for help to England and America. They stand on the bank and jeer at me. There comes a Russian straw. Drowning, I clutch at it. England and America on the bank shout at me on no account to clutch that Russian straw. But they do not help me. . . . I know it is a straw, but better than nothing."[2]

In 1922, at Sun's request, Morris Cohen arranged a contract with the Northern Construction Company of Canada to construct fifteen hundred miles of railway between Canton and Chungking and he went to Shanghai to complete the negotiations. His experience in real estate stood him in good stead for such a deal, for he had to sort out an enormous business muddle. Sun Yat-sen had in 1913 been head of the Central Railway Corporation, which at that time had signed a contract with the Pauling Construction Company of London for developing the railway, but that contract had never been completed because Sun had been driven out and civil war had ensued.

Having brought this deal to a satisfactory conclusion Cohen decided to throw in his lot with Sun and he was appointed third A.D.C. with the rank of colonel. He was, however, much more powerful than this. Sun had learned the importance in intelligence work of always giving a man a cover for any job he did. He had studied the espionage systems of other countries and had been impressed that the British system of concealing the identity of her chief intelligence officers was one which China should adopt.

It is worth noting that ever since, whether under Sun Yat-sen or Mao Tse-tung, China has maintained this system and, as the years have passed, has managed to make it work rather more effectively than have the British. Morris Cohen was not only an extremely faithful servant to the Chinese cause over many years, but he avoided the kind of publicity which would link him directly with intelligence work. After the advent to power of Mao Tse-tung it was inevitable that he should be publicised as an enemy of New China by the Communists. But he himself rarely gave a hint of his work and possibly the main reason why we know so much about him is through his friendship with one

Charles Drage, who had served in the Far East with the Royal Navy, and apparently met Cohen while engaged in espionage against the Japanese. The result of this friendship appeared in Drage's book *Two-Gun Cohen*.

Certain observations of Cohen show how closely he was linked to Chinese intelligence. He told Drage on one occasion: "The people I watched the closest were emissaries from the different factions in the north, who were always turning up on one pretext or another. This sounds odd, since we were at open war with them; and it seemed odd to me at first, till I came to realise that every civil war in China proceeds simultaneously on two fronts, military and political, and of these the political is the more important. While two groups of armies were fighting—not very hard—the two sets of leaders were constantly trying to come to terms with some faction on the other side. If they succeeded, they'd join forces and turn on the ones who'd been left out of the deal."[3]

Then again, concerning a spy incident, Cohen told of "the strangest of the humble folk I ushered into Dr Sun's office was a spy who'd been caught by our counter-espionage and sentenced to death. By all the rules his life was over except for a walk to the execution ground. Then he would kneel down and the executioner would put the muzzle of a Mauser pistol against the base of his skull and blow out his brains.

"We usually managed to keep that sort of event from the Doctor's knowledge, but someone slipped up this time and he got to hear of it and insisted on talking to the man himself. He saw him quite alone. Everybody was turned out of the room, including me, so no one knows what passed between them. Presently his bell rang and he sent Mah Sang for the head of the Intelligence and told him, 'This man will work for me in future!' From then on till his death that chap worked loyally for the Doctor. He gradually became more and more trusted and learned more and more of our secrets; but when the other lot caught him, he died without telling them a thing."[4]

This fascinating revelation, though it leaves quite a few unanswered questions, is especially interesting on two counts. It makes the first mention in modern times in writing of the existence of a head of Chinese Intelligence (prior to this such people were always given some other title), and, secondly, it reveals how Chinese psychology and perhaps even their unique gifts for extra-sensory perception, rather than what the Western world crudely calls "brain-washing", are the essential talents for winning improbable allies.

As is apparent from this last quotation from Cohen, Sun Yat-sen obviously needed to have tough, ruthless men around him who would carry out disagreeable but necessary punitive acts from which he personally shied away. Cohen had not witnessed the May 4 Movement in Peking, when China refused to sign the Treaty of Versailles and there was a wave of fury against the Japanese. But he saw its aftermath and was one of the first to convince Sun Yat-sen of how the revolution was getting out of hand and the need for at least a form of party dictatorship to re-unify China.

Suddenly the younger radicals had become intoxicated with the example of the Russians which, seen from afar, looked to them like a gallant peasantry overthrowing its own harsh imperialist armies out of Russia in the wars of intervention. They did not realise that the Russian peasants were then suffering as much if not more than they had ever done, that individual liberty was restricted even more than in the Czar's day and that mass executions in the name of Marx and Lenin were carried out daily.

Nevertheless Sun Yat-sen's position remained perilous because he faced danger on two fronts—from the wilder revolutionaries and from those warlords who still ruled as independent monarchs. It was the threat of the latter which brought the Kuomintang closer to the Chinese Communists and, for a time, collaborators with them in certain fields.

Unofficially Morris Cohen was intelligence adviser to Sun Yat-sen, but his military knowledge and experience was used extensively. In 1923 he spent a great deal of time travelling around with the Army, and also making a study of the methods used by some of the warlords' private armies. Chiang Kai-shek was at this time appointed Chief of Staff of the Chinese

Army and Cohen became his principal adviser and *aide*.

From that time onwards Chiang Kai-shek came to have a high regard for the flamboyant Jew and they remained allies for almost half a century.

18

Abbot Chao Kung: Man of Many Aliases 1916-1925

> What is in the end to be shrunk
> Must first be stretched.
> Whatever is to be weakened
> Must begin by being made strong.
> What is to be overthrown
> Must begin by being set up.
> From the *Taotehching of Laotse*

THE road to revolution in the years from 1919-22 lay across some surprising routes for China, for, while the agrarian revolution which Mao Tse-tung brought to fruition in the late 'fifties and early 'sixties was essentially Chinese in character, the revolutions of both the right-wing and moderate radicals and the left-wingers and Communists in those early years not only owed much to foreign influence, but increasingly relied on foreign aid. This was even truer of the Sun Yat-sen Secret Service and by degrees it became equally true of the embryonic intelligence service of the Chinese Communist Party.

Sun Yat-sen never lost his sometimes pathetic belief in the wisdom of American and British missionaries, some of whom undoubtedly supplied him with information; the loyalty of those with whom he had established a long friendship was never in question, but their wisdom often was. Morris Cohen used to remind him of an ancient Chinese saying: "Beware of the perfect saintly man; he is the stuff traitors are made of, for he is psychologically abnormal."

Cohen was convinced that the missionaries, while possibly supplying Sun with a few crumbs of intelligence, could not possibly be expected to behave as efficient spies, as it wasn't in their nature, but that they could through sheer ignorance support the most dangerous of the left-wing radicals because they spent so much time educating them. And Morris Cohen pointed to Mao Tse-tung as an example of this.

Sun Yat-sen realised as early as 1918 that the revolutionary left was growing in power and that an accommodation would probably have to be made with them. He had by now become convinced that Japan was China's number one enemy and that he could expect little help from any of the Western powers, except possibly the United States, in standing up to the Japanese. For these reasons he sought to find new allies in Germany and Soviet Russia.

There was no particular problem for Sun in seeking an ally in Germany. He had never approved of China taking even the smallest part in World War I so there was no fundamental switch of allegiance. He saw Germany as the vanquished nation, contemptuously treated by the other Western powers and, because of this and the poverty into which she had been plunged, already leaning towards revolution and an alliance with Russia. Sun, cautiously at first, never altogether convinced, but prodded by events into a flirtation with Western revolutionaries, began to see Germany and Russia as China's best allies against Japan.

At the same time he kept his lines wide open to the United States and insisted that priority in his Secret Service should be given to building up a network in that country: this was, he stressed, not so much aimed at spying on the U.S.A., but at organising the Chinese communities in that country to establish allies in America and to obtain the latest American intelligence on Japan. For the U.S.A. had proved a better ally than any of the Europeans; she had used her new strength to force Japan to back down on some of her demands on China and had managed effectively to abrogate the Anglo-Japanese alliance.

But there was still the Nine-Power Pact, supported by the U.S.A., Britain, Japan, France, Italy, Belgium, Holland and Portugal which, while appearing to give China equal status, most hypocritically maintained the "Open Door" policy which, in effect, meant grabbing all the Western powers could get in China. Probably each power saw different reasons for intervening in Chinese affairs; the U.S.A. for commercial reasons and to use as a bargaining counter against the growth of the Japanese navy; Britain and France for using China as a possible base for operations against Soviet Russia; the others simply for requiring concessional advantages of a commercial nature.

Once again Shanghai was a major centre of the espionage industry and it was from here that spies of all nations plotted to which particular warlord or favoured regional leader the surplus arms of World War I should be diverted. Mostly it was the spies and agents of the Western powers who made the overtures and decided the destination of the arms. It was left to the intermediaries of the Sun Yat-sen Secret Service to negotiate as best they could for their own arms, as, generally speaking, the European nations regarded Sun as weak and unable to control the drift of the Chinese people to communism and an alliance with Russia. Few had the good sense to see that Sun was the only answer to this drift and that, but for ill-health, he would probably succeed if the West backed him fully.

In the banking world it was the Americans and not the British who now dominated China, but in arms sales there was intensive competition between the U.S.A., Britain and Japan, with France intervening to a lesser extent. Sun Yat-sen still had to compete with the warlords and his Secret Service's task inside China was to detect which Western power was selling arms to which warlord. Japan backed Chung Tso-lin, a military dictator of the Fengtien organisation, while the British supported Wu Pei-fu of the Chihli faction.

Of course there were some solid reasons for the European fears of a communised China: in 1919–20 strikes had broken out all over the country and by 1922 the Chinese Communist Party had been formed, while shortly afterwards three hundred thousand workers went on strike, a movement that extended to the British colony of Hongkong and posed a considerable threat to that community's political stability. But, blinded in their obsession with the menace of communism, both Britain and France neglected the democratic alternative which Sun honestly if somewhat ineffectually offered, and just as they looked to fascist elements in Europe for support against Soviet Russia, so they made the even graver error of turning to a new chauvinistic, military caste-dominated Japan as an ally against China.[1]

There was a good deal of uncertainty in Chinese intelligence circles at this time as to which faction in Germany was the one with which they should establish links; that is to say, even Chinese intelligence officers could not always distinguish between right-wing and left-wing revolutionaries in the foreign country. All they knew was that the moderate forces in Germany were weak, corrupt and in the long-term a bad bet. To this extent the Chinese were right in their assessment. As to their uncertainty about the other factions, this was understandable because there were attempts both on the extreme right and the extreme left (including the German Communist Party) to seek an alliance with China. Extremists on the right were then anxious to win back concessions wrested from Germany by the Japanese and were quite prepared to lend senior ex-German-Army officers to China to train the Republican troops of Sun Yat-sen. On the other hand, immediately after World War I Communists everywhere were pinning their hopes for the decisive stroke in a global revolutionary victory in the establishment by a swift workers' coup of a Soviet Government in demoralised Germany. Thus both Germans of the two extreme shades of political thought and Russian Communists were all anxious to woo China.

Just how isolated China was at this time can be gauged from the fact that, because of the Western embargo on arms supplies to the Chinese Government of Sun Yat-sen, Sun had to beg Morris Cohen to form a team of spies to organise underground stocks of arms to be smuggled into the country. Cohen, who had quickly shown that he had a remarkable intuitive gift for accurately assessing long-term prospects, pinned his hopes on American and Canadian sources. He relied a great deal on the network of agents established along the west coast of the United States. Between 1922 and 1924 he made a number of visits to the U.S.A. to contact agents, to build up other networks in a modest way to lay the foundations of what later became known as the "China Lobby", even if this term became an abusive and contemptuous symbol in the 1950s. Cohen not only recruited personnel, but managed to buy materials for airplanes to be built in China. His missions over these two years were successful, but in his absence he found that the Russians had moved in as defence advisers and that the influence of communism inside the Sun Yat-sen Government was steadily increasing.

Lenin had founded the Third Communist International, or the Comintern, in 1919 with the object of fomenting a series of communist coups throughout the world, but concentrating on Germany and Central Europe, though even Britain was singled out. One by one these projected coups had failed; in Germany, upon which so many hopes had been pinned, no less than in Hungary where Bela Kun had staged one of the earliest communist insurrections. Yet curiously it was in the failure of the Bela Kun revolt in Hungary that the Chinese Secret Service won temporarily one of the strangest of all her allies.

This was an enigmatic, baffling character named Ignaz Trebitsch, a Hungarian Jew who was better known under his adopted name of Ignatius Timothy Trebitsch Lincoln, and whose story is so bizarre that it would sound more plausible as fiction than as fact.

Trebitsch had left Hungary under a cloud as a young man, gone to South America where he had acted as an adviser on oil prospects, then on to Canada where he had been ordained as a deacon of the Church of England by the Archbishop of Montreal. In 1903 he went to Britain and was appointed curate at Appledore in Kent. A few years later he insinuated himself into politics, striking up an acquaintanceship with David Lloyd George and joining the Liberal Party.

Then Seebohm Rowntree, the cocoa manufacturer and philanthropist of the Society of Friends, engaged Lincoln, under which name he had become a naturalised British subject, as a research specialist to investigate the conditions of the working classes in various European countries. Nothing could have suited Lincoln's purposes better than such a job for, under the guise of a student of philanthropic causes, he was able to travel freely and establish contacts for espionage.

In January 1910 this remarkable character, despite his broken English and eccentricities, his black beard and foreign appearance, fought and won Darlington as a Liberal Parliamentary candidate. What is more he fought the election with fanatical fervour on a left-wing brand of Liberalism, mainly on the issue of the people against the House of Lords.

Trebitsch Lincoln had all the audacity of the ambitious Jew: he may have adopted a left-wing line to become elected as M.P. for Darlington, but he also sought allies in right-wing circles, one of them being Sir Basil Zaharoff, the notorious arms salesman, for whom he appears to have acted as a kind of spy. Both Lloyd George and Zaharoff were at this time closely interested in the Galician oilfields and Lincoln was their principal informant on the subject.

Lincoln borrowed money from Seebohm Rowntree to invest in the oil industry in Galicia and Rumania, but he lost so much in speculation in this part of the world that he was unable to raise the funds to stand for Parliament at the next election. When his creditors were called together early in 1911 he had gross liabilities of £17,118 due, he claimed, to the investment of some £20,000 in the proposed amalgamation of certain pipelines in Galicia. Needless to say the money he had lost was not his own, but money he had borrowed from others.

By this time Lincoln's activities were being closely watched by other powers. The French suspected he was spying on behalf of the Germans and that he was a double-agent acting for Britain as well. Even on the eve of World War I French intelligence reports insisted that Trebitsch Lincoln was "feeding anti-French stories of speculation on the Paris Bourse to the English Chancellor [Lloyd George]".[2]

When war broke out Lincoln tried to obtain an official job in British Intelligence and he was interviewed by Captain Reginald Hall, the formidable head of Britain's Naval Intelligence Division. According to Hall's biographer, Admiral Sir William James, "he [Lincoln] produced some fantastic schemes for tempting the German fleet into the North Sea, which, he claimed, could be implemented if he crossed to Holland, and offered his services to the German Consul at Rotterdam. Hall soon summed him up and told him he had no use for his services."[3]

It is just possible that British Intelligence handled Lincoln badly, that they treated him with barely disguised contempt and forced him to turn his attentions to Germany. That is taking a somewhat charitable view in the light of the evidence that the French were convinced he was already a German spy. However he did spy for Germany and British Naval Intelligence discovered this. Curiously, however, he was not arrested and had ample opportunity to flee to New York when he learned that the British counter-espionage services were on his trail. Yet, despite having written a book in New York which made it clear that he was on the German side, when eventually he was arrested and extradited to Britain he was charged not with espionage, but with forging cheques. His sentence was three years' penal servitude after which he was deported to Hungary.

All of which was very strange. There was ample evidence that Lincoln was a spy for the Germans, so why was he not charged with this? Influential friends in high places? Fear of his ability to blackmail important British statesmen? And why, as he was a naturalised British subject, was he deported to Hungary? It can only be deduced that Trebitsch Lincoln was still in a position to make a deal with the British and the probable deal was an agreement to be deported in return for a promise of no charges for spying. How much the threat to blackmail leading British statesmen played a part in this is conjectural, but Lincoln's book published in the United States suggested that he had several aces up his sleeve if challenged by the British.[4]

So Lincoln went back to Hungary, but found the Bela Kun communist rule uncongenial, and promptly moved to Germany where he offered his services to Count von Bernstorff, formerly the German Ambassador to Washington. Here Lincoln was involved in the notorious Kapp conspiracy which aimed at staging a counter-revolution in Germany, planning to throw overboard the conditions of the Versailles Treaty, and to use right-wing forces on the one hand to make a deal with Soviet Russia on the other. But the attempted *putsch* ended in ignominy the following year.

It was after the failure of this *putsch* that in 1921 Trebitsch Lincoln established links with the Chinese Government. It is not clear who brought them together in the first place, but the probability is that Lincoln made the first approach through diplomatic channels in Berlin. Whatever decision was arrived at on the Chinese side it was not without certain reservations, for one report which went to Sun Yat-sen concerning Lincoln was that he was *"wu-ching"*, that is to say, cold-hearted and disloyal. The Chinese Secret Service made a careful check on Lincoln's notorious career and they did not at first feel he was a man they could risk trusting. Who could blame them? As Douglas Reed wrote of him: "He was born a Jew, in Hungary. . . . In his early manhood . . . he was a priest of one of the Christian confessions, in Canada. . . . A little later he was making a deep impression on those loving souls, the Quakers, in England. A little later still he was a good British patriot, a Member of the House of Commons. A few more years passed, the World War broke out and Trebitsch Lincoln proved to have been a spy—for Germany, a country to which he owed no allegiance. . . .

"Oblivion for a few years and then came the Kapp Putsch in Germany, the first of the Nationalist conspiracies to overthrow the democratic liberal regime that was so kind to the Jews, and reinstate the big business men, big landlords, monarchists and militarists in Germany. Who was a leading figure in this short-lived seizure of power? Trebitsch Lincoln, now a German die-hard. Among the other sympathisers was a relatively unknown man, one Adolf Hitler. Trebitsch Lincoln on the side of the anti-Semites? Of course, he was a Christian.

". . . Again a few years of oblivion and you heard of him in China, where men were fighting. By now he was either a good Russian Bolshevist or a good Chinese Nationalist. Then, again, news that Trebitsch Lincoln was a Buddhist monk, and the tardy post brought pictures of him in his little silken cap, his silken tunic, his funny pants. . . . A man without truth, without honour, without loyalty."[5]

In one sense there was no comparison whatsoever between the consistently loyal Morris Cohen and the basically disloyal and treacherous Trebitsch Lincoln. In normal circumstances one would have said that Lincoln was not one of those few types of Jew with whom the Chinese could have had any affinity. He was much more the type of which the Russians have made use and then later found themselves betrayed by, or whom the Western powers have engaged as agents only to find them double-crossing them to the Soviet Union. But to the subtlest type of Chinese mind Trebitsch Lincoln was the chameleon secret agent owing allegiance to nobody, but who could, by their ancient precepts, be won over as an ally.

If the Chinese engaged Lincoln and won him over to their side, they were acting on the rules laid down by Sun-Tzu in 400 B.C. and on the impulse of Sun Yat-sen in the incident of the condemned spy mentioned by Morris Cohen. Always, in analysing Chinese espionage, one must allow for their exceptional talents for winning over to their cause the man who seems totally committed against them. Nor does this imply a lack of sophistication on the part of Chinese intelligence men: on the contrary, it is symptomatic of their almost esoteric, near-telepathic gifts of vision.

No doubt Lincoln, through his links with Sir Basil

Zaharoff, then a major figure in the Vickers-Armstrong arms firm, with directorships in arms firms all over Europe, and a man devoted to selling to his enemies as much as to his friends as long as there was a profit to be made, had something to offer the Chinese. There was also the exploitable qualification that he had been imprisoned by the British (a much more important factor than that he had betrayed the British). Possibly there were promises of arms deals through undercover means and of German aid through certain channels, and again, almost certainly, links with leading Bolsheviks. But beyond this was that fact that Lincoln was psychologically an outsider, an exile, a man without a country he could really call his own and one who had learned to hate the Westerners as much as the Chinese did. It was this last factor which was the vital one.

In the Western World Trebitsch Lincoln had rarely been able to move about without his career being carefully documented. From 1900 until about 1921 there are no gaps in his history; his achievements, his treacheries and his wheeler-dealing are clear for all to see. But from 1920 onwards he truly went underground; he was protected in a remarkable way by the Chinese Secret Service and there is no evidence that he ever worked for them directly. There is, however, ample proof that he lived and worked under the name of Chao Kung. For his multifarious experience had even included a spell training to be an actor in Hungary before he went out to the Americas. A new rôle, a new identity, a new religion—all these things were part of the inspiration-mechanism of Lincoln's mind.

It could not be said that the Chinese acted hastily in receiving Lincoln into their ranks. In 1916, while he was in New York, hiding from the American detectives who were hunting him, he sent a letter to the newspaper, *The American,* stating that "Not all the forces of the United States Secret Service could have prevented me from carrying out my carefully-laid scheme. I am a past master in such work. The United States may find consolation in the fact that its Government is not the first I have outwitted, and from whose vigilance I have easily escaped." He went on to promise "a religious revival in the East among the Mohammedans, with which British rule in India and the whole of Asia will end. You will do well to watch the East, and when you hear of a great revival there, think of Lincoln. A similar revival will be engineered among the Buddhists and the blundering British Government will remember me."[6]

Even at this stage in his career there was a clear hint of his turning towards the East and the interesting point is that in 1916 hardly anyone either on the German or allied sides would have given much credence to the end of Western influence and power in China. One must remember that Lincoln was putting forward these ideas at the very time when he was supposed to be a spy in the cause of Germany.

How Lincoln established his links with the Chinese has baffled even his biographers.[7] There is the story, which they have borrowed from earlier newspaper reports, that Lincoln went to China after the Kapp *putsch* in Germany and joined the staff of the warlord, Wu Pei-fu. Ostensibly he may even have done so, but if he did he was undoubtedly double-crossing Wu Pei-fu, who was the very warlord the British were supporting at that time.

The fact is that Trebitsch Lincoln was employed by the Chinese Secret Service to infiltrate the camp of Wu Pei-fu and was promised total security after he had completed his mission. Apart from his having double-crossed the British, he had also deceived the Germans, for after the Kapp *putsch* he had sold various documents connected with the right-wing plots to the Czechs (who complained that they were forgeries) before he moved to the Far East. At that time there was the wooing of Germany by China and a few German right-wingers, forbidden under the Treaty of Versailles to develop their military strength to any extent, were plotting to offer their services as military advisers to China and to train officers and men out there.

What is clear is that it was the German-Chinese relationship which Lincoln exploited at this time, and whatever he may have done for Wu Pei-fu could only have been as a double-agent. There is, however, the suggestion of his biographers that, while spying for the Germans in China, he went back to the British War Office and offered his services, including a great deal of useful information and that this led to his working for Wu Pei-fu.

The truth is that, after his departure from Germany to the Far East, even Lincoln's biographers are as baffled by what he did, what he thought and how he acted as anyone else. It is possible that Trebitsch Lincoln, like Sidney Reilly, Guy Burgess, "Kim" Philby and a number of double-crossing pro-German rogues in World War II, may have fascinated the British Secret Service into believing against their better judgement that they could not do without him, and if there was a reason for this at that time it could be due to the notorious anti-Bolshevik bias of the British Secret Service. Yet, if Lincoln had at this time linked himself with Wu Pei-fu, the British-backed Chinese warlord, why should he be on record as having declared *at the very same time*: "I had long wanted to find ways by which I could strike a deadly blow at the British Empire. I had realised that it was only from China that India could be attacked with any prospect of success. And I knew the Bolsheviks were thinking along the same lines."[8]

It is clear that he was ostensibly the chief adviser to Wu Pei-fu and that he actually returned to Europe to raise funds for him. Wherever he went there were doubts: was he anti-British, was he pro-German, was he pro-Bolshevik, or was he just anti-Westerner? Nobody could ever be sure. What is certain is that Trebitsch Lincoln helped considerably in destroying the warlords and helping to build up first Sun Yat-sen's and then Chiang Kai-shek's Chinese Republic in the middle 'twenties.

This may seem like a hyperbolic special pleading for the rôle of Trebitsch Lincoln as a super-spy. In fact, it is nothing of the sort: what China required to consolidate her own growing power in espionage at this period was the experience of a man who knew a great deal about several Secret Services of the world. This experience was probably worth a great deal more than actual spying coups. It is possible that Lincoln was recruited by Morris Cohen, another man of Jewish origin. Certainly Cohen would have been consulted about him. At this time Sun Yat-sen was dying of cancer (January 1925) and Cohen had been somewhat neglected. He was in Canada on a mission at the time of Sun Yat-sen's death, but on his return to China was in dire need of money—he claimed this was due to the fact that he had not been well paid during his stint as Sun's A.D.C. because he never bothered to draw a salary, as he had a lavish expenses' allowance and, when in need, drew from his Canadian savings. On Sun's death he volunteered his services to Sun's son, Sun Fo, who was Mayor of Canton, and his services were accepted.

Then, in March 1926, it was reported from Ceylon that "Dr Leo Tandler, who for some time past has been staying at a small Buddhist monastery not far from here, is really Trebitsch Lincoln. Tandler, who stated he was an Austrian, came to Ceylon from Manila, with the approval of the local police, who had previously been in communication on the subject with the British Consul in Manila."[9]

Here again was an astonishing situation: Lincoln was barred from Britain, yet he was allowed into what was then a British colony, Ceylon. Who blundered, or who collaborated, in this extraordinary business? It would seem that once again Lincoln had fooled everybody—except the Chinese. He had obtained permission of the police to take up his residence in a small Buddhist monastery five miles from Colombo, where he lived the most simple life in a cell, his one meal a day being part of the food gathered by the monks during their daily begging expeditions. All who met him in Ceylon were impressed by his apparent sincerity, his swiftly acquired knowledge of Sinhalese and Pali, and his remarkable grasp of the fundamentals of Buddhism. But then so had various Archbishops been impressed by his grasp of the principles of the Church of England, and Canadian Nonconformists of his earlier religious enthusiasms.

A report in the London *Times* stated that Lincoln "left Ceylon on 5 February [1926] by the S.S.

Coblenz, taking a ticket for Genoa. At the hotel where he stayed before his departure he said he was bound for Germany. The police, however, were informed that Austria was his destination, though he told another acquaintance that he had business in England. On one occasion, in conversation with a local reporter, he said he had been a Political Adviser to the Chinese Government, but had given up this lucrative post in order to study Buddhism, which he loved. Shortly before his departure he intimated his intention to return to Ceylon and continue his studies."

So the mystery of Trebitsch Lincoln continues. By this time he had adopted the name and title of Abbot Chao Kung and it was under this name that he tried to re-enter England in March 1926, when his eldest son, a member of the Royal Artillery, was sentenced to death for murder. Despite all his faults, despite his having left his family behind, Lincoln was still prepared to risk imprisonment by trying to get back to England. Yet he had already told his wife in a letter that he could never live with her again "as man and wife" because he had become a Buddhist monk.

The son, who had broken into the house of a Mr Edward Charles Richards, of Trowbridge, Wiltshire, and killed him, when asked why he carried a revolver, said at his trial: "I have always done so because my father did." But Trebitsch was not allowed into England to see his son before he died. Instead his wife went out to see him in Amsterdam and, from all accounts, she still seemed to remain loyal to him.

But, as H. D. Ziman wrote in his review of the biography of Trebitsch Lincoln, "a thriller-writer who invented for his central character a career as complex and improbable as that of Ignaz Trebitsch (later Trebitsch Lincoln) would have difficulty, I fancy, in finding a publisher. It is all very well, he would be told, turning your Hungarian Jew into an English curate and then a Liberal M.P., and making him emerge as a self-confessed German spy in 1914. But to go on from there and represent him as a leading figure in the Kapp *putsch* in Germany, then political adviser to Wu Pei-fu in China, finally transforming him into a Buddhist monk—that is straining credulity too far."[10] It might well have seemed so even to the writer of this book but for the fact that, despite his apparent irrevocable retreat into a Buddhist monastic life in 1926, he emerged a year later as still being indisputably employed by the Chinese Intelligence.

When he was originally deported to Hungary by the British after World War I it does seem as though for a brief period Lincoln flirted with the possibilities of extending Bolshevism to the Far East. But a man who had tasted the good life in Liberal England, despite his extraordinary hatred for the land that had helped him, could never settle down under Bela Kun. Later his understanding of the German flirtations with Bolshevism may have shown him not only how to exploit this in his activities in China, but also how to advise China to avoid undue Russian infiltration. It is interesting to note that it was Lincoln who, in a dispatch to Wu Pei-fu, warned of "the rapid development of the organised strength and planned revolt of the working class in its links with the Chinese Communist Party". And it was after this message that in February 1923 Wu Pei-fu sent troops to kill or arrest workers' and Communist leaders in Kiangan.[1]

The understanding between Germany, Soviet Russia and China had been growing in the latter part of Sun Yat-sen's career. A great sensation was caused in September 1922, when it was reported from Hongkong that plans for the conclusion of a Sino-Russo-German alliance had been discovered. The papers revealing this were reported as having been left behind by Sun Yat-sen's Vice-Minister for Finance when he fled from Canton, though he had been given explicit instructions by Sun Yat-sen to burn the papers.

The Chinese Secret Service had been working in Berlin through a paid Chinese emissary named Chu Wochung, who had secured the co-operation of Admiral von Hintze, formerly German Minister at Peking and then Minister at Moscow, who, according to Chu Wo-chung, decided to give up all other political questions in order to concentrate wholly on this project, for the carrying out of which he proposed asking the German Government to send him to China.

The documents discovered included a signed letter

from Sun Yat-sen to the Vice-Minister, asking him to remit certain sums to Berlin for the continuance of negotiations. Sun Yat-sen stated that the scheme, especially the rôle which von Hintze was playing, must be kept secret from members of his own Government.

Chu Wo-chung reported in one letter that, since securing the help of von Hintze, the scheme was progressing well, and added that a bureau had been formed to carry out the project with von Hintze as director, acting in the capacity of adviser to Sun Yat-sen.[12] On his arrival at Hongkong he was to be secretly escorted to Canton and conducted to Sun Yat-sen's headquarters. Stress was laid on the need to use an assumed name in order to keep the project secret from the German public.

Chu Wo-chung referred to von Hintze as a man of moderate views, in full accord with democratic opinion. This ploy by the Chinese Secret Service anticipated the manifesto of the Chinese Communist Party which called for a united front to "eliminate civil strife, overthrow the warlords and establish internal peace; to overthrow the oppression of international imperialism and achieve the complete independence of the Chinese nation." It was clear from the discovery of these plans that the Sun Yat-sen Secret Service had established a bureau in Berlin and had paid out considerable sums of money to set negotiations going.

About this period it was possible to form some assessment of the organisation of what had turned from a phantom Secret Service into something much more official. To Sun Yat-sen must go the maximum amount of credit not merely for organising for the first time an effective Secret Service overseas, but for bringing in Western agents in limited numbers, and for developing bureaux abroad.

Dr Sun was an astonishing combination of the imaginative, the naïve, the kindly humanist, the devoted if non-Church-going Christian and the occasional Machiavellian. He not only possessed all these often contradictory qualities, but he imbued his Secret Service with them. Thus on the one hand we have the missionary influence, though this had faded by the mid-'twenties, the love of engaging foreign rogues and

220

what Lin Yutang calls the "enlightened scamp", the serious examination of the principles of Russian revolution, the military tradition of Germany, much more admired than that of the Allies, and, above all, for almost the first time, the acknowledgement of the need for a small, but efficient and impartial bureaucracy to control the Intelligence Service. The man picked by Sun Yat-sen to undertake the last-named task was Chen See-yen, who was nominally a representative of the Kuomintang, and who was responsible for all political screening and for checking on foreign agents. He was assisted by Li Lu-chao, who had been Sun's private secretary since 1915.

But Sun Yat-sen had been ailing for some time before there was strong pressure from the Russians on the Chinese Communists for co-operation with the Sun Yat-sen Government. Not even his opponents on the extreme flank of the revolutionaries denied Sun's incorruptible patriotism. They had only to compare it with the reactionary Peking "government" that had staged a presidential election won by the right-wing warlord, Tsao Kun, by bribing members of its puppet parliament with several millions of dollars from American sources. The left-wing revolutionaries' only concern about Dr Sun was that he sought to achieve national independence through co-operation with foreign capitalists. And in the long-term assessment the Chinese Communists were right: Sun's attempts to woo the Western capitalists had been spurned; instead the latter had often backed the warlords against him.

In 1923 Sun had had talks with the Chinese Communist Party leaders and established relations with a Soviet diplomatic representative. The Communists proved to be much more reasonable than he could have wished for and Sun revised his own views and developed what he called "three major policies", under which there was to be an alliance with Soviet Russia, full co-operation with the Chinese Communist Party and support for workers' and peasants' movements.

Thus, in effect, a new revolutionary government was established in Canton, creating the Whampoa Military Academy, which not only had the Kuomintang officer, Chiang Kai-shek as Dean, but the Communist

Chou En-lai as Political Director, to train a new type of army, revolutionary in character and trained to combat the warlords. It was also to be a training ground for spies. Certainly it was the first professionally-run school for Chinese agents in modern times.

Four foreign-born agents played a part in the Chinese Secret Service of this era: first, and in a strangely low-key note compared with his flamboyant personality, Morris Cohen; second, Trebitsch Lincoln, much remoter from the inner counsels of the Intelligence Service than any of the others, but in some ways perhaps much more a professional agent; third, Mikhail Borodin, the Comintern's nominee to the Kuomintang; and, fourth, "General Galin", whose real name was Vasili Blyukher, a general in his mid-thirties who had led the Red Armies to victory in the Urals and Siberia.

Borodin was yet another Jew, born in 1884 in Latvia, who in his youth had joined the Jewish Social Democratic Bund and later became a Bolshevik. He had avoided arrest in Russia early in the twentieth century by going to the U.S.A., where he studied at the Valparaiso University in Indiana and married a Lithuanian emigrant. When the Russian revolution succeeded in 1917 he returned to that country and was employed by Lenin first as an emissary to America and later to Britain (where he was imprisoned for six months), Spain, Holland and Mexico.

Borodin had been the Comintern's chief agent in London for a time and in those pre-Stalinist days he had a freedom of movement and power of negotiation with foreign allies which was swiftly ended in the purges of the 'thirties when the Comintern's authority was destroyed by Stalin himself. Early in 1921 it was clear even to the most optimistic world revolutionaries of the Kremlin that capitalism in Europe and North America was not going to fall before revolts of workers and there was a sudden switch of attention to the Far East.

Lenin had somewhat disparagingly regarded Sun Yat-sen as "the wide-eyed innocent of the revolutionaries", but he agreed to send Comintern agents to help organise the Chinese Communist Party. The Russians had, in fact, played quite a clever diplomatic game with the Chinese: they had maintained official diplomatic links with Peking, stressing the fact that they were willing unilaterally to disregard some of the concessions won by Russia under the Czarist regime, while also sending unofficial agents, such as Borodin, to make contact with Sun.

It was partly through the efforts of Mikhail Borodin that Sun admitted Communists into the ranks of his own Nationalist Party and agreed to accept a measure of Soviet help. In 1923 Sun sent his chief of staff, Chiang Kai-shek, to Moscow with instructions to discuss how China and Russia could help one another. It was then that the Russians sent Borodin to Canton without giving him any official title, his duties being rather vaguely described as that of "a permanent representative of the Soviet Government on loan to the Government in Canton".

It was one of Sun Yat-sen's fatal errors that he actually gave Borodin the title of "adviser" to the committee concerned with the re-organisation of the Kuomintang. On Sun's part this was simply intended as a friendly gesture to a man with whom he had speedily struck up a close working relationship. But it filled Sun's Western friends with dismay and it allowed Borodin not merely to plan the structural re-organisation of the Kuomintang, but to gain a foothold in the co-ordination of Chinese intelligence and in the Whampoa Military Academy to which he introduced other Russian "advisers".

Borodin's brief was to advise on a new, highly disciplined and authoritarian structure for the Kuomintang so that eventually it would be powerful enough to overcome and crush all internal opposition and to mount a nation-wide socialist (or, more accurately, communist) revolution. He had great personal charm, some of the qualities of a diplomat (for he had to placate militant Chinese Communists as well as the more conservative members of Sun's party); but, though he kept in the background as much as possible, Sun's gesture in making him an official adviser soon broke his original "cover" as a *Rosta* correspondent.

Han Suyin in her biography of Mao Tse-tung writes that Borodin "seems to have understood very little of the intrigues around Sun. He was almost hypnotised by Chiang Kai-shek's fluency and left-wing jargon . . . 'unity for all' was Borodin's motto."[13]

Borodin and Mao first met in 1924; the former spoke no Chinese and the latter no Russian and it is said that Mao was not impressed by the Kremlin agent. On the other hand Borodin was convinced that China was "a hundred years behind the times and not yet ready for communism". More even than the radicals of the Kuomintang Borodin believed in the policy of "making haste slowly".

It was the same in the sphere of intelligence. Gently, courteously, rarely giving a hint of the toughness underlying his real nature, Borodin, once Sun had promoted him to the new rank of "senior adviser", cautiously set about examining the structure of the Chinese Intelligence Service and infiltrating his own agents into its ranks, encouraging both Chinese and Russians to come to his office with secret reports. At the same time he maintained his own mini-intelligence section which consisted of his wife, who was his confidential secretary, translators who gave him a daily review of all foreign and Chinese newspapers and four Russians whom he sent around the provinces. There is some evidence that the Russian members of his staff were not of a high calibre and that they were often fooled or manipulated by the Chinese.

Vasili Blyukher, who was appointed chief of the Soviet Military Mission to China, arrived in 1924, and curiously, he worked under a pseudonym, that of "General Galin". This seemed quite an unnecessary subterfuge, as he had some forty Russian officers working under him and their presence could hardly fail to be noticed. He certainly achieved a great deal at the Whampoa Military Academy, creating the finest troops in southern China and developing among them a mutual espionage system that was guaranteed to weed out malcontents and those "politically undesirable".

On 12 March 1925, Sun Yat-sen died from cancer of the liver and one of his last acts was to send a letter, almost certainly dictated for him to sign by Borodin, to the Central Executive Committee of the Soviet Union. This read:

"Dear Comrades,
While I lie here stricken by a malady against which men are powerless, my thoughts are turned towards you, and towards the future of my party and my country.

"You stand at the head of a union of free republics—that heritage left to the oppressed peoples by the immortal Lenin. With the aid of that heritage the victims of imperialism will inevitably achieve emancipation from that international regime whose foundations have been rooted for ages in slavery, wars and injustice.

"I leave behind me a party which, as I always hoped, will be bound up with you in the historic work of the final liberation of China and other exploited nations from the imperialist order. By the will of fate, I must leave my work unfinished and hand it over to those who, remaining true to the principles and teachings of the party. . . . With this object I have instructed the party to be in constant contact with you. I firmly believe in the continuance of the support you have accorded my country.

"Taking leave of you, dear comrades, I want to express the hope that the day will come when the U.S.S.R. will welcome a friend and ally in a mighty, free China, and that in the great struggle for the liberation of the oppressed peoples of the world, both these allies will go forward to victory hand in hand."[14]

Thus far had Sun Yat-sen in his dying days moved from his original doubting, cautious and essentially pragmatic attitude to the Soviet experiment to one which almost amounted to an integrated alliance.

Chiang Kai-shek's Purge
1925-1936

Heaven does not hear a
forced oath.
Confucius

IT was not so much that Chiang Kai-shek, Sun Yat-sen's natural successor as head of the Kuomintang, believed that the alliance with the Soviet Union had been forced on China, but that, bearing in mind that most sayings of Confucius have several shades of meaning and many subtle implications, he suddenly realised that the effects of the alliance were almost the same as if it had been dictated at gun-point.'

More ruthless than Sun, quicker to see where the Russian alliance and the increasing presence of Soviet "advisers" were leading China and much less prone to trust foreigners, Chiang decided that the situation *vis à vis* Russia was not the same as had originally been envisaged by Sun. He also saw very clearly that things were not developing to China's long-term advantage and that the knowledge Borodin and others had obtained of the organisation internally, if not externally, of the Secret Service posed a real threat not only to the Kuomintang, but to China's future independence.

No doubt Chiang had seen something of Russian infiltration methods at the Whampoa Academy, of which he was president and of which Chou En-lai had been political director. Curiously, while mistrusting Borodin, Chiang got on extremely well with Vasili Blyukher even to the extent of calling him "a reasonable man and a good friend as well as an outstanding

Russian general", which, from Chiang, was high praise for a Russian. But here again Chiang was simply being a realist: the stark truth is that it was Vasili Blyukher who turned something little better than an amateur rabble of an army into a disciplined force.

It dawned on other members of the Kuomintang as well as Chiang that, though Borodin and Blyukher were nominally advisers, in effect they held a large measure of political and military control. Yet it was not easy, even on military or security grounds, to decry the aid Russia had given to the Kuomintang. Whatever Sun's limitations in the latter part of his life, when he was in ill health, he had seen the Kuomintang become all powerful and the warlords slowly eliminated. The Russians had not only given the Kuomintang a far stronger party structure, they had increased the army from nine hundred and sixty officers and men in 1924 to thirty thousand in late 1925.

One of the interesting facts about the introduction of Russian "advisers" to Whampoa Academy was that Blyukher not only brought in a corps of Russian instructors, but that he sold rifles so that Chinese troops could be taught how to fire, and the money paid for the rifles did not go back to Russia but was passed on directly to the funds of the Chinese Communist Party.

Chiang managed to inherit a Secret Service that was not totally infiltrated by the Russians; indeed, it was from this Secret Service that he learned that Borodin had tried to push Sun Yat-sen into a war with northern China in the hope of failure and the resultant elimination of Sun. It was a warning which Chiang bore in mind for the rest of his life.

When Blyukher returned to Russia in 1926 Chiang decided this was the moment to get rid of Borodin. In that style of imaginative logic (however much that may seem a contradiction in terms) for which the Chinese mind at its best is famed, Chiang used the discipline which Borodin had instilled into the bureaucracy and hierarchy of the Kuomintang to crack down on the Russians. It may well have been that this was the moment at which Mao Tse-tung first saw flaws in the Russian communist ideology. At least he must have realised with some bitterness that Soviet insistence on discipline had curbed the revolutionary ardour of Chinese Communists and that the fact that Borodin had insisted they should serve the Kuomintang had made it relatively easy for Chiang Kai-shek to take a tough line against the Communists in general.

The Intelligence Service was alerted, though great care was taken as to which sections were informed so that there should be no leaking of information to the Russians, and in a swiftly carried out operation several Chinese Communists and Borodin's Russian advisers were arrested. The whole operation was planned with the greatest care, as Borodin was away from Canton at the time. The whole purpose of the operation was to work out a compromise with Borodin, as Chiang realised full well that little could be achieved without continuing to work with the Russian.

Borodin was realistic enough to appreciate that he would have to come to terms with Chiang Kai-shek and that he must make the best deal he could. The compromise was an extremely subtle one: on the Chinese side, being sensitive to anything that smacked of losing face, they conceded that Borodin was still an adviser to the Kuomintang, while he had to agree that all Communist members of the Kuomintang must declare themselves as such and promise not to form any secret organisations within the Kuomintang. In effect, Chiang Kai-shek was playing for time: he knew that for a few years at least he could not divorce himself entirely from the Soviet umbrella.

Chiang was all for pressing ahead with a drive to the north, which was something the Russians had encouraged a few years previously, but which they now opposed. The successes of his armies belied Soviet criticism in late 1926 and Chiang succeeded in capturing and holding Changsha, Nanchang and Wuhan. This drive boosted the prestige of Chiang Kai-shek, made more people look askance at the Russians, yet remarkably confirmed Mao Tse-tung in his belief that the way to a real revolutionary victory for China lay through the peasants. He wrote later: "A revolution is not the same as inviting people to dinner or writing an essay or painting a picture or embroidering a flower. . . . A revolution is an uprising, an act of violence whereby one class overthrows the authority of another."[1] But it was the reaction of the peasants which inspired him.

Yet, adapting himself to the compromise imposed by Chiang, it was to the Kuomintang which Borodin clutched precariously, and not to the agrarian principles of Mao Tse-tung. This was Mao's first glimpse of the risks of relying too much on Soviet Russia, for shortly afterwards Borodin, intent on retaining control, if possible, of Chinese intelligence, stated that "the land is not yet a problem, because the peasant problem at the present consists of demands for the reduction of rent and interest, freedom of organisation, armed self-defence . . . to lead the peasantry away from the actual struggle for these demands . . . is to stop struggling."[2]

In short, in the beginning of the Stalinist era in Russia there was apparent the same contempt for the peasants in China as Stalin himself held for them in Russia. Thereafter Chiang played a clever game on both fronts. Knowing he was not yet strong enough to opt out of the Russian alliance, he maintained a strained but working relationship with Borodin, which became so uneasy by 1927 that it resulted in Chiang playing a double-game of attempting to play along with those Russians who did not agree with Borodin and by making renewed efforts to win advisers in the West.

"Two-Gun" Cohen was promoted by Chiang, who had a high regard for this long-tested servant of the new Chinese Republic. Cohen became a personal bodyguard to Chiang and was his constant prompter in using the large exiled Chinese communities in the U.S.A. as a powerful bargaining counter in acquiring American backing. It was a long haul to achieve this, but it was Cohen who prompted and boosted it.

Back into favour inside the Secret Service came the non-Russian agents and advisers. Morris Cohen acquired almost unprecedented powers for a secret agent when in 1927 he was given a post inside the Central Bank of China responsible for bullion vaults and with powers to issue a new currency to finance the Northern expedition. Cohen certainly prevented a run on the bank and acquired a considerable reputation in doing so, but the description by some newspapers of this period of his having held a position equivalent to a Chancellor of the Exchequer has certainly been greatly exaggerated.

Once again in this year—1927—Trebitsch Lincoln's name occurred in the headlines of the world's newspapers. Less than twelve months after his dramatic trip from Ceylon to Amsterdam in the hope of seeing his son, Bombardier John Lincoln, before he was executed at Shepton Mallet in Wiltshire for the murder of Edward Richards of Trowbridge, Trebitsch Lincoln was once again in Europe negotiating a secret £4,000,000 loan for the purchase of munitions for the Chinese Government. On this occasion it was reported in the *Daily Express* that "he was in Berlin a week ago and is now believed to have arrived in Switzerland, where he is presiding over a secret council which includes many of his old friends in Germany."[3]

The freelance spy who only a year or two before had declared he only wished to opt out of life and became a Buddhist monk, now stated that "If I have power anywhere on earth I have it among the hordes of the Far East. I do not want to go east, but if every door is closed against me, if I am brought face to face with the ever-recurring problem of no country and no capital, then my very sure refuge is with the Chinese."[4]

It is important to note the reply to the suggestion put to Lincoln by the *Daily Express* reporter that the Chinese "might not be anxious to trust him again after the manner in which he had played them false in 1924, when he was chief adviser to General Wu Pei-fu, and was forced to flee for his life".

"Wu is the most capable and most honest of all the Chinese generals," replied Lincoln, "and he is the one man with whom I care to work. If he refuses to hear me, I shall fall back on General Feng Yu-hsiang, who owes me something for the assistance I was able to render him when he was a defeated man. I shall persuade him to break with the northern army and to fight against Wu Pei-fu."[5]

China does not retain for long agents who publicise their internal conflicts and in this instance Lincoln was blatantly and arrogantly betraying confidences and showing his own hand. The fact was that he had become a broken reed, a freelance spy who no longer held out much promise to any side. In one sense Trebitsch Lincoln's permanent curse was his obsession with religion. Up to 1919 it might perhaps be argued that he had used religion as a means of advancing himself financially. But, while this was true up to a point, there seems to be abundant evidence that he was a religious addict: religion was to him what heroin was to others. And perhaps because of this he had always expected devotion to religion would ensure that —as was the customary belief in the Jewish religion from which he had sprung, but which he had eschewed —rewards would come to him much more quickly.

There was with Trebitsch Lincoln the extraordinary case of the rebellion in October 1924 of the Christian General Feng Yu-hsiang, who had no direct links with imperialism, but who rebelled against his master, Wu Pei-fu, marched to Peking and not only finished off the reign of the British-backed warlord, but also ended the reign of "President" Tsao Kun in Peking.

All this, if indeed it was organised by Trebitsch Lincoln, could explain how he wormed his way into the Chinese Secret Service while appearing to back a British-supported warlord. But a striking example of how he would always bite the hand that fed him is the fact that Feng Yu-hsiang, while ejecting from the "Forbidden City" of Peking the deposed ex-Emperor, Pu Yi, and his court, was ordered by Lincoln to organise sanctuary and Japanese backing for the ex-Emperor.

By this time it would seem that Trebitsch Lincoln was hedging his bets between a Bolshevik-Chinese alliance and a German-Japanese pact. On the surface there was nothing to incriminate Lincoln as far as the Chinese were concerned, but it should be noted that the ex-Emperor Pu Yi first sought shelter in the Dutch Embassy and then in the Japanese concession of Tientsin, later emerging as the "Emperor" of Japan's puppet state of Manchukuo.

Yet Lincoln continued to blow his own trumpet in a manner which hardly became a secret agent. "The reorganisation of China," he told the press, "will take about eight years, but long before that I shall be ready to strike. While world interest is focussed on the troubles in the Far East, trouble will silently but surely be fermenting in Europe. It is my plan, when all is ready, to invade French Indo-China from the Chinese provinces of Yunan, to attack Tibet, and to threaten the frontiers of India, drawing in Afghanistan and Persia.

"The colonial war in Indo-China will compel France to send large contingents of troops from Europe, which will provide an opportunity of striking at Europe from Germany." [6]

It is still not clear whose side this fast-switching freelance spy was on at this time. Five years previously he had entered China with only a few pounds in his purse, yet within three weeks had mastered the language sufficiently to be able to converse with the ruling powers and convince them that he had something to offer. Certainly under Wu Pei-fu he had achieved some measure of authority and affluence, living in a palace, having a bodyguard and being regarded as something of a miracle-worker. At the same time he was playing along with Sun Yat-sen's Secret Service as a double-agent. Three times he went to Berlin to negotiate loans and to bargain with a syndicate for the supply of war materials, although at that time there was a price of £1,000 on his head.

But Lincoln seems never to have been satisfied either with his self-deceptive quest for the one true religion, or his search for money and power. When sent to Europe to pay the first instalment on the loan for arms purchases he betrayed his trust, kept the money for his own use and made arrangements to flee to Java where he intended to buy a plantation and settle down for the rest of his life.

By now Lincoln's treachery as an agent was realised by the Chinese: not only had he misused funds, but he had already entered into traitorous relations with the Japanese. When, in November 1927, he arrived back in Peking, he was told to get out at once. His motives even then were far from clear, but, after entering Peking under the name of "Mr H. Ruh", and preserving this degree of anonymity for a whole month, he lived at the Hotel du Nord, predominantly a German institution. It was reported that he had called at the British Legation, disclosing his real identity and requesting that it be kept secret, as, so he said, "he was devoting himself to Buddhism and preparing to deliver lectures on that religious faith in China".[7]

He was promptly told by the Legation that he had "two minutes to get out, or you will be kicked out". Thereafter Lincoln became like the Wandering Jew of tradition, a man without a state, owing allegiance to none, and changing his politics and his religions as and when it suited him. There was just one difference from the Lincoln of the past: he now seemed to be totally committed to an oriental way of life and a hostility to the Western world generally.

Then on 7 May 1934 Lincoln was arrested on a deportation order when he arrived at Liverpool by ship. He was held in the Bridewell Jail and his "disciples" —five monks and five nuns—were placed in a boarding-house. He was still using the name of Chao Kung and his story this time was that he was travelling from China, had crossed Canada, with the intention of forming a Buddhist colony in the South of France. His "disciples" wore grey kimonos and their shaven heads were covered with black skull caps. His passport, issued in China, stated that he was of "no nationality". The same phrase was used on the passports of two of his ten disciples.

Discrepancies concerning Lincoln's form of Buddhism were pointed out by an official of the Chinese Consulate in Liverpool, interviewed by the *Daily Express*: "A Buddhist monk such as Lincoln professes to be a celibate. Yet Lincoln has two sons. Nuns are kept separate from the monks in Buddhist monasteries, but the men and women who follow Lincoln mix freely with each other."[8]

The monks and nuns held Chinese, French and German passports other than the two who were declared to have "no nationality". They declined to desert Lincoln, who was eventually ordered out of the country. Yet the latter part of Lincoln's life is even more mysterious than the events which preceded it. Some said he went into a lamasery in Tibet; others that he still travelled from place to place, a permanent fugitive from justice; and there is also the report that he returned to China, was allowed into the international settlement in Shanghai where he carried on the one trade he knew—that of a freelance spy. No doubt the Buddhist monk act was his cover, but, though he had been unmasked as a treacherous agent by the Chinese, this does not necessarily mean he would be refused admittance to China.

One must remember that with the Chinese the lesson of the "condemned spy" is firmly fixed in all their dealing in the world of intelligence. Both the British Secret Service and the Americans at that time were convinced that he was still being used by the Chinese, even if this amounted only to allowing him into the country and keeping a watch on him. Lincoln was the spider and the Chinese were quite happy to watch as he wove his web of intrigue: they fully understood his mentality, far better than most Westerners, and regarded him as much more useful as a somewhat fatuous double-crossing ally than as a man publicly condemned and therefore outside their control.

A former member of Chiang Kai-shek's Secret Service told me: "Lincoln was always a modest asset to us even in his old age and when we knew he was backing the Japanese. He had a complicated mind, but we probably understood it better than you Westerners. You think we were foolish still to retain an interest in him? No doubt you British would have locked him up. But lock up Lincoln and you would learn nothing; let Lincoln free and you might learn a lot. What always puzzled us is what you British did to Lincoln to make him hate you so. As far as his links with the Japanese were concerned, two points need to be made: first, we needed to have some kind of hold on someone who was in the Japanese camp, not that Lincoln could provide much worthwhile intelligence on Japan at that period of his life; secondly, knowing how the West had let us down so often, how even the treacherous Russians were, in World War II, allowed to have priority over us—and we had been fighting the Japanese for years—we realised that a situation might arise when we should need to make a separate peace with Japan and here Lincoln could have been a useful intermediary. After the abysmal defeat of the British in Singapore and Hongkong we Chinese did not trust or rely on anyone. We also knew that the Russians were quite prepared to sacrifice us if they could save themselves by doing so."

That statement may explain the Chinese attitude to Lincoln, but it does not tell us what he did. The last reports we had of him were that he was broadcasting Axis propaganda from Tibet in the early years of World War II. In 1943 there came the report of his death through a Japanese news agency. It just stated that Trebitsch Lincoln had died in Shanghai in October of that year.

Even after this the "Lincoln legend" did not easily die, for on 5 May 1947 reports in the British press appeared from such sources as Reuter and the *Times of Ceylon* that "Trebitsch Lincoln, former British M.P. and whose death was reported by the Japanese in 1943, is still alive". The report added that a local journalist in Ceylon had received a letter from Lincoln dated March 1947 with a Darjeeling-Bengal postmark.

But if the Jewish-born Lincoln had been a dubious ally, Morris Cohen's power grew daily under the Chiang Kai-shek regime. I have made several attempts to establish links between Cohen and Lincoln without success: if they existed, they were certainly well-guarded. But Cohen himself became an increasingly important figure in the Chinese Secret Service: when there was trouble threatening the Kuomintang, Cohen had invariably anticipated it. There was the attempt by the Chinese Communists to take over Canton in December 1928, which eventually seemed to have been a Russian-inspired coup. Cohen somehow got advance information of the take-over attempt and organised a counter-attack which resulted in three-quarters of the Russian Embassy staff being killed by Cohen's agents.

This was one of Cohen's greatest coups in the service of Chinese Intelligence. He ordered documents in the Russian Embassy to be seized and among these were found to be instructions for a Russian agent in Canton to contact a Chinese general (whose name was given in code) with the aim of establishing Communist cells in Indo-China.

Morris Cohen's next moves were partly concerned with intelligence and partly on the political level. Chiang Kai-shek wanted to establish new relations in London to replace the former diplomatic representation which had been held by a man who was pledged to the northern generals. Through Cohen's initiative a mission headed by Hu Hammin, and including Sun-fo, was sent to London. The following year Sun-fo became Minister of Railways and Communications and as a reward for services rendered he made Cohen his "adviser on foreign purchases".

Cohen advanced his career rapidly in the next few years. He became a staff officer for the new Governor of Kwangtung Province, General Li Chai-sun, and was given the title of "First and Principal A.D.C. and Liaison Officer with the Government of Hongkong and all Foreign Powers in South China". And Cohen's power and influence in the sphere of intelligence outweighed all else: when General Li fell from power, Cohen became A.D.C. to the new Governor, Chen Chi-tong.

Slowly Chiang Kai-shek was purging the Secret Service not only of Russian but of many other Western agents who had jumped on to the band wagon in the somewhat easy-going days of Sun Yat-sen. But he never wavered in his support for Morris Cohen. The erstwhile Cockney Jew was once again to the fore in rounding up the Bias Bay pirates in 1929. The head of these pirates was one Ah Hop, whose activities were reportedly backed by some of Hongkong's most prominent citizens who used to draw dividends directly from the pirates. Among these citizens was a man who was described as managing director of one of the biggest Chinese banks and a leading contender for the Legislative Council.

In 1930–1 when the rival provincial leaders began bickering and the South started to rearm, Cohen assumed his former duties under Sun-fo's continued appointment as adviser on foreign purchases, and he negotiated many under-cover arms deals for which he received two and a half per cent commission from foreign suppliers. Cohen had been one of the first to warn about the threat of direct Japanese aggression since the immediate post-war period and had devoted his intelligence activities to obtaining advance information about Japan's invasion of Manchuria, which came as no surprise in 1931.

In lining up various arms deals, which took him to Europe and the United States in 1932, Cohen never failed to return without an abundance of intelligence: "the man is a filing-cabinet, not a human being," declared Sun-fo. On a number of occasions his travels necessitated his calling at Japanese ports, but it is significant that he never left his ship, however long it stopped at any of these places. In the course of his travels Cohen also collected a formidable amount of data on Russian policy towards China and attempts to undermine the Chiang Kai-shek regime.

In the early days of the regime Cohen had not only done his utmost to check Russian influence in China and to advise how this might best be counteracted, but he had tried to convince the Americans, regarded by him as China's best long-term ally, that Chiang shared his suspicions of Russian motives for interfering in Chinese affairs. As early as February 1927, he had reported that Chiang and Borodin had had "a serious disagreement . . . a more or less permanent breach", and this message was passed direct to the American Consul-General in Canton. The gist of Cohen's message to the Consul-General was that "if the powers wanted to get the Russians out of China, they should establish direct contact with General Chiang. He was sure Chiang . . . was only co-operating with Borodin because the Soviet Government was supplying arms and ammunition which were absolutely essential for the success of the Cantonese forces."[9]

Chiang had to a large extent heeded much of this advice, but his military training had given him a mental rigidity and stubbornness which contrasted markedly to the more flexible Sun Yat-sen. He always tended to overreact to a critical situation and this applied in his relations as much with the Western powers as with the Russians. While admittedly he was not helped by the fact that the Western powers remained

237

mistrustful of China, for they were still worried about the extent of Soviet influence, he also blundered badly in his dealings with the West. Nor did the Secret Services of the foreign powers help their governments to arrive at an accurate assessment of the situation: most agents of European governments found that reports of Soviet infiltration in the Far East found much more favour with their masters than any hints of areas in which Russian activities might easily be counteracted by making friends.

So Chiang was forced to play a lone game against Soviet Russia, which he regarded as his main enemy. He was anxious that attention should be pinned on Russian rather than Chinese Communists in his early years, as he had not yet given up all hope of arriving at an understanding with the latter, providing they detached themselves from Soviet influence. In the meantime Mao Tse-tung, who had achieved extraordinary strength in Hunan Province, had increased the number of members of his peasant associations from 2 million in 1927 to 5 million by the early 'thirties.

Perhaps Chiang's compromise relationship with Borodin would have lasted longer and borne more fruit if Stalin himself had not intervened and with his cynical contempt for Asiatics informed Borodin that he must see that, while the Chinese Communists were to be encouraged to seize the lands of capitalist landlords, they should allow their warlord allies to retain their own lands (the warlord allies, it should be stressed, were even more reactionary than the forces of the Kuomintang), while at the very same moment urging Borodin to insist that Chiang should introduce a "revolutionary court" to try right-wing Kuomintang officers. How could Borodin, depending entirely on a slender and tenuous relationship with Chiang, be expected to put across such a policy?

It was, of course, impossible for a policy like this effectively to be implemented and nobody knew it better than Borodin, who at least had a mind that was attuned to international realities and an understanding of the Chinese. Stalin had been angered by the extent to which Chiang had consolidated his position: he looked upon the anti-Chiang warlords, feudal

238

reactionaries though they might be, as natural allies of the Chinese Communists. Perhaps Stalin also realised that, while he wanted to see Chiang crushed, he had himself failed sufficiently to encourage Mao Tse-tung's insistence on a purely agrarian revolution as a means of achieving communist power in China. This was why in a somewhat spiteful manner he had turned to seek support from some of the very warlords against whom he had previously fulminated.

By this time the Chinese Communists had formed a small but modestly effective intelligence organisation of their own, owing much not only to Chou En-lai, whose authority and knowledge of Western affairs from his earlier career while living in Paris gave him a distinct advantage, but to some of the Chinese allies among Indo-Chinese Communists. Minute as this shadowy Secret Service was it was at least sophisticated enough to know that Stalin was playing a nationalistic game and that the early revolutionary fervour of brotherhood through the Comintern had long gone overboard; or as one Chinese Communist leader, Chen Tu-hsiu, commented: "Obeying Stalin was like trying to take a bath in a urinal."

All Stalin achieved was to cause a few, but nevertheless important, defections from the Communist ranks to Chiang Kai-shek. Chiang's Secret Service swiftly acquired all the information they needed about the effects of Stalin's instructions on Chinese Communists with the effect that Wang Ching-wei sought a deal with the Kuomintang and the Communist general Feng Yu-hsiang made a secret agreement with Chiang to join forces with him.

Borodin knew that he could no longer be of use either to Chiang or to Stalinist aims in China. "I came to China to fight for an idea," he said sadly, "the dream of accomplishing world revolution by freeing the people of the East brought me here. But China itself, with its age-old history, its countless millions, its vast social problems, its infinite capacities, astounded and overwhelmed me, and my thoughts of world revolution gradually sank into the background. The revolution and the fight for freedom in China became an end in itself, and no longer a means to an end. My task was to grasp the situation, to start the great wheel moving, and as time has passed it has carried me along with it. I myself have become only a cog in the great machine."[10]

In July 1927 Borodin left China, sad and disillusioned. If he had failed it was not his fault, it was Stalin's. But it was Borodin who paid for Stalin's errors by being demoted to the post of editor of a minor Moscow newspaper.

The gradual build-up of the still minute Chinese Communist Intelligence Service was, ironically, to some extent helped by Chiang Kai-shek's purge of Soviet agents. Founded originally on Russian disciplinary rules, but moulded by its own peculiarly Chinese revolutionary fervour, it had often found itself at cross purposes with Soviet aims. For example, both Mao and Chou, through their brief honeymoon association with the Kuomintang, knew something of the organisation of Chiang's Secret Service. They were well aware even then that, however much they might need Soviet Russia as an ally, an independent Intelligence Service was vital to their interests.

There was also the fact that Chiang frequently promoted disillusioned Communists inside his own organisation. Mao Tse-tung had been a fellow student of Chen Kung-po when the latter was a Communist. In 1928 Chen had joined Chiang Kai-shek's side, repudiated communism and become chairman of the Political Bureau in Canton with some responsibilities, rather vaguely defined, in the field of intelligence, and he became as rabid an anti-communist as he had been an enthusiastic communist in his student days. As Mao astutely observed at the time, "In seeking out those who run away from the Communist Party, Chiang is only building up trouble for himself. Just as there is no Catholic so devout as a convert, so there is no Fascist so ardent and extreme as an ex-Communist." Thus it proved to be with a number of men employed by Chiang to purge communist influence in the Kuomintang Secret Service: several of them ultimately betrayed the Chinese to the Japanese, or actually served under Japanese puppet governments. It was the presence of such men in Chiang's camp which certainly caused the

British to regard the Kuomintang as at best a luke-warm ally and at worst as a potential appeaser of the Japanese in World War II.

One of the men on whom Chiang relied most in his early days was General Wu Teh-chen, formerly a chief of police in Canton, whom Chiang made responsible for all internal security in 1929. He was the driving force in purging the Kuomintang of communist agents and was ultimately rewarded by being made Governor of Kwantung in 1937. Morris Cohen served Wu Teh-chen briefly as his A.D.C.

Wu Teh-chen considerably enhanced Chiang's counter-espionage organisation and did as much as any man to enable the Kuomintang leader to establish a tight control over internal security. But life was always difficult for Chiang: it is easy to criticise him in retrospect, but one must bear in mind two factors: first, that primarily he was a military leader lacking in political know-how; secondly, that he was not only confronted in many parts of the country with strong, relatively honest and highly intelligent Communist opposition, but hindered and baulked within the Kuomintang itself by the many place-seekers and intriguers who had wormed their way into positions of power in the latter part of Sun Yat-sen's regime. A typical example was Wang Ching-wei, originally one of Sun's "bright young men", who had become an idol of the radical students on the strength of the story that back in 1906 he had thrown a bomb at the Manchu Regent, but who was an opportunist and thoroughly corrupt.

There was a time when Wang Ching-wei might have become leader of the Kuomintang, but just as Mao Tse-tung had weighed him up as being one who was "far too easily flattered" to be considered safe, so Chiang chose the moment when Wang was away on a mission in Europe to seize control of the Secret Service, the police and all party offices. Neither Mao nor Chiang (in both of whom Wang had confided at different times) trusted Wang from the very beginning and each was proved to be right. For in 1939 Wang went over to the Japanese side and became head of the puppet South China Government.

But if Chiang was right to mistrust Wang, he equally made many misjudgements of character, for the truth was that in purging the Kuomintang and the Secret Service of Chinese communist and pro-Soviet elements, Chiang laid himself open to the charge of encouraging pro-fascist allies in his own camp. If he mistrusted Wang, there were many others whom he did trust only to find that they were ready to support the Japanese as the armies of Nippon thrust deeper into Chinese territory towards the end of the 'thirties. Just before the outbreak of World War II it became apparent that Wang Ching-wei was preparing to make a deal with secret sympathisers in the Kuomintang to launch an all-out attack on the Chinese Communists in concert with the Japanese.

Apart from these constant wearing personality clashes inside the Kuomintang, Chiang was continually to be pressurised not only between the demands of the Russians and the Japanese, both of whom had designs on Manchuria, but by the devious policies of the Western powers towards China. He had realised too late after capturing Hankow, where the British Concession was overrun, and in entering Shanghai, where British troops were sent in to guard the International Settlement, that this was in part at least the result of a Russian plot with her allies inside the Kuomintang to antagonise the West against Chiang.

To sum up, at the end of ten years of attempting to purge Soviet elements inside China, Chiang was in a not much stronger position than before. True, his armies had gained a great deal of ground, but he was also confronted with almost as many problems with provincial warlords as Sun Yat-sen had had to face; the Japanese threat was now greater than that of Russia, while the Russians had still managed successfully to divide the country into two camps. And at the same time Chiang was a long way from winning anything like worthwhile support from the West.

In 1929 the Chinese Nationalists' seizure of the Sino-Russian administered Eastern Railway had led to a deterioration in relations between China and Russia. The Japanese capture of Manchuria ended once and for all the pretence that the League of Nations had an effective security system, and then in March of 1932 the last Ch'ing boy-emperor, Henry Pu-yi, was proclaimed Regent of the Japanese-controlled territory which was renamed Manchukuo. By the following year the Japanese had taken Jehol province and, by creating a demilitarised zone north of Peiping and Tientsin, manipulated a Chinese puppet regime to smuggle goods into North China.

Unquestionably some of Chiang's subordinates in his drive against communist subversion did more harm than good by their brutal methods. There were five anti-communist "extermination campaigns" between 1931 and 1934, but, as the authors of *East Asia* (Fairbank, Reischauer and Craig) make clear, "this effort to wipe out the practitioners of class war was represented by the Communists as class warfare itself, against the peasantry of whom they claimed to be champions". It was also pointed out that there seemed to be more concern to stamp out the Chinese Communist rebels than to fight the Japanese. Yet even in 1936 while the counter-espionage forces were arresting "Red agents", as they were called, there was the farcical situation in which Chou En-lai was able to travel freely in areas held by the Kuomintang and to be welcomed not only by his own followers, but sometimes quite openly by Kuomintang Party members.

Just as Sun Yat-sen had developed a shadow secret service which, by its intelligent use of exiled Chinese, had ultimately defeated and superseded the old-fashioned Imperial Intelligence Service of Empress Tzu-hsi, so in the 'thirties that which Chiang had inherited from Sun Yat-sen was slowly and almost imperceptibly being challenged by the embryo of a Chinese Communist Secret Service. It was only a small beginning, but in discipline, integrity, devotion to an ideal and growing independence of the Russians, the Secret Service of the future—that of the People's Republic of China—was already being forged.

Communist Advances and Chiang's Kidnap 1932-1938

It is difficult to be muddle-headed. It is difficult to be clever, but still more difficult to graduate from cleverness to muddle-headedness.
Chen Panch'iao in the 18th century

"THE praise of folly has never been interrupted in Chinese literature," once wrote Lin Yutang, and clearly he had this somewhat cynical and esoteric epigram of Chen Panch'iao in mind. But the problem for the Westerner is not merely to realise, in assessing all Chinese thought, literary, philosophical or political, that what may appear superficial cynicism can wrap up a great deal of wisdom to a Chinese, but to sift what is clever from what appears to be muddle-headed; and, a much more difficult task, as the Americans learned to their cost between 1943 and 1950, to ascertain what is totally muddle-headed in what on the surface seems eminently sensible.

But these same tests applied to a lesser extent in the 'thirties when so many of the Westerners still made the mistake of judging the Chinese leaders on their actions rather than analysing their motives. Thus Chiang Kai-shek was mistrusted by many Europeans because he had originally opposed the expulsion of Communists from the Kuomintang and the dismissal of Borodin. The fact that he later sent the Russian military advisers packing and that he conducted quite ruthless purges of Communists, including students, was overlooked. The reputation for devious behaviour was one which clung to Chiang for a long time, though this was more a European than an American view.

One powerful reason for this last statement is that Chiang, through Morris Cohen to a large extent, but also through his agents in the Chinese colonies in the United States, let it be known that a number of incriminating Communist documents had fallen into his hands. These told how the Russians plotted to eliminate the Kuomintang Party and replace it with the Communist Party and set up a Soviet state. These documents he revealed to justify the actions he took in his mass executions of Communists in Shanghai, Canton, Nanking, Swatow and elsewhere.

The Americans were permitted to receive a few tidbits of intelligence from Chiang because he had determined to use his Secret Service as a major instrument in forging a "lobby" in the U.S.A. It was Chiang himself who really laid the first foundation stone of what later came to be known as the "China Lobby". But if the Europeans regarded him as devious and still a secret supporter of the Russians, the latter, who had considered he would be easier than Sun Yat-sen to overthrow in due course, were astonished at what they regarded as his treachery in driving out the Communists. Perhaps they should have seen the danger signals, but Borodin, who understood Chiang rather better than most of his countrymen, had always insisted that China could not be treated like Russia and the U.S.S.R. must be patient in her dealings with Chiang. He was, of course, quite right: were it not for Stalin's obduracy and impatience to see a revolution setting up a Soviet China in 1927, Chiang might have remained at least a cautious ally of the Soviet Union.

But, as Joseph Keeley commented, "Chiang's successful action against the Communists took Moscow by surprise. Since he had kept his opinions about Communism and Communists to himself, the Kremlin considered him as tractable and subservient as other Chinese who had been indoctrinated in Moscow. . . . Many Communist functionaries, including America's gifts to the conspiracy, Earl Browder and Eugene Dennis, started turning up in China at that time, possibly with the idea that the Red risings were going to bear fruit."[1]

It was at this time that Chiang entered into a some-what circuitous relationship with the U.S. Intelligence Service through his own foreign agents. At the same time, realising that he needed to develop his own foreign intelligence service in the U.S.A., he ordered a reappraisal of the now creaking machinery of the Triads' section of the Chinese Secret Service, which had not been overhauled since the pre-World War I period.

The Triads had remained relatively dormant for some time except for their time-honoured rôle of self-protection and semi-religious principles dating back to when five Buddhist monks of exceptional, if not implausible, martial ability, calling themselves the First Five Ancestors, organised the Hung Family to defend the Ming dynasty against the Manchus in 1700. As we have seen, Sun Yat-sen developed branches of the Triads for intelligence purposes, though this was done in an amateurish fashion.

In the late 1930s the celebrated "14-K" Triad was resurrected and rejuvenated in Canton by the Nationalist General Koi Sui-heong, who operated it as a secret intelligence agency for the Kuomintang. One of the defects in using the Triads as a branch of intelligence had been—and this is still true today—that they had no tradition of loyalty to the state: they had been used over the centuries in desultory fashion by various sections of the community, sometimes commercial, sometimes warlords and other factions, not least by private armies. To try to make the Triads function for China alone was as difficult as it would be to make the Mafia work solely in the interests of Italy. Up to the end of World War II the Triads were rather more like the Masonic movement than, say, a gangster organisation such as the Mafia, into which category they gradually evolved.

But Chiang desperately needed a Secret Service which could develop his contacts overseas, with the emphasis above all on the U.S.A. One must bear in mind that within his own family he had problems that threatened his own intelligence organisation—no doubt one reason why European governments remained suspicious and aloof from the Kuomintang. The widow of Sun Yat-sen had sided with the Communists and had gone to Moscow to lend vocal support to their cause.

The "14-K" section of the Triads, which was specially developed to concentrate entirely on intelligence work and therefore put on a much more professional basis than anything envisaged in Sun Yat-sen's day, consisted solely of Kuomintang secret agents. It was extended to various centres inside China, to Hongkong, where it was extremely powerful, and to the U.S.A.

Nevertheless even when the "14-K" Section of the Triads became established on a professional basis, old-time formal initiation ceremonies were retained. Before smouldering joss-sticks on a Buddhist-style altar the candidates swore no fewer than thirty-six life-and-death oaths and drank from deep bowls of wine, cinnabar, rooster's blood and a drop or two of blood from their own fingers. They also bowed to the Ten Precious Articles, which included a red lamp (distinguishing the true from the false), a white paper fan (which strikes down all traitors) and a sword of peach-wood (which can decapitate enemies when merely flourished in the air).

Chiang had some success in his development of the Triads, but, even though the Nationalists have retained some control over them up to this very day, it has never been absolute and on occasion, despite the oaths of loyalty, has worked against them. This has not generally been realised in the Western World, but even just before World War I there were doubts in the ranks of some Triads about the desirability of backing Chiang Kai-shek. The truth was that the Triads represented in their philosophy the ancient tradition of the Chinese people that the best government was "when the Emperor was far away"—in short, the best government gave the maximum freedom with minimum interference.

Nevertheless, in the 'thirties Chiang gained considerable strength in his Intelligence Service both internally and externally through the Triad organisation. In the United States this even resulted, on a small scale, in Triad members who had been imbued with Western democratic principles and a cynical disregard for secret societies actually breaking away from the Triads, but providing much more useful intelligence independently to China.

One example of this will suffice. Andrew Chan, a curious combination of American and Chinese in his names, broke away from the local Triad branch in San Francisco and joined the American Communist Party. Over a period of five years he sent regular bulletins on American Communist activities back to China by carrier pigeons routed to an island not far from Los Angeles off the Pacific coast where they were passed on by boat to China. This was the information on which Chiang was able to build up a valuable flow of intelligence back to the United States, mainly details of American Communist activities, as much concerned with the U.S.S.R. as with China. It was this seemingly altruistic service of the Chinese Intelligence which helped as much as anything in the creation of a "China Lobby" in the U.S.A.

Stark adversity forced the Chinese Communists to try against all the odds to develop their miniscule Secret Service into a positively useful organisation within a few years. Though relatively well organised and disciplined, as an "Opposition Secret Service" it could not remotely be compared with that of Sun Yat-sen in the days when Tzu-hsi ruled China. It had no overseas intelligence coverage whatsoever except what the Russians deigned to pass on, which was relatively little.

But Chiang's military offensive against the Chinese Communists in 1930 changed all that; even in defeat they needed intelligence if only to survive while on the retreat. Possibly it was because Mao Tse-tung anticipated defeat that he determined to press ahead with at least an embryonic Chinese Communist State. In 1931 he held a congress and adopted a constitution for a Soviet China with himself as President. It was then that the tiny Secret Service was re-organised. Without it Chiang might well have dislodged the Communists much earlier, but sound intelligence managed to baulk the Kuomintang leader on at least six occasions before finally he dislodged the Communists from Kiangsi province in 1934 and then moved his troops in for the final drive.

From what appeared to be total defeat Mao Tse-tung plucked what ultimately became the beginning of a great victory—this was the Communists' celebrated "Long March", their retreat in disciplined order, with their women and children, citizenry as well as soldiery, a distance of two thousand miles to Shenshi province where the twenty thousand survivors made Yenan their capital. In this remote fastness they were more or less out of Chiang's reach.

In normal circumstances Chiang would probably have caught up with the Communists and eventually destroyed them, but the fight against Mao Tse-tung was only one of his problems. His minor battles with the warlords had cost him dearly in men, money and materials; so, too, had the battles with the Japanese, against whom he needed to maintain permanent vigilance. Also, by the end of 1931, Chinese forces had had to withdraw to the south of the Great Wall and by the following year the Japanese were attacking Shanghai.

These historical facts need to be stated to assess their effects on the two Secret Services. Mao's Intelligence Service's task was simple: it was simply to ensure the survival of the tiny Communist state remote in the heart of China. Chiang's was much more difficult: he required a Secret Service which would be vigilant internally against Communist infiltration, give him information on Japanese intentions, advise him on whatever moves or tricks the Russians were planning, as well as necessarily building up overseas contacts.

It may seem ridiculous, almost like comparing the gnat with the elephant, to measure the achievements of the two rival Secret Services of this period. But it is vitally important to do so because the sum total of the *two* Intelligence Services provides one with a much clearer picture of the potential of a modern Chinese Secret Service. Warring with one another meant that China's Intelligence Services could not possibly compare with those of the great powers of the world. Yet their overall achievements were formidable and enlightening.

On Chiang's side possibly his greatest achievement and the one which sustained him in power indefinitely was the remarkable success of his Secret Service manoeuvrings which led first to the "China Lobby" in the U.S.A. and then to the prolonged alliance with America. On the debit side he probably made less impression with the Europeans than did Mao Tse-tung, not perhaps in the early years, but certainly by 1943. Again he failed to obtain any worthwhile Russian or Japanese intelligence, while internally Chiang's Secret Service suffered from the faults of some of its predecessors—corruption.

The Communists made only modest gains, but these meant that year by year their own small Intelligence Service improved as Chiang's deteriorated. It was a slow progress because it was mainly aided by fanatical tenacity and honesty, qualities which usually pay very small dividends in the early years. Yet by cunning links with the Russians, who were still only partly trusted, they established a better system of intelligence regarding the Japanese than Chiang had himself. It was this bonus gained by the tiny Chinese Communist Intelligence Service which slowly won them admiration among the European powers. In some respects it secured for them a degree of sympathy that was never shown for Chiang. Thus in the matter of a few years were positions reversed; whereas previously the Europeans had backed the reactionaries against the radicals in China and the Americans almost alone had supported Sun Yat-sen, now it was the British and to a lesser degree the French who began to believe there was more hope of co-operation with the Communists than with Chiang Kai-shek. It is true that in public they continued to support Chiang to a lukewarm extent, largely in deference to American opinion, but in private they said the opposite. This was particularly true regarding British Secret Service reports.

In December 1936 Chiang Kai-shek was kidnapped

by some of his officers, headed by Chang Hsueh-liang and Yang Hucheng, and held prisoner for two weeks in Sian by the Communists. This was probably the most outstanding espionage coup of the era and one which at the time had most Western observers totally baffled. Even Joseph Keeley, author of *The China Lobby Man,* writing in 1969, stated that "the author of a novel dealing with foreign intrigue might well dismiss the plot as too fanciful, and indeed, the story has never been fully clarified".[2]

The Chinese Communist view of the background to this affair is that "the people of the whole country began to see . . . the kind of invincible, unbreakable force that was needed to drive out the Japanese invaders, who were menacing China's very existence as a nation. On 9 December 1935, renewed Japanese encroachments in North China were met by a great demonstration of the university students in Peking. These strikes sparked a nationwide movement under the slogan: 'Stop the civil war; unite to resist Japan!' " This is a facile view: at that period there was no coherent nationwide demand for anything like a united front and in any case the Communists' idea of a united front meant very much what it had meant in Russia, and later in Spain and in Britain—a front not of compromise in the face of a common enemy, but of communist-domination.

Nevertheless it was obvious that one way the Chinese Communists could turn their retreat into a quick victory might be by launching a propagandist campaign for a united front. But, under Mao Tse-tung's Secret Service, they did much more than this: they plotted a coup to ensure something of the sort could be imposed on Chiang Kai-shek, as nobody was more aware than the ultra-realistic Mao that slogans for a popular front did not win battles. Apart from this Mao was well aware that his party had to fight alone, as the Russians were now relatively cool towards him and continued to support the Nationalists. It is still not properly understood that until 1949 Soviet Russia was still basically backing Chiang Kai-shek mainly because of the Stalinist conception that successful revolution only came through industrial workers and not through peasants, on whom Mao Tse-tung based his strategy.

Borodin would have understood that Mao was right, but he had been withdrawn from China and was now in semi-disgrace in Russia. However the Chinese Communists did realise there was a great difference between the Comintern (of which Borodin had been a member) and Stalinist Russia, and between the G.R.U., the highly intelligent military espionage system of the Russians, created by Trotsky and still staffed largely by Cominternists, and the N.K.V.D., or the Stalinist Secret Police. One by one the Comintern old-timers were either removed from power or executed as Stalin purged his Secret Service, but Mao maintained slender links with some of the few Comintern old-timers who remained. Despite his poor relations officially with Russia, he made the fullest possible use of these. Mao had one trump card: if the G.R.U. really needed to develop an espionage service against Japan, it had to be based in China, and, if so, how better than with the backing of the Chinese Communists. In the Chinese Secret Service coup of kidnapping Chiang Kai-shek it was the Comintern allies, not the Stalinists, who aided Mao Tse-tung.

Chiang had been disturbed by reports from his secret agents of visits by the Communists to Shensi Province, particularly to Chang Hsueh-liang, "The Young Marshal", the son of the former ruler of Manchuria. Chang had a bitter grudge against Chiang: in the Japanese invasion of Manchuria in 1931 he had been advised by Chiang to leave Manchuria and to move to the north-west to fight the Communists. It was a tactical blunder on Chiang's part as Chang longed to fight the Japanese and hated being exiled from his own home. It was not difficult for Mao's Secret Service to capitalise on this, which they cunningly did through the capture of Chang's Manchurian officers.

These captured officers were specially well treated and the fact that Mao Tse-tung was anxious for a united front against Japanese aggression was stressed to them. It could even be said that they were fêted;

certainly the Communists treated them as comrades and released them within weeks. The whole idea was that propaganda should do the rest, though in a few cases some Manchurian officers became spies for the Communists. It is surely significant of the humane treatment afforded to these captured soldiers that three thousand of them defected to the Red Army in 1936.

These defections had been reported to Chiang, who became seriously concerned about the loyalty of Chang Hsueh-liang. The latter had written to him quite openly urging a united front against the Japanese and urging an end to the civil war with the Communists. Then came the news that Chang Hsueh-liang had invited the Communist commander, Yeh Chien-ying, to dinner.

So Chiang decided to go to Sian province to ascertain the facts for himself. He flew there on 9 December 1936, and made his headquarters at the Lintung Hotsprings, the former resort of a Chang dynasty Emperor. Some thousands of Manchurian students appeared to present him with a petition urging Chiang to resist Japan: foolishly Chiang's personal guard fired on them.

Chang Hsueh-liang immediately went to the Lintung Hotsprings to defend the students. There was a furious row between Chiang and Chang, the former recording in his diary that "I severely upbraided the 'Young Marshal'". He also threatened Yang Hucheng, present at the talks in his post of Pacification Commissioner and suspected of being a Communist sympathiser.

Then, just before dawn on 12 December 1936, some of Chang Hsueh-liang's officers surrounded Chiang's quarters and made the Kuomintang leader their prisoner. It was, in fact, a perfectly executed coup at a relative distance by the Chinese Communists, but so subtly manipulated that even now it is almost impossible to trace all the developments. But there is no doubt at all that the Chinese Communists had relied to a high degree over the previous few years on their winning allies inside the enemy camp by treating their prisoners well and by playing on the latter's well known hatred of the Japanese.

It is probably true that Mao Tse-tung's agents more or less nudged the supporters of Chang Hsueh-liang into action without having to make any positive plans themselves: this was not only in accordance with the best traditions of Chinese espionage, but it also explains why the full facts of the coup have not yet emerged. Even Joseph Keeley, who admits as much, goes no further than saying that to make sure that Chiang Kai-shek would become a partner in the drive against the Japanese in particular and the fascists in general, "the Communists staged the famous Sian incident of December 1936".[4]

Keeley, however, is vague enough to use the phrase "Communists" without specifying to which country they belonged; and, in the context not only of his previous remarks, but of those which followed, this leaves it conjectural as to whether he refers to Russian or Chinese Communists, or to both. It was, however, from all the available evidence almost entirely a Chinese Communist-inspired coup, though some agents of the Comintern can be given a certain amount of credit. The trouble was that at this time few Western observers could accurately distinguish between Chinese and Russian Communists, and often between Stalinists and Comintern agents.

Mao Tse-tung's biographers do not go into the kidnapping of Chiang in any great detail, but Han Suyin gets as near the truth as is possible when she states that "it is said that . . . the whole of Chiang's kidnapping was engineered by the Communists. Although there is no evidence, it is more than likely that without some 'suggestions' from the Communists the Sian manoeuvre could not have been carried out in so masterly a fashion."[5]

Joseph Keeley makes the point that "by a strange coincidence an American woman, Agnes Smedley, was in Sian on that historic occasion. Miss Smedley was an active propagandist for the Communists and was later identified as an important cog in the Sorge spy machinery."[6] She was certainly "an important cog" in

254

the network of Richard Sorge, the ace Russian agent. For years she had been a Communist sympathiser and she not only arranged for her apartment in Shanghai to be used as a base for the network's secret radio, but was primarily responsible for recruiting Ozaki Hozumi, a Japanese journalist, into the Soviet spy service while he worked as the Shanghai correspondent of the *Asahi Shimbun*. Indeed for a brief period Agnes Smedley was head of the Shanghai Soviet spy network.

Chiang's captors' main demands were that he should stop harassing the Communists and join in an all-out attack on the Japanese. When he at first refused to do this he was threatened with execution. Keeley makes the error of stating that "the Communists decided to kill him".[7] This is quite inaccurate, as it is abundantly clear from most reliable sources on both sides that only a few of the "Young Marshal's" officers wished to kill him. It is certain that Mao Tse-tung certainly never wanted Chiang to be killed, only to ensure his promise to fight the Japanese.

For the situation had become much more dangerous. Soviet agents had passed on to the Chinese Communist Intelligence the news that Wang Ching-wei, an arch enemy of Chiang Kai-shek, was on his way to China from Germany where he had reached an understanding with Hitler. Doubtless this "understanding" did not amount to much, but it was enough to frighten both Chiang and the Communists: if Chiang Kai-shek was executed and Wang set up his own "Nationalist" Government, then the way would be open for a Japanese-German drive to crush the Chinese Communists and threaten Russia's borders with China.

Almost certainly it was either on Comintern orders or Chinese Communist instructions that Chiang should be set free, and the circumstances strongly suggest not only that the Manchurian officers of the "Young Marshal" would have listened only to the latter but that there is good reason to believe that the *canard* about Wang Ching-wei was embroidered by Chinese Communist agents.

The kidnapping of Chiang had aroused world-wide interest and it was variously portrayed in the press, according to each paper's prejudices: to most of the Western press it was "a dastardly Communist plot", while the Soviet newspapers declared that the whole affair was "a Japanese plot". In Nanking the pro-Japanese Defence Minister, Ho Ying-chin, made the situation far worse than it was by threatening to bomb Sian and send in Chinese armies to co-operate with the Japanese in restoring law and order. Any such move would inevitably have meant Chiang would be killed.

Relations between the Chinese and Russian Communists were not good at this time and there seems to have been a distinct difference of opinion between the Stalinists in Moscow and the Comintern agents on the spot in China. A Kremlin underling is said to have sent a message to Mao Tse-tung ordering him to "free Chiang at once or we shall break all connection with you". It was a stupid message as Mao himself was far distant from Sian at the time.

There was no immediate agreement when Chiang was released, which suggests either that the forces of Chang Hsueh-liang decided to "cool" a dangerous situation, or that Chiang had verbally promised to give some assurance about fighting the Japanese. Eventually, on 22 September 1937, a period long enough for face-saving on both sides, the following agreement was reached on these four points between the Nationalists and Communists:

"1. The Communist Party shall strive for the realisation of Sun Yat-sen's three principles of the people, which answer the present-day need of China.

"2. It shall abandon the policy of armed insurrection against the Kuomintang regime and the policy of Red propaganda and the policy of land confiscation.

"3. It shall abolish the Soviet Government and institute a system of democracy, so that the nation may be politically united.

"4. The Chinese Communist Party shall disband the Red Army and reorganise it in a National Revolutionary Force under direct control of the Military Affairs Commission of the National Government and be ready to obey all orders to take part in resistance to foreign invasion."

From that date—in theory—Communists and Nationalists joined hands against the aggressor, but it was always an uneasy alliance, with neither side ever trusting the other, and if the Communists "proceeded to dishonour" these pledges from the start, as Joseph Keeley asserts, the Kuomintang's attitude to the war with Japan was always ambivalent and at times the pro-Japanese faction in the Party plotted for a negotiated peace with Japan.

What is abundantly clear is that collaboration between the Chinese and Russian Communists in the sphere of intelligence gradually lessened as World War II approached and was certainly markedly less after the uneasy alliance between Mao Tse-tung and Chiang. The Chinese Communists were forced to build up their own intelligence service for this very reason. They were given only such information that the Russians felt it was in the Soviet interest to give them.

The spy ring which Sorge built up for Russia inside China was known as the China Unit and, apart from Miss Smedley and some Japanese, he engaged Chinese and Germans, seeming to prefer them to Russians. He recruited agents in Canton, Nanking, Hanchow, Peiping and even inside Manchuria: his original brief had been to gather information on Chiang Kai-shek's Army but he quickly decided that his main aim should be to obtain intelligence on Japan and that information on Chinese matters was of secondary importance. Possibly for this very reason he found it easier to get people like Agnes Smedley and other Americans to join his network.

Mao Tse-tung managed to acquire some useful intelligence contacts inside Germany, making use of a Japanese Communist who posed as the correspondent of a right-wing Japanese newspaper in Berlin. Sometime in the summer of 1938 Mao's Intelligence Service received news from Berlin by this contact that secret talks were being conducted between the Germans and the Russians in Stockholm. It is probable that the actual venue of the talks was inaccurate, but the news gave Mao cause for alarm. It was on the strength of this that he sent a secret memorandum to Chinese Intelligence officers late in 1938: "The Sino-Japanese War gives the Chinese Communist Party an excellent opportunity to grow. Our policy is to devote 70 per cent of our effort to our own expansion, 20 per cent to coping with the Government [the Kuomintang] and 10 per cent to fighting the Japanese."

This document has been represented as an example of Mao's cynical betrayal of the spirit of his agreement with Chiang, but Mao had no doubts whatsoever that if there should be a Russo-German accord, this would immediately bring the pro-Japanese elements in the Kuomintang to the fore, probably causing them to try to oust Chiang. Thus it was that he laid down the principle that while "self-sacrifice should be made to show our outward obedience to the Central Government and adherance to the Three People's Principles . . . this will serve as camouflage for the existence and development of our party".

Orders were given to senior intelligence officers to obtain detailed reports of the strengths and weaknesses of the Kuomintang in all areas of China and especially "of military intelligence on the Central Government Army's movements and dispositions and their communications". This, it was explained, was to prepare for the final offensive phase "in which our forces should penetrate deeply into Central China, sever the communications of the Central Government troops in various sectors, isolate and disperse them until we are ready for the counter-offensive, and wrest the leadership from the hands of the Kuomintang".

Tai Li and K'ang Sheng Fight for Supremacy 1925-1943

> . . . success lies in retreating. Success lies in being able to retreat at the right moment and in the right manner. This success is made possible by the fact that the retreat is not the forced flight of a weak person, but the voluntary withdrawal of a strong one.
>
> From Commentaries on *I Ching*

Two men, both about the same age, were, unknown to each other, fighting for supremacy in the field of Chinese intelligence in the decade or so immediately preceding World War II. Each knew that the side the other represented was his enemy; each preferred to achieve power in the shadows rather than by any open battle. Both became at certain periods supreme masters of the Chinese Secret Service.

The one was Tai Li, who became master of Chiang Kai-shek's secret police and chief of the Kuomintang Secret Service. The other was K'ang Sheng, ultimately the Director of Intelligence of the People's Republic of China under Mao Tse-tung.

Their careers in the intelligence game lasted far longer than those of any other Secret Service chiefs among the great powers of the world over a similar period. Indeed K'ang's career has lasted well over half a century in espionage and Tai Li's continued for 25 years. The former has seen countless purges and changes in the hierarchy of the Russian Secret Service (with which for brief periods he co-operated in a cautious manner), while Tai Li saw the creation of the American Office of Strategic Services and S.A.C.O. and knew personally and worked with almost every chief of both organisations.

K'ang made the slower progress of the two, but then he had by far the more difficult task. His success, indeed his very survival, depended on building up an underground organisation and for many years constantly retreating from one headquarters to another. The quotation from *I Ching* at the beginning of this chapter must be indelibly engraved in his mind. No man, except Mao himself, made such a success of retreating, or revealed better judgment in knowing when to make a retreat and how to turn it into a tactical gain.

Born in the town of Chu-ch'eng in Shantung Province, half way between Peking and Shanghai, K'ang Sheng was one of the earliest members of the Chinese Communist Party. While he was still at school he developed such a fervent passion for radicalism that, so it is said, he changed his original name of Chao Yun to Chao Jung and later to K'ang Sheng as a mark of opposition to his father, who was a wealthy landlord, and a rejection of the middle-class habits, customs and capitalist creed of his family. For a Chinese youth of the early 1900s this was a totally revolutionary step in a community where respect for the family and above all one's elders came before anything else. Not perhaps an endearing trait, but a sure mark of his strength of character at an early age and his single-mindedness and determination to "go it alone".[1]

K'ang had a sound education according to the standards of that period, but brought to bear on this a marked originality and spirit of criticism. He went to Shanghai University, where there was perhaps more radical fermentation than at most other Chinese universities. Perhaps because he was already twenty-four when he went there he had already acquired sufficient maturity not only to absorb a number of exciting new ideas, but to take the lead in developing them. This university was founded as late as 1923 by Yu Yu-jen, a Kuomintang official, but it rapidly acquired a reputation for extreme radicalism and, being dominated by such leading Communists as Chu Ch'iu-pai, Teng Chung-hsia, Yun Tai-ying, Chang T'ai-lei and

Jen Pi-shih, was soon a breeding ground for recruits for the Communist Party. It was while he was here that K'ang, together with other students, joined the Communist Youth League.

He swiftly showed signs of organisational ability and administrative qualities together with a marked originality in translating classical precepts into modern pragmatism: like Mao Tse-tung he was fascinated by such works as *The Three Kingdoms,* and *I Ching.* No doubt he learned much of the "arts of retreat", which are so fully developed and explained throughout *I Ching,* for he is reputed to have quoted frequently from some of the "commentaries" to his subordinates later in life. Asked once why he insisted on retreating so often himself and caused his agents to be withdrawn with him, he replied: "In *I Ching* it is written that 'the mountain under heaven is the image of retreat'. This may be interpreted by the old-timers as a sign that the superior man keeps the inferior man at a distance. But for practical purposes it means that the man who retreats to the mountains, to a remote and safe headquarters, is being prudent, removing himself not only from contamination with wrong ideas, but enabling him to be self-supporting and self-reliant. He manages to survive in this way and, if he is to keep in touch with what the enemy is doing, he does not allow his agents to be overrun by and captured by the enemy, but withdraws them with him, to be sure he has the latest intelligence before he sends them out again. The British lost the initiative for two years in World War II by not realising the importance of this advice: they allowed all their networks in Europe to be overrun by the enemy."[2]

K'ang joined the Communist Party as a full member in 1924 and was given the task of being an organiser of labour in Shanghai together with Teng Chung-hsuia and Li Li-san. But from the very beginning he was plunged into espionage. He had an instinctive liking for intrigue and intelligence-gathering, not in any romantic way, but because his mind was attuned to the fact that the Communist Party of China would only succeed and survive if it had its own independent spy networks. Above all, he was pragmatic. Added to this he was loyal, obedient and undoubtedly brave and intellectually superior to most of his colleagues, a remarkable combination of qualities in a young radical.

Shanghai, as the major international espionage playground of China, was perhaps the perfect testing ground for his talents, and from the very beginning K'ang had decided views about the part he should play in the movement. Under his cover as an organiser of labour he developed his own spy service and kept the Party supplied with a steady stream of intelligence. Between 1925–7 he was appointed director of the Organisation Department of the Communist Party Shanghai District Committee, remaining in this post even after Chiang Kai-shek's anti-communist drive into Shanghai in April 1927.

This was the moment when he began to be a co-ordinator of Communist Party intelligence, for what existed at that time as a Party espionage service was in its most elementary stages. He seems to have taken great pains to safeguard his position by establishing some links with people inside the Kuomintang. In 1930 he was arrested in Shanghai and, in the circumstances then prevailing, he would normally have remained in prison, or have even been liquidated. However, he very soon got himself released through the intervention of Ting Wei-fen, a Kuomintang leader from Shantung, who seems to have been a secret ally. Nor did he then retreat from Shanghai—which, knowing K'ang's penchant for always retreating before it was too late, suggests that he retained some kind of protection from the Kuomintang, incredible though this may seem. At any rate, in January 1931 he played a prominent part in the Communist Party's fourth plenum in Shanghai, when the pro-Soviet faction gained control of many of the Party's principal appointments.

K'ang never allowed his individual quirks or political theories to impinge upon Party arguments: in all these he remained the quiet pragmatist on the sidelines, listening, offering advice and information when requested, but never forcing a point. Indeed he kept himself entirely free from any factions within the Party and this seems to have applied equally to the pro-Soviet group. But he was already respected as one of the most loyal and intellectual of all the younger Communists, and after this plenum he was appointed Director of the Party's Organisation Department.

In effect this meant that he was already a key figure in the Party's intelligence organisation, though his actual status in the Party, other than the post just mentioned, remained somewhat obscure. There is some speculation as to whether he was then already a member of the Politburo: there are conflicting reports on this. Already he was practising his policy of "retreat", for, while remaining in the Shanghai underground, he moved into the French concession in that international city, where he was safe from Kuomintang interference. He operated from a "secret house" in the concession and used this as a hiding place for other prominent Communists, such as Ch'en Keng, during 1932–33. He also acquired considerable knowledge of French intelligence methods and ingratiated himself with a number of French residents, some of whom provided him with intelligence links. That he acquitted himself efficiently in this period there seems little doubt, for in 1933 he was relieved of his Shanghai post and sent to Moscow to study Soviet security and intelligence techniques, an appointment which was in itself a tribute to his ability and trustworthiness.

In Moscow he quickly acquired a shrewd appreciation of the merits of the Comintern, already somewhat under a cloud, and of the G.R.U. (Soviet military intelligence), while quietly listening to but always mistrusting the N.K.V.D. and the Stalinists. The Chinese Communists could not have sent a better man to Moscow: he retained his integrity and all his devotion to the Chinese version of communism while having grave doubts about Russian loyalty to the Chinese cause, at the same time being sufficiently tactful not to antagonise the Stalinists. He also proved to be a most effective propagandist for the Chinese Communist Party and it is a mark of K'ang's approach to intelligence that he has always regarded propaganda as a vital part of the work of any espionage organisation.

His work in this sphere was prolific. Without giving away anything which was vital to his own Party's security, he published a series of essays in Moscow in 1936, revealing a certain amount of detail about the Chinese Communists' organisation in Shanghai in the late 'twenties and early 'thirties, the main theme of which was the Chinese Communist "martyrs". He also wrote a book—intended mainly for Russian consumption—entitled *Revolutionary China Today,* in which he greatly impressed the Russians by his claim that China had two million trade union members in the Communist-controlled areas and that the C.C.P. had three hundred thousand members. He was a lucid, compelling writer, sure of his facts and with a wealth of detail to support them.

K'ang probably realised from the beginning that what he would be allowed to learn of Soviet intelligence techniques would be extremely limited—limited, in fact, to the kind of techniques which the Russians thought he should have in order to supply them with information. Perhaps this is why he devoted so much time to propaganda for the Chinese cause: certainly his efforts in this direction were appreciated back in China. He acquired a working knowledge of the Russian language and also spoke a certain amount of English, French and German. (Some sources suggest his knowledge of English and French is rather better than he claims for himself.)

As to what intelligence he achieved for China during this period in Moscow it is not easy to say. K'ang has always been a man with a hunch, a gift for sensing the truth behind the camouflage and, despite some denials on this point, it seems certain that he used his powers of deduction to fill in the gaps with which Soviet secretiveness confronted him. He met Richard Sorge, the man who became Russia's "ace" spy in the Far East, and indirectly established an important link with him through Comintern sources and without the Stalinists knowing about it. He also had an understanding with some Dutch Communists. But his main aim throughout this period was to do his utmost to ensure support from Russia in the event of an attack by Japan and to promise to support Russia if she was attacked by the Japanese.

He made a number of lengthy and important

speeches—perhaps lectures would be a better description—during this period, and he saw to it that they were published in several languages, including English, one such edition being brought out in 1934 by the Workers Library Publishers in New York, in which he gave an account of the resistance movement in Japanese-controlled Manchuria.

All this was little more than a theoretical apprenticeship in the intelligence game, for none knew better than K'ang that the Russians still regarded Chiang Kai-shek as the master of China, however much they might wish to see him overthrown. But even in his absence from China such was the respect in which K'ang was held that, at the Second All-China Congress of Soviets held in Juichin in Kiangsi Province in August 1934, he was elected a member of the Central Executive Committee, and he was already a firm favourite of Mao Tse-tung.

A year later K'ang was one of the chief Chinese delegates to the Seventh Comintern Congress in Moscow and was one of the principal speakers in favour of a "united front against fascism", and for some time after this he was ostensibly more of a writer pleading the cause of China against Japanese and European aggression than an obvious intelligence chief. Few intelligence chiefs in history have entered so publicly and wholeheartedly into intellectual polemics and pure politics as did K'ang, but here again he showed his respect for team-work and eschewed power for its own sake by often collaborating with other writers solely for the sake of presenting a stronger argument. One striking example of this was his joint authorship with Ch'en Shao-yu of an article denouncing "as specious comparisons" Lenin's acceptance of the famous 1918 Brest-Litovsk Treaty with Germany (buying time by sacrificing space) and the situation in China *vis-à-vis* Japan. Their argument was that all Chinese must stand and fight. The article was published in Paris first and later quoted in a Comintern journal in 1936.[3]

But by 1937, when the situation of the Chinese Communists was becoming acutely difficult, K'ang was recalled to China to take charge of intelligence in the new Communist capital of Yenan in North Shensi. This was in many respects an admirable if remote headquarters for Communist intelligence, as it was close to the Mongolian border and enabled K'ang to maintain and build up some contacts inside Russia without the knowledge of the Soviet Government. For by now K'ang had few illusions about the deviousness of Russian communism: he saw quite clearly that whatever its professions—or rather, despite the idealistic professions of the now almost doomed Comintern—it was a regime which practised imperialistic power under the guise of being the friend of other nations threatened by imperialism.

From this time his exact official status was effectively masked. He preferred to work in the shadows of power and took great care to cover up his real assignment in the intelligence field. David Wise and Thomas B. Ross state that by 1939 he had apparently become "director of the Social Affairs Department, the long-standing euphemism for the party's central organ for security and intelligence".[4] The Biographic Dictionary of Chinese Communism (1921–65) puts it this way: "Once again there are reports that he assumed (or reassumed) a seat as a member of the Politburo, and still others that he also became a member of the Party Secretariat. But perhaps most important is the fact that he returned to his special field of security and intelligence work. For reasons of security the Communists [Chinese] have published very little about the chief security organ, the Social Affairs Department (She-hui pu), but it is probable that K'ang headed this department from the late 1930s."

There, for the moment, we will leave K'ang Sheng, for it will suffice to show exactly how he progressed during the period when the Chinese Communists were not merely in opposition and a minority in the nation, but constantly on the retreat. K'ang had arrived at a position of great power inconspicuously and despite a long absence from the country.

Curiously enough, despite the obscurity which K'ang Sheng courted during his career, Tai Li took even greater pains to cover up his origins. While a good deal of K'ang Sheng's early life is quite easily traceable, so much of Tai Li's is wrapped in mystery and half-truths and confused by the removal of evidence so that it is almost impossible to trace his beginnings with any degree of accuracy.

Tai Li is reputed to have been born in Chekiang Province, not far from the home of Chiang Kai-shek's family. It is, however, very doubtful whether his family was as distinguished as that of K'ang Sheng and the earliest positive reference to him is that in 1925 he was recorded as a member of Chiang Kai-shek's Military Police. By 1927 he held the rank of captain in the Military Police of the Kuomintang in Shanghai. On the other hand there is some evidence that for a time at least—between 1923 and 1927—he was secretly working with the Communists. There can, however, be little doubt that he did this solely as a ploy to safeguard his own future if Chiang Kai-shek failed to consolidate his position, or else as an attempt to infiltrate the Communist ranks.

It is fascinating to speculate on what would have happened if Tai Li and K'ang Sheng had been brought together, or if they had at this stage of their careers been brought into direct conflict with one another. They were both in Shanghai in the same period, but there is no evidence that they ever met, or even that they spied on one another.

The two men were in most respects totally different. K'ang was the quiet, short-sighted intellectual, hiding behind his thick glasses, with a thin dark line of a moustache, who smiled occasionally, but always, it seemed, with difficulty, and as though this was a grudging concession to anyone who made a humorous remark. He took life seriously and his relationship with his wife, Tsao Yi-ou, was almost a political partnership: they shared the same serious approach to life and indeed Tsoa Yi-ou became an outspoken radical in her own right later in life. Tai Li, on the other hand, though he took the same kind of pains to remove traces of his early life (having records burnt and people who knew him in his teens actually killed) rather like the late Sir Basil Zaharoff, was an extrovert. He could exude bonhomie and greet Western Intelligence leaders with gusto and a great show of hospitality. He not only liked to crack jokes with foreigners, but loved to try out his own ideas of espionage theory on them. K'ang would never do this. K'ang was rarely seen mixing with leading foreigners; Tai Li went out of his way to get to know them.

That Tai Li had already acquired important contacts as an intelligence agent was apparent when Chiang Kai-shek succeeded in his coup against Shanghai in 1927. It was Tai Li who gave him a list of Communists who should be arrested and eliminated and no doubt K'ang Sheng's name was among them. If so, he certainly foiled Tai Li on this occasion as indeed on many others.

But it was mainly on the strength of his ability to root out, arrest and to often ruthlessly execute without trial—sometimes without trace—opponents of Chiang Kai-shek that Tai Li rose so speedily to become chief of Chiang's Secret Police. But he also had influence with a number of bankers, guild chiefs and heads of secret societies, some of whom he was able to cajole into financing the Kuomintang in certain areas.

Horrific stories about some of Tai Li's summary executions are still told. André Malraux, the author and former Minister of State for Cultural Affairs under General de Gaulle, paid his first visit to China at this period and in his book *La Condition Humaine* he is said to have based one of his characters and one of the central incidents on Tai Li and his misdeeds.

"According to reports of this time, some of which were incorporated in André Malraux's novel . . . he [Tai Li] invented a new and efficient method of killing Chiang's enemies," wrote Oliver J. Caldwell.[5] "He lined up some locomotives on a siding, got the fireboxes red hot, opened their doors, tied down the whistles to shut out the screams, and one after another threw his living victims into the fiery furnaces. According to tradition, thousands of labour leaders and students and intellectuals were killed in a few days. A good many of them may have been Communists. Thus Tai Li earned the nickname of the Butcher."

Tai Li was the kind of striking personality who could make his presence felt at a distance, whereas the myopic K'ang might be passed by without a second glance. K'ang possessed many of the attributes of the intelligence agent in the field—which, of course, he had been. One could never imagine Tai Li being a spy: he would have attracted far too much attention. Unlike K'ang he had never been one.

Handsome, thin, with the kind of stiff, upright back which he must have copied from the Chinese Army's Prussian instructors, Tai Li took grotesquely long, quick strides when he walked, whether on or off duty. "At least," said one of his officers ruefully, "you can tell when Tai Li is coming. You can spot that gigantic stride of his fifty yards away. You can tell whether he is angry or in a good humour by the pace of his stride."

Politically and as far as Ministers were concerned, Tai Li kept in the background and, like K'ang, never interfered directly in purely political problems, seeming perfectly satisfied with the office he held and making no bid for higher honours. There was no reason why he should. After he had been made head of Chiang's secret military police and acquired the directorship of the whole of China's Intelligence Service, he had been made a General and was by the mid-'thirties one of the most powerful men in China.

Not an intellectual like K'ang, not nearly as well versed as the latter in Russian or even in European affairs, Tai Li was no ordinary soldier, or jumped-up military policeman. He had a personality that burned into those who met him: they were either terrified out of their wits and mesmerised by his sharp, piercing, darting eyes which seemed to take in every detail of an individual from head to foot, or fascinated and charmed by the play he made with his exquisite and expressive hands. As senior American generals were quick to learn in World War II, he possessed great power of command. To his own men he was a rigid disciplinarian, a smartly turned-out officer who would not tolerate slovenliness. He had a great sense of the theatrical and often stage-managed his public appearances to create the maximum impression whether on his own men or on visitors.

Gregarious, efficient, cruel, cunning and always in total control of himself, Tai Li, while not having a brilliant mind, was brimful of ideas and, if only he had had more experience of the world outside China, he might have come very near to being a great Secret Service chief. As it was he was a colossus who set out to give Chiang's China something like the first total espionage machine and co-ordinated Secret Service that she had known in modern times. It was an Intelligence Service which lacked the integrity of the Communists' far smaller organisation and was, not unnaturally, less well informed on Soviet Russia. But as far as internal security was concerned it was more ruthless and efficient than any of its predecessors; its brutal methods were never much publicised in the West, because technically Chiang Kai-shek was an ally, but they owed a great deal to ideas borrowed from the Germans, especially as regards interrogation techniques.

Tai Li was reputed to be the only officer who was allowed to wear his sword in the presence of Chiang Kai-shek. All the Kuomintang leader's Ministers, except those of the extreme right-wing, were fearful of Tai Li; and to those of China's masses who had heard whispers of his dread deeds and summary executions he was certainly a legendary bogeyman.

In many respects Tai Li was like a spy chief of fiction. He believed that two of the most important weapons in the espionage game were women and alcohol. He used both not merely to obtain information, but to bring foreigners, and especially Americans, under his power, and also to seduce them to his side. One of his greatest earliest successes was to lure Chang Kuo-tao, a leading Communist and one of the few ever to defect, from being an extreme left-wing Communist to an ultra right-wing supporter of Chiang Kai-shek.

When Tai Li heard in the early summer of 1938 that Chang Kuo-tao was being subjected to considerable criticism inside the Communist Party, he put out feelers to win him over, using an attractive female agent to act as go-between. Han Suyin writes that Chang Kuo-tao "in the compulsion to escape which seems to have been the mainspring of his actions . . . fled to the arms of Chiang's secret police, was greeted with honour by Tai Li, the number one hatchet man of Chiang Kai-shek, and began working as an informer against the Communist Party".[6]

Even in his use of women and drink Tai Li kept a tight rein on the techniques he employed with both these "weapons". He employed a large number of female agents, most of them hand-picked for their good looks as well as their brains. He insisted that they were kept under the same strict code of discipline as the male agents and several (usually the best looking, of course) came directly under his orders and, when not on assignments, were housed in various villas and pavilions which he owned and frequently visited.

While he regarded such perquisites as right for himself as head of the Secret Service, he did not permit any fraternising between them and his male subordinates. He mistrusted the influence of women on men in the Secret Service and disapproved of his chief officers and agents either being married or having permanent mistresses. "It is bad for discipline and can be highly dangerous," he told them. "Too close an association with women leads to two people learning what only one should know. Your physical needs will be provided for by the specially selected women I assign to you and in such places as you can satisfy your needs under tight security, but in comfort." He applied the same rule to servants who had wives and very often to visitors who wanted to bring their wives with them. The servants were told to leave their wives behind when they had to travel with their masters to one or other of the Tai Li "holiday camps", as one American sardonically described them.

Even Tai Li's deputy commander of the Secret Service, General P'an Chi-wu, was subject to his master's ruthless rules concerning women. P'an had been deeply in love with a Chinese girl and wanted to marry her. Tai Li had brutally forbidden the marriage. When P'an insisted that he was prepared to leave the Service in order to marry her, Tai Li shrugged his shoulders but said nothing. Shortly afterwards the girl died, whether from natural causes or because she was ordered to be killed by Tai Li is not clear. But when the heartbroken P'an asked for permission to leave the Service and enter a monastery, his request was refused. He then suspected that Tai Li would never allow him to leave the Service alive.

"Drink makes men talk and pour out secrets," was another of Tai Li's adages, "but not Chinese wine. There is not enough alcohol in it and it is no use plying Westerners, used to hard liquor, with Chinese wine."

This is a brief sketch of the man who tried to unify China by terror and failed in the end lamentably, yet one who reached the peak of his power in the mid-1940s when, as Chiang's Secret Service Director, he not only controlled several secret societies, but in status and in sharing information was on a par with Commodore Miles who was later to become head of the American O.S.S. It proved a one-sided arrangement, with Tai Li getting by far the best of the bargain.

22

The Four Rival Secret Services 1937-1945

I went to China as a civil affairs officer. Since there was no need for an officer trained to govern conquered territory, I drifted from one assignment to another until I suddenly found myself attached to the office of Strategic Services. . . . I was assigned to Chiang's Secret Military Police. . . . Here I was openly a double agent, working for my own army and for the Chinese. Soon I became secretly a triple agent when I agreed to represent the three great Chinese secret societies (Triad). . . .

Oliver J. Caldwell in *A Secret War*

BETWEEN 1937 and 1945 an increasing number of governments were operating in China at one and the same time. This situation of the divided rule of a vast territory reached its peak during World War II when, at one time, there were five such governments: the Kuomintang Government of Chiang Kai-shek, which ultimately had its headquarters in Chungking; Mao Tse-tung's miniature government in Yenan; the Japanese puppet government in North China; the Wang Ching-wei so-called Nationalist Government in Outer Mongolia; and a pro-Soviet Government in Sinkiang Province.

Apart from these five governments, the Americans, British and Russians, all in varying degrees, were participating in this chaotic situation of a war-torn and divided China and so this nation became the battle-ground of the spy services of all the great powers, with the Japanese as the invader often sending spies in ahead of their armies. The arts of modern espionage were learned in the hardest possible way not by any one single Chinese Secret Service, but by no less than four rival Chinese Intelligence organisations.

However, before naming and detailing the aims of all these four services, it is necessary to provide some background history if only to explain how the original three rival services ultimately split into four. Some surprising allegations, most of them unfounded, were made in the late 'thirties by both the pro-Soviet Sinkiang faction and the Chinese Communists that Chiang Kai-shek was dominated by German and Italian advisers and that he was aiming to come in on the Axis side against the Western world. Whatever Chiang's faults, however much his Kuomintang secret police may have had fascist methods, Chiang never had any sympathies with Hitler or Mussolini. Nor would it have made political sense for him to have made any move in this direction prior to the German conquest of Europe in 1940, for even his own spy service made it quite clear to him that the Germans and Italians were backing the Japanese.

He had used German military advisers, including the notorious General Von Seeckt, who had organised the secret rearmament and training of a German army after World War I, but it is not true, as has been asserted by some historians, that he made "the Nazi Captain Walter Steenes . . . chief of his personal intelligence".[1]

273

No foreigner would have been given such high rank by Chiang, who was himself intensely suspicious of most foreigners and in this respect totally different from Sun Yat-sen. Though Morris Cohen was still high in his favour, this was because by this time Cohen was something of a living legend with a privileged position—almost, in fact, an honorary mandarin. The fact that Cohen was still high in Chiang's esteem in the late 'thirties and early 'forties effectively gives the lie to the pro-Nazi influence, for one can be quite sure that Cohen would never have tolerated working with a regime that permitted Nazis to run an Intelligence unit.

One proof of Cohen's influence at this time was that when the Japanese made use of poison gas in the Sino-Japanese war Cohen was largely responsible for providing the Kuomintang with a cylinder of the gas which, after analysis, enabled them to confirm to the world that this deadly weapon had been used against them.

But Cohen's intelligence career was cut short for a period in 1942 when he was sent to Hongkong to rescue Madame Sun Yat-sen, who refused to leave. He was finally trapped by the Japanese, spending the remainder of the war in a Japanese concentration camp until he was repatriated to Canada.

The civil war between the Communists and Nationalists and between all the various factions in China continued secretly (and sometimes hardly even secretly) after the accord between the Kuomintang and the Communists. Neither side took the accord seriously, each knowing that, regardless of whether or not Japan was defeated, sooner or later there would have to be a showdown between Kuomintang and Communists as to who was to rule China. The two ideologies, which might have seemed close enough together for a rational compromise in Sun Yat-sen's time, gradually drew further apart, Mao Tse-tung moving even further to the left, while Chiang adopted more authoritarian measures and right-wing policies.

Early on, Chiang's forces put up some stiff resistance to the Japanese until the fall of Hankow and

Canton, but the Generalissimo had the stupendous task of facing the enemy with only a part of his armies. Chiang could not risk all his forces against Japan, even if he had wished, for he still had to be on his guard against treachery from a number of sources, individual warlords as well as Communists.

To be fair, in the early stages of the war with Japan and after the accord with the Communists, Tai Li did his best to expand the Secret Service into a powerful "third force" to be used against the enemy both inside Japanese-occupied China and in China itself. Chiang Kai-shek, as we have seen, had much earlier made use of certain branches of the Triads, but Tai Li's plan was to summon the leaders of the Triads and some of the smaller secret societies and ask them to form intelligence networks to spy on the Japanese and to carry on the war by sabotage and the planting of agents behind the Japanese lines. What Tai Li was really seeking was to incorporate into his own Secret Service an informal arrangement that had existed since the mid-'twenties, but, partly by cajolement, partly by playing up the theme of patriotism and, if necessary, by threats, to make a bold bid to take over all the secret societies of China. In the beginning the plan succeeded and Tai Li managed to get himself elected as the President of an amalgamation of secret socieites. This, of course, did not mean that the individual societies lost their identity or their own prerogatives, though Tai Li would have preferred it to have been that way.

By this period some of the Triads had already switched from being purely protection societies of a relatively benevolent nature to the pursuit of crime. Up to the time of the Pacific War the "Greens", or, more accurately, the Green Circle, were the dominant secret society of the Shanghai underworld. They maintained an iron code of discipline and an authoritarian hierarchy to which the quasi-Triads of today could never pretend. The Green Circle had a million members in the Yangtse Valley alone and probably as many as a hundred thousand members in Shanghai. They dealt directly with the French police in the French concession of the international city and the latter welcomed their co-operation in solving crimes in which the "Greens" had no financial or "protection" interest. Not unnaturally, in view of this association with the French, the "Greens" were mixed up in espionage and had been courted by more than one power and more than one of the rival Secret Services of China. Their two head men were Dou Fu-seng and Wang Hsiao-lai, who managed to combine directorship of the Green Circle with banking, commercial and municipal interests as well as careers in extortion and murder. The Green Circle was easily the largest of the secret societies and some estimates put its membership as high as four million at one time. They identified themselves by the way in which they lit a cigarette, pushed a tea-cup across a table to a waiter, or waved a greeting in the street.

During World War II the titular ruler of the Green Circle was Tu Yu-sung, an astute man who had managed to cover up traces of his earlier life, lived in the French concession where he could not be touched by the Chinese police, and who was reputed to control prostitution and drug rackets. He was also an intermediary between businessmen in Shanghai and their workers, his brief being to check any hostile moves against the bosses, while seeming to serve the workers' interests. A particularly nasty racketeer in a country where on the whole leading racketeers were sophisticated operators with a sense of style and even a redeeming sense of humour, Tu Yu-sung also specialised in kidnapping. Yet in the Chinese *Who's Who* he was listed as a "banker and philanthropist"!

His most daring attempt at pushing his protection racket was when Chiang Kai-shek once visited Shanghai long before the Japanese occupation and Tu sent the Generalissimo a note asking whether Madame Chiang would like "protection" while she was in the city. Chiang tersely and angrily replied "no". Soon afterwards Madame Chiang received a note asking her to visit her sister who was sick and a car was sent to pick her up. When Chiang found his wife was missing he immediately telephoned Tu's office and was told that some of the "Greens" had seen Madame Chiang riding around the streets of Shanghai and had taken her into "protective custody" for her own safety.

"You see," said Tu, "Madame was in a strange car and this can be a dangerous city. We thought it was safest to look after her. Of course this has cost my men a great deal of time and effort and no doubt, Generalissimo, you will be happy to pay them for their services."

It was an indirect challenge to Chiang and he paid up. The sum involved was reputed to be "substantial, but modest", whatever that might imply, but ever afterwards the Chiangs paid protection to Tu when they visited Shanghai and thereafter, so the rumour goes, the Green Circle became more respectable and began to establish links with various Buddhist orders, to give protection to small farmers and to dabble rather less in prostitution except where it used the latter as a branch of the intelligence service which Tai Li, after striking a hard bargain, established with Tu. It is probable that the links with the Buddhists were for espionage reasons and not out of a piety which Tu never pretended to profess.

The Green Circle had a "class structure" of officers, known as "Brothers", and of rank and file members who had to swear total allegiance to their officers. For this reason alone, quite apart from its huge membership, it not only had a great influence in China, but was courted both by the Kuomintang and Japan. On the whole the Green Circle was pro-Kuomintang, though Tu Yu-sung himself took the precaution of moving from Shanghai to Lanchow in the North-West where he was outside the influence both of the Japanese and of Chiang Kai-shek.

Yet the Green Circle typified the kind of secret society which Mao Tse-tung detested and against which he warned all his followers. In this respect he was not only fully backed by K'ang Sheng, but the Communist Intelligence chief took the greatest pains to ensure that no member of his organisation, small as it was, established any links with any secret society: as a Communist he condemned the membership of such societies as rigidly as the Vatican forbade membership of the Masonic fraternity to Roman Catholics. This may have robbed the Communists of some useful information in the early years of their exile, but in the long run it paid handsome dividends. Thereafter it was clearly understood that while, in certain circumstances, infiltration might be permitted, the enrolment of secret societies as allies was banned. That this decision was absolutely right is indisputable: the secret societies today have deteriorated and become so involved in criminal enterprises and commercial piracy wherever large colonies of Chinese exiles gather that none of them could be trusted as a reliable and patriotic ally.

Mao had learned the lesson which the Americans failed to learn when they so enthusiastically backed the Mafia exiles in the U.S.A. prior to the invasion of Sicily in 1943. Mussolini had successfully stamped out the Mafia; the U.S.A. by releasing Mafia gangsters from jail and putting them back into Sicily, paved the way for a revival of this world-wide criminal secret society after World War II. Successive Italian governments have suffered ever since from repeated failures to put down the Mafia due to its infiltration into so many Italian political parties, not least the so-called Christian Democrats. And in the U.S.A. itself the Mafia has achieved far greater power and influence than it ever had before.

Emulating Mussolini, Mao Tse-tung drove the Triads out of China and they sprang up in such tarnished outposts of colonialism as Hongkong where they operate in much the same way as the Mafia, increasing their membership by threats and blackmail, seeking not only to control big business and criminal enterprises, but to infiltrate police and civil service. A depressing measure of their success has been the corruption of the higher ranks of the British-officered Hongkong Colonial Police Force which has resulted in a number of scandals in recent years. According to the latest official figures from Hongkong's Police Force approximately eleven thousand young criminals have been enrolled today in the "quasi-Triads" (as they are called), while the elderly ranks of the conventional old-time Triads have been declining to well under ten thousand. But it is doubtful if this estimate is anywhere near accuracy and the true figures are almost certainly higher. As for the Chinese Communists, they have been quite happy to see some of their criminal citizens escape across to Hongkong to join the Triads and so rid themselves of a crime problem.

This sudden peep into the present day is important even if it disturbs the chronology of the book because it shows how a Secret Service anxious to take a long-term view of its requirements cannot afford to make short-term accommodations with gangster societies. When Tai Li made his bid to mould the secret societies into his own organisation, though some of them were deeply involved in protection rackets, others were merely benevolent protection societies for their own members and in some cases both semi-religious and patriotic. But the trend towards crime had already begun, as is evidenced by the Green Circle.

In South China the dominant secret society was the Red Circle, smaller numerically than the Green Circle, but powerful in its own sphere of influence. Its total membership was probably about two and a half millions. Prior to the Japanese invasion its headquarters were in Canton, though it had branches in Hongkong and, so it was rumoured, in other places where there were Chinese exiles or emigrants. When the Japanese armies moved into China the Red Circle set up its headquarters in Kweilin where it made smuggling its chief source of revenue.

Like the Green Circle, the Red Circle was also a Triad to which the rival Secret Services, always excepting the Communists, paid close attention. The head of this society was Ming Teh, a tall, strikingly dominant man who affected a shaven head and monk's attire and who most willingly offered the services of his society to Tai Li for guerrilla activities against the Japanese.

There were many such societies, some of them too small to be of any value to the rival secret services, and some, indeed, whose motives were purely religious or whose rôle was merely that of a benevolent welfare club. Such societies were the White Lotus, a Buddhist organisation, though one which many years before had been anti-Manchu, and the Red Spears, who flourished mainly in the valleys of the Yellow River: they were prepared to fight the Japanese, the Kuomintang and the Communists, as and when either of these threatened their well-being in any way. Even the Roman Catholic community, which had to struggle against oppression and downright persecution in the North-West provinces in this period, managed to organise its own secret service, designed mainly to keep a watch on the Communists, regarded as their principal enemies. Its aim was partly for self-protection and to establish an early warning system when Communists were planning action against them and partly to counter Communist activity. For the latter reason the information supplied by it was eagerly sought by foreign Secret Services, especially by the Americans.

One of the most interesting of the secret societies was that of the Ko Lao Hui, or Society of Elder Brothers, which was in effect the third society in the Triad—i.e. the third group after the Red Circle and the Green Circle. From a Secret Service point of view this was in many ways the most important of the Triads: historically it had a record of political activity and could boast that Sun Yat-sen had been one of its members.

Ko Lao Hui had done much to ensure a successful outcome to the revolution of 1911, but latterly it had become a society of wealthy merchants. But, with that whimsical disregard for logic which Chinese secret societies have so often displayed, while Chiang Kai-shek was the titular leader of the society the real head man and the one who held the power was Feng Yu-hsiang, the so-called "Christian general", who in October 1924 had rebelled against his master Wu Pei-fu, marched to Peking and ended the rule of the American-backed "rump president", Tsao Kun. Feng Yu-hsiang, it will be recalled, was the general Trebitsch Lincoln threatened to support if Wu Pei-fu declined to listen to him. He was an interesting character, not without many merits, if somewhat ambivalent in displaying them.

The Ko Lao Hui was particularly strong in Szechwan and some of the North-West provinces: it was therefore an ideal organisation to use for spying both

Chien-lung, Emperor of China, who gave audience to the British
Mission in 1793. From a print published in 1801. *(Mary Evans)*

Kuang Hsu, a reformer who made enemies *(Mary Evans)*

林則徐〔公元一七八五—一八五〇〕

100 郵民國華中
REPUBLIC OF CHINA

Lin Tse-hsu, the counter-espionage chief appointed to tackle opium smuggling. This picture of him appears on a one-dollar stamp of Taiwan, recently issued *(From the author's collection)*

The gardens of the Imperial Palace, Peking *(Illustrated London News)*

The last Empress of China, Tsu Hsi *(Illustrated London News)*

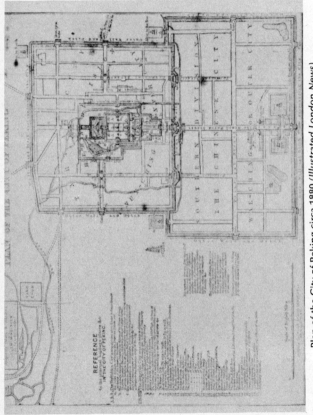

Plan of the City of Peking circa 1880 (*Illustrated London News*)

Above: The defence of the Peking Legations: Russians repelling the Boxer attack on the barricade *(Illustrated London News)*.
Below: A detachment from H.M.S. *Terrible* in action against Boxer marauders, 1900 *(Illustrated London News)*

Boxers travelling on the Imperial Grand Canal, which extends
from Canton to Peking *(Illustrated London News)*

"Two Gun" Cohen. General Morris Abraham Cohen was for
more than thirty years intelligence adviser to successive Chinese
Governments *(Associated Press)*

Ignatius Trebitsch Lincoln, former British MP, who was engaged in intelligence activities in China during the early days of Chiang Kai-shek's regime

Trebitsch Lincoln's visiting card, showing his Chinese pseudonym

Abbot CHAO KUNG

POPPE ROAD
FU SHAN LI 6/8
Third Special Area

TIENTSIN

China

照空大和尚 收啓

禰善里八號 七緯路

天津特別三區

Chiang Kai-shek, photographed during the 'thirties *(Thomson Newspapers)*

Dr Ch'ien Hsue-shen, lured back from the USA to China to take charge of China's nuclear programme, after spending fifteen years working on US rocket programmes *(Associated Press)*

A corner of Yokohama where two Chinas are fighting. *Above:*
First the Republic of China put its own notice-board on a plot of
land which had been vacant since the war—"No Entry, the
Ground of the Republic of China Consulate General in
Yokohama." *Below:* However, Communist Chinese supporters
burnt down the signboard and put up their own to say this was
the land of the People's Republic of China. Fearing reprisals, the
Japanese Government, the local authorities and private individuals
dared not purchase this ground, which the Taiwan Government
wished to sell. In such a situation, and with such well-organised
local Chinese support, it is obviously not hard to pursue an
ideological offensive, and easy to influence both Chinese and
Japanese to help Peking intelligence efforts. *(Operation Jackdaw
photograph)*

လုံၿြံစြာသြားလာခြင့်လက်မှတ်

SAFE CONDUCT PASS

THE BEARER IS A PATRIOT WHO HAS DECIDED TO
ENLIST IN THE FORCES OF LIBERATION. ASSIST HIM
IN EVERY WAY. PROTECT HIM FROM HARM AND
FEED HIM AND CARE FOR HIS WOUNDS. GRANT HIM
EVERY COURTESY AND ESCORT HIM TO THE   NEA-
REST PATRIOTIC FORCES H.Q.

ၿမိဝလကျာ

General Let Ya
Chairman of the War Council
Patriotic Forces

Taung-Gyi-Ko-Lone

Safe-conduct pass issued to Chinese-backed ''patriots'' of the
Burmese Liberation Forces *(Operation Jackdaw photograph)*

Above: Wang Kuan-cheng, head of the Chinese General
Chamber of Commerce, Hongkong, which normally sent out
invitations to China's two trade fairs *(Hongkong Standard)*. *Below:*
Ho Yin, Chinese community leader in Macao, with the Governor
of Macao at a reception *(Hongkong Standard)*

Li Chu-sang, deputy chief of the Hsin Hua News Agency at the funeral service of Chiang Sze-chao, member of the Chinese Congress who died in Hongkong *(Hongkong Standard)*

Fei Yee-ming, publisher of the *Ta Kung Pao*, shows up at a protest parade outside the Hongkong Government House in 1967 *(Hongkong Standard)*

Assembly shop for missiles being built at Lop Nor *(Thomson Newspapers)*

"Lucky Brand" opium produced by the Chinese Communists *(Operation Jackdaw photograph)*

幸運商標

道地原料 精工監製

如假包換 老少無欺

LUCKY

TRADE MARK LUCKY BRAND

Lin Piao

Sun Yat-sen *(Topix)*

Chinese Communist Deputy Foreign Minister Chia Kuan-hua, left, laughs with Ambassador Huang Hua after taking their seats in the UN General Assembly *(Associated Press)*

The Red Chinese advance party being greeted at the United Nations. Kao Liang is shaking hands with Byron G. Castrounis, a UN protocol official *(Associated Press)*

Gerrard Street, centre of London's Chinatown *(Thomson Newspapers)*

on the Communists and the Russians. Not surprisingly it had the reputation of being a quasi-fascist front.

Finally, there were the Blueshirts, a most untypical Chinese society, based not upon the age-old principle of *pao-chia,* or "family espionage", but upon European fascist ideas. They were dangerous for a short period when they launched sabotage operations under the directions of Tai Li, but in the long term they did not prove of much importance.

Oliver J. Caldwell, an American who was born in China, educated there and who loved the country and felt himself emotionally involved with the Chinese people, had some considerable experience of Tai Li and his organisation during World War II. While disagreeing with his statement that "the Secret Military police of [Tai Li] was frankly modelled after the Gestapo",[2] much of what he has to say about Tai Li is valid. Of Tai's formation of a coalition of secret societies he states that "for a while things apparently went smoothly. Nearly everyone was patriotic in the early days of the war. Intelligence nets were organised and guerrilla bands operated successfully at great cost to the Japanese. . . . But as the years went on, something went wrong. Tai Li had a tremendous weapon in his hands. He used it to strengthen his control of the Chinese people rather than to fight the common enemy. . . . It was the boast of the organisation that there was not a single village in China in which there was not a Tai Li spy to report on subversive activities. By terrorising a man's family it was easy to keep the man in line."[3]

The boast was certainly exaggerated: there were areas of China where Tai Li could justly claim such spy coverage, but many others that he had only partially penetrated. Also it is doubtful whether the coalition of secret societies ever lasted effectively for more than a few years.

Twice Chiang Kai-shek was forced to make indirect approaches to the Japanese through his Intelligence Service, so desperate was his position. There was no great popular uprising throughout China against the

Japanese as Communist mythology has propagated, and the United States did nothing to give Chiang any hope of their intervening on his behalf. By the outbreak of World War II Chiang knew that ultimately he would be faced with two choices: either he would win full American aid and so stave off Japanese and Communist aggression and retain power; or he would be forced to come to terms with the Japanese, especially if the Axis powers won.

In short, for the first three years of the war Chiang had little choice but to adopt a Machiavellian policy and to use his Secret Service to keep some contacts with the enemy as well as with his American friends. Such chicanery may not have been virtuous, but it was pragmatic and essential for the self-preservation of the Kuomintang. Soviet Russia, always an admirer of authoritarianism and Machiavellianism in an adversary, probably kept on good terms with Chiang only because they saw him as a realist.

Thus the U.S.S.R. signed a non-aggression pact with China in 1937 after the all-out Japanese onslaught on the Chinese mainland. And, despite the Russo-German pact of 1939, the Russians managed to put across even to the ultra-suspicious Chiang Kai-shek Government, with whom they conducted a curious flirtation, sometimes at the expense of the Chinese Communists, that they were more anti-Japanese than either Britain or the U.S.A.

That they succeeded is clear from what Madame Chiang Kai-shek, who was probably more anti-Communist and anti-Russian than her husband, wrote in an American magazine: "Eighty per cent of Japan's war supplies come from America . . . and 95 per cent of the aviation gasoline which was used by Japan in her ruthless bombing was American. Throughout the first three years of resistance Soviet Russia extended to China, for the actual purchase of war supplies and other necessities, credits several times larger than the credits given by either Great Britain or America . . . at the meetings of the League of Nations it was Russia who took an uncompromising stand in support of China's appeal that active measures should be adopted to brand Japan as the aggressor . . . Russian help has been unconditional throughout." [4]

Where the Chinese Communists gained inostensibly in this tangled situation was not through Soviet aid, but through the fact that they had no real external allies and were forced to be self-reliant. Also, whereas Chiang had an old-fashioned, formal and orthodox army, the Communists by reason of adversity turned themselves into a small guerrilla army and, in due course, as experienced guerrillas and with more trustworthy and dedicated agents, were able to infiltrate behind the Japanese lines much more effectively than any of Chiang's men. To a limited extent the Chinese Communists also had links with the Soviet network in Japan, the key link here being, however, not Richard Sorge but Agnes Smedley.

Possibly because they had to cope simply with a small rural area in Shensi province, the Communists were able to make their small state seem a model of efficient administration in contrast with the disorder, corruption and uneven government to be found in Chiang's China. The small Communist state had not only schools, but even a tiny university.

K'ang Sheng was determined that his still modest Intelligence Service should have the backing of an educational system which would turn out first-class agents. Although there is a certain ambiguity about his status at this time he is known to have held a high position in one of the leading "Party schools" in Yenan; and Edgar Snow, the American journalist stated in July 1938 that the Communist Party School was under K'ang Sheng and Ch'en Shao-yu and that it had about five hundred students. This is confirmed by other reports that during the Sino-Japanese War K'ang was "vice-president of the Central Party School".[5] Much of his intelligence work in this period was devoted towards sabotaging the activities of the warlord Wu Pei-fu.

There is some evidence that early on in World War II the Chinese Communists began to supply British Intelligence with information on China, this being passed through intermediaries in New Delhi and Calcutta. From personal experience, when I was in India in 1943, I know that many orthodox Establishment figures in the then British administration of India were highly impressed by Chinese Communist good faith and that this was working to the detriment of Chiang Kai-shek. Almost overnight there came about a change of heart and mind among very many, if not a majority, of British officials in India.

Some of the intelligence supplied to the British by the Chinese Communists was embroidered to make Chiang Kai-shek appear about to make a deal with the Japanese at any moment. It is true that when Japan was winning big victories in the Pacific and Soviet Russia was suffering under the Nazi push towards Moscow, Chiang Kai-shek had resumed undercover contact through his Intelligence Service with Tokyo. It was not true that the Nazi Walter Stennes was a key figure in these deals, but it was partially true that the Japanese Secret Service was given protection by Chiang in Chungking: the exact truth was that one of the senior Japanese Secret Service officials, Kuroda, was allowed to live in Chungking and had protection (and no doubt surveillance as well) from Chiang's secret police.

Of course all except the most fanatical of the "China Lobby" knew that Chiang's was a police state and as near to an autocratic dictatorship as one could get. Not even the glamorous, highly intelligent personality of Madame Chiang, one of the famous Soong sisters, could hide the anti-democratic sentiments of the military-minded Chiang.

To prove this point I have quoted at the beginning of this chapter from Oliver J. Caldwell. Let us look at what Caldwell said in detail on the subject of his war-time service in China: "Before my military experience I was intensely pro-Chiang Kai-shek and an admirer of the Kuomintang. But when I left China I was convinced that Chiang and his party would lose China to the Communists . . . I went to China as a civil affairs officer . . . I suddenly found myself attached to the Office of Strategic Services. This was a very tough organisation, the forerunner of today's Green Berets and of the C.I.A. I was assigned by the O.S.S. to Chiang's Secret Military Police, headed by General Tai

Li. Here I was openly a double agent, working both for my own army and for the Chinese. Soon I became secretly a triple agent, when I agreed to represent three great Chinese secret societies (Triad) in their effort to secure American support to oust the Generalissimo [Chiang Kai-shek] and to establish a new moderate democratic government. This effort failed and the Communists eventually ousted the corrupt Chiang regime because it was repudiated by a large proportion of the Chinese people."[6]

This is an admission of enormous importance when one considers the U.S.A.'s hysterical support for Chiang in the immediate post-war period and the paranoic view that anyone who was against Chiang was against America, an idea largely fostered by the multimillion dollar industry of the "China Lobby".

On the other hand let it not be thought that this is the view of a pro-Communist observer. Caldwell himself stressed that "those of us who are critical of Chiang Kai-shek should not forget the enormous material progress which took place in China under his leadership". And Miles Copeland, an objective observer, has this to say on Caldwell: "The first Central Intelligence Agency, formed in about 1950, was a dull place. . . . It was brightened from time to time by a guest lecturer. . . . The brightest star of all was Oliver Caldwell, or 'Captain Caldwell', as he was known to his friends, lecturing on China. Caldwell's Lectures were standing room only because they were like nothing else at the C.I.A. . . . Caldwell . . . convincingly demonstrated the 'stupidity' of American generals who, he insisted, had backed Chiang Kai-shek uncritically and had committed us to a 'disastrous China policy'. Even sophisticates like Richard Helms, presently director of the C.I.A. and at that time head of the Western Europe division, came three or four times to hear the same talk. . . . Caldwell is the genuine article—he had 'been there'."[7]

At the beginning of this chapter it was stated that at one period of World War II there were no less than four rival Secret Services in China, all working against one another. These four services were, first, the Secret Police and Personal Intelligence Service of Chiang

Kai-shek, controlled by Tai Li; second, the small but rapidly improving Communist Secret Service; third, the Wang Ching-wei organisation; and, finally, the suddenly emergent anti-Kuomintang branch of the Triads, who, wearied of Chiang's dictatorship and essentially military mind, conscious that Tai Li was using them to keep the Chinese people rather than Japan under control, and anxious only for freedom from political restrictions, plotted to create a democratic alternative to Chiang's form of government.

Not one of these Secret Services could have survived for long without outside backing. Chiang claimed American support and so, too, to a limited extent did the Triads (as will shortly be seen). Wang Ching-wei had some slight assistance from the Japanese and Germans, while the Chinese Communists, though mainly relying on their own efforts, had the benefit of some snippets of information through Sorge's Far East network, though Soviet Russia kept their Chinese "brothers" starved on information on Europe.

On the whole, however, it was the Chinese Communists who survived longest with the least outside backing and who remained the most independent, the most self-sufficient and, potentially, the most promising of these four rival Intelligence services. That of Wang Ching-wei quickly disappeared; Chiang's problem was that he had to fight against all the others and depended a great deal on American support. As for the anti-Chiang branch of the Triads, they were probably too devoted to individual freedom and the motive of family protection and the "closed society" ever to create a Secret Service strong enough to defeat Chiang Kai-shek, or anyone else. Nevertheless, for a while, the Americans believed that they could use the Triads as effectively as they used the Mafia in the taking of Sicily from the Axis powers.

To understand the reasons for the yearnings of some of the Triad leaders to break away from Chiang Kai-shek one must appreciate two things: first, that the Triads put their own members and the family as a unit above the state, and, secondly, they had come to hate Tai Li. There was also another vital factor: whereas the Communists had remembered and indeed built up their strength among the small farmers and peasants, Chiang Kai-shek, in the eyes of the Triads, had neglected the farmers. In the long term it was to prove a fatal error; in the short term it was the cause of the breakaway of some of the Triad leaders from the Kuomintang. And after Chiang was forced to leave Nanking and to set up his government in Chungking the rift between the Triads and the Kuomintang became acute.

The Triads' rebels had one strong complaint—that Chiang's taxation measures were unfair to the small farmer. They had, while supplying intelligence to Tai Li, also kept a certain amount of intelligence for their own use. What the Triads had built up was a knowledge of who was who in the American civil and military affairs departments working in China. On the strength of this inside information they made approaches to some of the Americans—Caldwell was one—for a new Secret Service with the aim of overthrowing Chiang and, with American co-operation, setting up a new, democratic government under the presidency of General Li Tsong-jen of the South-West China Command. While conservative Triads were mainly to the fore in this move, they also had some backing among Chinese intellectuals in the universities.

Caldwell said he "wondered how many middle-aged American army captains had received such a proposition". However, he agreed to think things over and was told he would be put under the protection of the Society of Elder Brothers. If ever he was trying to escape from the Japanese, he was told, he must go to the nearest village, walk down the main street and find the biggest shop. There he would ask to see the proprietor and, when the latter appeared, he must ask him: "Where is my old uncle?" Then he would be taken under the protection of the society.

The Communist Espionage Machine Expands 1943-1946

One way of starting a revolution is to capture the capital. . . . The French Revolution broke out in Paris and the English one in London. . . . But the nature of these revolutions is different from ours. . . . We cannot rely on the ignorant and easy-going Peking populace. . . . Therefore we can only start in one province and hope for simultaneous uprisings in all of the others.
General Huang Hsing, from a speech in 1903

WHAT General Huang Hsing said in 1903 was still applicable in 1943 and indeed Mao Tse-tung's revolution had taken firmer roots precisely because it was in a terrain where life was hard and the populace could not afford to be easy-going. But, though there had not been simultaneous uprisings in the Communist cause in other provinces, great progress had been made. In 1937 the Chinese Communist Party had only one base in a remote and drought-stricken area of North-West China where there was a population of only one and a half million. By the end of the war, by using guerrilla tactics based on meagre but accurate intelligence reports, and employing agents inside Japanese-occupied territory, the Communists had managed slowly but surely to incorporate into the area they controlled something like eighty million people.

Much of the success of this operation was due to the efforts of K'ang Sheng in that he realised from the earliest years that to achieve total victory the Chinese Communists needed a Secret Service which would not only defeat the Kuomintang, but match those of the other great powers of the world. It is probably no exaggeration to say that he was the greatest Chinese spy chief since the era of Sun Tzu.

One of the arguments used by the Triads' rebels for setting up a new Secret Service, backed by the Americans, was that it would remove the Chinese people from control by Chiang Kai-shek's Secret Police, and that General Li Tsong-jen, as head of the largest army in China, could carry this with him not only to defeat the Japanese, but, by establishing a more democratic government, to weaken support for the Communists.

K'ang Sheng from all accounts had somewhat belated information of the Triads' plot and took certain measures to ensure that he heard of later developments. This is understood to have been achieved by infiltrating agents into General Li's army. This part of K'ang's career is necessarily shadowy because he was involved in security work. Though there does not appear to be any identification of K'ang as a Politburo member until December 1954, he obviously held high rank in the Communist Party during World War II as he was one of only fifteen members of the steering committee of the seventh National Congress of the C.C.P., held in Yenan in June 1945.

To organise an Intelligence Service on an efficient scale from a remote province with poor communications was in itself a considerable achievement, but K'ang also had to contend with the Kuomintang's blockade of the Communists, aimed at preventing the latter from obtaining arms supplies. K'ang's only hope of effectively by-passing this blockade was to be able to influence the Americans and in this respect he was fortunate in that one of the advisers to General Stilwell, appointed by President Roosevelt as military adviser to Chiang Kai-shek, was none other than Agnes Smedley. She strongly urged that arms should be sent by the Americans to the Communists to be used for mounting an offensive against the Japanese in North China. Stilwell, despite vehement protests by Chiang Kai-shek, strongly supported this plea, though purely on military grounds.[1]

The exact rôle which Agnes Smedley played on behalf of the Chinese Communists is to a large extent masked by the fact that she was also working for the

Russians. When, at the time of the hysterical anti-communist drive in the U.S.A. in the early 'fifties, she was named as "one of the enemies of the nation" it was as a Soviet agent that she was attacked: her Chinese connections were largely overlooked, probably mainly because it was discovered that she had been a key member of Sorge's network. But there is no doubt that, before, during and after World War II, her real sympathies in fact lay with the Chinese Communists and that at no time did she allow her allegiance to the Russians to stop her from helping the Chinese.

It is all very well to argue that there was no conflict between working for the Russians and helping the Chinese, yet the fact remains that as a Soviet agent she took considerable risks in serving two masters. But then Agnes Smedley was an exceptional woman—brave, idealistic, yet incredibly discreet and probably at one stage of her career equally valuable to the Americans, Russians and Chinese, all of whom she was serving simultaneously in various capacities.

Richard Sorge, who, though himself a womaniser, mistrusted women as spies, said of Smedley that she had a good educational background and a brilliant mind. . . . In short, she was like a man".[2] She continued to keep the Chinese Communists informed of her activities during the period she served as an adviser to Stilwell. K'ang was the chief beneficiary of this intelligence and through Smedley learned all about the Americans' links with Chiang Kai-shek and Tai Li and probably something of the Triads' revolt. One of Agnes Smedley's closest contacts among the Chinese Communists was their Commander-in-chief, Chu Teh, who later on was commander of the Chinese armies fighting against the Americans in Korea. A curious feature of Agnes Smedley's will, revealed when she died after World War II, was that she bequeathed her ashes and her estate to Chu-teh. She was buried in Peking in what at the time was described as "the new cemetery for revolutionaries"—a high, if posthumous, honour.[3]

However, though Smedley's advice seems to have been accepted by Stilwell, the U.S. general was recalled by President Roosevelt on the representations of

Chiang Kai-shek and he was replaced by General Wedemeyer, who reversed Stilwell's policies and forbade arms supplies being sent to the Communists.

After Pearl Harbour and the American entry into World War II China was flooded with American officers, bureaucrats, advisers and spies. They soon fell foul of one another. The intellectuals and liberals were, generally speaking, appalled at the corruption and harshness of the Kuomintang's rule, urging that Chiang should negotiate with the Communist Party, though most of them made the stipulation that this need only last as long as the war against Japan continued. The U.S. Government's brief that full backing should be given to Chiang was rejected even from within the U.S. State Department by their academic advisers, such as Owen Lattimore.

Oliver Caldwell soon found that the U.S. Army hated the intervention of civilian advisers, or even officers of the newly created Office of Strategic Services: There was throughout the war a tremendous clash between the Army, only just finding its feet and in consequence blundering along, and the university-educated advisers of the Roosevelt "brain trust". The ultimate tragedy of the intended co-operation between one group and the other was that the Army became increasingly obsessed with the Communist bogey, while the academics practically risked their future careers in warning where the Army policy would lead the U.S.A. A decade later they were to pay for their advice by being smeared and in some cases destroyed by Senator Joseph McCarthy's anti-communist lobby.

Early in the war the U.S.A. had a very poor intelligence service and Roosevelt was using the Shavian device of exaggerating in order to tell the truth when he informed Major-General William J. Donovan, whom he chose to form the O.S.S., that "you will have nothing to begin with. We have no intelligence service."[4]

It was not until June 1942 that the new Intelligence body was named the O.S.S. and operated in the China-India-Burma sector. "Much balderdash has been written about the 'brilliance' of the work of the O.S.S.," wrote the military historian, Hanson Baldwin, "but some of it was brilliant—particularly in China and South-East Asia. But much of it was inefficient, some of it was stupid."[5]

Any brilliant achievements in China and South-East Asia by the O.S.S. were achieved against great odds. The Americans found themselves fighting a war among themselves, sometimes against the Japanese, sometimes against restoring British or French imperialist rule; they supported Chiang Kai-shek, yet some of them tried to overthrow him; some were openly for the Communists while others were just as determined to destroy them. And, most ironical of all, they then admired the frail old man holding out against the Japanese in Indo-China: it was an O.S.S. doctor who once saved the life of Ho Chi-Minh!

When Oliver Caldwell went to New Delhi nobody in General Stilwell's headquarters would admit to having heard of him. There had obviously been no real co-operation between the U.S. Army and the O.S.S. on this posting, or someone in the former had been deliberately obstructive. Indeed it was only when the determined Caldwell impressed on the military that he could speak both Mandarin and Foochow Chinese and various other dialects and had scored 100% in an Army examination in spoken Japanese that he was at last given an assignment. He was sent to Chungking to serve as an interpreter for the American Army in China.

Caldwell gradually became convinced not only of the necessity of U. S. support for the Triad rebels against Chiang Kai-shek, but that Tai Li was not merely obstructing American policy in China, but in many respects sabotaging the war effort. However, not even his detailed report on the Chinese situation, recommending backing for the secret societies' coalition against Chiang, was accepted in Washington. It was considered at Cabinet level, but turned down by a small majority. In the meantime lack of adequate U.S. support for the secret revolt combined with the ruthless efficiency of Tai Li's Secret Service spelt this scheme's ultimate doom.

Tai Li gave orders for the arrest of some and the secret assassination of other distinguished liberals and university professors, some of whom had backed Li Tsong-jen and his group. In 1943 Wen I-to, one of China's greatest literary figures of the 'thirties and a leading member of the "Third Party" (as the rebels called themselves) and his son were shot down on the steps of Chungking University. They, like Professor Li Kung-po, of the Democratic League, were killed with special silent pistols supplied to Tai Li's men by the U.S. Naval Intelligence. Students were also shot while they slept in their dormitories. When challenged some years later by President Truman about these killings, Chiang Kai-shek merely dismissed them as "mistakes by subordinates". He might have informed Truman that the weapons were American, for the President seems to have been unaware of this.

"The history of mankind might have taken another direction had Li Tsong-jen and his group, supported by the three great secret societies, received American encouragement," wrote Oliver Caldwell: ". . . Mao Tse-tung might not now be in Peking and American troops might never have fought in Korea and South-East Asia."[6]

Certainly the Communists gained from the collapse of the "middle-of-the-road" revolt, but after Stilwell was recalled the Americans foolishly blundered right into the hands of Tai Li, who, more than Chiang himself, seemed to dictate the day-to-day war policy in China. They did this by launching the joint Sino-American project S.A.C.O., which initials stood for Sino-American Co-operative Organisation. This body comprised at its head Tai Li, Commodore Miles of the U.S. Navy and some O.S.S. personnel. In fact the whole affair was manipulated by Tai Li to his own advantage and to the detriment of the Americans. Miles was dominated by Tai Li, while the O.S.S. were not allowed to operate without the Kuomintang Secret Service chief's permission.

The S.A.C.O. headquarters were incorporated inside the grounds of Tai Li's own establishment, which he had cynically designated the "Happy Valley". Thus Tai Li not only knew everything that was going on among the O.S.S. officers, on whom he was able to spy, but who their operatives were. All Americans attached to S.A.C.O. were given agents of Tai Li as servants or chauffeurs.

The Chinese Secret Service chief himself promised the utmost co-operation in launching a secret war of espionage behind the lines and guerrilla tactics against the Japanese, but nothing ever happened. His long-term aim was to ensure that neither Japan nor the U.S.A. won the war, but that each nation would in due course be persuaded to withdraw from China. In some instances he actively sabotaged American efforts against the Japanese, while making undercover deals with the enemy through his intermediaries. Once, when some U.S. officers had trained some Chinese students in the arts of sabotage and the latter had blown up a bridge on the Yellow River and thus delayed Japanese railway traffic for three months, Tai Li recalled the officers, rebuked them for acting without his authority and broke up the team of students.

Caldwell reports how matters once came to a head when Tai Li and Major-General Donovan met at a dinner party at the "Happy Valley". An argument developed between the two men and the O.S.S. chief bluntly told Tai Li that if the O.S.S. could not perform their mission in co-operation with him, then the O.S.S. would operate separately.

Tai Li angrily replied: "If O.S.S. tries to operate outside S.A.C.O. I will kill your agents."

Donovan answered back: "For every one of our agents you kill, we will kill one of your generals."

"You can't talk to me like that," shouted Tai Li.

"I *am* talking to you like that," said Donovan.[7]

He was probably the only man, American or Chinese, who dared to address Tai Li in such terms.

On the other hand Tai Li could afford to take this rebuff: he worked well with the U.S. Navy and Commodore Miles and was able to take advantage of the naval-military rivalries of the U.S. Forces to exploit his dislike of the O.S.S., which, as he knew full well, was a foreign Secret Service operating in his own territory. But Tai Li continued to work with the O.S.S. because he was most anxious for Chinese to be trained and used as U.S. agents so that he could learn their techniques. But whenever the Americans seemed likely to be able to employ their Chinese agents successfully against the Japanese—or, perhaps more accurately, in a highly successful manner as against an occasional coup—Tai Li would manage to have the operations postponed.

Tai Li was aided because Commodore Miles was practically his lackey. The Communists gained indirectly because they benefited from the failures of both sides—Chiang Kai-shek and the Americans. They were also able to recruit defectors from the Kuomintang armies, who were badly clothed, badly fed and badly led. As World War II drew to an end the main exercise of K'ang Sheng was to organise regular defections from the Kuomintang armies. By this means and by reason of a much better intelligence service behind the enemy lines he paved the way for the ultimate success of the Communist Party in winning the minds, if not the hearts, of a vast number of uncommitted Chinese people.

K'ang Sheng gradually began to cast his net further afield and eventually he managed to infiltrate two key agents into the "Happy Valley" to spy on both Tai Li and the Americans. This was a considerable achievement, but it was not difficult to bring off, bearing in mind the crude brain-washing tactics employed by Tai Li. In this respect K'ang Sheng was very clever: he did not attempt to make direct infiltrations into the Chiang Kai-shek camp, but he carefully selected able, trusted and well disciplined members of the Communist Party and arranged for them to pose as defectors to the Kuomintang, or, more usually, to allow themselves to be arrested by the Secret Police. Whichever method was adopted the end was the same: the defectors or arrested persons were sent to a correction camp to be brain-washed by Chiang's agents.

The methods of the latter were not merely crude, but inefficient. Without any real tests being carried out it was generally accepted by the Kuomintang that those who had undergone this "training" would emerge as "reformed characters". Yet a few of these Communist agents were actually recruited into Tai Li's organisation. All the information they obtained was sent back to Communist H.Q.

Thus the Communists were able to seize the initiative in the field of espionage and slowly not merely to catch up with Tai Li, but to overhaul him, to absorb much American intelligence and to establish networks as far afield as Calcutta and New Delhi, Rangoon and Singapore.

As to the failure of the Americans to influence events, this can be exemplified not so much by their inability to establish worth-while links with the Communists, but by their absolutely disastrous liaison with the Kuomintang. Oliver Caldwell has summed it up as follows: "We never accomplished anything except to spend American money. It took real talent to be as unco-operative as were Tai Li and his aides. It was like trying to fight a ghost. We knew the opposition was there, but we could never see it. Never were we permitted to accomplish anything while part of Tai Li's Secret Military Police. The only exception to this record of failure was when some of us succeeded in getting into the field, far away from Tai Li's headquarters."[8]

Towards the end of the war Tai Li, far from losing control of the situation, was actually manipulating Americans as his agents and he succeeded in controlling joint Sino-American spy networks in such far-flung places as Outer Mongolia and Chinese Turkestan.

Belatedly there was an American mission to Yenan —the area controlled by Mao Tse-tung—as "observers". But by this time it was too late for the Americans to make any worthwhile impact with the Communists. They were as suspect to Mao Tse-tung as were the Kuomintang and the Japanese. Nevertheless members of this mission were impressed by what they saw and they urged co-operation with the Communists.

But by late 1944 the Communists' Intelligence had already had information from their spies inside Tai Li's network, confirmed by their agents in the U.S.A., that Roosevelt was a dying man and that the American Government was swinging violently to the right. Truman, the new Vice-President, was marked down by the Communists as their most virulent enemy. The Korean war would prove them to be right. Meanwhile they began to prepare for what would be the final show-down with the Kuomintang.

Yet in the very last days of the war in Europe some Americans were still complacent on the subject of the growing power and influence of the Chinese Communists. John Stewart Service recorded that "Hurley [the U.S. Ambassador in China], Lt.-Gen. Wedemeyer and Commodore Miles discussed the Chinese military problem with the Chiefs of Staff on 27 March 1945. They were all of the opinion that the rebellion in China could be put down by a comparatively small assistance to Chiang's Government."[9]

The S.A.C.O. chiefs were totally bewitched by the charm and magnetism of Tai Li and they just could not believe that any other force in China could equal his in the field of espionage. The paradox of political thinking at the time was that the academic-minded Chinese specialists warned of the disastrous path upon which Tai Li was leading the Kuomintang, while the right-wing militarists were so blinded to reality that they ignored even such positive evidence as that Tai Li was *organising the kidnapping of American agents in places as far afield as Calcutta.*

That Tai Li's agents could reach out so far beyond their own territory was due only to the fact that they more or less controlled S.A.C.O. and certainly had every opportunity of keeping a watch on O.S.S. agents. There were several incidents in Calcutta after the U.S. had sent an official mission to Mao Tse-tung. Tai Li intended his kidnappings to be partly a warning to the United States not to meddle with other forces inside China and partly to smear some of the O.S.S. agents to the U.S. Army, with whom, as we have seen, the O.S.S. was never popular.

In two instances American officers were kidnapped, while the O.S.S. discovered that two Chinese girls in Calcutta were not only agents of Tai Li, but were relaying information to the Japanese as well. Not even the revelation that Tai Li's agents were working for the common enemy seemed to change the minds of the stubborn men in S.A.C.O.

One of the most tragic cases was that of an American officer who was about to throw a party for his Chinese girl friend to announce their engagement. By this time the O.S.S. had learned that the girl was also a spy for the Japanese, with Tai Li's permission. The O.S.S. in Calcutta ruthlessly intervened and told the U.S. officer that, though his bride was an enemy agent (which was something he found hard to accept), the engagement party must go through. Yet despite a close watch the girl that the O.S.S. expected to arrest disappeared.

It is not surprising that in dealing with the Americans the Tai Li Secret Service became careless and arrogant. They began to make the assumption that all other nations were fools in comparison with the Chinese. Thus, when they operated in India, Burma and elsewhere, they always seemed to assume that discretion was unnecessary.

The Communists did not make this mistake. They had a much greater respect for their enemies, even when it was for reasons of hostility, than did Chiang Kai-shek and his men for their allies. The result was that they built up inside India a useful minority of support for themselves and a small but effective Intelligence network that kept a close watch on what Tai Li's men were up to.

Communications posed one of the chief problems for the Communist Intelligence network in these early days and to overcome this agents were used in various parts of India to buy up surreptitiously and singly—never in bulk—various components for the construction of radio transmission sets. It was a complex operation, because caution dictated that the purchasing must be carried out slowly and casually. Agents were ordered to move from one centre to another in quest of material, never to go back to the same shop or dealer if they could avoid it. Every agent was given a cover story as to why he was buying such goods, if ever he should be questioned. The material was passed back to the area supervisers with the same caution and patience. At the same time agents were also requested to obtain technical books on radio science and even to buy up books and magazines covering the subject. In this manner the Chinese Communists built up their own radio techniques for espionage purposes and wisely avoided depending upon Russian know-how as they had in the past.

Certainly the Communist Secret Service had expanded fast between 1943 and 1946, but whether it had actually infiltrated the O.S.S. is a question which has not yet been satisfactorily answered. Without doubt some of the personnel and interpreters attached to O.S.S. officers by Tai Li were double-agents and at least two of these were secret Communists. Therefore it seems logical to assume that they had links with the Communist Secret Service. Some American equipment was certainly smuggled out of the "Happy Valley" to the Communists, though this mainly concerned radio components.

Oliver Caldwell tells how, one day shortly after the war when Tai Li took off from Nanking in his aeroplane, "it exploded in mid-air. A man who could have known the facts told me an O.S.S. limpet (magnetic) bomb might have been attached to an engine of his plane."[10]

The killing of Tai Li was a devastating blow for the S.A.C.O. school of Americans and a boon for the Communists. It could also have been a blessing for the O.S.S. On the other hand the planting of the bomb on the plane could well have been the act of the Communist Secret Service, using O.S.S. equipment. The evidence of the inquiry into this affair was kept secret and the full truth may never be known.

24

The "China Lobby" Revelations 1945-1952

To take no notice of the basic frictions which animate this kindly, dogged, energetic, modest and intelligent man, would be to render an imperfect tribute to Alfred Kohlberg. . . . I know him well enough to venture to say that the first thing that went through his mind on being asked whether he would consent to being honoured by us was, "Hm. A good opportunity to state again the case against the recognition of Red China."
William Buckley, Jnr., speaking at the Alfred Kohlberg testimonial dinner, 26 July 1960

IN the context of an examination of the history and development of the Secret Service of the People's Republic of China any reference to the "China Lobby" must essentially be controversial. To utilise material and evidence of Chinese Communist espionage as culled from "China Lobby" sources is immediately to lay oneself open to the charge of accepting tainted witnesses. Yet to fail to study the vast amount of research and detailed documentary evidence which this admittedly biased organisation produced would be at best an act of intellectual prejudice and at worst a downright neglect to any historian's duty.

It is fashionably assumed today that the "China Lobby" was a combination of right-wing reactionaries employing unscrupulous and heavily bribed intermediaries to build up a case at all costs, regardless of the evidence, against the Chinese Communists, and as a means of bolstering Chiang Kai-shek. But the truth is not nearly so simple as that. Certainly the "China Lobby" was in many respects a highly suspect propa-

gandist source and the hysteria of its leading lights
prevented a truly objective look being taken at the evidence it collected. Nevertheless it would be foolish
to deny that, but for the activities of those working
for the "China Lobby", some of the machinations of
the Chinese Secret Service would not be known today.

A major error of the "China Lobby" was their
wild assumption that communism was the same in
all countries and that what was happening in China
was being totally controlled by Russia. This was a
wrong assumption even in 1945. Partly because of this,
much of the "China Lobby's" evidence defeated its
own ends. The manner in which this evidence was
presented made it appear that the Soviet Union was
master-minding Chinese intelligence whereas the contrary was in fact true.

Alfred Kohlberg, the originator of the "China
Lobby" in the U.S.A., graduated from Lowell in 1904
and, after a spell at the University of California,
worked as a reporter for the *Oakland Enquirer* and
later for the *Daily Californian*. With his family he entered into partnership in a printing business which was
later beset by union troubles. He then went into the
real estate business with his father.

Kohlberg first developed an interest in China in the
Pacific Exposition of Panama at San Francisco in 1915
and this led him into exploratory business tours of the
Far East. His first ventures out there seem to have been
with the Japanese, and it was only in the 1930s that
he developed a business in China—a peculiar trade in
that, working from offices in California, he was an im-
porter of handkerchiefs, made from Irish linen purchased in Belfast, shipped out to China where Chinese women embroidered them. No doubt Kohlberg
was already forming his own ideas as to how a "China
Lobby" could be developed, but he had no political
influence in this period.

To his credit he seems to have been an honest em-
ployer of Chinese labour, making it a principle to visit
his work people frequently and, by the standards of
the time, to pay them a decent wage for their work.
It was after World War II that Alfred Kohlberg devoted most of his energies to public affairs and to

formulating a "China Lobby" which played right into the hands of Senator McCarthy and his witch-hunt against communists in public life.

Kohlberg had continued business almost normally until the Chinese Communists finally seized the country in 1949. He himself was not a spy in the sense that he served any government, neither that of the United States, nor that of Chiang Kai-shek. But he was twice decorated by the Government of the Republic of China (Chiang)—in 1941 for his work on behalf of the American Bureau for Medical Aid to China, and in 1948 for what he said were "my activities on behalf of the truth with regard to the China situation".[1] Nevertheless he was engaged in a kind of espionage, if only on his own account and for the "China Lobby" which he had created. Because of his frequent trips to China he managed to get hold of various items of intelligence data which provided evidence of the growing "communist menace" in China and the involvement of various American officials in promoting its growth.

His activities included participation in A.B.M.A.C. —the American Bureau of Medical Aid to China— until 1943, when he found on a trip to China that Dwight Edwards, the field director of A.B.M.A.C., was sending back reports alleging corruption in the use by the Kuomintang Government of funds meant to help the needy, and he suspected that the organisation was being infiltrated by persons with communist sympathies who were using A.B.M.A.C. as a front for their activities.

Kohlberg was also active in the American China Policy Association, of which he was a co-founder in 1946, and for a brief period his chief propaganda organ, in addition to his vast correspondence with officials and newspapers, was *Plain Talk,* a pocket-sized magazine which he financed for the purpose of enlightening the public on the dangers of communism.

Until the Communists took control of China in 1949 Kohlberg had reputedly been drawing an annual income of between one and two million dollars. But in the 'fifties he was devoting his efforts almost entirely to gathering evidence on the involvement of American

302

officials in what he called "the communist plot". He had no difficulty in obtaining backing from prominent people, including J. B. Powell, doyen of American newspaper correspondents in China, and Clare Booth Luce.

While allowing for the fact that Kohlberg was a right-wing reactionary and totally obsessed with the communist bogey, one must admit that much of what he uncovered was truth. As to whether he interpreted this truth wisely is another matter. But there was in academic circles in America—and they were by no means confined to the left—such a virulent hatred of imperialism and colonialism, which they associated with everything for which Britain stood, that it was relatively easy to find many honest, patriotic citizens in high places who took a sympathetic view of the Chinese Communists.

One of the organisations attacked by Kohlberg's "China Lobby" was the Institute of Pacific Relations, founded in 1925 as an outgrowth of the Honolulu conference of religious leaders, scholars and businessmen from Pacific countries who "realised the need for greater knowledge and frank discussion of the problems of Asia and the relations of Asia and the West". Largely financed by the Rockefeller and Carnegie Foundations, this was essentially a research organisation. Among its many publications was a magazine called *Far Eastern Survey,* while its trustees included Owen Lattimore, Frederick Vanderbilt Field, and Alger Hiss. I.P.R. was the subject of many days of inquiries during the McCarthy hearings into un-American activities and was one of the chief targets of Kohlberg's campaigns. He accused I.P.R. of being a Communist-front organisation and on 18 March 1947 published the statement that Owen Lattimore, the China expert, "maintains liaison with heads of the Communist Party—reportedly an operative for Soviet military intelligence".[2]

This last allegation was typical of some of the wild, unsubstantiated, totally malicious and inaccurate statements which emanated from the China Lobby. Nobody would deny that Owen Lattimore, now a Professor of Chinese Studies at Leeds University in Britain, was more sympathetic to the Chinese Communist cause than to Chiang Kai-shek, but to suggest he was "an operative for Soviet military intelligency" was the quintessence of "Reds-under-the-bed" madness. The most charitable reply one can objectively make against the China Lobby of this period is that they had neither the integrity nor the knowledge to differentiate between Chinese and Russian Communists. Indeed, in putting a pro-Soviet label on people of Liberal persuasion who were prepared to take a moderately benevolent view of Chinese communism, the China Lobby not only prolonged the cold war, but delayed recognition of the fact that the Chinese and Russian conceptions of communism were in many respects totally opposed.

During World War II the American Bureau for Medical Aid to China was largely funded by the United China Relief Fund, which was part of the U.S. Government-organised National War Fund. It received an average of two million dollars annually for its work in China. The Secretary-General of I.P.R., Edward C. Carter, participated in the distribution of funds and this was a subject of controversy which Kohlberg exploited.

Carter replied to the Kohlberg charges by saying that ". . . we are up against a vastly complicated, abundantly financed movement which is employing the classical Nazi methods in attacking liberals, leftists and middle-of-the-road Conservatives. Mr Kohlberg is one of the spearheads of this nation-wide intrigue. He is carefully planning his timetable and is moving with great skill from objective to objective. To the I.P.R. he has added the F.P.A. [Foreign Press Association] and to that he has recently added an attack on Alger Hiss, the very able but by no means leftist successor to President Nicholas Murray Butler as the new President of the Carnegie Endowment for International Peace."

Nevertheless, despite the Kohlberg failure to discriminate between Chinese and Russian communism and between the supporters of Chinese communism from a purely detached, liberal point of view and those who actually worked for the Soviet Secret Service, out of this probe into the Chinese situation there emerged a substantial amount of evidence of the recently developed scope of the Communist Secret Service.

What not only precipitated the Kohlberg "China Lobby", but carried it into the realms of a witch-hunt was the quite unexpectedly swift collapse of the armies of Chiang Kai-shek and the smoothness and totality of the Communist take-over of China in 1948–9. This was, wrote Oliver Caldwell, ". . . followed by a witch-hunt to find Americans to blame for Chiang's defeat. General George C. Marshall, together with a few China specialists, including Davies, Service, Atcheson and Lattimore, became scapegoats."[3]

The military experts had repeated so often the theme of the impending defeat of the Communists that when, against all odds, the latter brought off a series of resounding victories there was a widespread but erroneous feeling that there must be treachery in high places. Yet just how ludicrous such allegations by the China Lobby often were can be deduced today by the linking of Dean Atcheson with these names. Atcheson was always a realist, regardless of ideological or party considerations: in fact he was probably the most honest American politician of the past fifty years. Today he appears as a stalwart of the right-wing and it is hard to imagine how in 1948–49 he was regarded not merely as a friend of the left, but "soft" on Russia and China. This is not to suggest that Dean Atcheson changed his beliefs during this period, but that whereas in 1948–49 he saw that the China Lobby had so distorted evidence that they had created mass hysteria in a swing of public opinion to the extreme right, so today he has put forward right-wing policies because he has seen equally distorted and tainted evidence, backed by similar hysteria, creating what he feels to be an undue swing to the left—not only in the U.S.A., but especially in Britain and to some extent in other parts of Western Europe.

There is no question but that the vast amount of so-called evidence produced by the China Lobby was either manufactured or based on *non sequitur* deductions. Nevertheless a modicum of the Kohlberg evidence did throw light on the Chinese Communist Secret Service and, though the manipulation of this evidence may be suspect, it does, when thoroughly sifted, show the ramifications overseas of the Chinese Secret Service of this era.

In the 1945–9 period there were already signs of marked differences of policy and tactics between the Chinese and Russian Communists. Even inside the British Foreign Office a tendency to equate the Chinese and Russians was actively encouraged by such top traitors in high places as Donald Maclean, "Kim" Philby and Guy Burgess, all of whom were to some extent able to influence British thinking on the subject of Russia and China. A British Intelligence officer with considerable experience of the Far East over a period of thirty years made a report to the Foreign Office in 1950, suggesting that a split between Moscow and Peking seemed likely. A copy of this report was later returned to him with some caustic comments written in the margin, saying that the author should have his head examined for making such a fatuous suggestion. The signature to this comment was that of Guy Burgess, who defected to the Soviet Union with Donald Maclean in 1951.

Great play was made by the China Lobby with the notorious *Amerasia* case, which threw a good deal of light on Soviet espionage in Asia, but which they clumsily presented so that the links between *Amerasia* and the Chinese Communist Secret Service were only cursorily examined and never properly investigated. Kenneth E. Wells, a member of the O.S.S., read with astonishment a copy of the *Amerasia* magazine of 26 January 1945 and found that an article entitled "The Case of Thailand" contained information he had supplied in a highly confidential memorandum describing the lack of harmony between British and American policies in that country.

Wells suspected there had been a serious leakage and probably a purloining of top secret documents. He reported the matter to his chief and an immediate investigation was carried out. There were some thirty persons who had had access to the report and the O.S.S. decided that to investigate each person separately would take too long; so instead it was agreed to probe the organisation behind *Amerasia.*

This probe turned up some interesting information. Philip Jacob Jaffe, *Amerasia's* managing editor, turned out to be the proprietor of a printing company that produced good profits, whereas the magazine ran at an annual loss of some 6,000 dollars. He had been born in the Ukraine in 1897, emigrated to the U.S.A. at the age of eight and was naturalised when he was twenty-six. In 1934 he had made a trip to China, visiting the Communist-held areas, and when he returned to New York he organised a group calling itself "American Friends of the Chinese People". He was affiliated with the American Council of Soviet Relations. His assistant editor, Kate Louise Mitchell, a graduate from Bryn Mawr, it was learned, had visited Moscow in the 'thirties to establish a working relationship with the chief of the Far East Division of the Communist International.

As a result of these discoveries the *Amerasia* office was raided on 11 March 1945, and in the words of Frank Brooks Bialaski, who led the raid, "they had a photocopy machine and developer pans all around the shelves . . . I went into the office of Jaffe. His desk was covered with originals and freshly made photo-copies of documents, every one of which was secret in character. . . . Some of them were from military attachés in China and other places. . . . There were documents from the British Intelligence, Naval Intelligence, G–2 State Department, Office of Censorship, Office of Strategic Services."[4]

No immediate action was taken and the inquiry was passed on to the F.B.I., presumably with the idea of trying to track down the whole network of suppliers of secret information to the *Amerasia* office and in the hope of uncovering bigger fry.

One principal proved to be John Stewart Service, the son of an American missionary in China, who had spent some time in that country and had become friendly with Sun Yat-sen's widow, who was a sympathiser with the Communist cause. During the war he had been appointed to Chungking as a political analyst on General Stilwell's staff. When he returned to the

U.S.A. he was one of *Amerasia*'s chief informants. Another was Mark Julius Gayn, a journalist, born of Russian parents in Harbin, who had moved to China in 1927 before finally coming to America to work for the newspaper *PM* in 1939. Gayn, notwithstanding his Russian associations, was more a Chinese sympathiser than a Soviet spy.

Indeed nearly all these people were in the main friends of the Chinese Communists rather than secret agents as is shown by the fact that neither Jaffe, Mitchell, Service nor Gayn were charged with espionage, but simply with being in illegal possession of Government documents. Some six thousand documents had been discovered in the *Amerasia* offices. As I wrote in *A History of the Russian Secret Service,* "It was perhaps one of the biggest hauls of confidential information in history and must have benefited the Soviet Union to a great extent. Service had worked out a code for use by the network . . . Madame Chiang Kai-shek was 'Snow White' and the Chinese Communists were referred to as 'Harvard'." [5]

However, in retrospect, and in the light of my inquiries into the Chinese Secret Service of the period, I am now certain that a great deal of this information was passed direct to the Chinese Communist Secret Service and not merely relayed to them via Moscow as was originally thought. Indeed, putting together the evidence again, I should say the Chinese obtained far more of the documentary information than did the Russians for the very reason that Chinese Communist Secret Service tactics were not as heavy-handed as those of the Russians. They do not expect their agents to work in such a manner as to incriminate themselves as spies, but to adopt as far as possible legal means of obtaining information. Thus material that was "written up" for articles to appear in *Amerasia* was regarded as relatively "safe". That the Chinese arguments were to some extent justified by events is proved by the fact that six persons were tried, but Gayn, Mitchell and Service were acquitted. Indeed Service was not only acquitted, but actually reinstated in the State Department as an administrative officer in Japan.

The China Lobby continued to stir up a great deal

of mud, but most of it was past history, such as Agnes Smedley's links with both the Soviet and Chinese Secret Services. They succeeded by their campaign against Agnes Smedley in driving her out of the country, but they never uncovered the full extent of her network.

While enormous sums of money were spent in backing Chiang Kai-shek's propaganda and in building up anti-Communist news services, and large salaries were paid to some officials, in the long run the China Lobby became a sick joke. This rapidly became apparent when Chiang Kai-shek, his Government and Secret Service were exiled to Taiwan which was hardly the best centre for obtaining objective or even accurate intelligence on mainland China.

25

The Crimson Dawn Cracked Slowly 1949-1974

The night was long and the crimson
 dawn cracked slowly;
For hundreds of years demons and monsters
 danced frantically;
Our five hundred million people were disunited.
Once the cock has crowed and all beneath the
 sky is bright,
Music rises from the Khotan and a thousand places
To fill the poet with unparagoned inspiration.

Mao Tse-tung

THE "crimson dawn" of the new Chinese Secret Service may have "cracked slowly", but unobtrusively and steadily it made spectacular strides between 1949 and 1956, achieving far more in a quiet way than any other major power gave it credit for doing.

There has been—and there still is—a tendency to dismiss the Chinese Secret Service as something that hardly exists and that is about as elusive as the Scarlet Pimpernel. Dennis Bloodworth, a most discerning student of Chinese affairs, writes that "it is dangerous for a Chinese ambassador or agent overseas to present a score-sheet that makes nonsense of Mao's ideological arithmetic".[1] A leading Chinese expert in London told me that he did not believe "the Chinese have a Secret Service of any consequence" because he had found they were filled with misconceptions about the rôle of the British Labour Party! He added: "I do not believe the Chinese have any intelligence network in this country."

I find the arguments used by both these distinguished Chinese experts unacceptable and unconvincing. If the Chinese were so badly informed by their Intelligence Service overseas, would they have brought about so secretly, swiftly and smoothly their rapprochement with the U.S.A., their number one enemy until the late 'sixties? One can hardly let Dr Kissinger take all the credit for that. Again, could China have not only acquired nuclear secrets, but actually developed the most up-to-date nuclear weapons, without an efficient overseas Intelligence Service? The answer to this last query will be given in a subsequent chapter in some detail.

As to the tight control which the Chinese maintain over their Embassy staffs, this in itself is not all that different from Communist Embassy practice all over the world. It merely means that the Chinese have maintained a more rigorous internal security than most other Communist powers in their embassies. As to the second picture of a Chinese officialdom which appears ill-informed about the British Labour Party, this hardly seems a good example, for it must be very difficult for any foreigner to know just where that party really stands on any question for long, at least in the past decade.

The fact is that the Chinese are extremely adroit at appearing uninterested, or even ill-informed when it suits them to be so. They do not publicise their intelligence work as the Russians have done in recent

310

years. Again they logically believe that the first task of a Secret Service is to remain secret and, even in the era of their closest relations with Soviet Russia, they never had the kind of close association of Secret Services which the Americans and British had in World War II or the early part of the "Cold War". In the Western World there is certainly a detailed knowledge of the methods and systems not only of each other's espionage organisations, but of the Russians' as well. Yet neither the Western World nor the Soviet Union know anything like as much about the Chinese Secret Service as they do of one another.

Very rarely indeed are Chinese spies caught and fewer still defect. This is partly due to tighter discipline and better morale, but also to the totally different approach to espionage by the Chinese. They regard much of Russian espionage as being "in the capitalist tradition" and as clumsy, extravagant, wasteful and outdated. They do not believe in risking hordes of agents in situations where they lay themselves open to arrest, nor do they regard spies as expendable. They use their agents sparsely and as unostentatiously as possible.

Their attitude to the spy game is, quite simply, that it is a quest for knowledge. Indeed the prime aim of their Intelligence Service overseas is that of self-education: they wish to acquire technological, industrial, scientific and academic information over a very wide range. What is not generally realised is that eighty per cent of their intelligence gathering is not so much conventional espionage as the legitimate collection of valuable information which is available to any persistent intelligent person if he sets out to find it. This includes the winkling out of secret information by diligent research and probably very often the collection of a good deal of irrelevant details which in time have to be discarded. Whereas the Russians will spend vast sums in infiltrating agents into foreign Government departments, or in bribing or blackmailing foreign officials, the Chinese are more likely to obtain similar information by patient plodding which does not even break any laws—that is, by discreet observation, by collecting text-books, pamphlets, hand-outs, scientific articles and studying Diplomatic Lists and then, by analysing what they learn in this way, trying to make the right deductions.

This may be a laborious process and it can lead through lack of experience to arrival at the wrong conclusions on occasions. Nevertheless, at its best, this method has produced some surprising results. Perhaps the most perfect example of it is that three times in the last few years the Chinese Secret Service have cracked the identity of two heads of the British Secret Service —D16—and one head of MI5, the British counter-espionage organisation. This has not been achieved by espionage in the occidental sense of the word at all. The simplicity of their methods is so breath-taking it is almost laughable.

On 7 February 1973 the German magazine *Stern* revealed that the head of D16 was Sir John Rennie, attributing its information to a "Hongkong source". The same day the London *Evening Standard* announced that "the previously unnamed son of the head of D16, who is facing drugs charges in London is Charles Tatham Ogilvy Rennie", adding that the arrest of Rennie and his wife and the fact that they were facing drugs charges had first been reported on 15 January, "but at that time and ever since a D-notice—a Government request to the press—inhibited identification of either the son or the father".

As *Stern* had published all these details, restrictions of identification in the British press were then withdrawn by the D-notice Committee. Almost immediately it was announced that Sir John Rennie would retire from his post.

Stern's source of information was not, of course, the Chinese Secret Service. Nevertheless it will be noted that they obtained the news from Hongkong where the Chinese Secret Service has a key analysis post for sifting British and Commonwealth intelligence. By some discreet inquiries both in Hongkong and elsewhere I was not only assured that the Chinese Secret Service had details and dossiers on the heads of all Soviet and Western Intelligence chiefs, but was given details of the technique they used to obtain this information.

"It is relatively easy to get information on the Russian, American, French and many other Secret Service chiefs, because their countries make no secret of their appointments. Having got the names, all the Chinese have to do is to build up dossiers on them, adding scraps of information as they come in from their agents. With the British it was originally much more difficult for the simple reason that, traditionally, they have always kept the identity of their Secret Service chiefs carefully hidden.

"The Chinese Intelligence Service reads, sifts and analyses foreign newspapers in great detail. All this is tabulated and filed under various headings—personalities, policy-making and even public opinion. When Harold Wilson was the British Prime Minister the Chinese noted as a result of this diligent reading of newspapers that he mistrusted professional Intelligence officers as heads of the Secret Service and that he was seeking to bring this office under more rigorous control of the Foreign Office.

"They at once rubbed their hands with glee. This trend would enable them to spot much more quickly who was head of the British Secret Service. Instead of learning of it long after the Russians and the Americans they could, with care, probably get it first. I am not saying they did, but this is how they worked:

"Orders went out for a careful scrutiny of the Diplomatic Lists, making a careful note of changes of appointment, backed up by diligent reading of *Who's Who*. A Chinese intelligence officer once told me that *Who's Who* was one of the finest aids to spies he knew.

"What the Chinese would look for would be anything unusual in Foreign Office appointments, as they would now assume that the head of D16 would be a professional diplomat, thus reversing previous practice. At the same time they would study their *Who's Who*. Regarding Sir John Rennie they would, quite apart from noticing some curious designations for his work in the Diplomatic Lists, see in *Who's Who* of 1970 that the last entry

313

concerning his work was that he was 'on loan to Civil Service Commission during 1966'. After that there was no entry. An intelligent spy chief would find this worth further investigation.

"He would then note that Sir John Rennie's recreations were listed in *Who's Who* as 'electronics, painting'. For a diplomat to be interested in electronics would be remarkable enough—especially a British diplomat—but to the Chinese this would point immediately to espionage.

"The next step would be slowly to build up a more detailed picture of the man, to keep a discreet watch on his whereabouts (*Who's Who* gave no address, but named all his clubs), what he seemed to do and, not least, his family. Another important point the Chinese would have noticed would be that in 1953–58, after having been in the Warsaw Embassy, he was Head of Information Research Department of the Foreign Office. This would be the kind of euphemism, or appointment used, for somebody being groomed for a high job in Intelligence.

"In the case of Sir John Rennie I believe the Chinese were so cautious that they refused to accept their own suspicions for a long time. Confirmation finally came when Sir John's son was arrested. They did not have far to look as his son's wife used Gerrard Street—almost a 100 per cent Chinese quarter of London—as a rendezvous for obtaining Chinese heroin.

"This, if you like, was an unexpected bonus for the Chinese, but they were remarkably quick to maintain this perfectly legitimate method of tracking down heads of Britain's Secret Service. By this time the Chinese were building up their contacts with the West. They were beginning to receive American and British delegations and it was important that they should be known to be relatively well informed. As one Chinese diplomat said to me, 'Our academic friends in the West do us a great disservice in suggesting we are ill-informed on important matters. They make these statements in good faith, hoping to suggest that we are not like the Russians in flooding their country with spies, but nevertheless this can do us much harm.'

"So, when it was known that Rennie was to go and a new head of the Secret Service to be appointed, they turned again to notices of new appointments in the Diplomatic Lists. Here the Chinese are rather clever. They not only study the current edition of *Who's Who,* but compare it with those of the past ten years. Thus, while carefully watching the Lists, they would notice that in the 1970 *Who's Who* Maurice Oldfield had served in the Intelligence Corps in the Middle East in World War II, that he had been in the Office of Commissioner-General for the U.K. in S.E. Asia in Singapore in 1950–2—an area where a check could easily be made—that he had also been a Counsellor in Washington and that they had all his addresses in London and Derbyshire.

"Thus as early as mid-1973 the Chinese had Maurice Oldfield tabbed as head of D16. How did they find out? They put two and two together and decided that the fact that he had been given the title of 'Head of the Research Department of the Foreign Office' was merely a blind. In the mean time they had built up a complete dossier of the man as having been a specialist on S.E. Asia and having done a stint in Washington as senior liaison officer with the U.S. Central Intelligence Agency, which I might add, is sometimes a normal preliminary qualification for a Secret Service chief. When Philby was sent to Washington there is no doubt that some high officials saw this as a grooming for his eventual promotion to head of the Secret Service and, but for Burgess and Maclean, he might well have achieved this.

"Again, in January 1974, the Chinese had even tabbed the head of MI5, owing to the fact that he had been named in the New Year's Honours List. Yet until this happened the name of MI5's head had been kept carefully secret."

This is the statement given to me by a contact who is well versed in the methods of the Chinese Secret

Service. I suspect that some of the leakages to the press of this information come from the Chinese, who have a very high regard for the British Secret Service. Possibly one fault of their espionage system may have been to place too high a priority on British Secret Service matters.

The Chinese were quick to realise after 1949 that the Russians were reluctant to give China as much aid as they could, particularly in the military field, because the Soviet Union feared that the Chinese, as the most numerous people in the world, could pose a great threat if they became too powerful. Thus, secretly on the part of the Chinese, the break between China and the U.S.S.R. was developing as early as 1950.

Not surprisingly the first really independent move away from Russian influence came in the Chinese Secret Service. Suspicions engendered in World War II, when Soviet Russia was still officially supporting Chiang Kai-shek, were never fully dispelled and both Mao Tse-tung and K'ang Sheng were determined to keep their Intelligence Service free from Russian infiltration. This was by no means easy, for, under guise of friendship and support for the People's Republic against the Chiang Kai-shek regime in Taiwan, the Soviet Union sent an increasing number of "advisers" to China. Mao Tse-tung found himself in much the same position as Chiang Kai-shek had been during the Kuomintang's early flirtation with Moscow.

By the early 1950s the number of advisers had grown so rapidly that it was a matter of grave concern to the Chinese leaders. For example, in 1951, one of Mao's Secret Service aides reported to him that the Russians had infiltrated the Chinese Institute of Mathematics and, in doing so, had acquired control in the sphere of "electronic computer techniques in engineering and scientific problems, aerodynamics and nuclear physics". Mao decided that the Chinese were becoming over-reliant on Russian technology. He also suspected intrigues between some of his Army commanders and the Russians: as a result of what he discovered the Minister of Defence and the Army Chief of Staff were both dismissed as being too pro-Soviet.

K'ang Sheng was now a major figure in the hierarchy. In a speech given on 1 April 1948 at a cadre conference Mao Tse-tung had referred to K'ang's work in the Lin-hsien area, though while he gave K'ang full praise for this, he was also mildly critical of the fact that K'ang had appeared to espouse the policy of "doing everything as the masses want it done", whereas Mao believed the masses required leadership and being told what to do.

A directive of Mao's in February 1949 also referred to the fact that K'ang had been instructed to proceed to the headquarters of the Second and Third Field Armies and "to turn your rear-area work over to the Shantung Sub-Bureau". Later in 1949 K'ang was identified as the Shantung Governor as well as the Political Commissar of the Shantung Military District.[1]

But by the end of that year K'ang had become a member of the Central People's Government Council and he was also appointed to the First Executive of the Board of the Sino-Soviet Friendship Association (1949–54) through which organisation he was able to keep a watch on Russian activities. This was indeed one of his main tasks in the early 'fifties and he made no public appearances until 1954 when, coincidentally enough, his attendance at public meetings occurred at the very moment that Kao Kang, Jao Shu-shih and Hsiang Ming were being purged from offices in the Party. One suspects that K'ang Sheng had something to do with these purges.

His work at this time covered a much broader field than purely intelligence and internal security. He was active in promoting the usage of "the common national language", attended many educational conferences and was senior liaison officer with all foreign Communist Parties. There is a good deal of evidence which suggests he used this last post as a means of building up an important dossier on Soviet tactics and policies towards China, just as he saw his educational work helping to speed up the means of having an effective analysis of Chinese intelligence reports. Certainly he was one of the first to insist on the complete separation of the Chinese Secret Service from the Russian and one of the earliest critics of what he denounced as Soviet espionage in China.

K'ang went to Moscow on two occasions between 1959 and 1960, on the latter occasion being leader of the Chinese "observer" delegation to the Warsaw Treaty Political Consultative Committee. At this conference he made it quite clear in a forceful speech that China disagreed strongly with Soviet policies towards the West, especially on the subject of disarmament, and he bluntly stated that any disarmament agreement reached without China's participation would not have any binding force.

So K'ang Sheng himself stressed the rift between China and Russia long before it came out into the open, and sometimes even in the face of opposition in the Politburo he continued to hark on this theme. His task after 1952, according to the most diligent students of Chinese affairs, was ostensibly mainly concerned with the unusual combination of higher education and liaison with foreign Communist Parties. But he made the fullest use of his work in the higher educational sphere to strengthen, improve and revolutionise the Chinese Secret Service. He demanded a higher standard of education among both Intelligence executive officers and agents in the field.

Generally speaking, it can be said that Chinese Intelligence since the Communists took over has worked in accordance with an old Chinese saying, "sowing wide to reap thinly"; in other words, operating on a broad front and expending considerable efforts for possibly modest gains. Without being too cynical, one could perhaps say that far too much time and effort was spent in establishing the identities of the various heads of British Intelligence. On the other hand, as the Chinese know, espionage is very much a matter of "keeping up with the Joneses" and this alone can give them extra strength and authority in diplomatic negotiations which from now on they will increasingly have with the Western world.

Every time the Chinese make a further step in establishing diplomatic contacts so they develop a parallel espionage set-up. This is achieved more often than not through relatively innocuous sources—trade offices, news agencies and cultural associations. Embassy staffs have been used as a cover for espionage in much the same way as the Russians utilise such personnel, but with the difference that the Chinese are much more cautious and employ only a few key Embassy officials in such work and even then not in every capital.

Contrary to the views of most Western Intelligence observers who believe that the Chinese employ hardly any non-Chinese agents today, there is abundant evidence that anyone (especially foreign students) who applies for a visa to visit China has his background carefully checked by local diplomatic personnel in collaboration with the Intelligence Service to decide of what use the visitor will eventually be to China. Once the visitor has arrived, though this applies more to the student visitor, cultural organisations play an important rôle in these activities.

As to the modern structure of the Chinese Secret Service it should be stressed that it is all-embracing to an extent that no other Communist nation's Secret Service has yet achieved. Fundamentally, it is more authoritarian, yet in its scope much more democratic and flexible, more anxious to learn even from dissidents than, say, are the Russians. The whole apparatuses of internal security, espionage at home and abroad and counter-espionage are all interlocked and tightly controlled. The County Military Service Bureau is for example linked with the Army, the Secret Service and the Public Security Bureau. A high degree of secrecy and security-consciousness prevails. There is a well-defined security system with comprehensive rules on how written materials and other information should be handled. There are varying degrees of secrecy, but much material that is classified as top secret is of a type that most Western nations would regard as routine or even desirable to publish.

The Korean War following so quickly on the creation of the People's Republic of China, and the fact that at times China seemed poised for an open clash with the U.S.A., forced the Communists to speed up the development of the Chinese Secret Service. Work that would normally have taken ten years to complete had to be hastily compressed into two or three years and, not surprisingly, some mistakes were made on the organisational side.

All government and civic departments have their intelligence organisations which contribute to the Central Control of Intelligence. There are three main channels for this: first, the Party channel, which includes the investigation department, a powerful team of professional intelligence officers; secondly, the Central External Liaison Department, which, at the time of writing, is headed by one Keng Biao, and which is concerned with the kind of analysis of foreign intelligence mentioned earlier on; third, the State Council, which does not have contact with the professional intelligence agencies, but which indirectly is concerned with intelligence gathering through the Ministry of Foreign Affairs, the New China News Agency, the Ministry of External Trade and the Ministry of External Economic Liaison (in charge of foreign aid disposal); fourth, the Military Intelligence Department of the General Staff which controls Embassy military attachés and other personnel, collecting military intelligence and sometimes linking up with the Investigation Department of the State Council.

It has only been in the last decade that these various branches of the Secret Service have been developed to a higher degree of efficiency, but the basic concepts of such an all-embracing Intelligence Service were well laid in the mid-'fifties. By degrees this all led to the creation of the *Cheng pao k'o*, or Political Security Section, responsible for counter-espionage against enemy agents and control and investigation of overseas Chinese, the latter being an increasingly important factor in espionage, and the *Chi pao k'o*, or Organisational Security Section, focussing its attention on personnel in government agencies, factories, schools, etc.; and, finally, the Social Order Section which divides its time between routine administrative duties such as census registration, investigation of crimes and traffic control, with some espionage investigation.

At the time of the Korean War China began to build

up and extend its still very small network among the Chinese overseas. This was essentially a slow and cautious business as the Communists were fully aware that from Taiwan Chiang Kai-shek still maintained his own Secret Service which depended almost entirely on exiles from China. Thus great care had to be taken to avoid recruiting double-agents among the Chinese exiles whose first loyalty might be to the Taiwan Government. On the other hand a number of attempts were made to infiltrate Chiang's network.

Though priority was given to Chinese who actually lived overseas, major attention was also given to Chinese who had returned to China from exile (this involved very thorough screening) and to families and relatives actually residing in China of overseas Chinese. Some of the returned overseas Chinese were gathered together in special areas. An "Overseas Chinese New Village" was created for this purpose: here the residents had special privileges in return for being recruited as spies.

Espionage was also financed from contributions sent back home by overseas Chinese, and Hongkong became a key centre for the receipt of such contributions, in the financing of agents, and in developing the overseas espionage network.

For most of the 'fifties and part of the 'sixties China was isolated from the rest of the world largely through her own decision. This undoubtedly put her at a disadvantage in gathering intelligence overseas, but it was also a stimulus and unquestionably led the way to short cuts in finding the right answers and to the simplified system of intelligence gathering already mentioned. But perhaps its great advantage was that it avoided the errors of the Soviet Union who, in the 'twenties and early 'thirties, made such an enormous espionage drive all over Europe that their agents were caught and rounded up in scores. The Chinese Secret Service maintained an excellent record of losing fewer agents to foreign counter-espionage organisations than any other Intelligence Service of this period.

The main intelligence battle, however, between 1949 and 1956 lay in combatting the joint threat of the U.S.A. and the forces of Chiang Kai-shek in Taiwan and the offshore islands of Quemoy and Matsu. The intervention of China on behalf of the North Koreans was simply a natural self-preservative reaction to this: from their own need to survive they dared not do other than challenge American might in this theatre. What appeared to the Western World like aggression in those years was in fact almost entirely defensive. At the end of the Korean War China emerged with enhanced prestige, but at the cost of slowing down for ten years the external espionage of the nation. The sole task was to concentrate on defending North Korea, withstanding the threats of the megalomaniacs in the Pentagon who wanted to use nuclear weapons on China, and containing the moves from Taiwan to "liberate" China. Foreign intelligence was devoted almost entirely to this end.

In this period the shock troops of Chinese espionage overseas comprised largely the disciplined and fanatically patriotic personnel of the New China News Agency. It was a cautious, strictly financially controlled and highly experimental operation in external espionage which, if it achieved only modest results, avoided too much adverse publicity (later, however, it tended in some areas to overreach itself and to suffer in consequence). But the N.C.N.A. became in effect an instrument of the Secret Service and it was directly subordinate to the State Council.

Two of the N.C.N.A.'s earliest and ablest directors in this field were Chiao Kuan-hua, latterly chief delegate to the United Nations General Assembly; and Huang Hua, first Ambassador to Canada. This exemplifies the close link between the agency and China's foreign policy-makers. Chiao was the foreign news editor of *Hsin-hua Jih-pao* (*New China Daily*) during World War II when the N.C.N.A. was really an appendage of this newspaper. He wrote several commentaries on world affairs under the pen name of Chiao Mu and from 1946–9 was head of the N.C.N.A bureau in Hongkong. Apart from some discreet intelligence gathering Chiao also had the tasks of providing information for Western correspondents in Hongkong and attempting to influence businessmen and Chinese intellectuals in the colony. Similarly Huang Hua was

322

an N.C.N.A. correspondent in Chungking during the last days of World War II and because of his fluent English was active among Western journalists and diplomats.

The pattern of dual rôle of newspaper correspondent and liaison officer with Western journalists and diplomats has always been maintained in the N.C.N.A. Not only do they obtain information, but they evaluate it and even make proposals for foreign policy-making. "They are," writes Alan P. L. Liu, Assistant Professor of Political Science at the University of California, "a vital source for the small group of top leaders in Peking who determine China's strategy in international affairs. N.C.N.A. is thus an indispensable part of Communist China's foreign affairs establishment."[2]

Such a systematic, if often over-bureaucratic, approach to Intelligence work curbed adventurous activities in the first ten years of the People's Republic. In the whole period the only recorded instance of an aggressive espionage act was in November 1950, when, in Bombay, a group of Chinese Communist agents attacked one Anadan Andrew in an attempt to steal coded diplomatic messages he was delivering to the U.S. Consulate.

26

The Rift with Russia
1956-1974

Behind all the ideology, the rôle of the nuclear weapon
in the feud [between China and the U.S.S.R.] has been
clearly discernible from the outset. It was the bomb
issue which prompted Peking eventually to describe
Moscow's leadership as China's 'Enemy No. 1.'
William L. Ryan and *Sam Summerlin* in *The China
Cloud*

SUSPICION and hostility have, except for relatively
brief periods, marked relationships between China and
Russia over the centuries. It was to keep out "the
barbarians in the West" that China built the Great
Wall. Memories of the many invasions from that quarter lingered on into the nineteenth century. But above
all else most arguments between the two nations inevitably centred around the question of maps, for each
country had (and still has) its own views of who owns
what.

In the fifteenth century Muscovite Russia and Ming
China were at the nearest point more than two thousand miles apart, separated by deserts, mountains,
steppelands and a variety of peoples, both settled and
nomadic. But as the nineteenth century drew to a close
the expansionist tendencies of both the Czarists and
the Manchus narrowed the gap so that by the 1880s
the two great giants were separated only by the prin-
cipalities of Russian and Chinese Turkestan.

The Treaty of Chuguchak in October 1864, fixing a
frontier in Russia's favour, had deprived China of three
hundred and fifty thousand square miles. For some
time after that, border limitations fluctuated, the Russians gaining some more ground in Kuldja in 1871,

when they moved in "to restore order", and the Chinese recovering this area ten years later under the Treaty of Ili.

China's frontier with the Soviet Union today runs for some two thousand miles from the north-east corner of the Mongolian People's Republic to the Pacific coast south of Vladivostock. The truth is that on the territorial question China has a strong moral case against Russia in that most of the land was wrested from her in the days of Czarist imperial aggression and the U.S.S.R. has made no gestures towards restoring such territories. Much the same applies to certain border areas of India, and Chinese demands for correcting the old imperialist-fixed frontiers are not nearly as unreasonable as they are frequently depicted.

A Peking Communist newspaper (1963) stated the unembroidered truth: "In the hundred years or so prior to the victory of the Chinese revolution the imperialist and colonial powers consisting of the United States, Britain, France, Czarist Russia, Germany, Japan, Italy, Austria, Belgium, the Netherlands, Spain and Portugal carried out unbridled aggression. They compelled the Governments of old China to sign a large number of unequal treaties, the Treaty of Nanking in 1842, of Aigun in 1858, of Tientsin, 1858, of Peking, 1860, of Ili, 1881, the Protocol of Lisbon, 1887, the Treaty of Shinionoseki, 1895, the Convention for the Extension of Hongkong, 1898, and the International Protocol of 1901. By virtue of these unequal Treaties they annexed Chinese territory in the North, South-East and West and held leased territories on the seaboard or in the hinterland."

The Chinese case was that Soviet Russia was being hypocritical in denouncing past imperial aggression while actually defending what she had gained from it. But while this was a significant factor in the gradually worsening Sino-Russian relations, the underlying, if unmentioned, cause of the rift was Russia's possession of the nuclear bomb. They saw the nuclear bomb as a Soviet weapon with which to bully China. But it was when Khrushchev came to power and launched on his brash, back-slapping campaign to defuse the "Cold War" and make a deal with the U.S.A. that the Chinese foresaw that in collusion the Americans and the Russians could isolate China completely. Finally, the Chinese greatly resented the Soviet policy of showing favours to India, which they looked upon as a decadent, corrupt capitalist country.

K'ang Sheng gave instructions for a lengthy dossier of hostile actions by the Soviet Union against China to be compiled. As one of the earliest of the anti-Soviet members of the Politburo he was eager to substantiate his case. He put his finger on the one single subject which would clinch his case—cartography: Chinese agents were ordered to obtain the latest Russian maps showing the Sino-Russian border. He suspected that these had been falsified by the Russians for two reasons: first, to claim more Chinese territory than they had already annexed; and secondly, to introduce a measure of censorship into maps covering the border areas, designed to mislead the Chinese by deliberately altering the location of certain places and installations.

K'ang's agents managed after great difficulty in proving that not only were the maps doctored, but that the K.G.B. had to a large extent controlled Russian cartography, falsifying many details. Latitudinal and longitudinal details had been altered by a few kilometres, these distortions being stepped up where the Asiatic borders were concerned.

The quest for Soviet maps and the demand for the production of more up-to-date Chinese maps to counteract the Soviet distortions became an important task in Chinese Intelligence. K'ang himself hammered away at the Russians, making his critical views even more forcefully when he attended the Third Congress of the Rumanian Workers' Party at Bucharest in June 1960. Using all the knowledge he had acquired from his anti-Soviet dossier, he made a point of giving interviews to all foreign Communist leaders who came to Peking. His power and authority grew as Peking hardened its attitude to Russia and by the early 'sixties he had suddenly risen from twenty-fifth to fifth place in the Politburo of the Chinese Communist Party.

Chinese espionage in Russia has always been extremely limited. In the past, even before World War I, the Chinese sought to recruit Europeans for intelligence purposes in Russia on the grounds that members of their own race were too noticeable. In this connection some of the White Guard Russians who fled to Manchuria after the revolution provided a source which by now, however, has become virtually exhausted, and few Russians, whatever their political beliefs, could be enticed to serve the present Peking regime.

Back in the 'fifties before the rift developed thousands to Chinese students were enrolled in various schools and universities in the Soviet Union and even then, together with a number of Chinese teachers and professors, they always formed tightly knit, highly disciplined groups. Doubtless some among their members had assignments to gather intelligence, especially in the economic field and in classified areas. At that time their task was relatively easy, but virtually all of these had departed by 1962.

The really serious trouble between Moscow and Peking started in 1960. That spring the Chinese Embassy in Moscow began mass distribution of pro-Chinese propaganda material in Russia until the Soviet authorities finally stopped it. Meanwhile in China itself a campaign of harassment began against Russian personnel, including efforts to intimidate and recruit them to the Chinese cause.

Chinese espionage against Russia was stepped up in those fields left open to it and it was a markedly aggressive campaign. The drive to win agents among Russian personnel in China was so massive that Moscow ordered the re-patriation of a large number of their advisers and diplomatic personnel from China.

In June 1960 there was a mass incursion by peasants with their cattle from the Chinese side of the border into Soviet territory and, despite Russian protests, they stayed across the border, raising livestock until the snows came. It was a carefully master-minded preliminary intelligence probe. Peking did not expect to gain any worthwhile intelligence out of it, but they saw it as a means of alerting them as to how to prepare for a more serious effort at infiltration later on.

This was merely a prelude to what happened in 1962 when, with the beginning of spring, thousands of Kazakhs and Uigurs came flocking to the Soviet border without visas, having been informed by the Chinese authorities that they would not need any. The number exceeded forty-six thousand in a few months. When the Soviet authorities tried to persuade these immigrants to return to China and apply for proper visas the Chinese refused to let them back. By the end of the year the Russians were forced to close their Consulates in Urumchi and Khlezag. Doubtless they suspected with some justification that this mass influx without frontier formalities was deliberately engineered by the Chinese as a cover for infiltration of political agitators and intelligence agents.

Much of this is still simply cautious probing on the part of the Chinese, but there has been some evidence latterly that the operation has been taken a stage further and that some of the border tribes inside Russian territory have been in part won over as secret allies of the Chinese.

Chinese Intelligence and the foreign policy makers in Peking worked closely together at this period to extend Chinese influence in those areas bordering on both Russia and India. Indeed, despite Nehru's blandly friendly gestures to Peking in the 'fifties, the Chinese always suspected that he (and more important, those around him) were closer to Russia than to China. A big diplomatic effort, linked with a Secret Service operation, was made to counteract this by establishing close links with Pakistan and to infiltrate Tibet, while consolidating the Chinese position *vis à vis* Mongolia.

The spy network in Tibet was set up well before the takeover of that country by China. From the Secret Service point of view the policy was to direct espionage networks against both Russia and India from these two centres.

Secret pressure from 1956 onwards led the Chinese to press for a socialist revolution in Tibet, and a rising in Lhasa in March 1959 led to the flight of the Dalai Lama to India, repressive measures by the Chinese forces and the take-over of the country. China's aim was control of the strategic route between Tibet and Sinkiang Province.

From that moment the Chinese made Tibet one of their vital listening posts *vis à vis* India and Russia. Organisations like the Commercial Academy and the Border Affairs Office which sprang up in Tibet were in actuality training schools for agents, disguised as traders. For Chinese Intelligence was concerned about the efforts being made to win over the neighbouring tiny satellite states of India—Sikkim, Bhutan and Nepal—by Soviet Russia.

One permanent tactic of Chinese Intelligence in a situation such as this is not so much direct espionage as the deliberate infiltration of agents to propagate the Chinese cause. The argument here is that the appearance of Chinese in great numbers can by the size of its impact have a strong political influence.

Nevertheless espionage was not neglected and the Commercial Academy in Lhasa, the Tibetan capital, became the headquarters of a special section devoted to "civil intelligence". This had eight classes running concurrently, each with eighty members enrolled for six months. Most of the members were either Chinese students from the dispute area of East Tibet, or Tibetans coerced to join. They were taught elementary trading techniques and given language courses in Nepali, Hindi and Bengali. Then, when they had completed their courses, and after they had been carefully vetted, they would be sent to one of three infiltration training schools.

As far as can be ascertained both the training and screening of potential agents was extremely thorough. An élite class was singled out comprising Chinese college graduates, all speaking some English, whose political backgrounds were impeccable. It has been reported from one source that the instructors here included Russian as well as Chinese instructors. If so, they were certainly Russia defectors, which in itself as far as China was concerned is somewhat remarkable.

Training classes for agents were limited to fifty students and the course lasted for one year. They were all taught Indian dialects and at the same time every effort was made to perfect their English. Some four hours a day were devoted to a study of Intelligence techniques.

Later they were sent out to India either as traders or members of missions.

There was a certain amount of specialisation: one school of agent-training was concentrated entirely on espionage in Nepal: it included two hundred Chinese and one hundred Nepalis, many of whom had crossed over from Sikkim, which has a large Nepalese population, into Tibet. This school was situated in Lhasa with a front-line border office where agents were trained for the last three months in the customs and manners of Nepal. One of the directors of the school was a Nepali, Dr Singh, who had defected to Tibet.

Another training school was devoted to students who would be sent as agents to Bhutan and Sikkim. The Sikkimese and Bhutanese languages have close affinities with that of Tibet, so training in infiltration was made relatively easy on this account. Sometimes agents were sent into these countries as traders, occasionally as teachers or monks.

The Border Affairs Office was rather more secret in its activities. It was situated in an isolated building, closely guarded, near the headquarters of the Chinese Army in Lhasa. This was the headquarters where five top Intelligence men from Peking, with a staff of eighty, directed operations into India, Nepal and Sikkim. But the Border Affairs Office also had three subsidiary offices, one in a small town named Chung Petan in a steep valley of the Himalayas between Tibet and Sikkim, where there was a detachment of the Police Army, another in Nelammo, north of Mount Everest and close to the Nepalese border, and the third in Tsona, near the Bhutan and Assam borders.

K'ang's insistence on the importance of cartographic research as a vital part of intelligence work was developed in Tibet. More than three hundred Chinese cartographical experts were deputed to make surveys in the disputed areas along the borders of Tibet, Nepal, Bhutan and parts of Northern Assam, as well as Sikkim and Kashmir. The result of all this was a new atlas of the world published by the Chinese which laid claim to something like a million square miles of Russian-ruled territory, quite apart from areas in India, Nepal and Sikkim. A strong case was put forward denouncing the fact that Imperial Russia had fastened itself on to autonomous Mongolia since 1912.

There is a peculiarly Chinese feature of the Peking Government and its Secret Service's attack on Soviet Russia which reminds one of Danton's advice of *l'audace, toujours l'audace*. In seeking a confrontation with Russia, China, though totally isolated at the time, made no effort to devote her propaganda to winning allies other than Communist countries to her cause. The gist of her attack was in fact that which was most likely to exacerbate still further China's relations with the West. Peking objected to the assaults by Khrushchev on the menace of Stalinism, to Soviet suggestions that war was not inevitable and that revolution could be achieved without violence. All this was an outrageous piece of bluffing, supported only by the findings of the Chinese Secret Service, which more or less informed Mao Tse-Tung that the harder and more extreme a line the Chinese took the longer it would buy them time and the more it would leave both Russia and the West guessing.

Peking's judgement proved accurate. The intemperance of the Chinese Communists' declarations took both the Western powers and the Soviet Union by surprise: both began to suspect that China might be on the verge of acquiring nuclear weapons. There was panic among the Sino-Russian border communities. Mongolia complained that before 1962 Peking had published maps showing Mongolian territory as part of China. Sometime later more than twenty thousand booklets in Mongolian were smuggled into the country and distributed via local Chinese activists. A box purporting to contain medical supplies delivered to the Chinese hospital in Ulan Bator was found to hold thousands of posters with portraits of Mao Tse-tung and Lin Piao, the commander-in-chief.

There were, of course, swift counter-attacks by the Russians and their satellites. In 1963 the New China News Agency was ordered to be expelled from Prague because of allegations of involvement in espionage. Up to this date Prague had been one of China's most important espionage bureaux in Europe, and had been almost the first European centre in which the

N.C.N.A. had set up an office, as far back as 1948. Other European Communist countries also took a tougher line against the Chinese.

Albania was the last of the East European countries to recognise the Chinese People's Republic in 1949 and Ambassadors were only exchanged in 1954. Nevertheless Albania was soon to become China's firmest friend in the European Communist world.

After the Hungarian revolt she firmly supported China and relations between the two countries rapidly became cordial. At the Bucharest conference in June 1960 Albania backed China, while at the Moscow conference in November of the same year Enver Hoxha, the Albanian party leader, strongly defended China and attacked Khrushchev. In February 1961 China offered a £45 millions loan for Albania's third five-year plan, which compensated for the withdrawal of Soviet aid. In December 1961 the U.S.S.R. broke off relations with Albania and the next year China offered a further £35 millions. Offers since then are not known in detail, but in November 1968 Hoxha declared that the aid then given by China was "the largest credit aid, interest-free, that China has given to our country".

China urgently needed a Communist ally in Europe and Albania soon became not merely a perfect venue for a listening-post for Eastern Europe and the Balkans, but also an admirable site for Intelligence Service radio monitoring. In fact the Chinese moved in as the Russians moved out, for the latter had previously been firmly installed in Albania with an elaborate naval base in the south.

Details of the Secret Service organisation which the Chinese have built up in Albania are essentially sketchy, for Albania guards its secrets and rigorously restricts the number of foreign visitors to it, more so than any other Communist nation. But what is clear not so much from visitors to Albania, who have come away with relatively little information, but from radio hams and radio experts generally, is that China has its own reception and transmission stations in Albania and that these are manned and directed by some of their finest Intelligence brains.

I quote from one ham radio analyst on this subject: "Without doubt the Albanian broadcasting services are under the influence of P.R. China. Radio Tirana's transmitters are used to relay the broadcasts of Radio Peking and these broadcasts seem to be beamed to North America. Also at least two of the transmitters being used in Albania were previously in use in China itself.

"There exists between Albania and P.R. China both RTTY and other code links. The RTTY codes never use the standard frequency shifts. In fact they don't use any one frequency shift for very long—on occasions I have noted changes in shift being made two or three times in a day. This tactic of using nonstandard shifts and continuously changing the frequency of the shift makes it difficult to copy their RTTY transmissions. I would add that China also does the same in its RTTY transmissions."

The problem of accurate interception of all such transmissions depends upon the construction of an RTTY (radio teleprinted link) terminal unit which would allow the operator to vary the shift in accordance with any standard that is being used. Needless to say the construction of such a unit presents problems both technical and financial, but the mere fact that the broadcasts in question are made as difficult as possible to intercept indicates that the contents of the transmissions are of a secret nature.

Constant monitoring of Albanian transmissions—as distinct from Chinese transmissions from Albania—over the past few years have not revealed a great deal of significance as far as the subject of this book is concerned. As regards the purpose of the transmissions, the Radio Tirana Station is almost exclusively concerned with propaganda—both anti-Soviet and anti-Imperialist. The only countries that seem to be favoured in their broadcasts are China, some countries of S.E. Asia and those countries in Africa and the Middle East and Central and South America which are governed by People's Revolutionary Governments or similar administrations. Chinese technicians and engineers are involved in Albanian broadcasting and telecommunications services and this collaboration extends to mutual espionage.

To illustrate the point made in the last sentence, I have before me the text of a monitored transmission from the Albanian point-to-point radio station which was made at 21.40 hours on 12 January 1973. This quoted "Moscow sources" (obviously unofficial sources) as saying that Soviet submarines had been engaged in placing detecting and recording equipment at key points of NATO activities. Their source stated that it was necessary to create and maintain this method of surveillance to offset advantages gained by NATO through breaches made by U.S. espionage of the Warsaw Pact of Security. There followed a resumé of espionage by both sides since World War II, asserting that the Russians had successfully infiltrated Western military establishments. They also referred to the fact that East-West defections had been much greater than those going the opposite way, which seemed to balance up the overall picture and to enable them to draw the conclusion that treaties and talks were only side-shows "while the Soviet Union and the U.S.A. are clearly determined to maintain a state of terror for all the world's peace-loving peoples".

On one or two other occasions Albanian broadcasts have indicated the movements of Soviet submarines, mentioning one that had been in the vicinity of Britain's Polaris base, while at the time of the detection of an unknown submarine on the sea bed of a Norwegian fiord, the Albanians gave an explanation within a few days that it was a Russian submarine, some of whose crew had mutinied, and telling how the remainder of the crew took charge while another Russian submarine towed it to safety out of the fiord underwater, despite NATO ships hunting for the craft.

Obviously the Chinese have access to this kind of information and there seemed no reasons to doubt that it is with their approval that such information has been broadcast, primarily as anti-Soviet propaganda, secondly to make the Western world alive to the continuous Soviet threat.

In October 1963 Stephen Constant in the London

Daily Telegraph reported that "a major difficulty facing the Chinese leaders as a result of their growing isolation from the rest of the world is how to maintain a flow of intelligence and other vital political, economic and military information from Peking. Whatever help China may have received from the Soviet bloc intelligence services in the past . . . has now ceased."

As we have seen, China was fully alive to this problem from the beginning of her rift with Russia and after the expulsion of N.C.N.A. correspondents from Prague. Stephen Constant added that "Chinese intelligence is also severely hampered by the difficulty of communications . . . the full dangers of the situation became clear to the Chinese after last summer's crash in Russia of an airliner carrying two Chinese diplomatic couriers to Albania. The Chinese Government is anxiously looking for alternative air routes bypassing the Soviet Union."

Many of these difficulties have long since been overcome, though not without a certain amount of trial and error. Their choice was two-fold as regards replacing their sources of Soviet bloc intelligence—to use the services of agents or sympathisers of other nationalities, which involved normally a heavy expense in hard currencies, and, either alternatively or additionally, to infiltrate and use the small Chinese communities in some of these countries.

Albania gradually came to provide an ideal base not merely because of its friendliness to China, but due to its tight internal security and the fact that it needed Chinese aid and technicians. But discreet infiltration in other areas paid off and great use was made of Chinese merchant seamen who, after undergoing elaborate training in China, were used as couriers between Peking and Chinese agents in the field. Though the use of seamen as agents and couriers is usually kept to what is known as low-key activity, which is to say they are not employed on aggressive espionage in the Russian manner, a carefully selected few of them are sometimes instructed to cajole, threaten and even blackmail overseas Chinese who may seem reluctant to cooperate.

The development of an espionage service inside

Pakistan, with a certain amount of co-operation from the Pakistani authorities, was governed both by hostility to India and Russia. Naturally the N.C.N.A. moved in, for they always flourish in such a situation. But Pakistan is a country in which security as regards intelligence machinations is far below that of, say, Albania, and leakages of information are considerable. Though the Chinese may have gained some intelligence from Pakistan, they soon found that Western observers in Pakistan were—to quote the words of a colleague who has served both in the Far East and in Pakistan—"getting as much information in Pakistan on China as I did from Hongkong".

In Moscow today the Chinese Embassy has a diplomatic staff of thirty-three, including the Ambassador, four Counsellors, three military attachés, three First Secretaries, one Second Secretary, seven Third Secretaries and thirteen attachés. Only nine wives are indicated and it is significant that all the attachés are single and so are all but one of the Third Secretaries. In addition there are two correspondents of the N.C.N.A., one of whom is married. All members of the Chinese colony live within the spacious Embassy compound which was built in the 'fifties before relations between the two countries soured. In addition to those with diplomatic status all service employees are Chinese, including the drivers and yard men. The present strength of personnel in the Embassy represents a considerable increase over what it was at the height of the Cultural Revolution in 1967, but only a fraction of what it was in the 'fifties.

The Soviet Union is well aware of the dangers of infiltration from China. Officially there are some twenty-eight thousand Chinese with Soviet nationality and ever since the rift the U.S.S.R. have kept them under strict surveillance as far as is possible. But in truth, as has been seen with the border incidents of 1962, there are in the desolate and difficult to control Sino-Russian border areas more than twice this number of Chinese. Extensive attempts to infiltrate Central Asians, mainly Kazahks and Uigars who live in Sinkiang Province, into principally Soviet Kazahkstan, where the inhabitants belong to the same tribe, have been made.

Leftwingers and rightwingers have both alleged that the disagreements between China and Russia are superficial and that the two powers would quickly come together again in an emergency. The fact that the two extremes of opinion take this view is yet another example of wishful thinking. Much has happened in the past ten years which would have borne out this theory had it been valid. The reverse is true.

In January 1974 five members of the Soviet Embassy in Peking were expelled for espionage after being held incommunicado for four days. According to Moscow's version, "two Soviet diplomats and their wives were out shopping . . . and were arrested after they had dined at an hotel in Peking. . . . They have been named as Mr V. I. Marchenko, the First Secretary, and his wife, and Mr A. A. Kolosov, an interpreter in the office of the Soviet military attaché."[1]

This version conflicts markedly with the Chinese account of the arrests. The Chinese Note accused the five Soviet diplomats of meeting a Chinese collaborator, Li Hung-shu, on the outskirts of Peking on the evening of 15 January. The Chinese statement added: "They handed over and received intelligence, counter-revolutionary documents, a radio transmitter and receiver, means of secret writing, forged border passes and other facilities and money for espionage activities. They were caught on the spot by Chinese public security personnel and militia-men. With the culprits and material evidence at hand, their crimes are conclusively established."[2] The Note went on to accuse the Soviet Embassy of carrying out over a long period espionage in China and "surreptitiously setting up counter-revolutionary organisations aimed at subverting the dictatorship of the proletariat in China".

The Chinese had for some time been keeping a discreet watch on Soviet activities and the evidence against the Russians had been built up over a long period. The only surprising thing is that the Russians risked such tactics by Embassy personnel despite the tight watch kept on all foreigners by the Chinese counter-espionage organisation. The Chinese had quite overtly stepped up their watch on foreigners in the week or two preceding the arrests as they had stopped

337

every car carrying foreigners as it left the built-up areas of Peking in this period.

This represented a new low ebb in Sino-Russian relations, with stern and uncompromising threats from the Chinese and a strongly worded protest from the Soviet Ministry of Foreign Affairs at what it described as "new anti-Soviet provocation". (The Russian version of the arrest was that some of those detained had their hands bound and were subjected to filming by cameramen in front of a large crowd). Yet the Soviet Embassy, despite the differences between the two countries, had remained until January 1974 one of the largest in Peking, and Chinese officials had constantly expressed concern at its unofficial activities and scope for espionage. But, perhaps wisely, the Chinese Secret Service had decided that the Russians should be given enough rope to hang themselves.

There is little doubt that this is what happened. The Russians were deliberately lulled into believing they could not only hoodwink the Chinese authorities, but conduct major espionage activities against them inside Peking itself. The Chinese had given orders that every aid to counter-espionage—bugging, filming and shadowing by microphone—should be carried out. The N.C.N.A. version of what happened is interesting. This agency claimed that Li Hung-shu had confessed what happened, that he admitted receiving a telegram from Moscow on 27 December, ordering him to go to the Soviet Embassy in Peking. One might well query whether Moscow would have taken any such risk. However, they further alleged that Li first talked with the Russians by radio as a result of which he began collecting information on the Chinese Communist Party and the Army which he wrote and hid in a white medical mask. Such masks are worn by a good twenty per cent of the Peking population in winter as protection against the cold.

The Russians, according to the N.C.N.A., also gave Li a password, "Alen", and told him to meet them under the Paho River bridge about four miles from the centre of the city and a mile from the Soviet Embassy. There, it was claimed, Li and an unnamed companion met U. A. Semenov and A. Kolosov from the

Soviet Embassy. The Russians were said to have disguised themselves in Mao jackets and to have been driven to the rendezvous by V. I. Marchenko, the First Secretary. Li handed over the medical mask and received a suitcase containing a radio transmitter which had been covered with the Chinese Communist slogan, "Serve the People". The suitcase contained times and tables for receiving instructions and sending intelligence information to Moscow.

The Chinese claimed they were able to make a film of the whole incident prior to the arrest, presumably with infra-red lighting. They further alleged that Li was recruited by the Russians as an agent and that he had left China secretly for the Soviet Union in 1967. He had, according to them, received special training from a military intelligence agency of the U.S.S.R. before being ordered to go back to China via Sinkiang in 1972.[3]

The truth was that Li was a highly skilled agent of Chinese counter-espionage. In just under seven years he had been able to expose Soviet tactics towards Peking.

27

China Secures Nuclear Secrets
1946-1966

The intelligence activities of Red China have brought about an increase in our responsibilities . . . and the work can be expected to mount . . . In this country Communist Chinese agents have mounted a concerted effort to obtain highly sensitive data for their homeland. This material goes to Red China by various means. For example, two individuals have been forwarding electronic components, which could be used in a multitude of military equipment, to Communist China through an intermediary in Hongkong.

From a testimony by *J. Edgar Hoover,* late head of the F.B.I., 23 February 1968

J. EDGAR HOOVER, in the latter part of his life at least, was ever an alarmist, but in his statement of 1968, two years after China had successfully launched her first nuclear weapon carried by a guided missile, he was by no means exaggerating. To those in the Western World who tend to play down the importance and efficacy of the Chinese Secret Service, there is one argument which no amount of casuistry or cynicism can counteract: it is the fact that, against enormous odds, China's Intelligence Service master-minded the wresting of nuclear secrets from the West.

This in itself was a tremendous achievement, far greater in comparison than Soviet Russia's admittedly much earlier capture of the same kind of secrets. One must remember that Russia not only had a highly efficient network of agents inside the U.S.A. and Canada in World War II, when she was an ally of the West, but that she also had the benefit of information obtained from captured German scientists and technicians, as well as the advantage of having secured the services of such dedicated scientific spies as Klaus Fuchs and others. But the Chinese Communists had to concentrate on trying to obtain this intelligence while they were still fighting Chiang Kai-shek—and therefore had a relatively small overseas Intelligence Service—and after they had broken with the Russians. They also suffered from the defect to which Stephen Constant has referred—"a Chinese is easily identifiable in a white community, and thus severely handicapped from the start".[1]

It is not easy to assess just when China started a systematic operation to obtain nuclear secrets. There are some indications that the Chinese Communists had obtained hints of the development of a super-weapon by one or other of the Western powers as early as 1944. If so, one can only presume this intelligence came from the Soviet Union. But it is abundantly clear that as early as 1946 they were mounting an operation to get details of the atomic bomb.

This was a team operation, but if credit is to be given to a few, then those who stand out as the masterminds are K'ang Sheng, Chien Wei-chang (more familiarly known as Jimmy Chien), Ch'ien Hsue-shen and Chao Chung-yao.

Curiously enough, one of the first tips about work on a secret project involving the creation of a super-bomb to be built by the United States came to K'ang Sheng from one of his spies inside Tai Li's headquarters in 1944. The spy in question was a chauffeur to a U.S. officer in the S.A.C.O. team. He overheard a conversation between a S.A.C.O. and an O.S.S. officer in which the phrases which stuck in his memory were "we're on the way to making a super-bomb which could finish the war with Japan in a matter of days" and "top secret research at Pasadena".

The spy was no technician and these phrases were all he managed to absorb, but K'ang was immediately impressed because he had already formed the opinion from a few clumsily worded Russian inquiries that the U.S.S.R. were also on the trail of such a secret weapon, and he saw the possibility of this being used to attempt to blackmail the Chinese Communists into surrender at some future point. Naturally at this stage he visualised the main danger being the U.S.A. using such a weapon to uphold Chiang Kai-shek and destroy Mao Tse-tung.

K'ang hoped to get some further confirmation from the Russians of what his spy had overheard, but at the same time he decided the Chinese Communist Intelligence must make their own efforts to ascertain these secrets. He knew that in the 'thirties a large number of promising Chinese students, many of them scientists, had gone overseas to complete their studies, mainly to the U.S.A., but some to France, Britain and Germany. He at once ordered the compiling of a register of all known Chinese scientists or scientific students who were living in the West or employed by the Western powers, especially the U.S.A. Once the list was compiled he was astonished to see that more than two hundred of the names were those of highly promising students in the field of higher mathematics and technological research.

K'ang then ordered a dossier to be compiled on each one of these students, with instructions that the names and addresses of all their relatives in China must be obtained as well as detailed information on their strengths and weaknesses, their politics and technical qualifications and whether any of them had secret sympathies or links with the Chinese Communist movement.

By this time the first atomic bomb had been dropped on Japan and K'ang felt that his suspicions had been more than justified. He gave orders that preliminary dossiers were to be sent in immediately, even if they amounted to "a small toe of the Dragon". Further reports, however short, even if they added only a single fact, were to be dispatched as fast as possible afterwards.[2]

K'ang sent for the spy who had been in the Tai Li camp and demanded that he should remember exactly what had been said about Pasadena. "Well, there was mention of a research college—a name like Caltech —in Pasadena where many of the top brains in the scientific world were working on nuclear physics," was the reply. "And he happened to mention that there were some Chinese engaged there."[3]

K'ang took a quick look through his dossiers, which were being added to week by week. He saw that at the California Institute of Technology in Pasadena (Caltech) there were the following Chinese: Chao Chung-yao, Ch'ien Hsue-shen, Kuo Yun-huai, Chien Wei-chang and five others.

"Look at this," declared K'ang excitedly. "We have an important ally on the spot. His name is Chien Wei-chang, he is a member of the Chinese Communist Party (or at least he was) and he took part on the Long March. Now in California there are large Chinese communities. We must use our friends and agents among them to track down and contact Chien Wei-chang."

The exact details of K'ang's work at this time still remain masked to a large extent. While covering a wide range of activities, he increasingly became a political and executive principal of the Politburo rather than a head of Intelligence, but he never relaxed his grip on this work. In 1946 he was succeeded at the Social Affairs Department by Li K'o-nung, an old colleague of his from the days of furtive espionage in Shanghai in the late 'twenties. Li K'o-nung held the post of head of this particular Intelligence Department until he died in 1962.

But on the broader front K'ang was still the star Intelligence executive of the Communist Party. His gradual progress up the ladder of the Politburo enhanced his power and he not only influenced but actually created the new structure of the Chinese Secret Service, modelling it to some extent on the Soviet system which he had studied in depth and fully understood, by putting internal security and foreign intelligence under the control of a single officer—in this case K'ang himself. Thus K'ang, possibly even more than any other Intelligence chief in the world, was able to control foreign espionage, internal security and counter-espionage. It was this absolute control which enabled him both before and after the Communists came to power to keep such tight wraps on the probing of nuclear secrets from the West.

Though prior to the Communists coming to power K'ang Sheng had relinquished his directorship at the

office of Social Affairs to Li K'o-nung, after the establishment of the Chinese People's Republic he was
given overall authority in the Intelligence field at the
Central Intelligence H.Q. at No. 15, Bow Street Alley,
in Peking. Here he was a co-ordinator of all Intelligence Services.

K'ang Sheng's first task after he had obtained the
dossiers on Chinese technicians and scientists overseas
was to recruit the services of the United Front Workers Department and the International Liaison Committee. These organisations, both closely linked, were
technically speaking outside the scope of the Intelligence Service until K'ang saw the possibilities of utilising them. In China their main task was to win friends
and influence non-Communist specialists and technicians. K'ang sought to use them to forge links with the
several millions of Chinese living abroad and by doing
so to recruit spies.

For K'ang had a knack of being able very quickly
to assimilate the right way of setting about a complicated problem. One of his mottoes at this time was
that "the right way is the simple way". He was sufficient of a realist to know that the infiltration of agents
into the U.S.A. and Britain to probe nuclear secrets
would at best take too long and at the worst end in
total failure. Thus in the early stages, while doing his
best to obtain information from the U.S.S.R., still the
most obvious but a not very co-operative source, he
believed that the quickest and simplest methods of getting results were through top Chinese scientists in
exile.

Statistics in his department showed that at the end
of 1949 there were more than three thousand five
hundred Chinese students at colleges in the U.S.A.
and that between eighty and a hundred of these were
engineers, physicists, chemists or mathematicians. If
they could be persuaded either to defect to China, or
to pass on information, K'ang felt sure this would enable his country eventually to catch up with the U.S.A.
and the U.S.S.R.

One Chinese scientist in whom he was particularly
interested was Ch'ien Hsue-shen, the son of a prosperous Shanghai businessman, known by repute to K'ang

344

over many years. Ch'ien had had a brilliant career at Chiaotung University before going to the United States in 1935 at the age of twenty-five. What had encouraged K'ang to mark down Ch'ien as the likeliest candidate to help him in his quest was that he, together with other promising young Chinese scientists such as Chao Chung-yao, had been educated and trained in the U.S.A. through the Boxer Rebellion Scholarship Fund. K'ang discerned that the sponsorship of their education by a fund devoted to the memory of an essentially anti-foreign organisation should give them close ties with the mainland.

Ch'ien Hsue-shen had been further educated at the Massachusetts Institute of Technology, where he took a degree in aeronautical engineering and at the California Institute of Technology where he took his Ph.D. His work as a scientist and his all-round efficiency quickly won him many admirers. Ch'ien was well mannered, quietly but immaculately dressed, sober and gentle in demeanour and only rattled when confronted with men of inferior intelligence: he could not suffer fools gladly.

There have been some suggestions that the Russians made early efforts to win Ch'ien as an agent. If so, he seems to have been unaware of them, or, if he suspected anything, pretended not to understand. His sole diversion from his studies was a love of classical music and he frequently attended concerts of the Boston Symphony Orchestra. He became a member of a scientific experimental team at Caltech in Pasadena under the famous scientist, Dr Theodore von Karman, who wrote of him: "Even as a young student he helped to clear up some of my own ideas on several difficult topics. These are gifts which I had not often encountered. He was quickly noticed by other professors on the campus."[4]

Another man at Caltech was Chao Chung-yao, who had already made a name for himself for research into the field of atomic science. He was slightly more gregarious than Ch'ien, but shared the same passion for music and, like his colleague, often felt intensely lonely and missed his homeland.

Before long Ch'ien Hsue-shen developed an interest in rocketry and, in collaboration with others at the Department of Aeronautics, carried out a number of experiments with model rockets. Though never showing any apparent interest in politics and seemingly totally absorbed in his work, he was sometimes seen in the company of left-wing intellectuals at informal parties in Pasadena.

There was during World War II a big drive to win members for the Communist Party of America in Los Angeles County and the F.B.I. (U.S. Federal Bureau of Investigation) had infiltrated its membership. Years later, during the McCarthy quest for subversives in the U.S.A., the F.B.I. testified that Ch'ien Hsue-shen had been registered as a member of Professional Unit 122 (Pasadena section) of the American Communist Party. This Ch'ien emphatically denied and no proof was ever produced of his having signed an application for membership, or of his having a membership card.

In World War II Ch'ien had been sent to Washington as Director of Rocketry in the U.S. National Defence Scientific Board, in which post he had access to a great deal of top secret information. Theodore von Karman gave his opinion that "of all the experts whom I suggested for the Air Force Scientific Advisory Group in 1945, my friend, G. S. Tsien [the American version of Ch'ien Hsue-shen's name], was an undisputed genius whose work was providing an enormous impetus to advances in high-speed aerodynamics and jet propulsion."[5]

Ch'ien was given the honorary rank of colonel in the U.S.A.F. and went to Germany to interview the captured Nazi scientists who had been engaged on rocketry and missile building. After his return to the U.S.A. he was awarded a commendation for "meritorious civil service and outstanding performance of duty". Part of his work at this time was a top secret report on *New Horizons—Science as the Key to Air Supremacy*.

By now Chinese Intelligence in Peking had had detailed reports on all the leading Chinese scientists overseas and the dossiers compiled on them were supplemented by clippings from articles in scientific journals and notes of lectures given by some of the leading nuclear scientists. Several universities were infiltrated by small teams of student-agents of the Communists, whose task it was to make shorthand notes of lectures, to ferret through waste-paper baskets for notes, to obtain text-books, copies of diagrams and anything that might add to the general fund of knowledge on nuclear physics, rocketry and the like. All this material was sifted by scientists employed by Intelligence in Peking and put to immediate use in various technical research departments.

But K'ang Sheng was now so deeply concerned with China's need for scientific intelligence that almost immediately after the establishment of the People's Republic he had formulated a plan for luring Chinese scientists back to the mainland. This, he insisted, must be carried out cautiously and discreetly: there must be no gangster methods or clumsy efforts at kidnapping. Where possible scientists should be encouraged to come back by invitation and flattery in the case of those known to be sympathetic to the Communist cause. Such a man was Chien Wei-chang, who as a youth had taken part in Mao Tse-tung's "Long March" and who worked at Caltech on the problems of high speed flight. Others who were playing a part in the development of U.S. nuclear weapons in varying degrees were Chao Chung-yao, Wang Kan-chang and Hua Lo-keng. Wang Kan-chang had studied at the University of Berlin, specialising in Beta rays, and had moved on to the University of California at Berkeley where he was a research physicist, while Hua Lo-keng had arrived at the University of Illinois via England. But Chao Chung-yao was the man Chinese Intelligence especially wanted because, from a conversation their agents had overheard when Chao was having a Chinese meal in his local Chinese community in the U.S.A., it was known that he did not need to rely on or keep files or notes, because he could memorise perfectly any scientific data.

Early on, the Chinese Communists appreciated the value of Chinese restaurants as listening-posts, though in the early days this was mainly employed for the obtaining of information of Kuomintang movements and, of course, spying on prominent exiles. In the case of Chinese scientists generally this policy paid off handsomely as the one place they usually sought out for relaxation and free talk was one of their local Chinese restaurants. From this moment on all Chinese restaurants in areas close to such key technological centres as Pasadena became listening-posts for Chinese Communists. Whenever possible waiters were employed as agents.

The main tactic in luring back scientists to the homeland was the sending of letters urging them to return to China. There was nothing stereotyped about this: each was varied according to the individual case. Sometimes relatives were forced to write letters begging them to return; on other occasions there were promises of splendid posts with handsome homes to go with them; if a relative was found to be ill, or dying, a message would be sent begging the scientist to come back. In a few—but a very few cases—there were threats. Usually even these threats were subtly indirect. A relative would write to say that if a "loving son" or "a beloved brother" would return, life for him or her would be made that much easier by the authorities.

Opportunities for such action had been few while Chiang Kai-shek was still in power. For example when Ch'ien Hsue-shen's mother died in Shanghai in 1946, the Communist Intelligence passed a message to an agent in the Chiang Kai-shek-occupied territory asking him to see that someone in the Chiang camp informed Ch'ien. When Ch'ien eventually received the news of his mother's death he asked for and got permission to go to China.

Contact with Ch'ien was discreetly established by the Communists who had also had an unexpected piece of luck: Chiang Kai-shek's Minister of Education turned down a suggestion that Ch'ien should be made president of his former university on the grounds that he was "too young and inexperienced". Ch'ien did not forget that snub, even though he met and married Yin Tsiang, the daughter of one of Chiang's generals.

No doubt this marriage provided Ch'ien with an excellent cover as far as American screening went at that time—it was as lax then as it was to become ultra-thorough a few years later. I am assured that Ch'ien was partially debriefed by Intelligence agents posing as Chinese scientists even on this visit, but that they took the view that no useful purpose would be served by kidnapping him. They had the intelligence to sense that Ch'ien could, for a while at least, be more useful to them if he returned to the U.S.A. He seems to have convinced himself that Chiang was on the way out and that Mao Tse-tung was bound to come to power. Yet back in the U.S.A. he became Goddard Professor of Jet Propulsion and seemed seriously to be considering taking U.S. citizenship.

In late 1949 Ch'ien received a disturbing letter from China which said that his father was very ill and anxious to see him and that "Mother China wanted him to come back", that his efforts were needed to help in "the great task of reconstruction under the heroic Mao Tse-tung".[6] It was an appeal to the most conservative instinct of the Chinese—love of family. Ch'ien sensed there was an element of threat in the letter, as he had heard of other Chinese scientists in the U.S.A. getting similar letters. Indeed some of them, under the impetus of K'ang's subtle drive, had already been lured back.

The technique would sometimes be the offer of a good post in the homeland, and plane tickets, already paid for, which would be delivered by a neutral embassy. Geneva in those days was a centre for rerouting the return of prominent exiles. By this time the Chinese Communists were fully aware that Ch'ien was a marked man: the McCarthy drive for Communists in high places was gaining impetus. While Ch'ien pondered what to do for the best, his security clearance was withheld from him: the authorities claimed he had been registered as a Communist Party member in 1938. Despite all the efforts of the authorities this allegation was never proved, but after being interrogated by the F.B.I. and held in custody pending an inquiry Ch'ien underwent all the horrors of persecution in the McCarthy era. He was removed from his various governmental posts and word went out that on no account must he be allowed to leave the country.

Attempts were also made to incriminate Chao

349

Chung-yao, but no evidence could be collected to justify holding him. The Chinese Secret Service did everything they could to smooth his exodus from the U.S.A. They gave him a farewell dinner party in Los Angeles Chinatown and saw him safely aboard ship with all his crates of material and some instruments. But when his ship stopped at Yokohama, U.S. military police went aboard and arrested him and three other Chinese students. They were all held for "plotting in alliance with Dr Ch'ien Hsue-shen to deliver nuclear secrets to China". They alleged that Chao was carrying top secret documents from Caltech. However, within a few days the Chinese were released and went on to Hongkong and from there into China. Soon afterwards a Jet Propulsion School was set up in China with Chao as one of its advisers.

After the Korean War started and when the McCarthy anti-communist drive was at its height and the China Lobby making its loudest—and very often its most blatantly lying—allegations, the U.S. administration acquiesced in the restrictions put on many Chinese scientists that they could not leave the U.S.A. in any circumstances. Ch'ien Hsue-shen was one singled out for this treatment.

Many of these scientists did not want to return to the mainland as long as it was under Communist control, others would have liked to visit relatives but not to stay permanently, while a growing minority would, through sheer bitterness at their treatment by the U.S. authorities, have opted for Communist China immediately.

Then the Immigration Service of the U.S.A. started to panic: they switched from not wanting the Chinese to return to ordering their deportment. James Reston wrote in *The New York Times* at this period that one professor had stated that "it is criminal to send back our friends and idiotic to send back our enemies—since all of them are so highly trained."

On the instigation of the Chinese Secret Service, Peking played heavily on the subject of the persecution of Chinese students and scientists in the U.S.A. Propaganda letters, requests to such people urgently to come home, had their effect. But, as the Immigration

Department clamped down on such people leaving the country and as a constant watch was kept by the F.B.I. to prevent them from going, all manner of subterfuges had to be adopted. With the less important students it was relatively easy. They would be contacted in a Chinese restaurant and told to wait for instructions: later they would be smuggled into Mexico and from there sent by ship or plane to China. Others would be picked up by fishing vessels off the California coast. One island off that coast was used as a Chinese Intelligence rendezvous point for escaping students and scientists for several months.

Chien Wei-chang, the gregarious, cheerful and highly intelligent open Communist sympathiser, was perhaps so blatantly opposed to Chiang Kai-shek that nobody imagined he could possibly be any danger. "If he wished to trick us, we thought he would have disguised his sympathies," said one U.S. official ruefully: "But goddam it, he never seemed a fanatic. Why, he even liked dry Martinis, which is rare for a Chinese. Yet he got away all the same."

Whatever K'ang's ploy was to get Chien Wei-chang out of the U.S.A. he kept it very secret. Chien returned to China in early 1947—two years before the Communist take-over. He disappeared from Caltech without leaving any trace of an escape route, or clues as to his future plans. But in the *Far Eastern Economic Review* of 19 August 1965 it was reported that "on the missile side, the programme is headed by Ch'ien Hsue-shen . . . with the help of Chien Wei-chang . . . no one doubts the quality of talent that Peking has been able to assemble."[7]

And Ch'ien Hsue-shen? Denied any participation in the U.S. nuclear developments, he had worked on quietly on the theory of space-craft being able to travel to the moon until, in August 1955, he was told that the Immigration Service had ordered that he should be deported. It was true that this was done under the guise that the ban on his travelling movements was suspended, but there was a reason for this. Communist China's Secret Service had urged that China should barter eleven American airmen, who had been imprisoned after they had been chased into Chinese territory during the Korean War, for some key Chinese technicians in the U.S.A. It was, of course, a ridiculously one-sided bargain—the equivalent of exchanging eleven quite ordinary airmen for four armoured divisions (or so said one Pentagon expert afterwards). But the clamour for bringing the boys back home was at its height in the U.S.A. and, though neither the State Department nor any other official body admitted as much, this is what had happened.

"Swop for U.S. fliers as scientist sails for Red China" was the headline in the *Los Angeles Times*.[8] The State Department indignantly denied this, but Ch'ien Hsueshen and his family left by ship from Los Angeles after meetings in Geneva sponsored by U.S. officials and Chinese Secret Servicemen. Perhaps the U.S.A. thought that as Ch'ien had not been allowed any access to classified information for the past few years it was safe to let him go.

Ch'ien arrived in Hongkong and from there crossed into China with the other Chinese students who were included in the exchange deal. In Hongkong there was a brief press interview with Ch'ien in which he parried most of the questions in non-committal fashion, but when asked whether he had all his books and luggage, he said "the majority of them". But he admitted that part had been confiscated.

Only long afterwards was it realised in the U.S.A. that even in these last few years, when debarred from official secrets, Ch'ien had used Caltech to develop many more of his theories and to bring himself almost as up-to-date as if he had been a member of a Governmental research team.

Once back in China Ch'ien was given red carpet treatment by the Chinese Government and warmly welcomed by Chien Wei-chang and Hua Lo-keng. He was appointed Director of the Institute of Mechanics in the Academy of Sciences and became chairman of the China Aerodynamics Society. The drive to set up China's nuclear research establishment and to build her first nuclear weapons was now under way. Ch'ien found he had a host of defecting Chinese scientists and students to help him, including Chien San-chiang, who had worked under the Communist sympathisers

Frédéric and Marie Joliot-Curie, in France, and Nieh Jung-chien, an army general as well as a physicist with European training. There were now approaching two hundred top Chinese scientists from overseas who had been lured or blackmailed into returning to their homeland. Many had returned much earlier than Ch'ien, including Hua Lo-keng, who had been imbued with communist sympathies when at Cambridge University and who, having received letters from China making threats against his family, quietly escaped from the U.S.A. in February 1950, going via Hongkong to Peking. He was immediately given a key post at the Academy of Sciences. The *New York Times* referred to his case on 11 May 1952, when they stated that "the case of the professor of mathematics who taught at the University of Illinois is indicative of what happens to American-trained Chinese scholars once they return [to China]. After receiving several letters, half-promising, half-threatening, the professor agreed to go back to China."

Despite this mass defection of top Chinese scientists to Peking, remarkably enough the Chinese Secret Service managed to keep its networks in the U.S.A. intact. Nobody ever discovered for sure how some of these scientists were persuaded to part with information before they left America, or how some of them were smuggled out. Some of them were certainly enrolled as Chinese agents before they left the U.S.A., yet the one who was mainly persecuted was one against whom the least evidence could be offered—Ch'ien Hsue-shen.

The gathering of scientific intelligence in the U.S.A. takes many forms. It has been helped in recent years because, since a change in the U.S. Immigration laws in July 1968, the number of Chinese entering the country has swelled to more than twenty thousand a year, most of these going to San Francisco. In the Chinatown section of this city Chinese Intelligence has several networks. Many of the immigrants come from China via Hongkong and a small proportion of these include deliberately infiltrated Communist agents.

"Peking's intelligence activities in the United States," write David Wise and Thomas B. Ross, "are limited largely to the massive collection of unclassified material. Peking will buy virtually any book, magazine, newspaper or technical journal it can lay its hands on . . . the collection of overt intelligence is co-ordinated by the Chinese through Post Office Box 88 in Peking, which serves as the mail drop for Guozi Shudian (International Bookstore) and Waiwen Shudian (Foreign Language Bookstore)."[9]

Some of this material is obtained by agents in the U.S.A., but much else is often purchased or winkled out by Chinese agents living in Europe, using European names. Maps, technical publications and even confidential blueprints are sometimes gathered in this manner and then relayed on to Peking. Quite often a Chinese agent in, say, Paris or Amsterdam will put an advertisement in American newspapers asking for a pen-friendship with a fellow scientist for an exchange of information on some seemingly innocent subject. When this is followed up a new probe for intelligence is launched.

An uneasy period of trying to co-operate with Russia in the nuclear field followed Ch'ien's move to China. It was symptomatic of the suspicion which China had about Russian intentions that one of the delegations to probe nuclear matters, under Chien San-chiang, the chief of China's new Physics Research Institute in Peking, had gone to Moscow in 1953, accompanied by Lo Jui-ching, the sinister Minister of Public Security. Some somewhat desultory research was carried on between representatives of both countries at the Joint Institute of Nuclear Research at Dubna, near Moscow. Lo Jui-ching reported back to Peking that he was convinced that Russia was stalling.

A few years later as the rift with the U.S.S.R. developed, China made up her mind to "go it alone". In June 1958 she was confident enough to announce through her Foreign Minister Chen Yi that "soon we shall have the nuclear bomb". But this move was made only after the Russians had in October of the previous year signed an agreement promising co-operation on nuclear matters which Krushchev had reputedly repudiated, arguing that China had no need for nuclear weapons as long as she was under Soviet "protection". By 1960 all Soviet technicians had been withdrawn from China. Then came two major shocks in the Communist world: Khrushchev was ousted from the Kremlin leadership and China exploded her first atom bomb.

The latter was an event which helped to change history, and certainly paved the way to the U.S.A. seeking an understanding with China as well as with the U.S.S.R. The Americans first attempted to denigrate the Chinese experiment and suggested that China lagged far behind the U.S.A. and Russia, and then rapidly became alarmed at the speed with which China had acquired nuclear technology. Aerial spies had pin-pointed roads built in the Sinkiang Province and further research into the Chinese experiment revealed that China was using in her new weapon not plutonium, but the rare isotope of uranium, U-235. This meant that China had progressed much further than the U.S.A. had believed possible in so short a time.

Then came the second nuclear test in May 1965. This showed that China was well on the way to making a really powerful H-bomb and that soon she would have intercontinental missiles as well.

Nor have the efforts to win more exiled Chinese in any way slackened off. In recent years Yang Chenming, an American-educated physicist, has paid at least two visits to China and the U.S.A., one in May 1972, and he appears to have contacted other U.S.-educated Chinese and persuaded them to make similar visits. Li Chen-dao, the Nobel Prizewinner and another nuclear physicist, is now in Peking and was probably engaged by Yang back in the U.S.A. Another such visitor was Ren Tzu-kung. All these visitors are known to have met Ch'ien Hsue-shen, who is now in charge of China's nuclear development. Nobody can tell what their rôles are, but it would be interesting to know why the U.S.A. has permitted these visits to China.

Much imaginative nonsense has been written about China's nuclear centres at Lanchow and Lop Nor—and then again a fair amount of accurate detail about them has been published and rashly dismissed as third-hand journalism. What is clear is that Wang Kan-chang is in charge of the nuclear weapons programme and that former American-employed technicians have been specially used by the Chinese Secret Service to think up ways of misleading and thwarting the C.I.A., whose task has been to get information on these remote nuclear outposts. All China's nuclear projects are not only kept top secret but are totally controlled and protected by a special branch of the Intelligence Service. For example, the Chinese are well aware of American spy-satellite photographic probes in this area and they are convinced that the C.I.A. do not know where the exact Lop Nor missile base is sited. The Chinese have built several dummy sites which, they insist, cannot be distinguished from the real site from the air.

These nuclear centres in Sinkiang Province are not, of course, at a great distance from the Russian border. This may partly explain why yet another section of Chinese Intelligence is master-minding a gradual infiltration of Soviet territory across that vague never-never-land of nomadic frontiers. The Chinese are spreading into Ugihur and Kazakh territory and through the Production Construction Corps of the Chinese Army, have planted border areas with crops, dug canals, built houses, schools and hospitals and aimed at winning over the nomadic tribes of the buffer states.

It is not "Intelligence" or even "Secret Service" work as the West understands it, any more than the ultra-simplistic Chinese plan for gaining nuclear secrets was, but it is just as, if not more, effective. They have even won over to the Chinese Communist Party many members of the Russian Communist Party in these areas.

Meanwhile the probe for nuclear secrets goes on into the mid-seventies. According to a Washington assessment in 1973, China was developing an intercontinental missile that would be bigger than anything Russia or the United States possesses, with a range of up to seven thousand miles, which would mean that it could hit targets almost anywhere in Russia or America, while at the same time President Nixon's strategic advisers believed that China had developed a nuclear deterrent powerful enough to discourage the Russians from attempting a preemptive attack to knock out the Chinese. Stephen Barber, the London *Daily Telegraph* correspondent in Washington, reported that "qualified

American defence experts have been amazed at the speed with which the Chinese have caught up with Russia and the West in developing weapons and technology. One said they had overtaken France two years ago . . . the latest unexpected development to be reported is a test of a submarine-launched missile working on the same principle as the American Polaristype."

Without question the main reason for this swift advance is the perfect co-ordination between China's military and scientific chiefs at Government level and the various branches of the Intelligence Service. No item of information, however seemingly irrelevant, is ever neglected: the quest for every scrap of scientific data is avidly pursued. The rule is "today it may mean nothing; tomorrow it could be all-important".

One example into which I inquired specifically was the placing of an order by the Chinese Government with the British firm of Pye Unicam of Cambridge for four Pye 104 Gas Chromotographs, standard machines for examining moon dust. There had been a British industrial exhibition in Peking at which news of this machine leaked out quite innocently: it was explained that its object was to see whether there were organic traces of life on the moon. A Pye company spokesman: "It's a complete mystery why they should want these machines. We did not know they had any moon dust." The instruments, which cost £10,000 each, are the standard moon dust equipment used by American and British scientists. The Chinese Embassy in London said of the moon-dust machines: "We don't necessarily know what China is doing when dealing direct with this country and on this issue we know nothing."

My information is that the machines were ordered in anticipation of the smuggling of some moon dust specimens into China. "You can be sure that if the orders were placed, the Chinese Intelligence were fairly sure of obtaining a specimen of moon dust," was the reply I received from a student of Chinese technological development in Hongkong. "Each Chinese student who has been leaving for China in the past ten years was asked to find a replacement—Chinese or otherwise—who would keep him not only informed on spe-

357

cific projects, but with samples of anything brought back from space probes by the U.S.A."

Another intercepted broadcast from Albania in mid-1973 reported that "an unnamed American scientist" had informed them that the U.S.A. had developed a new bomb triggered by a laser beam instead of fission, thus causing a much cleaner explosion with only a fraction of the radio-activity created by the existing H-bomb. I was interested to learn a few months later that "a clean nuclear device with a yield of only a few ounces of T.N.T. will probably be detonated in an American laboratory shortly. . . . A laser trigger in a weapon would be required to work once only, and in these circumstances it might be possible to devise new methods of driving lasers to get far more power out of much smaller equipment."

28

Chinese Intelligence in Japan and Singapore 1950-1972

By the mid-1960s Ceylon was, besides Mongolia and India, the only place in Asia where the pro-Moscow wing was dominant and still actively engaged in promoting revolution. In the rest of Asia, and in Australia as well, the K.G.B. had become so bogged down in counter-intelligence operations against the Chinese that its subversive activities had practically come to a standstill.

David Wise and Thomas B. Ross in The Espionage Establishment

IF in the course of the last few chapters the author may have seemed occasionally to wax over-enthusiastically about the Chinese Communists' Secret Service, he has meant no more than to give credit where it was due.

Its operation in obtaining nuclear secrets was a remarkable achievement by any standards. However, this is not to say that the service has been without blemish. It has made some mistakes and at times even behaved with foolishly flamboyant tactics and at others with sinister intent.

This has certainly been true of many of its operations overseas and especially in the Far East. There the Secret Service has too often allowed itself to be portrayed as an essential instrument in Marxism-Leninism and the stirring up of revolt in neighbouring countries. It is the classic error of all Communist Parties who are in a hurry.

One must remember that, unlike Russia, China had actually been exploited for more than a hundred years by foreign nations. Therefore the new regime had much excuse for pursuing a virulent attack on imperialism wherever it was to be found, but especially in her neighbouring territories. And from 1949 until the end of the Korean War China lived under the fear of American-backed attacks on her mainland from Taiwan or Japan, as well as having been deeply involved in Korea. Thus it was that in the early 'fifties the stirring up of revolt, the encouragement of bands of anti-imperialist guerrillas, of parties who were anti-imperialist and the actual incitement to revolt in territories still occupied by U.S., British or French forces were main aims of Chinese Intelligence.

Normally speaking, Chinese Intelligence activities are not "aggressive"; they are cautious, often operating within a legal framework and essentially low key. There is not the preoccupation of the Russians with putting pressure on employees in ministries in foreign countries by blackmailing or bribing them into spying. The Chinese approach is much more subtle and possibly in the long run more insidious: those who work for Peking are invariably totally dedicated and completely incorruptible, one reason why "defectors" from the Chinese side must be treated with so much caution.

While China is typically "unaggressive" in her overall espionage, she does on occasion embark on "aggressive" espionage in an extreme manner. This may seem a total contradiction, but it needs to be stated that

359

the two techniques are quite separate. One can put it this way: ninety-five per cent of Chinese espionage and intelligence work is low-key and unaggressive, five per cent of it is violent, open and brutal aggression. Often such tactics may appear to have nothing in common with Secret Service work.

After the rift with the Soviet Union a prime aim of China in the Far East became to undermine not only the position of the United States, but of the Soviet Union as well. It was, as the quotation at the head of this chapter shows, highly successfully carried out and in a very short time. Some of these successful coups will be examined later, but the fact is that the Russians not only were forced to mount counter-espionage operations against the Chinese in the Far East, but in some cases to change their regional spy headquarters. Nowhere have the Russians been more worried about their set-backs in the Intelligence game than in Tokyo where for years they had such a powerful network, both civil and military.

In the early 'fifties much aid was given by the Chinese to the Chinese Malayan guerrillas who were fighting the British in the jungles of what was then the British colony of Malaya, now the self-governing territory of Malaysia. Nobody was able to advise these jungle guerrillas better than Mao's men, who had probably had more experience of disciplined guerrilla warfare than any native soldiers in the Far East. This Vietnam-style revolt was staged by the Malayan Communist Party, backed by the Chinese, but it proved a costly and ineffective uprising, and was finally defeated by the British, not so much militarily as by sealing off areas that had been liberated and giving them the protection to live in peace while paving the way to self-government.

As this campaign was more a military than an espionage operation there is no need to dwell on it other than to say that the Chinese Intelligence, both civil and military, learned a great deal from its failure and these lessons were later exploited in Vietnam, Laos and Cambodia as well as Thailand, When the Malayan revolt died down, the Chinese communist movement in the new Malaysia was forced underground (it was bitterly opposed by the Malayan Moslems), but it flourished in schools and colleges, and in Sarawak and Borneo, where a clandestine Communist network bent on stirring up a rising was uncovered in the early 1960s. Similar riots were fomented in Singapore, where in 1964 there were violent clashes between Chinese and Moslems.

The trouble in Singapore was organised by a Chinese secret agent named Sim Siew Lim, who had slipped into the city from Shanghai in 1960. In 1965 he was arrested together with twenty other agents and charged with plotting the assassination of leading Singapore politicians and the head of Government.

When the Korean War ended the Peking Government decided the time had come to set up a spy network in Japan where, of course, it had not yet been able to establish diplomatic relations. With the United States still keeping a close watch on the newly independent Japan, it was vital for China to have a co-ordinated system of intelligence on this important neighbour. Chinese policy in such a situation is usually to send in a delegation, trade mission or a branch of the N.C.N.A., but in this case Peking dispatched a team of the Chinese Red Cross ostensibly to handle the repatriation of Chinese in Japan. The titular head of the mission was a charming and disarming female, but the Intelligence chief who used the cover of the Red Cross to start up his network was one Liao Cheng-chih, later to become ambassador to Burma.

There is today no law in Japan against the gathering of secret information from Japanese sources, however strange this may seem. Paradoxically, during the same period, the collecting of secrets concerning United States troops in Japan, and about American weapons offered for use by Japan's Self-Defence Forces, has been punishable by law. Public servants are liable to prosecution for giving any state secrets away under the National Public Service Law.

The Chinese have undoubtedly exploited to the full loop-holes in the security laws and one Japanese political commentator, Kazuo Kuroda, wrote in the *Japan Times* in 1965: "Japan has renounced war in its constitution, but whether it is necessary to go so far

361

as to open the country for espionage cannot readily be affirmed."[1] He recommended incorporating anti-espionage legislation into the Criminal Code. North Korean intelligence agents, who appear to abound in Japan and some of whom probably work for Peking as well, are generally charged with subsidiary offences —illegal entry, transmitting without a licence, but the penalties are light and Tazuo Furuya, writing in March 1969, described Japan as "a principal base for international spies".[2]

To a large extent China has pursued a cautious intelligence drive in Japan, notwithstanding the ease with which spying can be carried out. The tactics have been similar to those pursued in the U.S.A., concentrating on collecting theses and data on missiles, space development, electronics and especially on the production techniques of Japanese computers. All such material has found its way from Tokyo University to certain libraries in Peking, according to reports made by Japanese visitors to Peking. It is believed that these theses and data are sent to China by bookshop agents handling left-wing publications in premises in Kanda, near Tokyo University.

Students at the Engineering Department and the Research Institute of the University are said to co-operate in the micro-filming of documents. The micro-films are then enlarged and put into book form. The students are not public servants and thus cannot be prosecuted under the National Public Service Law. The Japanese police, though aware of these activities, have so far been powerless to act.

Chinese missions to Japan are another means of collecting intelligence. Such missions come here to inspect facilities for making cars, ships and electricity and, while their main task is industrial espionage, they do keep a watch for other data, too. One party is said to have obtained full details on the workings of the Central Power Supply Control Office of the Tokyo Electric Power Company, the key to Tokyo's power supply. Another team inspected a national research laboratory concerned with studies of vacuum tube instruments used for missiles on four occasions and an actual vacuum instrument plant in Yokohama twenty-four times!

This is typical of the disciplined thoroughness of Chinese espionage. The rule is never to dawdle and thus arouse suspicion on one visit to a laboratory or factory, even if it means missing some details. Quick mental notes are made, they are discussed later to ascertain what further details are required and the aim then is to pick up the rest of the information a little at a time on subsequent visits.

Liao Cheng-chih has retained his interest in Japanese affairs for more than twenty years now. Two years ago he headed a Goodwill Mission to Tokyo, taking with him experts in the field of industry, chemists, doctors and even acupuncturists as well as writers skilled in compiling reports. According to a Tokyo police source this Mission was a blatant intelligence gathering operation and the Mission split up into teams which covered the whole of Japan from Hokkaido to Okinawa.

The establishment of diplomatic relations with Peking was not a subject which evoked much enthusiasm in police circles in Japan when Chou En-lai and Tanaka signed their agreement. They merely regarded it as creating more work for them, for their view is—to quote one senior officer—"the Chinese are engaged in an ideological offensive and all kinds of intelligence activities under our noses. Diplomatic recognition means we have had to increase our personnel to maintain a watch on the steady stream of missions from China." These missions range from engineering teams to visiting dancing and ping-pong teams, and plain clothes, Japanese police shadow them in cars with video-cameras. But, as the senior police official ruefully confessed, "they rarely put a foot wrong, or make any suspicious move. They just use their heads."

As far as can be ascertained there are no records of arrests for supplying information to Peking, thus since nobody has been found guilty (and the law makes it exceedingly difficult to arrest anyone), one has to rely on police assumptions of who is guilty of such activities. China relies overwhelmingly on Chinese residents in Japan for her agents and of the fifty-eight thousand Chinese in the country about half owe their allegiance to the Communists.

China Town in Yokohama is an area from which officials of the Republic of China (Taiwan) embassies and consulates in Japan have kept well away in recent months. There has been constant friction here between Chinese Communist and Taiwanese factions: since the diplomatic recognition of China by Japan the Communists have been the more aggressive group. Some two thousand six hundred Chinese live in this area, operating restaurants and other businesses. The Yokohama Chinese League has been used as a cover for some intelligence operations and its *Seinenkai,* or Young People's Group, is perhaps the hard core of the network. Its office is in a shabby room in the middle of China Town, watched at a distance by plain clothes Japanese police, while the actual office is guarded by youths armed with baseball bats.

The young activists appear to keep close links with extreme left-wing Japanese students and to obtain their financial backing from "Communist" restaurant owners in Yokohama. This office feeds back information to Peking, sometimes through members of visiting missions, occasionally and more discreetly by radio transmission. Japanese police say that where they have caught radio operators transmitting to China the only offence they can be charged with is failure to take out an operating licence. Thus Peking is capable of wielding considerable influence in local affairs in such a centre as Yokohama. Help and encouragement was given by Chinese agents to Japanese groups fighting against the transportation of U.S. tanks from the Sagami supply depot to Yokohama port for shipment to Vietnam.

In Yamashita-cho in Yokohama there is a plot of ground overgrown with weeds, patrolled by hungry cats, where China built a consulate a hundred years ago. The buildings were destroyed by bombs in World War II and the Taiwan Government never got around to rebuilding them. Taiwanese officials were planning to sell the land when relations with Peking were established by Japan. The pro-Communist Chinese put up big notice-boards with slogans such as "Long Live

Japan-China friendship" and "Liberate Taiwan" and, to discourage any potential buyer, they set up another huge notice in the centre of the plot of land stating "as this land belongs to the People's Republic of China its sale or rent is strictly forbidden". No Japanese is willing to take the risk of trying to buy or rent it and the Japanese Government and police have been careful not to interfere in this quarrel between the two rival Chinese factions.

Again this is not typical of what spies of other nations do, but it is typical of the special Chinese technique of "aggressive espionage".[3]

According to one knowledgable source in Yokohama, Peking has less need for the services of foreigners than any other Intelligence service in the world, with the possible exception of Israel. This is certainly true of Japan and nearly all the Far East. Where specialised information is required, however, the same source maintains that the Chinese have little difficulty in recruiting a usefully-placed Japanese. The China-Japan Friendship Association is one meeting place for Chinese and sympathetic Japanese: many of its members are Japanese businessmen eager to please in order to make a trade deal.

The Chinese in Japan do not indulge in wining and dining sprees which are a method of recruitment commonly employed by Soviet attachés in softening up men from ministries. They depend chiefly on ideological commitment.

A Japanese police spy, an informant of mine, has explained something of the ways in which Japanese are employed as Chinese agents:

"I was watching a Japanese in his early fifties—let us call him S. He had served for a period in the Intelligence Department of the American Occupation forces after the war. He had made several journeys to China and appeared to be engaged in selling Chinese products to department stores in Yokohama. He was a member of the Friendship Association through which channel he had received invitations to visit Peking.

"S also maintained close contact with local Chinese friendly to the Taiwan Government and in fact I would not altogether rule out that he is a double-agent, though you can be pretty sure that his real allegiance is to the Communists.

"The chief reason why the Public Security Force is interested in S is that he still keeps good relations with his former employers, the U.S. Army, and often visits bases in the Yokohama area."

One can also be sure that the Chinese Intelligence obtained an enormous amount of useful information on resident Chinese from the Red Cross team that first went to Japan. This team would swiftly ascertain which resident Chinese had relatives back in China, who they were and where they lived. Having gained that information it would be relatively easy for the Chinese Secret Service to establish a hold over such of their nationals still living in Japan and who were not repatriated.

29

Watching Taiwan and the C.I.A. 1950-1972

In the Chinese mind Taiwan is primarily one of those territories lost to Chinese control during a century of weakness and humiliation, a century whose memory they are anxious to expunge. To the Government in Peking Taiwan remains the outstanding territory in this task of restoration.

Richard Harris

FROM the earliest days of the Chinese People's Republic one of the most difficult of the many tasks the Intelligence Service had to perform was keeping a watch on Chiang Kai-shek's regime in Taiwan and the American C.I.A. at one and the same time. Increasingly the two tasks became inseparable. With the close and special relationship between the Taiwan Government and that of the United States, with the State Department, the Pentagon and, above all, the C.I.A. involved, the Chinese Secret Service was constantly trying to find the answers in the U.S.A. to reports emanating from Taiwan, and vice versa.

The Central External Liaison Department is, of course, still the intelligence co-ordinating and policy-making body covering the Far East as well as the rest of the world, assessing the information that comes to it mainly from the Department of Investigation, the Ministry of Public Affairs and the Intelligence Division of the General Staff. It also promotes special operations through the United Front, already mentioned as a vital factor in obtaining nuclear secrets. Nevertheless the branch of Intelligence which is responsible for intelligence links with Taiwan (and also Macao and Hongkong) is the Ministry of Public Affairs, which controls internal security.

There was originally an excellent reason for this in that intelligence from all these centres very often directly concerned China's internal security and called for action inside the People's Republic. The Public Affairs Ministry has a quarter of a million members of the armed Popular Police Force, which is in the ratio of one police officer to every two and a half thousand inhabitants. On a local level another instrument of the Intelligence Service is the "Street and Lane Committee" in the cities and the "Team Authorities" in the countryside. "Shadow" Committees of a smilar, but smaller and of course inconspicuous, nature exist in Hongkong and Macao, but not, it is thought, in Taiwan, where the counter-espionage service of Chiang Kai-shek has always been formidable. The police also use their discretion in building up where necessary citizens' and housewives' committees in certain streets and areas of large cities. From these is obtained a vast network of informers and nowhere is this more important than in Macao and Hongkong.

After the Sino-Japanese war of 1894–5 Taiwan was ceded to Japan, but at the Potsdam Conference in

1945 it was decreed that it should be handed over to the Kuomintang. It was here that Chiang Kai-shek set up his government after he had been driven from the mainland, while retaining control of the islands of Quemoy and Matsu.

Since then both the Communists on the mainland and the Nationalists on Taiwan have followed the precept of Sun Tzu that "to defeat the enemy psychologically is the superior strategy" and each side has avoided any head-on confrontation, though there have been occasional minor skirmishes, mainly a testing out of each other's defences.

Thus the Central External Liaison Department, headed by Keng Biao, has had a rôle in formulating intelligence tactics towards Taiwan and it is suspected that they use the United Front organisation to seek to subvert pro-Taiwan supporters in the U.S.A. These tactics have been going on for the past twenty years, but with Chiang Kai-shek now a very old man and with Taiwan steadily losing all her diplomatic privileges to the People's Republic, there is probably even greater scope today for winning defectors. It is reported that more than two hundred million U.S. dollars were allocated for United Front operations abroad in 1973. The chief of the People's Association for International Friendship, Wang Kuo-chuan, was charged with directing Peking's infiltration in the U.S.A.

It is difficult to find out much about specific cases of mainland spies apprehended in Taiwan. The Garrison Command and Investigation Bureau refuse to discuss the matter and are eager to give the impression that, however vulnerable other nations may be to Peking's spies, Taiwan's tight security measures prevent any such infiltration. Nevertheless occasional irruptions, which are not reported in the press, and cases concerning prominent individuals which are leaked from Hongkong or elsewhere, give some clues that the Taiwanese official picture is not quite true.

One morning a few years ago a young Taiwanese girl—she was the secretary at a police station—was cycling to work when she saw some pamphlets thrown over a fence on to the road. She turned back, picked one up and saw that they were mainland propaganda.

Then she noticed a man running away. Having watched him go back to his house, she reported the affair to the police who promptly arrested him as being a Peking agent.

Such cases do not get reported in the press and one only hears of them from private sources. In a similar case another man was caught throwing pro-communist material in leaflets from the top of a building in downtown Taipei. One gets the impression that the Taiwan authorities are as frightened of petty incidents like this as of a major spy scare and that they go to any lengths to hush them up. My information on this leaflet-throwing from non-Taiwanese sources is that the use of Peking agents just to perform acts like these is considered valuable psychological warfare.

A list of prisoners smuggled out of one of Taiwan's political prisons throws a little light on mainland Chinese activities on the island, but must be treated with some caution, since the offences involved probably do not always constitute actual spying even if that is the interpretation which the Taiwan authorities choose to put on them. On the list are the names of people charged with violation of Article 9 of the Statute for the Investigation and Eradication of Rebel Spies, promulgated on 13 June 1950. For example, Lin Tao-p'ing, then aged twenty-five and a student in National Taiwan University, was sentenced to two years' jail under Article 9 in August 1968, but his actual offence was not working for the mainland, but being a member of the Taiwan Independence Movement. "Rebel spies" is a catch-all label for anyone considered dangerous to the Government.

Therefore it is difficult to assess whether many of the people in Ching-mei Prison, where the list originated, were spies in our sense of the word. One's impression is that the mainland Chinese make relatively few efforts to infiltrate Taiwan with their agents, but that they rely largely on bogus defectors. However, some cases do point to the fact that even the highly-guarded, security-minded police state of Chiang Kai-shek, surrounded by seas which are closely patrolled, can be penetrated by Peking agents.

The planting of defectors by Peking is made easier

by the fact that the Taiwanese authorities love to make propaganda out of such cases. In August 1967 there was a report in the *China Post* about Wu Shu-tung, a 61-year-old of Wuchin, Kiangsu Province, who went from Hongkong to Taipei and was described as "the highest ranking Communist official to defect to date". He had been a member of the Hongkong-Kowloon Anti-Persecution Struggle Committee and chairman of its publications branch during the 1967 riots. Besides being a member of the Kwantung Provincial Committee of China's National Political Consultative Conference, Wu had been president of the communist-operated Chunghwa Book Company in Shanghai and head of its Hongkong office. Wu was said to have given information that the Committee he represented had four sections—combat (responsible for terrorist activities), transport (in charge of smuggling and distribution of arms and ammunition), United Front and propaganda. He also claimed that he had been to Peking once or twice a year since 1950 and had met such Chinese leaders as Chou En-lai and Shen Yu-pin.

Does a man who has been an active Communist for more than twenty years suddenly defect at the age of sixty-one? Is the conversion genuine? Was he in disgrace with the Peking authorities? Or, for that matter, would China send a man of this age as an agent to Taiwan under the guise of a defector?

In any event, whether a defector is genuine or a plant, he will be closely watched for a long period by the iniquitous but highly efficient Secret Police of Taiwan, organized in something like Soviet style by the President's son, Chiang Ching-kuo, who is said to have gambled on his ultimate survival by having long ago established secret links with the Russians and, more recently, indirect links with Peking.

That the authorities are extremely nervous of any suspicion of subversion is typified by the fact that Li Ao, Taiwan's best-known writer, was tailed by sixteen secret agents of the Taiwanese before his arrest in 1972. He was sentenced to ten years' imprisonment for having passed secret Government information about political prisoners in Taiwan's jails to foreigners. Yet one of the "foreigners" in question, Mr Lynn

Miles, an American now living in Japan, has stated that an Independence Movement activist, and not Li Ao, had given him the documents. For the record Li Ao was originally a mainland Chinese refugee.

No doubt the Independence Movement has been infiltrated to some extent by Peking agents, or at least they have been able to manipulate it. Some Taiwanese secret police suspect this, but have not been able to prove it. This was probably one reason for the harsh sentence on Li Ao—a deterrent to other would-be dissidents.

Propaganda is the main function of the Chinese Secret Service both in Taiwan and outside of it. They have handled this propaganda much more skilfully than some of their cruder efforts in Africa and the Middle East. It is almost as though, because they are combatting their fellow-countrymen, they instinctively employ more subtlety. The propaganda always appears to come from a non-Communist individual, or a non-Communist organisation like the Independence Movement.

A short story is published, escaping the Taiwanese censor, but being cleverly exploited by Peking in other exiled Chinese communities, expressing in veiled form the disillusionment shared by many post-1949 refugees from mainland China. The central figure is a Chinese who fled from the Communists in 1949 and became a coffin-maker in Taiwan. That in itself is subtly symbolic. The story goes on to tell how he lives with a Taiwanese mistress, whom he cannot bring himself to marry, and his father who escaped with him. The latter shut himself in an upstairs room without windows years ago and nothing is heard from him except the monotonous query: "How's the weather, boy?" The old man still clings to his hope of returning to the mainland.

The story can hardly be faulted even by the Taiwan secret police, but the principal target of criticism is not the old man, but the Nationalist Party who brought the refugees across but are too corrupt and impotent to take them back to the mainland.

Similarly letters are smuggled out of Taiwanese prisons telling stories of brutal treatment by the secret police and their interrogation methods.

On 3 April 1964 a report in the *China Post* stated that a *New York Times* correspondent had been made to spy for Peking. This derived from the disclosures of Chu Pao-heng, a former Chinese editor in Hong-kong, who defected to Taiwan in late March 1964. Chu said the Communists first paid the *New York Times* correspondent, whose name was not mentioned, 10,000 Hongkong dollars for this work. At the same time this correspondent was also a staff reporter on the Hongkong *Tiger Standard,* according to Chu.

It was said that the *New York Times* man had tried to commit suicide, but failed, and that he was still un-der pressure to work for Peking. Chu added that "the source of the pressure was the New China News Agency" and that he had been told this by the man in question, who was "an old friend". Further, Chu alleged that the Chinese Communists were "expert in luring foreign correspondents to work for them", first trying to induce them to live an extravagantly luxurious life and then, when they needed money des-perately, giving them cash but with strings attached. "To promote their infiltration and propaganda cam-paign in Hongkong," stated Chu, "the Red agents have also bought over many of the writers and report-ers of the Chinese language newspapers in much the same way."[1]

Chu went on to tell of his personal experience. He went to Hongkong from the mainland in 1948 and joined the independent Chinese language paper, *Sing Dao Bao,* where he served as cable news editor for eleven years. During this period he was influenced by leftwingers and began working for the Peking regime. He was sacked by the paper along with seven other leftwingers in 1959. They then set up a newspaper themselves with funds supplied from Peking, and worked under the direction of the United Front. He confessed that he had fabricated many reports in which the Taiwan Government was "viciously criticised" and that these were then attributed to "special correspon-dents in Taiwan". The *China Post* report concluded: "Chu said he decided to defect when he was compelled

372

by the Red agents to buy over many of his old friends now working with the newspapers in Hongkong loyal to Taiwan."

Many reports of defectors to Taiwan I have found to be thoroughly suspect and, though they might have been accepted as evidence ten years ago, now appear artificial and unconvincing, little more than a desperate Taiwanese effort in propaganda and not very skilful at that. When one tries to find corroborative evidence of some of these stories the quest yields nothing at all. This is not to deny that there are a few genuine defectors with positive evidence, but in some instances the defectors are plants and in others their stories are doctored and embroidered to serve the Taiwanese propaganda department.

More interesting, however, is the sentence of life imprisonment in December 1971 by a military court in Taipei of Li Ching-sun (alias Johnson Li), former board chairman of the *Great China Evening News* and vice-president of the Broadcasting Corporation of China. He was accused of having been engaged in communist subversive activities. Yu Chi, former deputy editor-in-chief of the *China Daily News* in Tainan (Southern Taiwan) was sentenced to five years in jail for being a Communist Party member. He had confessed to all his activities during the investigation period, and his relatively brief sentence was said to be due to the fact that his confession had led to the arrest of Li Ching-sun.

The military prosecutor read out a long statement charging that the defendants had been members of the Chinese Communist Party since 1935 and had engaged in subversive activities against the Government. Yu disclosed that he and Li belonged to the same "cultural movement sub-committee" of the C.C.P. in Fukien Province in 1938 when they were both working at the *Nanfang Daily News*. Yu went to Taiwan in 1946 and said that Li contacted him after his arrival in Taiwan in 1949.

Li, however, denied the entire contents of his alleged "self-confession", charging that he had written it under the threats of his interrogators and claiming that he had never been a member of the Communist

Party. The prosecution alleged that Li had followed directives to use newspapers as weapons to launch "a bloodless revolution" in Taiwan and that as far back as 1949 he had been ordered by his Communist boss, Pu Hsi-hsiu, head of the "cultural movement sub-committee", to accomplish three missions: (1) to protect his newspaper until the liberation of Taiwan; (2) to strengthen communist United Front operations in the press in Taiwan; (3) to destroy the prestige of the Government in order to alienate the people from it.

But while Chinese espionage in Taiwan could at best be only low-key in all these years, their attitude towards the C.I.A. had to be much more determined. Here again they used the United Front as a spearhead on a number of occasions and one of their earliest successes in stifling a C.I.A.-Taiwanese plot was that of the defection of General Li Tsung-jen to Peking in 1965.

General Li, a former Vice-President of the Kuomintang, had stayed in China as Acting President of the Nationalist regime until 1950—a year after the Communist take-over, which should have made even the C.I.A. suspicious. True, he had a record as a loyal Kuomintang man, but he had disagreed with Chiang Kai-shek, declined to follow him to Taiwan and ultimately gone to the U.S.A.

The Chinese Secret Service had made oblique approaches to General Li before he left China. They knew all about his disapproval of Chiang and his feeling that the attempt to set up an exiled Government in Taiwan was doomed to failure. As Li had admitted to the Chinese Intelligence officers who had contacted him "the Taiwanese are totally different from the mainlanders and all Chiang can do is to set up another police state. It will not really be much different from when the Japanese administered it."

So Li was Peking's man when he went to the U.S.A. and he was encouraged to make contacts with the U.S. authorities and to do all he could to create an atmosphere of mistrust of Chiang. Li went to live in Englewood Hills, New Jersey, where he was not particularly happy and where his wife was frequently ill and pined for her homeland. Chinese Intelligence regarded Li as potentially such an important recruit to their cause that they ordered two of their agents to keep in close touch with him, sometimes in New York, at others even in Englewood Hills. No suspicion was aroused because eventually the Communist agents were believed by the F.B.I. and the C.I.A. to be Li's informants.

Which of course they were—informants of what was going on in Peking and, as far as Peking could find out, what was happening in Taiwan, while at the same time persuading Li to find out various American opinions on the policy to be adopted towards the Chiang Kai-shek regime. This ploy worked better than probably Peking had believed possible in the first place. Li told the U.S. authorities that he thought Chiang was a loser and that the U.S.A. were wasting their time supporting him. This was no easy task for, as President Truman stated: "What I don't think most people understand is that the China Lobby was very strong in this country when I was in the White House. They had a great many Congressmen and Senators lined up to do pretty much what they were told, and they had billions of dollars to spend. They wanted to put old Chiang back in power. And the first step in this direction . . . was trying to get Chiang's army into the war in Korea, which I was not about to let happen in any way."[2]

But before long one or two U.S. Senators took a keen interest in Li and saw him as possibly a more amenable and less corrupt successor to Chiang Kai-shek. The C.I.A. took an interest and a plan was hatched by which Li would be used to arrange a coup in Taiwan to overthrow Chiang.

The Chinese Communists were interested not because they believed such a coup was possible; they were more realistic than the C.I.A. and were certain it was not feasible. But they saw that, if Li could be persuaded to return to China and defect officially to their side, it would be a splendid propaganda coup and cause a rift between Taiwan and the U.S.A. once news of the plot was leaked.

Li reported back to Peking through two agents in the U.S.A. that "the C.I.A. is childish in its madcap ideas of overthrowing Chiang, but the details of their plans

375

will give you an indication of how their minds work and how dangerously they plunge into the unknown".[3]

In 1965 Li went to Peking via Switzerland, then an acknowledged staging-post for defecting Chinese from the U.S.A. and elsewhere. He was seventy-four years of age, not anxious for power, but longing to be in his homeland. Using American phrases he had picked up, he gave out a specially staged news conference that in 1955 an "American Republican 'big-wig'" had sought his services in a plot against Chiang Kai-shek.

According to Li, this Republican was convinced that as he (Li) had been Acting President and commanded an army, he must have some forces on his side lying low in Taiwan and that on the basis of this he could arrange a coup. The idea, he explained, was that U.S. forces would be landed in Taiwan to link up with the rebels and force Chiang to abdicate so that Li could come to power.

Nor was this unconfirmed evidence on Li's part. It was a subject of acute embarrassment for the U.S. Government as, during the first Eisenhower administration, the Chiang Kai-shek lobby in Washington had indignantly asserted that General Li had been employed by the C.I.A. to destroy Chiang. Senator Styles Bridges, a Republican from New Hampshire, had even demanded a statement from the C.I.A. on rumours to this effect. Yet Washington had not attempted to stop Li's departure from the U.S.A. Peking claimed Li as one of their most important defectors as, despite his age, his propaganda value was considerable.

But if Peking could fool the C.I.A. through Li, the C.I.A. frequently gave the Chinese Communists some severe headaches. Late in 1958 a special two-man team on a radio interception project on the Chinese mainland developed a new technique for infiltration. After a few weeks' training in Taiwan the two agents were sent in a small, high-speed craft to within easy reach of the Chinese mainland. They dropped over the side into a rubber raft and set out for a small cove where they unloaded their radio and other equipment and were met by three native Chinese C.I.A. agents.

Such efforts have been sporadic and have not

376

yielded many worthwhile results. Indeed Peking has usually mopped up such infiltrations quite easily and their vigilance in this respect has unfortunately resulted in many unjustified arrests of Westerners, though the Chinese policy has been "it's better safe than sorry."

In 1973 it was announced that China had decided to commute the sentence of John Downey, a pilot for the C.I.A. who had been captured in 1952. This decision was made after it was learned that Downey's mother had suffered from a severe stroke and was critically ill in her Connecticut home.

Downey's aircraft disappeared in 1952 during the Korean War and no word of his fate was heard until 1954, when the Chinese Government announced that he had been captured and was sentenced to life imprisonment on espionage charges. Yet during his term in prison he was visited five times by members of his family.

Downey refused to discuss his mission when he was released by the Chinese, but there was a hint that he could have been released earlier if the U.S.A. had only acknowledged that he was a C.I.A. agent. Downey, one of a dozen Yale graduates who had been recruited direct from the campus, had only been in the C.I.A. a year when he was captured. But already he was regarded as one of the best young agents in the Far East where he was employed training Taiwanese in the arts and crafts of the cloak-and-dagger game.

Later his job was to see that these trained Taiwanese agents were dropped into China. He need not have accompanied them on such trips, but on one occasion he did so. This particular mission was intended not only to drop agents, but to pick up a Taiwanese agent who was already inside China. The plane was then to continue on to the mountains of Manchuria and parachute seven other Taiwanese into China to set up a communications base.

Downey's plane never reached the mountains. The Chinese arrested the Taiwanese agent Downey was to have picked up before Downey's plane left for China. They also intercepted radio messages being sent to the

Taiwanese agent which alerted them to the time and place of the pick-up.

Thus Downey and all his men were caught along with another C.I.A. agent, Richard Fecteau. The seven Taiwanese agents were summarily executed as spies and the same fate may have been meted out to the Taiwanese pilots. Downey was sentenced to life imprisonment and Fecteau to twenty years.

According to the *Washington Post,* Downey "said he told his captors everything he knew in those first ten months [of captivity]. He was quoted by newsmen interviewing him. . . . 'I would say I revealed every bit of information I had.' "[3]

When he had made these revelations he was taken out of the leg irons in which he had been placed, but kept in solitary confinement for another fourteen months, during which time he was not allowed to talk to anyone. Later he was put in prison with the crew of a B-29 that had been shot down over Korea. The Korean War had ended before the Chinese announced Downey's capture and conviction, but from that moment they began negotiations with the U.S.A. to arrange an exchange of prisoners. But poor Downey was not on the American list submitted to the Chinese because John Foster Dulles would not allow it to be admitted that he had been working for the C.I.A. Had the Chinese had proof of this they would undoubtedly have tried to barter him for a Chinese scientist held in the U.S.A.

What is of interest is that after more than twenty years in Chinese incarceration Downey was physically fit, in good spirits and at the age of forty-two could "run ten miles, do one hundred push-ups and as many as fifty chin-ups". He came out of prison speaking Chinese and able to read and write Russian which he had learned from Russian cell-mates and from the Russian novels his Chinese captors let him have. Had he been a Chinese agent caught by Chiang Kai-shek's police it is extremely doubtful if he would have been in anything like the same fit condition.

Nor did C.I.A. activities against China slacken off after the Korean War. On a mountain top outside Taipei a U.S. Air Force Chinese-language specialist regularly tuned in on mainland China's air-defence network and started a tape. Across the continent a supersonic aircraft named the SR (strategic reconnaissance)-71 then probed with its radar recording electronic pictures of missile installations. Targets for the SR–71 were often suggested by the C.I.A. and as time went on the aerial spy probes over China greatly increased.

In 1971 it was reported from various sources that U.S. spy raids were being made two hundred miles inside China. The C.I.A. refused to confirm or deny these reports, but the Washington press stated that teams of men were being sent "several hundred miles into the Yunan Province of Southern China".[4] It was alleged that these teams were recruited, equipped and trained by the C.I.A. to infiltrate Chinese territory and obtain information on troop movements and political developments.

Michael Morrow, of the Dispatch News Service International, cabled from Vientiane in Laos that "armed reconnaissance teams organised by United States Intelligence are penetrating two hundred miles into China. They are composed of Laotian hill tribesmen armed with American weapons, dispatched from a secret C.I.A. outpost in Northern Laos. According to sources close to the C.I.A. and confirmed by Western diplomatic sources in Vientiane, the C.I.A. always maintains at least one team inside China, equipped with radios and equipment to tap telegraph lines. . . . Teams are usually gone from three to four months, maintaining radio contact with Nam Lieu and with planes which fly close to the China border."[5]

Exaggerations of effective espionage are more likely to come from the Americans than the Chinese. One cynical diplomatic view, somewhat typical of the Nixonian school of secret diplomacy, is that a certain amount of publicising of such spy probes does more good than harm in negotiating with the Chinese. "It gives an extra kick to the Martini we offer them. Once they have swallowed that, they are ready to talk turkey."

U.S. diplomats may deceive themselves into thinking Peking is impressed by this kind of braggart talk on espionage, but it appears to be met only with impassivity. It neither helps nor hinders attempts at agreements between the two countries. On the other hand those Westerners, especially Europeans, who read stories of Americans and Europeans being held for years as spies by the Chinese—often on the slenderest of evidence, or on mere suspicion—must try to realise that for approaching a quarter of a century China has had to contend with joint attempts by the Taiwanese and the C.I.A. to send spies into China and from non-stop harassment and infiltration. In the circumstances it is surprising that men like John Downey survived so well.

Most hill tribesmen used by the C.I.A. in the infiltration operations belong to the Yao tribe. The Yao are used because this tribe lives in large numbers in Laos, Burma, Thailand and in China, where there are approximately two million of them. Quite often the task of using such tribesmen has been hopelessly bungled by the C.I.A., of whom one Chinese Intelligence officer boasted that "for every tribesman the C.I.A. try to use against us we send back two to spy on them". Several of the teams sent into China by the C.I.A. have been captured and some have switched their allegiance, returning to Nam Lieu as counterspies.

It is not the purpose of this book to enter into the domestic controversies of American politics. Suffice it to make the point—an important one in the context of this book—that on the whole the U.S.A. and the world generally have been somewhat safer under a sedulously devious Nixon than under an honest but inept Eisenhower. In 1973 President Nixon privately ordered a ban on all manned and unmanned spy flights over China, according to various reports from Intelligence sources. This officially put a stop to the SR-71 flights. But here again the Chinese were not fooled by this gesture, though outwardly expressing appreciation of it. For they knew perfectly well that the gesture was something to be leaked to the outside world as a by-product of secret diplomacy, whereas all Nixon was doing was to substitute Milsat (Military Satellite) operations from Vandenberg, California, for the SR-71s.

While ruthlessly combatting C.I.A. activities inside

China and imprisoning many Westerners on the slightest pretext as a deterrent, in the U.S.A. itself Chinese Intelligence suffered for years from the fact that she had no diplomatic headquarters. The diplomatic base used for directing espionage in the U.S.A. was the Chinese Embassy in Canada where the Ambassador, Huang Hua, was himself an Intelligence executive of long standing. Thus the fact that up to about 1968 not a single Chinese Communist agent had been arrested in the U.S.A. was as much a pointer to the low-key nature of Chinese espionage in America as to efficiency in protecting their agents. They relied heavily on a small but cleverly organised courier system, linking up with the Embassy in Ottawa as well as directly with China and Hongkong, on the networks in the cities where there were large Chinese populations, and on such institutions as the *China Daily News,* a newspaper launched in New York in 1949, on about four Chinese restaurants (two in New York, one in San Francisco and one in Los Angeles) and for a brief period (until it came under suspicion) the Sino-American Petrel Club in Chicago.

Once the United Nations recognised the People's Republic of China in 1971 Chinese Intelligence was rewarded with a strong diplomatic base in New York. It is interesting to note that when Peking sent in a fifty-two member team of diplomats, headed first by Chiao Kuen-hua, no effort was made to disguise the fact that two key Intelligence officers were among the delegation. One was Huang Hua, the Ambassador to Canada, to whom Chiao handed over the charge of the delegation; the other was Kao Liang, who came with the advance party. The C.I.A. knew all about Kao from his subversive activities in Africa, where he had been one of the top secret agents under cover of the N.C.N.A.

Kao Liang is not only an able Intelligence officer of wide experience in many parts of the world: he is an extremely gifted diplomat, well versed in African, Middle East and Far Eastern affairs.

From Korea to Thailand and the Philippines 1951-1973

Shock brings success.
Shock comes—oh, oh!
Laughing words—ha, ha!
The shock terrifies for a hundred miles,
And he does not let fall the sacrificial
    spoon and chalice.
From the commentaries of *I Ching*

THE Central External Liaison Department of the Chinese Secret Service, which is the real master-mind of its intelligence, is an amorphous, all-embracing entity with no exact equivalent anywhere in the world. It uses policy-making to advance espionage which, to a Westerner, is very much like putting the cart before the horse. But always it aims at shock in order first to anger a potential ally, then to make him worried, finally to win him over.

A perfect example of this is to be found by examining the rôle of China in Cambodia and to compare a statement made by Prince Sihanouk of 13 March 1968 with what has happened to this enigmatic and astute Prince latterly. Then he said:

The Khmer have nothing to fear because the Communist nations have made a pretence of being our friends—that is, officially. But under cover they are also playing a dirty game, because the Khmer Reds are their offspring, as all the world knows. By the way, all the documents we seized originated there. There were also documents from China and certain of their agents who we have succeeded in arresting came from Hanoi, ha, ha, ha! They came from Hanoi and the documents came from China . . . the other day we seized a junk carrying a great amount of weapons of all sorts coming from China in particular."

This would appear to suggest a close tie-up between Chinese and North Vietnamese Intelligence operations in Indo-China, with China as the supplier of arms and know-how; but the situation in Hanoi is very involved, with China backing Hanoi, yet spying on Soviet activities at the same time. This is a sensitive area for espionage as far as China is concerned and the Intelligence Service is well aware that the Russians would quickly exploit this to their detriment whenever possible.

In South Korea there are thirty two thousand Chinese residents—the largest foreign community—and on the surface all are ardent supporters of President Chiang Kai-shek, thus markedly contrasting with the open support for Peking among large numbers of Chinese residents in Japan. In South Korea, however, the stringent National Security Law and Anti-Communist Law, enforced by South Korea's own American-style C.I.A., are sufficient deterrents for most Koreans and Chinese who, under different conditions, might openly admit to sympathy or at least a sneaking admiration for the Peking regime. Fear is an ever-present element of life in South Korea, much more so than in Taiwan.

Despite this, three Chinese residents have in the strictest secrecy supplied some information which helps to throw light on the Chinese Intelligence operations inside both North and South Korea. Peking's relations with Pyongyang, the capital of the North, though outwardly harmonious, are not remarkable for their warmth. North Korea has consistently played down the rôle of "Chinese volunteers" in the Korean War; and Soviet Russia has undertaken a much more important rôle in the North Korean economy and has been the principal supplier of arms and aircraft.

There is a situation in Pyongyang not unlike that in Hanoi with the U.S.S.R. and China both competing for influence, but in many respects China has less influence here than in North Vietnam. For this reason Peking tends to operate her principal Korean network in the police state of the South, where the Government is opposed to China, rather than among the relatively few infiltrators and resident agents employed in North Korea.

The resident Chinese in the South, while fearful of the strict laws and the long arm of the South Korean Central Intelligence Agency, and even though they may have been born in the country, feel distinctly superior to the Koreans among whom they live. At heart they have no allegiance to the Republic of Korea. What is useful from Peking's point of view is that all Chinese here carry Taiwanese passports and they are only hindered from travelling overseas by the same restrictions which apply to South Koreans. In practice it is not difficult for Chinese wishing to go to Taiwan, Hongkong or Japan to do so. In both Hongkong and Japan, Chinese residents of South Korea occasionally meet friends and relatives from the People's Republic of China. This is one of the channels of the courier service for intelligence between Seoul and Peking. Indeed since most Chinese on the mainland cannot travel freely in and out of the country, such contacts between relatives would only be sanctioned by Peking for such a specific purpose.

Despite their Taiwanese passports and nominal support for Chiang Kai-shek very many of the Chinese residents of South Korea secretly but strongly resent the somewhat harsh paternalistic control which the Taiwan Embassy attempts to establish over them. Once when the then Ambassador from Taiwan, General Liang, sold off a slice of the Embassy garden to a department store about a thousand Chinese marched on the Embassy in protest. There are also complaints of bullying by Taiwanese officials and some suggestions that, in league with the South Korean Government, the latter sometimes organise the disappearance to Taiwan of Chinese residents—almost certainly suspected agents of Peking.

During the Korean War a number of Chinese who had lived for many years in Korea were found guilty of spying for the Chinese Communists and were handed over to the Taiwanese authorities who had them summarily executed. The families of these men still live in South Korea.

The importance of South Korea from an intelligence view-point has not diminished since the Korean War: the peninsula is of interest to China, Russia and Japan. The Chinese Communists certainly make South Korea a prime target for intelligence gathering and they use Chinese residents (known to dislike the Americans more than they do the Koreans) in preference to Koreans who are, generally speaking, not trusted.

The kind of information Peking seeks here concerns strength and disposition of the U.S. forces, locations of missile bases, new types of weapon in use, factors affecting U.S.-Korean relations, Washington's trade and aid policy and—an interesting point—details of all offences by U.S. military personnel against the Korean population.

The South Koreans frequently round up North Korean agents, but there have been no known arrests of Chinese agents in twenty years, though there may have been a very few cases in which the Taiwanese have been tipped off about suspects.

In one respect China has a curious parallel intelligence link with Russia—that of having maintained what is known as the Cambridge cell, a small network consisting mainly of graduates of Cambridge University. In this it resembles the Soviet spy network which operated at Cambridge University in the late 'twenties and 'thirties and which produced such agents as Peter Kapitza, Allan Nunn May, "Kim" Philby, Donald Maclean and Guy Burgess, all of whom were at Trinity College.

Illustrative of this is the curious case of Pak No-su, who was arrested by the South Korean secret police soon after he had returned from Cambridge in 1969 and taken up a senior post in the office of South Korea's President. He was accused of master-minding a spy-ring based at Cambridge University and recruiting Korean intellectuals in Europe for the North Korean cause. In fact all the evidence, especially some of his links in Cambridge and on the continent of Europe, pointed to Pak No-su working for the Chinese cause. He could well have been an agent for North Korea as well.

Pak was rounded up with thirty-two others. The hard core of the case against him was that he had made contact with North Koreans in Europe and visited the Communist North himself. But part of the case rested on "confessions" obtained under torture and it is probable that even this forced "admission" was a cover story. One of the unhappiest factors of this case was that Pak's wife co-operated with the prosecution against her husband and thus got off with a very light sentence.

Pak had been offered the job in the President's office as a bait to bring him home to Korea. For more than two years he lived under sentence of death and almost his last wish, made to a Roman Catholic priest when he was in the death cell shortly before his execution, was that his 4-year-old daughter should be sent to England to give her a fresh start in life.

Pak was fervently pro-British and even had pictures of the Queen on the walls of his cell. He had spent 1968–9 at Fitzwilliam College, Cambridge, as a postgraduate student. A few years earlier the West German and French Governments had put pressure on South Korea to save students who were forced to return from Europe to face similar charges to those levelled at Pak.

While in prison Pak made the odd remark to a fellow-prisoner that "spiritually I am more British than Korean". Efforts are still being made to obtain a British passport for Pak's daughter as there is a family in England anxious to adopt her.

A close friend of Pak's told me:

"He was an astonishing mixture, being strongly pro-Chinese Communism in secret, rather more cautiously pro-North Korea and, at the same time, fascinated by and adoring British institutions from the Royal Family to the parliamentary system. His favourite reading included the biographies of British kings and queens. He was very tight-lipped, but you can take it that he was an active member of a

Cambridge-based spy network that operated for China, but was allowed by the Chinese to use the cover of North Korea, North Vietnam, Burma or Singapore, as best suited the operation of the moment. Perhaps the phrase 'Cambridge-based network' is somewhat misleading, as most of the operators really get to work only when they leave Cambridge. But the recruiting is done partially in Cambridge and partially in Geneva, though the actual Cambridge network dates back to the late 'thirties when some of China's present nuclear science team were there."

The Chinese Secret Service has been so successful in Thailand that it is said in Intelligence circles there that they forced the K.G.B. to make Kuala Lumpur rather than Bangkok their main H.Q. in the Far East. This is perhaps somewhat of a distortion of the real facts, but there is an element of truth in it.

The New China News Agency announced in January 1966 that "the Malayan National Liberation League, formerly a part of the Malayan Independence Movement in Djakarta, has set up a mission in Peking, joining the Thailand Patriotic Front". This was the first major mention of the discreetly formed Thai Front in 1965, its principal aims being to drive out the U.S. forces from Thailand and to overthrow the "fascist" Bangkok Government.

Chinese tactics in Thailand were simple: they knew that the mass of the Thais were devoted to the King, so rather than waste time wooing them they concentrated on the three million minority of Chinese, Vietnamese, Laotians and hill tribesmen. Special agitators were sent into Thailand to whip up a revolt, circulating at first with great circumspection among the Lahu tribe.

The tactics were to work on local folklore and superstitions. One of the first tasks of the shock Secret Service unit master-minding this operation was to find a malleable Lahu tribesman with sufficient presence that he could be produced as the "deliverer" of his tribesmen. One such was chosen, on the basis of Lahu tradition, that by "magic hammer, magic rope and magic knife", as folklore decreed, he could destroy all their enemies however powerful they might be. Although this plan had a certain success no major result was achieved.

The Thai Government may have its own reasons for exaggerating the Communist threat to Thailand, if only to go on getting foreign aid and perhaps prolong military rule, but there is no doubt that Peking is more active here than in most Southeast Asian countries. The Thais produced a White Paper entitled *Disturbances and Destruction of the Thai Communists.*[1] Unquestionably it overstates the case, but not altogether without justification. The first chapter points out that the Thai and foreign Communist Parties' ultimate goal is to rule Thailand, while the third chapter claims that the Chinese Communists support and control the Thai Communists, giving them military, political and economic training, asserting that the department in Peking responsible is the Central External Liaison Department.

It is true, of course, that this Department is responsible for overall strategy, tactics and policy-making, but it is the United Front which really takes charge of operations in Thailand. They have been backed by broadcasts from the Voice of the Thai People, a clandestine radio station located in North Vietnam or South China. Day-to-day decisions on Secret Service policy towards Thailand are taken in the Chinese Embassy in Vientiane in Laos.

A dispatch from the A.P. reporter, Maurus Young, in Taipei on 23 January 1973 reported that Chinese troops in Thailand were using a Thai-Chinese translation textbook of military terms. This had been obtained by an Intelligence unit in Taipei. A sample translation was, according to the report: "My uncle, don't be afraid, we are the troops of Chairman Mao. We are coming to fight for your interests. When your enemies have been destroyed, you will lead a better life. Please be our guide. We will pay you." The date of the textbook was 1965, and Taipei Intelligence sources say it is the first example of such teaching material to be brought out of China.

Lesson 12 of the textbook dealt with "Three Commandments and Eight Points for Attention": they were listed as not taking so much as a needle or thread from any household, and turning over all confiscated property; politeness, fair trading, returning items borrowed from the people, compensation for any damages, not beating people or cursing, avoiding damage to farms, not flirting with women and not treating prisoners badly.

Particular attention has been paid by Chinese Intelligence to the secretive, ultra-neutralist Burmese whose country has remained so very much of a mystery ever since it was given independence by the British after World War II. The Chinese have in fact had their own outlawed White Flag movement waging underground war in Burma since 1949.

The White Flag was a Burmese movement which the Chinese gradually infiltrated and to a large extent controlled, giving a number of the White Flag leaders special training in China. I have in my possession a copy of a safe conduct pass given to Chinese-approved Burmese personnel, signed by General Let Ya, Chairman of the War Council Patriotic Forces. This states that:

"Copies of the enclosed SAFE CONDUCT PASS are appearing everywhere in Burma. Supplied by the Elected Government of the Union of Burma, Provisional H.Q. Taung-Gyi-Ko-Lone, Eastern Burma, the leaflets are circulated by the combined patriotic forces of the UNITED FRONT and by elements of the Burma Armed Forces.

"All who receive the SAFE CONDUCT PASS are called upon to align themselves with those militant men and women who have taken up arms for restoration of democratic freedoms and institutions. . . ."

The resignation of Burma's head of state, Ne Win, from his Army command as "general" to lead a reorganised government in Rangoon in April 1972 reflected growing anxiety over the continuing menace of intransigent border tribes. The threat to his rule came from the formidable anti-Rangoon minority tribesmen along the Chinese and Thai jungle borders who still demand local autonomy. In North-east Burma the tribal minorities, armed with Chinese weapons and supported by Chinese "advisers", permitted the operation of a direct land link between China and the active Communist terrorists in North-east Thailand.

The picture of United Front operations extends far and wide in South-east Asia. There have, of course, been failures from over-enthusiasm, or from stirred-up revolts getting out of hand. Nowhere was this more marked than in China's untypically incautious drive in Indonesia where they nearly brought off a total coup in September 1965. The Peking Indonesian Communist Party, heavily backed by a policy of extorting money from members of the Chinese trading circles in Indonesia, developed so swiftly and successfully that the drive to take control seemed too easy. A Secret Service training school was set up in Djakarta with the aim of directing operations in the Philippines.

But here the Chinese overreached themselves and the backlash came with the ousting of Soekarno from power, a massacre of many Chinese in Indonesia and almost a total defeat. It set back Secret Service long-term planning for at least three years and resulted in a ruthless drive against Chinese agents in Indonesia. Nevertheless the Chinese Intelligence Service is still re-grouping inside this country and, in January 1973, the official Antara News Agency in Indonesia announced that twenty Communist agents who worked in sawmills in the port of Teolakair, West Kalimantan, had been arrested by Indonesian Security authorities. Antara stated that the agents had been ordered by their leaders to "infiltrate among other Chinese and influence them to support the Communists".

In 1973 Indonesia refused to readmit an estimated ten thousand former Chinese residents who had gone to China in the mid-'sixties and who were now stranded in Macao and Hongkong. These Chinese Indonesians went to China hopefully, but became dissatisfied with conditions and were granted exit visas by the Chinese. But the Indonesian authorities are so fearful of infiltration that to date they have maintained the ban on their re-entry.

Djakarta was for some years a major Chinese Intelligence H.Q. for operations not only inside Indonesia, but directed against Malaysia, Sarawak and the Philippines. Early successes intoxicated them and several foolishly provoked risings which failed were the result. More agents have been thwarted in this part of the world than in any other.

The Djakarta-based drive against the Philippines was in the early days concentrated on whipping up the Huk movement. A training school for agents was set up in the Southern Philippines and attention was paid to training guerrillas. Thus the Marcos Government in the Philippines has been as anxious as were the Thais to create the impression of "Chinese involvement" in the country. "Outside support" for Communist insurgents was one of the reasons Marcos cited for invoking martial law in September 1972, specifically in connection with the seizure of arms in June of that year from the motor vessel *Karagantan* in Palanan, Isabela province, stronghold of the New People's Army, the military wing of the Maoist-oriented Communist Party of the Philippines. Despite intensive propaganda, the Government failed to convince knowledgeable foreign observers that the source of the arms was China.

Although some of the leaders of the New People's Army may have received their training in Peking, the movement is essentially home-grown, owing relatively little in leadership and material support to China. Peking's chief source of strength in the Philippines probably lies somewhere within the Chinese community, numbering between 455,000 and 600,000, of whom 118,000 are citizens of Taiwan rather than the Philippines. As in South Korea, sympathisers with China are obliged to keep their views to themselves for their own safety, but with the eventual recognition of Peking— much talked about in Manila and likely in the near future—the dividing lines between pro-Taiwan and pro-Peking residents may begin to show themselves.

At the moment the principal instruments for political and intelligence influence are the Chambers of Commerce and the Federation of Philippine-Chinese Chambers of Commerce. These "Chinese" Chambers of Commerce are in control of large funds which they use to buy political protection and favours. They are the key to influencing and penetrating the Chinese community, though here again the Taiwan Government as well as Peking has some say. It is a secret battle for power between the two, with the odds on Peking in the long-term.

After the Indonesian disaster the Chinese are playing a very discreet Intelligence game in the Philippines, hoping when recognition comes that they will retain a Chinese minority and that the Taiwanese-Chinese will not become Philippine citizens. The Chinese community here has no record of sabotage, espionage or subversion, since non-citizens are vulnerable to deportation.

According to Father Charles J. McCarthy, an authority on the Chinese in the Philippines, "no responsible agency has arrested Chinese and proven them guilty of subversion in the last fifteen years (the Yuitung brothers might be mentioned as an exception: however, their trial had little credibility inside or outside the country)."[2] The Yuitung brothers, respectively publisher and editor of a Chinese-language newspaper in Manila, were deported to Taipei to stand trial for publishing "subversive materials sympathetic to Peking", despite the fact that Quintin and Rizal Yuitung were born and educated in the Philippines and had publicly renounced Nationalist Chinese citizenship, though they had not become Philippine citizens.

The "New People's Army", officially founded in December 1968, does seem in its early stages at least to owe some debt to the People's Republic of China, though to what extent is still a matter of some dispute. It is known that the NPA's secretary-general, Jose-Maria Sison, visited Peking in 1967 (from which time Radio Peking and the Chinese press began issuing statements about the re-establishment of the Philippine Communist Party on Maoist lines). Certainly some Filipinos have been to China for training and this much was admitted by Chou En-lai to President Marcos when the latter made a secret trip to Peking in 1972. Chou En-lai added that no guarantee could be given that such training would not continue.[3]

31

Defectors and Brain-Washing 1949-1973

No type of mind is so like the extreme right as the extreme left.

Albert Pauphilet

UP to 1973 there have been far more defectors to China than of exiled Chinese going back to the homeland. On the other hand very few indeed of the defectors from China have been members of the Chinese Secret Service, and there is no doubt that a fairly high proportion of the defectors leaving China have been agents posing as escapers from the Peking regime.

The easiest and most used method of escaping from China is via Hongkong, swimming from the mainland across Mirs Bay or Deep Water Bay, which takes anything from four to eight hours, usually attempted at night to avoid the Chinese patrol boats. Swimming is dangerous as there are many sharp rocks en route and oyster beds in the shallows. Many swimmers carry floats of some kind, football bladders and even pieces of wood.

If a swimmer succeeds in landing in Hongkong he is at once classed as an illegal immigrant, but at the same time is given an identity card and aid in finding a home and a job. Every "illegal" is closely examined by experts (*a*) for information about China, working conditions, popular feelings, etc., and (*b*) to make sure he is not an agent.

In 1971 there were thirteen thousand "illegals" and in 1972 there were fourteen and a half thousand. The figures have been rising by on an average seven hundred and fifty a year since 1959. Not all escapes are in twos or threes. In July 1972, ten families (fifty-six people in all, including children) overpowered a five-man junk in a Chinese harbour. They locked the crew in the hold and after a twelve-hour voyage landed in Hongkong.

It is possible to be smuggled out of China by sea. This is done in what the Chinese call "snake-boats". There are believed to be at least three hundred and fifty junks operating this type of escape. "Illegals" are charged anything from £100–£400 for the trip which usually takes place at night and is controlled by professional operators who carefully plot the courses and times of patrol boats.

Escapers from China, if caught by a patrol boat, face penalties of ten years in a labour camp for first offenders and twenty-five years for "undesirables" —those who have tried before. More than seventy-five per cent of those escaping do it by swimming. Most of them are dissatisfied youths who have been sent to communes to gain experience through manual work and the majority of those detained in Hongkong are between sixteen and twenty-two years of age.

Along the seventeen-miles' land frontier is a twelve-foot-high barbed-wire fence which is heavily patrolled by troops with orders to shoot and some two hundred police dogs trained to kill. The "season" for escaping is approximately six months long, from April until the autumn. It is about four to six miles from border to border. In Hongkong the Geneva-based International Social Service and the International Refugee Service operate re-orientation programmes for the refugees. Amnesty International unofficially reports that some of these "freedom swimmers" have been sent to West Germany.

It should not be thought that Peking's attitude towards the flood of immigrants into Hongkong is always rigidly opposed. On occasions measures to prevent escapers are tightened up, at others—for example twelve years ago—an exodus from the mainland to

Hongkong has actually been encouraged. A branch of the Intelligence Service controls the whole question of escapers and would-be immigrants, sometimes using escapers as agents to infiltrate the colony of Hongkong, at others gladly letting known criminals and trouble-makers get away to make a nuisance of themselves to the British.

It was in the early 'sixties that Communist Army guards mysteriously and impassively encouraged a flood of seventy thousand men, women and children to trample across into Hongkong in a twenty-five day period, and, just as impassively, allowed harassed Colonial authorities to intercept and return most of the refugees. Even in recent years there has been an unwritten agreement between the Hongkong authorities and those on the Chinese border to permit a maximum quota of fifty Chinese with legitimate immigration permits to enter Hongkong each day. For a short while this number was actually doubled and steps had to be taken to check it.

Immigrants originally permitted to leave China under the fifty-per-day quota usually comprised the elderly, unskilled and disabled, but latterly Peking has even permitted some skilled workers and technicians to leave and find work in Hongkong. These have caused most embarrassment in overcrowded Hongkong, especially the Indonesian Chinese who responded to China's "return to the homeland" drive in the mid-'sixties, but some of whom are now dissatisfied with conditions and want to go back to Indonesia. The Indonesian authorities refuse to accept them on the ground that they have already rejected their Indonesian citizenship. Thus they become permanent and unwanted Hongkong residents.

An ambivalent game is sometimes played by Intelligence forces on both sides of the border, with both Peking and Hongkong occasionally turning a blind eye to known agents crossing backwards and forwards. There was the case of "Two-Gun" Cohen who, after he had been repatriated to Canada, paid at least two more trips to China after the Communist take-over. The first visit was in 1956 and said to have been arranged by Madame Sun Yat-sen, when he went to both Taiwan and Peking. He was said to have arranged some business deals and to have acted as a go-between for informal messages between Chou En-lai and Chiang Kai-shek. Again, in November 1966, he attended centenary celebrations for Sun Yat-sen in Peking. Cohen died at the age of eighty-one in England.

When the Japanese were rounding up suspects in the Sorge spy-ring in World War II, among those arrested was Kinkazu Saionji, a consultant to the Japanese Foreign Ministry. One of Sorge's biographers, Richard Storry, refutes the suggestion that Saionji was a member of the Sorge set-up, stating that he was found guilty by the Tokyo District Court of "no more than careless talk; and this was why he was given a suspended sentence of eighteen months' imprisonment".[1]

It is not strictly correct to say that Saionji was merely given a suspended sentence for "careless talk". He was found guilty of "having violated the Military Secrets Protection Law" and the "National Defence Law", in particular Clause 6, dealing with the leakage of information to others. He was without any doubt whatsoever a member of the Sorge spy ring and its sole survivor, only escaping with a suspended sentence because he was the grandson of Prince Saionji.

Kinkazu Saionji, who is now approaching seventy, was a former graduate of Oxford University, and he worked for the Russians against the Japanese in both Shanghai and Tokyo as far back as the 'thirties. He was fortunate to have survived the break-up of the Soviet network in 1941 and it is suspected that, apart from his aristocratic connections, he saved his life by giving the Japanese some valuable information. Quite possibly he worked for the Japanese Intelligence for a brief period afterwards. Significantly, he was contemptuously ignored by the Japanese liberal-aristocratic elements whom he had betrayed and was later expelled from membership of the Japanese Communist Party.

But Saionji unquestionably has a brilliant mind, a shrewd Secret Service operator's knack of surviving the most difficult moments and his experience alone is worth a good deal to at least four Intelligence Services even today. Curiously, when at Oxford, his ambition was to become a playwright and it was only after he had failed to achieve success in this direction that he decided to apply for a post in the Japanese Foreign Office. After the war he seems to have regarded the whole Communist world as being in a state of flux and for this reason to have played a waiting game while lying low. For a time he was nominally a Japanese Communist, but in 1957 he went to Peking where he made a Maoist-style recantation of "former errors" and worked first with the Chinese Communists against his former Russian comrades (this was before the Sino-Soviet rift became official) and later with Peking against his Japanese comrades.

Saionji once claimed he was the founder of the Japanese Council Against Atomic and Hydrogen Bombs, but he modestly dropped this claim when China tested its first bomb. Then, in 1970, after being given a farewell banquet by Chou En-lai, then the Chinese Foreign Minister, Saionji surprisingly returned to Japan, stopping off at Hongkong where he was the guest of one of that colony's leading Communist bosses, Dr K. C. Wang.

At that time Saionji had spent twelve years in Peking and this in itself suggests that he must have been working closely with the Chinese Secret Service. In Hongkong he was as smooth and nimble-witted as he had always been, but with much greater assurance and a touch of grandeur. He said that he liked to call himself "Japan's unofficial envoy to China" and referred to his Peking residence as "the little Embassy".

One cannot stress too much the relatively small number of defectors to the West from China. The nation with the largest population in the world has proportionately far fewer defectors than the Soviet Union or the U.S.A. The sense of being Chinese always in the end outweighs all other considerations, and a good deal of evidence suggests that among the defectors there is a higher proportion of hidden Peking agents than one would get from a similar number of defectors from Soviet Russia.

The most important defection in recent years was undoubtedly that of Liao Ho-shu, who was chargé d'affaires at the Hague. But he belongs more appropriately to another chapter. Here is a list of notable Chinese defectors in recent years:

A Chinese Army general (name not disclosed) is reported to have fled to Hongkong on 3 February 1972 and to have hidden away with anti-Communist sympathisers. It is probable that he has now moved elsewhere as the Communists would have swiftly tracked him down had he remained long in Hongkong. He was believed to have fled from the purge which was going on after the downfall of Defence Minister Lin Piao. Three generals and sixteen other officers who had attempted to escape across the border the week before were stopped at gun-point by Chinese guards. In 1971 a total of twenty-seven Army officers were reported to have been arrested while trying to escape to Hongkong.

Chang Shi-jung: This thirty-one-year-old Chinese agricultural adviser, who had been serving in Algeria, was detained by the police at Orly airport outside Paris on 28 April 1971, where a dozen or more Chinese comrades were carrying him, unconscious from a heavy dose of drugs, to board a Shanghai-bound airliner. He recuperated at the Hotel Dieu Hospital in Paris, but in May was reported to have requested permission to return to China. The French counter-Intelligence organisation was reportedly involved in this case and Chang had allegedly attempted earlier to defect in Algeria.

Ma Szu-tsung: This 54-year-old violinist and director of Peking's Central Conservatory of Music escaped to the U.S.A. with his wife and two children in 1967. He is reported to be living with a brother in New York City.

Lau Yvet-sang: A 43-year-old New China News Agency home news editor, Lau defected to Taiwan from Hongkong in November 1966.

Tung Chai-ping: Assistant cultural attaché at the Chinese Embassy in Bujumbura, Burundi, he defected to the U.S.A. in August 1964.

Professor Wang Minchuan: 40-year-old Director of Chinese Studies at the University of Baghdad from October 1959, Wang defected into Greece in June 1961, reportedly bound for the U.S.A.

Miao Chen-pai: 29-year-old former member of the

Chinese Foreign Aid Delegation in Damascus, who defected to New York in July 1966.[2]

Chou Hung-chin: 44-year-old member of a technical delegation to Tokyo, who in October 1963 was reported to have defected to Russia.

Chou Hsiang-pu: Second Secretary in the diplomatic mission in London since 1957, defected with his wife and two children to Russia in October 1963. He was *en route* to Peking via Leningrad aboard the Soviet liner Baltika, which docked in Leningrad.

Chao Fu: 27-year-old former security officer at the Chinese Embassy in Stockholm, who requested political asylum in Bonn in August 1962.

Two Chinese pilots (names not disclosed) who defected to South Korea in September 1961.

Four Chinese Army officers (names again not disclosed) crossed the Himalayan passes from Tibet and sought political asylum in India in October 1966.

Sun Wei-kuo: Aged twenty-five, assistant information officer in the Chinese Embassy in New Delhi, he defected in September 1966.

There is nothing to suggest that many of these defectors have been able—or willing—to give much information to the West. Certainly the capture of a Chinese defector is generally speaking of less value than that of a Russian defector.

There are exceptions to this rule, but even when the defectors give information it is so hedged about with play-acting and disinformation (sometimes this is a natural reflex action and not done to deceive) that Western Intelligence officers have been known to shriek for alcohol or to take sedatives after long bouts of interrogation. Nobody in the world—and this really should be underlined—can con Western observers, whether of an Intelligence Service, or those serving newspapers, into writing reports which are sheer unadulterated waffle, as much as can the Chinese.

The Chinese mind is in many respects impervious to attempts to penetrate it by occidentals. On the other hand, while it may fail to understand all the nuances of Western thought (though this is a dangerous proposition to count on), it can and often deliberately does baffle the Westerner. Highly intelligent, experienced Western journalists go to China, intent upon putting over an objective, unbiased viewpoint: they end up by writing almost exactly what the Chinese want them to write. Nor is this from a fear of censorship: it frequently occurs when they have returned from China. As a footnote to this assertion perhaps I should add that the nonplussing of journalists is less prevalent in the female of the species! There may be a lesson for Western Intelligence officers here.

Chinese Intelligence not only closely watches resident foreign journalists, but keeps their numbers down to a figure easily controllable by constant vigilance, deliberate isolation from other contacts and a low-key, but even more efficient, technique of remote-control brainwashing than the Russians could ever manage.

This raises the question of the treatment which the Chinese counter-espionage authorities give to prisoners. One gets the impression that Chinese methods of treating prisoners and interrogating them are much more humane than those of the Soviet Union, the Taiwanese or the South Korean authorities. On the whole, as we have already seen in the case of a C.I.A. agent such as John Downey, the Chinese do not employ the Russian tactics of treating a prisoner so badly that his health suffers, and then suggesting that, if he is to survive, an exchange deal should be arranged.

Admittedly this is partly due to the fact that the Chinese regard a captured agent of theirs as one who has failed to do his job: for this reason the return of captured spies does not—at least, so far—worry them unduly. On the other hand there would appear to be an experimental, if not a positive, attempt at more sophisticated treatment for captured spies by the interrogation officers.

This may be partially due to the fact that many of those arrested are held only on the slightest of suspicions and therefore more carefully treated. But the Chinese also believe that even the most hardened "reactionary" can eventually be won over. For this reason they make painstaking efforts to "reform" their foreign prisoners.

It is easier to know when these "reforming" tactics

fail than when they succeed. George Watt, born in Belfast and a constructional engineer with the firm of Vickers-Zimmer, who worked first in the U.S.S.R. and later in China, was arrested at the time of the sacking of the British Mission in Peking in 1967. He was charged with being a spy and appeared before the People's Court in Lanchow, after which he spent three years in the Ideological Remoulding Prison in Peking.

Watt later wrote of his cell, consisting of one chair, one small table, a bed of four wooden planks without a mattress and a pail:

"Before long I was marched off to the office of a man who spoke English and who was introduced as my tutor in Maoism. For many months to come he was to be virtually the only person I would speak to, for it was made clear to me that I should not, under any circumstances, attempt to communicate with fellow prisoners.

"For me this was a cruel, soul-destroying punishment, but the Chinese had their reasons for imposing this ruling. In the first place they didn't want prisoners due for early release to be disclosed— they didn't want prisoners due for early release to return to the free world and reveal the names of those still held in custody. But there was another reason, too: any social contact with other prisoners would upset the plans of the Communists to 'condition' minds . . . the Chinese feel they have the right to use force and to brainwash a prisoner with Communist ideology."[3]

In the early 'seventies the Belgian banker, Frans van Roosbroeck, was released from prison in China after twenty years' detention and four years' solitary confinement in Shanghai Prison.

Van Roosbroeck, now reunited with his family in Brussels, did not choose to repeat to the Belgian press what he related to a few pressmen in Hongkong after his release. In 1949, when the Communists came to power in China, Roosbroeck was only twenty-nine and he remained at his post, under house arrest, until his detention in June 1968—a curious gap of nineteen years before he was "formally arrested".

During this period he had married a Korean girl and they had children. This was a measure of the "freedom" given to him. Yet in the four subsequent years he was never once allowed out of his Shanghai cell even for exercise. He had been charged with offences which ranged from "counter-revolutionary activities" to espionage, but which were more acutely related to the United States' freezing of the dollar assets belonging to the Belgian Bank during the Korean War. He had to awake and face the Judas window of his cell at five o'clock in summer and six o'clock in winter each morning to bow to the scrutiny of the People's Guard. He was denied letters from his wife and family.

Roosbroeck had admittedly been indiscreet during the lull between his twenty-year detention and four years of solitary confinement. He came forward voluntarily to help the terrified family of the British Consul, Hewitt, aboard the plane to Peking when that British representative and his escort were assaulted and spat upon by Red Guards. He also attended the Party auction of the Hewitt effects to bid for personal and treasured belongings of the expelled Consular family. These auctioned possessions were later impounded with Roosbroeck's own belongings when he was arrested.

There is an interesting finale to Roosbroeck's departure from China. One of the escorts conducting him to the border warned him that as "a confessed criminal" he should expect no welcome home, and added with a smirk: "Remember, your Korean wife has been separated from you for four years and that is too long to expect her to have remained faithful to you."

The closing episode was a dispute at the border between his guards over whether Roosbroeck should himself carry his small hand-bag, or have it carried for him. The guards eventually withdrew, presumably to telephone Canton, and Roosbroeck, standing correctly to attention, waited until they returned after fifteen minutes and directed him to carry his belongings himself for the fifty yards separating him from the People's Republic and the colony of Hongkong.

I have examined carefully some twenty-four accounts of people held as spies by the Chinese and my deductions from these—both written accounts and personal interviews and cross-examination of the individuals concerned—are that while Chinese methods and techniques vary considerably from one area to another and more so from one period to another, they are not as a general rule physically harsh, but that mentally they can have a devastating effect. The success of such tactics depends on highly skilled interrogators and brain-washers (or "tutors" as they are designated) and quite often these fall below the required level, or else the prisoner in question is not susceptible to such methods.

It is easy to criticise and even to satirise Chinese methods of brainwashing, but I should like to cite the opinion given to me by a Briton employed by the American C.I.A.:

"One of my jobs was to interview people who had been imprisoned by the Chinese. We had come across cases of brainwashing among prisoners-of-war in Korea, and we suspected that the Chinese might have similar methods. Some of those imprisoned had been agents, yet I discovered that not a single one of them had been tortured or illtreated in a physical sense.

"What was fascinating about these interviews was that they revealed that considerable brainwashing had been carried out without the prisoners being aware of it. It was all much subtler than some of the so-called confessions which the Russians obtain by cruder brainwashing. Of course, the Chinese did sometimes obtain 'confessions' which read as though they had been brainwashed, but more often than not this was a symbolic prelude to release, a kind of diplomatic, face-saving device on both sides, which each side understood.

"One agent of ours who came back from Shanghai seemed to be more hostile to his own country, because he claimed the U.S.A. had done nothing to get him released, than towards the Chinese who had arrested him.

"He insisted he had not been badly treated, though admitted he had been kept in solitary confinement for several days without being allowed any exercise or having been questioned.

"The Chinese would hint that the C.I.A. did not seem greatly concerned about his fate. I am certain that he talked a great deal to the Chinese and gave them information he should have kept to himself. But where the Chinese were clever is that they did not ask him obvious questions about his work, or what he was doing in China. They encouraged him to talk on generalities—computers, aeronautics and technical matters—often luring him into indiscretions by the most innocent of questions. I am sure he was given a truth-drug, probably in his food. My own guess is that he was given marijuana in his food. Later I learned he had become a pot addict. Very cunningly the Chinese decorated his cell with paper streamers and gave him a farewell banquet the night before he left prison."

32

Infiltrating Europe 1950-1974

When a man does not boast of his efforts and does not count his merits a virtue, he is a man of great parts. It means that for all his merits he subordinates himself to others. Noble, mature, reverent in conduct, the modest man is full of merit and therefore he is able to maintain his position.

I Ching

SINCE the People's Republic was established China has approached Europe warily and shown none of that brashness and open aggression she has displayed in Indonesia, Thailand and parts of Africa. Certainly the Chinese Secret Service treats Europe with far greater respect than it shows either the U.S.S.R. or the U.S.A. This may be an unconscious residue of reluctant respect for the forces of imperialism, but it would be truer to say that in the long-run Chinese Intelligence sees Europe as a potential ally.[1]

For that reason China is prepared to play a modest, patient game in Europe as far as intelligence gathering is concerned, and not to take risks. Not only does the Chinese Intelligence Service deliberately maintain a low-key activity in Europe, but this has lulled some European countries into believing that either it does not exist inside Europe, or that it is totally insignificant. This is both dangerous and foolish thinking.

In the early 'fifties the Chinese Communists, having relatively few links with Europe and few large communities of exiled Chinese to rely on for recruiting agents, depended heavily on their diplomatic personnel inside the Soviet bloc. They made their principal espionage headquarters in Prague until they were forced out by the Czechs in 1963. Since then they have relied on Albania, as already mentioned, for a watch on Eastern Europe, and on Switzerland in Western Europe.

After 1963 Berne was the headquarters of Chinese espionage in Western Europe, though today the emphasis has been switched to Paris and Vienna, partly to spread the load and partly for political considerations. Nevertheless Berne, and to a lesser extent Geneva, remain two key areas where the direction of Chinese espionage is carried out and master-minded. The Chinese are well aware that the Swiss secret police are extremely efficient and well versed in the Intelligence manoeuvres of most of the great powers in their country and for this reason even up to 1974 the rule has been for a low profile exercise in espionage with their efforts mainly focussed on information gathering. On the other hand a good deal of planning of espionage efforts outside Switzerland, particularly in France and Germany, is done in Berne and Geneva.

Sometimes the zest for information gathering, despite the low profile image (or perhaps because of it), goes to comic lengths. At a National Day reception in Geneva in 1973 a Western journalist was questioned closely by the Assistant Air Attaché of the Chinese Embassy in Berne on what he thought about the "East-West German situation" (although he had never more than passed through Frankfurt airport and could only repeat what he had read about it). Nevertheless the conversation ended with the presentation by the attaché of his card and a "Do come and see us the next time you are in Berne".

To ultra-sophisticated Western minds this approach may seem amateurish. This again is a foolish interpretation of two factors of Chinese intelligence gathering: first, the legal, candid approach; secondly, the concentration on sources of information which most professional European spy-masters would neglect. It is more than probable that something the journalist said whetted the Chinese appetite.

In the summer of 1965 the Swiss Foreign Ministry communicated with the Chinese Ambassador, Li

Ching-chuan, to protest against activities which could not be tolerated by the Confederate authorities. This followed, among other things, rather lengthy visits to the Embassy during the weekend by Frenchmen. Three of them picked up for questioning before they returned to France said they had been having "cultural discussions". Two of them had each $200 on them, and all were members of the (French) *Cercles Marxistes-Leniniste,* the pro-Chinese Communist movement. Papers in their possession showed that some of the organisational problems of French Communists had been debated. A few days later more French visitors to the Embassy were picked up. All of them were forbidden to return to Switzerland. It was believed that the key man in the discussions at the Embassy had been Chou Chen-chung, the cultural attaché.

Then, in April 1966, a Chinese Embassy secretary and a senior Chinese Nationalist (Taiwanese) official at the World Health Organisation in Geneva, Dr Tsung Sing-sze, were expelled from Switzerland, the latter on the grounds that he had been acting as an informant for the People's Republic. From all accounts Dr Tsung Sing-sze seems to have been one of their most successful part-time agents, completely unsuspected and friendly with all Chinese Nationalists resident in Geneva. He had been with the W.H.O. for twelve years, having headed the occupational health section, and was an efficient administrator.

He and his wife, Joan, who, with their daughter, later followed him to Peking, were well known for their hospitality. "They provided the best Chinese food in Switzerland," said a W.H.O. colleague. Before coming to Geneva the doctor had taught at Hongkong University. Apparently he was a Kuomintang man both officially and by personal conviction until 1948, when he secretly switched his allegiance to the Communists. However, even at parties both he and his wife gave the impression of being vehemently anti-imperialist and of having a modicum of sympathy with Peking. It was probably this outspokenness rather than any slip-up by the C.P.R. representatives in Berne that led to his being discovered. The impression one has on speaking to his former colleagues in W.H.O. is that, expressing his views so freely, he could hardly have been used by the Peking Chinese as an under-cover agent. It may have been that it was only by expressing his pro-Peking attitude in public that he was able to convince the Chinese authorities that he was on their side and wished to defect. His expulsion from Switzerland would seem to have been due to his having been present repeatedly at Berne propaganda meetings and that he might have been given an occasional specific assignment which brought him to the attention of the Swiss counter-intelligence.

Dr Tsung Sing-sze was lively, gregarious, candid and popular. His wife, whose mother was British, was apparently educated at a boarding school in England and spoke impeccable English. She was extremely active in the international women's circles in Geneva and started a psychology course. It is suspected that she used this as a ploy for obtaining information. The daughter, Linette, who was about sixteen when they left Geneva in 1966, had been educated at the International School and one who knew her says, "Linette, like her parents, was well indoctrinated with left-wing views."

Dr Tsung Sing-sze, and his wife and daughter who followed him, left Switzerland via Karachi for Peking. Once they had arrived in China, according to reliable reports, they were treated as "overseas Chinese" and therefore sent to Sinkiang Province for an indoctrination course. In a postcard to a W.H.O. colleague Dr Tsung Sing-sze indicated that he and his family were living an austere life compared with what their Geneva existence had been. He is now in the Ministry of Health in Peking.

His exact rôle in working for Peking remained mysterious after the story of his expulsion broke, as were the circumstances of his unmasking by the Swiss counter-espionage service. It may have been that he was given away by documents found in the possession of Mr Y. A. Kuo, the cultural attaché at the Nationalist (Taiwanese) Embassy in Brussels, who later sought asylum in Peking, and who was a regular visitor to Geneva. Kuo was a Nationalist Chinese delegate to UNESCO in Paris in addition to his work in Brussels. He attended meetings of the International Education Bureau on Geneva, subsequently taken over by UNESCO.

At the time of the Tsung Sing-sze incident, while only thirteen diplomats and forty-four diplomatic employees were officially registered at the Chinese Embassy in Berne, the actual number of persons employed during 1965–6 had been as high as three hundred. Swiss newspapers stated at the time that Ambassador Li Ching-chuan was in charge of an information and propaganda network extending throughout Western Europe and there is no doubt that at this time all direction of espionage was done almost solely from Berne. It was believed that subsidies were being paid to pro-Chinese splinter groups within the Communist Parties of various countries, with the largest sum probably going to Belgium where the pro-Chinese faction controlled the party. Here the key-man and one of the few Europeans employed by the Chinese Secret Service was Jacques Grippa, who appeared on the platform at a Peking gathering at the start of the Cultural Revolution in August 1966. It is calculated that something like $120,000 a year is paid to further espionage in Belgium by the Chinese.

The press attaché's office in Berne, which was in a separate building, had a staff of more than twenty in 1965–6 and had telex links with the New China News Agency offices in various cities. In Geneva the N.C.N.A. occupied a large house on the outskirts of the city.

In 1965 a Swede living in Lausanne was asked to leave Switzerland after it had been ascertained that he was engaged in turning out propaganda material for the Chinese which was being sent to other European countries. About the same time a Chinese was stopped at the frontier near Geneva with a large quantity of propaganda material, the Swiss feeling that this was not compatible with their neutrality. Some of the Chinese in Berne were at the same time very busy establishing relations with French student organisations.

Even now in Switzerland there are one or two small publications cyclostyled rather than printed, carrying the Chinese line—*L'Etincelle* (from Lenin's *The Spark*), published by the tiny pro-Chinese *Parti Communiste Suisse*. This, of course, is quite separate from the *Parti du Travail*, which is the Swiss Communist Party proper and is pro-Russian. Yet curiously the *Parti Communiste* seems always to be in chronic disagreement with the Lenin Centre in Lausanne, which publishes a monthly called *October* and which is also pro-Chinese.

The leader of the latter group is Gilbert Etienne, who can be described as an intellectual Maoist, and is reported as having believed that his activities are under close observation by plain-clothes security agents. *L'Etincelle* is produced by Gerard Bulliard, well known as a militant and apparently too outspoken to be popular with the Chinese in Berne.

Today the general view is that Berne is no longer the chief headquarters for Europe. All the indications are that the Chinese here have a great respect for the Swiss counter-intelligence service, that they use their own Intelligence Service mainly for gathering of legitimate information and for supporting the various Swiss pro-Chinese associations of a cultural nature and to sponsor the showing of Chinese films and exhibitions. But underneath this low-key operation they still employ a number of Swiss agents, and set out to cultivate as many Swiss people as possible. They are entertaining much more today and rapidly extending their contacts, though in an exceedingly discreet manner.

There are now only about a dozen on the diplomatic list, a figure that has remained constant over the past few years. The Geneva mission to the U.N.—formerly the Consulate-General in Geneva—is building up its staff quite steadily and now has ten on the diplomatic list. There are two ace agents in Switzerland at present, a man-and-wife team who have a small Chinese staff —four or so including a driver and cook.

The best summing-up of the Chinese Intelligence Service in Switzerland was given to me by a contact in Berne: "They could be doing anything. They are discreet and don't attract security attention and they have a great deal of scope in a country such as Switzerland. The authorities give the impression of being a bit complacent and it might take them a while to notice a new ploy, especially by an individual who had been here recently."

What is very significant is that the Chinese here have latterly ceased to worry about contacts with the press, which, as a general rule in the Chinese Intelligence game, suggests they are more interested in bigger game. They send in much larger delegations—on the opening day of the Sea-Bed Conference they had twelve men and one woman—and the impression is that they learn very quickly.

A carefully formulated policy of the Chinese Secret Service was to set up a base in Switzerland—at Berne —and then to follow this up with a second base in Geneva and gradually to develop worthwhile headquarters in Paris and Vienna. At the same time a drive was to be made to establish networks in Holland and Sweden. The story of the Dutch network deserves a chapter to itself, but those in Stockholm, Paris and Vienna belong essentially to this chapter.

Peking discovered early on that the Swedes tended to be sympathetic to their cause, having found an admirable agent in Nils Andersson, the Swede who was asked to leave Lausanne in 1965, and who had been turned out of France for political reasons. Despite this, the Chinese have adopted an even more low-profile attitude in Sweden than they have in Switzerland, possibly because of the proximity of Sweden to Russia. SAPO, the Swedish secret police, have not so far uncovered any positive evidence of Chinese intelligence in Sweden, judging from the fact that in World War II, when 1,837 spies were arrested, not a single Chinese was caught here, and that no arrests have been made since.

On the other hand Stig Wennerstrom, who was a Soviet spy for fourteen years (1948–63) told the Swedish security police that he had visited the Chinese Embassy in Stockholm several times in his official capacity as chief of the Command Expedition of the Swedish Ministry of Defence, and in charge of keeping contacts with foreign military attachés in Stockholm. He said that China's opportunities for intelligence on other countries' war potential, military strength, weapon technique and NATO contacts were mainly worked along official, legal channels, while other information at that time was collected through the Soviet Embassy.

The N.C.N.A. have two correspondents in Stockholm and, in contrast to the Soviet Tass Agency people, who behave in a somewhat arrogant overtly intelligence-gathering manner, they seem to concentrate solely on objective reporting.

Vienna has gradually come to assume more importance in the Chinese mind because it is the headquarters of various important European agencies, not least those concerned with nuclear energy and sciences. Over the past few years it has become an increasingly vital centre of the Eastern European network aimed at supplementing and checking information from Albania. Today the so-called executive headquarters of Intelligence is in Paris, while the "subversive" or information gathering H.Q. is in Vienna. But Paris remains the control centre and the policy-maker.

The Albanian base is an extended arm of the Paris headquarters, while the principal duties of the Vienna headquarters is to gather facts, assess situations and to recommend lines of action. On minor schemes an indicated line of action can be recommended direct to Paris, the executive branch of the European operation, but, on all major policy, recommendations, fully documented and reasoned, have to be submitted for approval to Peking in the first place. If approved, action is then ordered direct to Paris.

At present activities in Vienna are concentrated on Communist Europe, including Yugoslavia, but it is intended that Vienna will eventually cover the whole of Europe, even Britain, operating, perhaps, branch offices in Paris and London. These, however, will be entirely separate units, and not under the control of the Paris executive, which will be responsible solely for operational rôles. Conversely a small Paris unit has now arrived in Vienna to co-ordinate moves with the strategists or tacticians based on Vienna.

The Vienna headquarters is a large villa in its own grounds, surrounded by a high wall, at 50 Weimarerstrasse in the residential district of Vienna

18. There are only seven diplomats attached to the Chinese Embassy: Wang Yueh-yi, the Ambassador, a trade expert who speaks Chinese and Albanian and, apparently, nothing else; Sung En-fan, counsellor; Chin Ching-san, commercial counsellor; Lin Hai-cheng, second secretary responsible for press and cultural affairs; Hsu Tung-e, third secretary; Wang Ching-yu, third secretary; Liu Hsiao, attaché: and to these should be added two press correspondents, Chen Wen-kue and Li Chung-fa, representing the N.C.N.A. In addition there is a small army of retainers, about forty-five strong, though the numbers seem to change with bewildering speed, no doubt to keep the Austrian State Police on their toes.

What is interesting as regards the Chinese Intelligence set-up in Vienna is that the Taiwanese maintain the nucleus of a miniature Secret Service here, ostensibly merely to watch what their Peking opposite numbers are up to. The Taiwanese Intelligence chief in Vienna has an adequate cover and, though he carefully conceals the fact, he was a general in the Kuomintang and associated with Chiang Kai-shek during World War II. One must always suspect Taiwanese intelligence, but his view of the Communist Secret Service's operations in Vienna is that they rely far less on espionage and counter-espionage in the accepted sense than on demoralisation, infiltration and the skillful manipulation of human weaknesses.

"They make full use of subversive elements wherever they may be found," he said, "to practice infiltration, avoiding all direct moves wherever possible, and, in order to dissemble on Peking intentions, make all possible use of the U.S.S.R. as a stalking horse. Their aim is to lend colour and credence to the notion, widely held by capitalist observers, that the Soviet Union and China are serious rivals and will eventually cancel each other out to the benefit of the capitalist world, and at the same time to weaken the Soviet Union's self-appointed rôle of leading communist nation."

This is fairly certainly a broadly accurate assessment, though probably applying only to Austria. Having won Albania as an ally, the next Chinese move is to achieve similar recognition in Rumania and, of course, to exploit any uprisings, such as that of Czechoslovakia, in their long-term interest. They also pay a great deal of attention to Yugoslavia, where through a few itinerary contacts they have established a useful network aimed at exploiting tribal discords in their favour.

China's biggest espionage coup in Vienna has been that of winning European nuclear secrets through the Euratom Agency. Having had considerable experience of extracting similar scientific data from the U.S.A., Peking's agents have obtained an enormous amount of similar up-to-date intelligence through Vienna. I am told that because of the success of this operation on a low-level contact basis Peking has deliberately withheld its main Vienna-designated agent from taking up his post. Or, as the Taiwanese agent sadly puts it: "They have always remembered what happened in Switzerland. You will not find the real spy chief in Vienna on the diplomatic list. The Vienna headquarters is still in the developing stage and my guess is that the ultimate 'man in charge' has not arrived yet."

In many European bases of the Chinese the Embassy interpreter is often the real espionage boss and in effect has the edge on his Ambassador.

It was not until November 1970 that diplomatic relations between China and Italy were established. In May 1971 the first Chinese Ambassador to Rome arrived. He was Shen Ping, a 53-year-old considered to be one of the main Chinese experts in the economies of Western Europe.

Shen Ping is an extremely able operator, having become Deputy Director of Finances in the Fukien region at the age of thirty-one and eight years later Director-General of the Chinese Customs. Afterwards he was appointed Vice-Minister of the Finance Ministry and spent several years commuting between the various Chinese commercial offices in Europe.

Not surprisingly the emphasis on Sino-Italian relations under the influence of Shen Ping has been the development of trade relations between the two countries. Though Taiwan broke off relations with Italy after the latter recognised Peking, the Chiang Kai-shek Government still has an embassy in Italy accredited to the Holy See. However, it is possible that here, too, Taiwan may break off relations in the fairly near future, as the Vatican has been making contacts with the Chinese Communists ever since the beginning of 1971. The dialogue between the Vatican and Peking has been promoted by Monsignor Agostino Casaroli, and after a series of soundings the Chinese decided to accept periodic meetings in Dar-es-Salaam with the Church's representative there, Bishop Pierluigi Sartorelli. Another protagonist of the Sino-Vatican dialogue is Father Louis Wei Tsing Sing, a Chinese priest resident in Paris, who is highly regarded as an intermediary by the Chinese Communists.

One can be certain that most complicated diplomatic moves in Italy and especially those concerning the Catholic Church are vetted and masterminded by the Chinese Secret Service. In this sphere they probably act as the directing force. Again there has been an emphasis on secret diplomacy and on low-key operations. For example the New China News Agency did not come into Italy until February 1973, when three correspondents were appointed to set up a bureau in Rome, this having been achieved on the basis of an exchange of journalists between the two countries.

The Chinese have shown in Italy in particular a marked fervour for the Common Market, stating quite openly that they hope to see a totally integrated, both politically and militarily, United Western Europe. There are various suggestions that Chinese Intelligence operations in Europe have in the past few years been devoted to pressing for greater integration in Europe rather than espionage itself. The object of this, of course, is to combat Soviet influence.

But the Secret Service agents' other aim is to provoke splits in the Italian Communist Party and to favour factions who are favourable to European unity, like that of Giorgio Amendola, inside it. This general orientation is reflected in the relations of the Chinese in Rome with the pro-Maoist groups.

The first trace of a strictly pro-Maoist organisation in Italy was in 1962 when a group led by V. Calo split away from the Italian Communist Party and founded in Padua a "Long Live Leninism" organisation. This later dissolved and its members joined the League of Marxist-Leninist Communists, which had little importance, and in turn formed the nucleus of the Red Star, which several leftists consider is infiltrated by some curiously individualist, non-Communist people. There were various divisions and splinter groups formed among the anti-Soviet Communists in the late 'sixties, but in 1965 there originated the New Unity Movement, to which the group concerned with the Oriental Editions (publishing the *China Note-Book*) adhered.

In 1968 various pro-Maoist students and former Trotskyites formed the Union of Marxist-Leninists of Italy, but despite, or perhaps because of, their fanaticism there is no evidence that this latter group has any support from China. Those who enjoy China's cautious backing are the Communist Party of Italy (Marxist-Leninist) formed in 1966. A delegation from the Chinese Party led by Chao I-min came to wish them good luck. But this party has also been subject to splits and the Chinese have been even more cautious latterly in backing any group until it was well established. They have, however, given their blessing to a faction which broke away to form a weekly magazine called *New Unity,* printed at Leghorn. The chief of this party is the former Pisa pharmacist, Manlio Dinucci, secretary of the Party, who is regarded as Mao Tse-tung's trusted supporter in Italy. He has been to Peking on a number of occasions.

Though Maoist thought has penetrated extensively to many corners of Italy, it has so far failed to stop itself splintering into relatively small and uninfluential groups. No doubt China has several potential agents among the Italians themselves, in Italy, but they have shown a reluctance to use them and so far it has been impossible to trace a single discovered case of Chinese espionage in Italy, though there are some indications that prior to the recognition of China by the Italian Government the Albanians, who have an embassy in Rome, did some work of this nature on behalf of the Chinese. One Albanian diplomat was expelled quietly from Italy between mid-March 1969 and

March 1971, but the whole affair was hushed up. The suggestion was that China was involved in this, but that as negotiations were going on for recognition of Peking at this time details were kept secret.

"In nine cases out of ten Chinese agents in Europe are posing as journalists," states a C.I.A. agent, "and for that matter the few remnants of the Taiwanese Intelligence do much the same. For example, the Chinese News Agency representative in Bonn negotiated diplomatic relations with the West German Government and once the papers were signed promptly changed his job to become the new *chargé d'affaires*."

Because of China's steadily improving and increasing diplomatic links with France after General de Gaulle became President word went out that the Chinese Secret Service in France was to remain fairly passive. It was considered to be more important to make the best of Paris as "special relations" base for diplomacy and close exchanges with the French Government than for the Chinese to compromise themselves with intelligence operations on French soil.

Since 1970 this situation has changed somewhat, though the emphasis is still on using Paris as a "consulting base" rather than as an executive base for espionage. The Chinese Embassy is now once again the one on Avenue George V, formerly occupied by the Taiwanese authorities. The French took it away from the Taiwanese and handed it over to the People's Republic when they recognised the latter in 1967, but the Peking diplomats did not really move in until early in 1972. Up to a few months before that they continued to give their Embassy address as that of the Ambassador's apartment in a fairly low-cost block of apartments in Neuilly. The confusion caused by the Cultural Revolution in their diplomatic establishment probably had something to do with their slowness in moving. Up to the end of 1972 there was only one representative of the N.C.N.A. in Paris, Mr Chen Chi, and this in itself is significant of the unostentatious trend of Chinese Intelligence in France. It is also noteworthy that there are only twenty-three diplomats accredited to Paris.

However, earlier on the N.C.N.A. was much more active in France and Western Europe generally. Yang Hsiao-nung, who was formerly director of the N.C.N.A. in France and Switzerland, was one of the leading Chinese intelligence agents in Europe and specialised in information on Africa affairs as well.

Yang was active in fomenting revolts in various parts of Africa through financing various splinter groups and he was particularly active in thwarting Russian influence in the Congo and establishing a Chinese network in that country. He was able to do this owing to the fact that China's flow of intelligence from Belgium and France was extremely good in this period.

China is currently eager to do nothing to spoil the special relationship with France and to ensure that as far as co-existence is concerned she is not put at a disadvantage *vis à vis* Russia. Indeed one of the prime objectives of the Chinese Secret Service in 1973–4 was to aim at an exchange of intelligence with France in certain carefully defined spheres of common interest, this being a euphemism for the U.S.S.R.

A great deal of intelligence on Vietnam was passed on to the French and also a certain amount of information on Soviet moves in the Far East. That this has impressed the French can be gathered from the fact that Alexandre de Marenches, the chief of France's S.D.E.C.E. (espionage and counter-espionage), recently flew to Peking for talks with the chiefs of the Chinese Secret Service on arranging a regular system of exchanging information. As far as can be gathered from independent sources this appears to concentrate on intelligence concerning Russia.

Latterly China has shown an interest in peripheral and marginal areas of European influence such as Malta and Iceland. In 1973 Peking sent Chen Tung as Ambassador to Reykjavik together with a staff of nine, including one Icelandic speaker. There is no doubt that this was a counter-move against Russian activities in Iceland, for the U.S.S.R. has by far the largest embassy in Iceland.

Unostentatiously and without any publicity an estimated three hundred Chinese came to Malta in 1973, the Maltese Government having put a former school in Valletta at their disposal. Among them were engineers and technicians to help the Maltese Government build a dry dock and quay capable of accommodating ships of 300,000 tons, a chocolate factory and a factory to make ornamental glass. These projects were to be financed from a loan of £16.93 millions which the Chinese made to Malta interest free. Russia has long been seeking if not a base, at least considerable port facilities in Malta and one can only interpret the Chinese move as a counter to the U.S.S.R.

33

The Strange Case of Liao Ho-shu 1966-1969

"The shock terrifies for a hundred miles." If one causes fear far and wide and has concern for what is near by, one may come forth and protect the temple of the ancestors and the altar of the earth, and be the leader of the sacrifice.

I Ching

HOLLAND has from the earliest days of the People's Republic of China been such an important centre of Chinese espionage that it deserves a chapter devoted to it alone. Both Amsterdam and the Hague have been used as headquarters for Chinese intelligence work, which originally assumed special significance because of the large number of Indonesian or half-Indonesian Dutch who returned to Holland and the even larger number who emigrated there during the worst excesses of Soekarno's rule.

Among this polyglot population of rootless people adapting to a new life were many who were potential allies, and others (some of them Indonesian Chinese) who were possible agents. This called for a highly skilled, experienced and senior director of the Dutch network and the man chosen for this post was Liao Ho-shu, then in his early forties, married, with two daughters, who was given diplomatic cover at The Hague.

Amsterdam and The Hague became increasingly important as a major Chinese espionage centre—first, after the Chinese were clamped down on by the Czechs, and, second, after the Swiss counter-intelligence put pressure on the Chinese in Berne. There was also the fact that the Dutch are a liberal-minded people with probably far less racial prejudice than any other nation in Europe. Many Chinese had been living in Amsterdam for more than forty years. Most, perhaps, were anti-Communist, being wealthy merchants and lawyers, but their real devotion, as always with the Chinese, was to China.

Amsterdam was also the port through which a vast amount of Far Eastern goods flowed into Europe, and this trade opened up an obvious route for recruiting spies to operate a network which was beginning to extend to Paris, London and Stockholm, as well as Rome and Berne.

The Dutch police began to take an interest in the ramifications of Chinese espionage only after one or two mysterious beatings-up and the death of a suspected double agent were brought to their attention. One night a Dutch police officer noticed two Chinese running down an alley between two canals and across a narrow bridge into the warehouse district of the city. Just afterwards he came across the body of a murdered Asiatic who, it was learned, had been importing goods from Eastern Europe. The murdered man was suspected of having worked for the Chinese, but of having double-crossed them by passing on information to the Russians as well.

On 5 December 1965 Professor Richard Follis, an American scientist, supposed to have been a C.I.A. man in Iran, disappeared in Amsterdam. He was seen with a woman who was never traced. Eventually his body, heavily weighted, was found in a canal on 5 January 1966. The police could never prove anything, but once again there was some evidence of a link with Chinese intelligence.

It soon became apparent to the Dutch that an astute man was master-minding Chinese espionage in Holland, for there were underground hints of more ambitious attempts at espionage coups. One such was a move to lure Alexei Golub, a Russian scientist, to pass over information. He had actually defected to Holland in 1961, but the following year had changed his mind and gone home to Russia.

There is a great deal of evidence that both the Chinese and the Russians were competing—with no holds barred—in a period of aggressive espionage in Holland in the early and mid-'sixties. The exact rôle of Liao Ho-shu in all this was not, however, discovered until early in 1966, and then the Dutch police were astonished at the extent of the Chinese network and how it had reached out to the furthermost parts of Europe.[1]

It all began with the discovery on 16 July 1966 of a man lying on the pavement in front of No. 17 Prins Mauritslaan, a three-storey house in The Hague. He was Chinese and obviously in great pain. A person looking out of a window nearby, having seen the groaning Chinese, telephoned the police. They swiftly arrived on the scene of the incident, but by that time the man had disappeared. Inquiries revealed that the house at No. 17 was the home of a Third Secretary in China's diplomatic mission and that the man, 42-year-old Hsu Tsu-tsai, an engineer, had been carried into the house.

Dutch police are painstakingly thorough in their inquiries, polite but persistent and not easily thwarted once they sense that all is not as it should be. Their first inquiries were made at the home of their informant, who told them that the man had been dragged inside No. 17. Knocking at the door of that house, they wanted to know what had happened.

It transpired that the man was living there with some eight other Chinese delegates to the annual assembly of the International Institute of Welding, which had been holding its meeting in Delft. The police became suspicious when the Chinese occupants refused to allow them to enter the house. Eventually one police officer and an ambulance driver were admitted. Hsu Tsu-tsai was then put into the ambulance, though accompanied by two Chinese, and driven to the nearby Red Cross Hospital. There he was found to have a fractured skull, broken ribs and an injury to his spine.

The two Chinese who went with Hsu to the hospital alleged that he had fallen out of a window of the house. Shortly afterwards more Chinese arrived at the hospital, led by Liao Ho-shu. If the Dutch police had merely suspected before that Liao was a senior executive of the Chinese Secret Service, now they must have been sure. For while he kept the doctors in conversation, Hsu was kidnapped from the X-ray department. It was such a skilfully managed operation that it had obviously been planned by one experienced in such techniques. Hsu was driven away to the office of the *chargé d'affaires*.

The *chargé d'affaires* was summoned to the Dutch Foreign Ministry and informed that the removal of the engineer from the hospital was a breach of the law and requested that he should be returned. No action was taken by the Chinese and when the *chargé d'affaires* was again called to the Foreign Ministry, he announced that Hsu had died.

This affair had now become an international incident. The New China News Agency stated that: "Secret U.S. agents, with the connivance of the Dutch Government, used every sordid means to induce, illegally and repeatedly, members of the Chinese delegation to desert and betray their own country . . . Hsu, incited by U.S. agents, jumped down from the building where he was lodged in an attempt to run away, and injured himself."

The Dutch police were sure that Hsu was trying to defect. They demanded that they should have custody of the body and the right to interrogate the eight other delegates. The Chinese refused these requests, but compromised by calling in an undertaker who gave the body to the police for an autopsy. This showed that Hsu had been the victim of violence.

Then the Dutch Government expelled the Chinese envoy, Li En-chu, from Holland while police put a guard around the office where the eight colleagues of Hsu had been staying ever since his death and which they had refused to leave. Meanwhile the Chinese Government declared the Dutch *chargé d'affaires* in Peking, G. J. Jongepans, *persona non grata,* but told him he could not leave the country until the eight engineers had safely left Holland. This diplomatic stalemate continued for some months. All this time the Dutch maintained a rota of police guards around the Chinese Legation in The Hague and it was made clear that if the eight engineers left the building they would at once be arrested.

This whole affair is perhaps worth mentioning in some considerable detail because it is the only incident in the past quarter of a century in which the machinations of the Chinese Secret Service have attracted considerable public attention. Crowds of sightseers poured out daily to see the office where the engineers were hiding out and reporters and television cameramen remained in constant attendance.

At last, on 29 December, the battle of wills ended. Officials of the Dutch Foreign Ministry, together with lawyers, and accompanied by an interpreter, were allowed into the Chinese offices. It was far too short a visit for the Dutch to carry out any adequate and detailed inquiries, but it was accepted by them as a way out of the impasse and a means of letting their own envoy in China have a chance of release.

The Chinese story had changed somewhat. They now alleged, in line with the N.C.N.A., that Hsu had been approached by American agents. This in itself was a curious admission to make and untypical of the Chinese. It needs to be noted carefully in the light of what happened a few years later.

Thereafter the Chinese engineers flew home, obviously carefully drilled as to what they should do and say. Each wore a badge bearing Chairman Mao's picture and before they left they arranged themselves in a circle at Amsterdam airport and recited some of the sayings of Mao Tse-tung.

The deadlock between China and Holland lasted six months. The agreement was unsatisfactory: the engineers were allowed to leave without their having given any worthwhile evidence about the death of their colleague. Then, on 3 January 1967, the Chinese envoy in Peking returned to Holland.

What was behind all this? Careful research has shown that it was not merely a question of a would-be defector, but that the origin of the matter lay in a laboratory in the Polish town of Zyrzyn some few years before. Here a Polish scientist, Professor Stanislaw Ostrowski,[a] had succeeded in manufacturing a deadly gas. C.I.A. men in Washington heard news of this and also of the complicated formula: they were alarmed that it could all be contained in a tiny capsule.

The C.I.A. decided they wanted the gas before the secret could be handed over to Russia or China. It is not quite clear why the C.I.A. thought that China could be involved, but the suggestion was that they had had information that China was either directly interested or had become concerned in the matter.[3]

As a result the C.I.A. sent an agent to Holland, supposedly about April 1966. He met a Dutch contact man who arranged a meeting with a German known as "Willy". The C.I.A. man and "Willy" met regularly for some days, but the former was quick to notice that they were being shadowed, and suspected this was being done by Chinese Intelligence. He knew that Rotterdam was an important centre for ships landing Chinese agents.

The C.I.A. man returned to Washington without having discovered anything worthwhile, but the Dutch Intelligence (B.V.D.) found out that the two men had been shadowed not by the Chinese, but the Russian G.R.U. This raises the interesting query as to why the C.I.A. man suspected the Chinese. Had information been planted on him?

"Willy" was summoned back to the U.S.A., so one must assume he was also in the pay of the C.I.A., or some similar agency. The C.I.A., despite a total lack of confirmation of any suspicions of Chinese involvement, immediately carried out a probe into Chinese intelligence operations in Europe. Until this moment they had not been convinced that the Chinese had any effective intelligence system on the continent. Now they noted with some concern the size of the Chinese diplomatic representation in Paris, Berne, Geneva and The Hague. They also learned that in the Legation building in Holland there was a powerful short-wave transmitter in touch with Peking.

More interesting, however, to the C.I.A. was the hint of a competitive struggle between the Chinese Intelligence in Berne and Paris. The chief of the Western European network of the Chinese Secret Service was an old hand in the espionage game, Colonel Li Changhuan, the Ambassador in Berne. It became clear that instructions for Paris were going through Berne and then in Paris Intelligence channels were split into two separate departments, one for London and the other for The Hague.

A double-agent, working for the Chinese and the Americans, mentioned that a valuable man to win over to the Western side was Hsu Tsu-tsai, a Chinese welding engineer, who was well versed in the progress being made in Chinese rocket construction. The C.I.A. then told their double-agent that he must offer Hsu one million dollars to desert to the U.S.A. This must be arranged when Hsu attended the International Congress of Welding Technicians in Delft. In addition the Chinese intermediary of the C.I.A. was offered three million dollars if he managed to buy the poison gas from the Polish Government and handed it over to the Americans. The plan was that the Chinese agent would see to it that a capsule of the poison gas and the formula were handed to Hsu Tsu-tsai during his stay at The Hague, and the latter was to pass it on to an American agent.

In Vienna the C.I.A. man contacted the Chinese intermediary and offered him the reputed payment of three million dollars if he could obtain the poison gas. From that point onwards the story becomes more and more like a fictional fantasy. The Chinese intermediary is said to have double-crossed the Americans by offering the gas to Peking for ten million dollars. China was prepared to pay that sum in order to keep the gas away from the U.S.A. Then the Chinese intermediary contacted Hsu Tsu-tsai and offered him a million dollars for deserting and handing "a parcel" to the U.S. Embassy in The Hague.

In Poland, a Polish security officer was ordered to fly to Prague with a small parcel and from there to travel by train via Vienna to Zurich. In the railway station at Zurich he was to meet his Chinese contact man in a restaurant and hand over the parcel.

This assignment was carried out and the Chinese contact man delivered the parcel to his Ambassador, Li Chang-huan. As far as can be ascertained this deal was finalised about 6 July 1966. Two days later a Belgian travelled by train from Belgium to Holland. He had had close connections with the small pro-Chinese Communist Party in Belgium of which Jacques Grippa was the leader.

The Belgian had received a parcel that morning from somebody looking like a half-caste Chinese in the Cathedral St Michel in Brussels. His instructions, which he followed to the letter, were to meet Hsu Tsutsai somewhere in the vicinity of the Prins Mauritslaan at The Hague, where the welding experts had just arrived, and to deliver the parcel to him.

Hsu was in fact the leader of the delegation to the welders' conference. Opening the parcel he found inside it the capsule of gas and some micro-film. He decided, foolishly for him as it turned out, to hand over the gas, but to keep the film for a few days with a view to demanding extra money for this.

Next day he handed over the capsule to the C.I.A. agent in a park, telling him "The rest costs more" and asking for eight million dollars. The C.I.A. man told Hsu that the request sounded like "madness" to him, but that he would refer the matter to his superiors.

It is possible that Chinese Intelligence in Peking had had some inkling of this sell-out as they had ordered a special group to proceed to The Hague at once. The C.I.A. heard about the arrival of this special counter-espionage squad in Holland and so, too, did Hsu, who immediately regretted that he had not handed over the micro-film with the gas capsule.[4]

Whether or not the hierarchy of the Chinese Secret Service had had information that they were about to be double-crossed, they regarded this whole operation for obtaining the gas as a major espionage task. It had been meticulously worked out as a detailed, closely time-tabled plan under the title of "Operation Nanking": the orders from Peking were that the gas was to be put aboard a Chinese ship in the port of Rotterdam. But the Chinese intermediary had started his part of the plan prematurely and it was because he had not kept to the timetable so carefully laid down that Peking became suspicious.

Secret orders went out from Peking that the Chinese intermediary was to be arrested. This obviously meant that by now they suspected some kind of a double-cross with the Americans.

The Chinese counter-espionage team in The Hague and elsewhere launched a series of interrogations. They ordered the Ambassador in Berne to eliminate the original intermediary if he could be found, and on 16 July they interviewed the Belgian, who told them: "I handed the parcel to a Chinese in The Hague almost a week ago."

Heated messages were exchanged between Peking and The Hague Legation. Instructions were given that the members of the welding delegation should be interrogated and searched. Upstairs in his room Hsu Tsu-tsai had been asked to get ready to leave for "a reception" in the Legation with other members of his delegation. He now sensed that he was in dire danger and that he must try and make a getaway. He slipped out of the front door and crossed the road to where the C.I.A. agent had been stationed watching for him.

"Take me to your Embassy," he pleaded. "I am going to ask for political asylum."

The C.I.A. man, not sensing the real urgency of the situation, hedged and said he would do nothing until he was given the micro-film. Equally foolishly and greedily Hsu demanded money. The door of No. 17 opened up and four Chinese ran into the street. It is believed that Hsu handed over the micro-film just in time and then started to run. The C.I.A. agent lay low, but wondered why Hsu had lost his nerve.

The Chinese shouted out to the driver of a car that had just come round the corner: "Look—someone is trying to escape. Stop him." The driver immediately drove straight at Hsu, knocking him down and pushing his body on to the pavement.

When Liao Ho-shu arrived at the hospital later he had with him the local team of Chinese counter-espionage agents. He appears to have taken complete charge of the situation, no doubt realising that he would be blamed if Hsu escaped alive. But once Hsu had been kidnapped from the hospital he remained quietly in the background while his diplomatic chief bore the brunt of Dutch demands for retribution after Hsu's death.[5]

The sequel to this somewhat involved plot came three years later when, in January 1969, Liao Ho-shu asked the Dutch Government for political asylum. He was without doubt the single major defector from the Chinese Intelligence Service to the West in the past quarter of a century.

What lay behind the defection is still a matter of conjecture. There are various theories, each one of which may be partially true. The first is that Liao was in disgrace after the Hsu Tsu-tsai affair and that he sensed that his days were numbered as a senior member of the Chinese Secret Service. Certainly everything points to the fact that until this time he had been one of, if not the most important Chinese spy chiefs in Western Europe.

Another story, which somewhat smacks of Western propaganda, is that Liao was a brilliant spy chief whose reports and advice were consistently ignored by Peking and that, because they would not listen to him, he decided to throw in his lot with the West. Had Liao been a Westerner and one of their spy chiefs, this might have made sense, but anyone who knows and understands the Chinese mind would doubt such a reaction by a Chinese. Let us say that it is possible, but highly improbable.

A third version is that for some few years Liao had been a "Chinese Philby", that he had already been engaged in selling secrets to the West and working on behalf of the Americans while actually still operating inside Chinese Intelligence, and that his actions at the time of the Hsu affair were merely to cover up his double-dealing. In other words he had to kill Hsu before Hsu was interrogated by the counter-espionage team from Peking.

Whatever the truth there are indications that Peking's Intelligence executives were not too happy about the management of espionage in Holland even before Hsu's arrival there. For them to send in a team of counter-espionage agents from the mainland was not a typical move.

The Dutch, when questioned about Liao's defection, merely said somewhat guardedly that he was "acting *Chargé d'Affaires* at the Hague [as he was by this time] and that he has been asked to go to a location where he will feel safe from reprisals". At the time this was taken as an oblique reference to the 1966 incident.

The Chinese were swift to launch a massive protest against Liao's flight, saying they had "incontrovertible evidence" that it was "an anti-Chinese action deliberately carried out by the Netherlands Government after long preparations". The Dutch denied these allegations, but they did not seem surprised by Liao's defection. They had granted his request to provide him with a temporary place to stay after he had entered the headquarters of The Hague police at 4.30 a.m. on 24 January 1966, wearing only pyjamas and a raincoat, and had told the officer on duty that he wanted to end his work at the Chinese Legation.

There was a suggestion that what had finally prompted Liao to seek asylum was that he had been ordered to return to Peking to be given a "loyalty test" and for an investigation into the Hsu affair. Chinese officials tried desperately to find out where Liao was hiding and the whole affair became somewhat farcical when the Dutch police started shadowing the questing Chinese and the press started following the Dutch police.

Then on 5 February it was announced that Liao Ho-shu had been flown to the U.S.A. and was now in the hands of the C.I.A. Little was revealed from Washington beyond the suggestion that Liao feared an assassination attempt by Chinese agents. Mr Robert

McCloskey, the State Department spokesman, said: "We have taken Mr Liao to a secret place and he is under protective custody. He has applied for asylum in the U.S."[6]

Liao, tall, bespectacled, serious-looking, was a familiar figure among diplomats at The Hague in his dark grey, high-collared suit, and he was unquestionably the highest ranking Chinese Communist ever to desert to the U.S.A. Over the previous four years his rôle in the Intelligence game, though masked by his diplomatic status, had been queried by Western counter-spies: it had long been rumoured that he had switched the main direction of Chinese espionage from Switzerland to Holland.

There is no doubt that the incident of the kidnapping three years earlier had been of far more importance than was realised at the time. For example the eight "welders", or "welding-engineers" as they were officially described, were much more than this designation suggests: they were scientists, and Hsu Tsu-tsai himself was an expert in electronics and bugging devices.

Since then China has returned to its policy of "low profile" Intelligence activities in Holland. The staff at The Hague is now relatively small, comprising only seven diplomats, three of whom have wives with them, while the wives of the other four are registered as "absent". This suggests very tight control from Peking.[7]

Hongkong: Spy Centre
of the Far East
1950-1974

To promote their infiltration and propaganda campaign
among the Chinese population in Hongkong, the Red
Agents have also bought over many of the writers and
reporters of the Chinese language newspapers there.

Chu Pao-heng, former Chinese editor in Hongkong
who defected in 1964

HONGKONG today, with its teeming millions, is perhaps
the number one city of the world for espionage as an
industry. The great powers between them probably
together employ more spies in this British colony linked
to China by a causeway than are to be found in any
other territory of comparable size. Certainly the People's Republic of China regards it not only as a key
listening post, but as its chief spy centre in the Far
East, and, above all, the best centre they have for discreetly financing espionage. It is also an ideal staging
post for sending agents into various parts of Asia.

Keeping watch on what the Chinese are doing in
Hongkong are agents of the C.I.A., the Pentagon, Britain, France and other powers to a lesser degree, though
curiously Soviet Russia has faded from the picture as
regards espionage in Hongkong in recent years. Ever
since the rift with China the U.S.S.R. has drastically
scaled down its Intelligence effort in the colony, having
switched its attention to other areas. There is, of course,
a small Soviet spy cell in Hongkong, but their earlier
agents were nearly all unmasked by the Maoists. A
recent "top man" of Soviet Intelligence in Hongkong
was known to live aboard a ship for his own protection,
which caused much hilarity among the Chinese agents.

Most K.G.B. agents only pay brief visits to Hongkong by ship from Nahodka, according to the Chinese, and then they meet their contacts aboard ship, which they rarely if ever leave.

The Chinese Intelligence organisation in Hongkong is vast in its ramifications, which extend from the New China News Agency and various newspapers to the Bank of China and some other banks, with some support no doubt from such agencies as the China Travel Service, which is reputed to be a post office for Intelligence courier services and which also issues visas on orders from Peking.

"Disinformation" is one of the chief commodities peddled in Hongkong and, apart from the problem of sifting it, there is the added complication that even the most honest of the experts disagree on the subject of who directs Peking's espionage operations in the colony and what those operations are. Li Tsung-ying, editor of *Eastern Horizon,* a pro-Peking monthly, says that "the object of interest, obviously, is People's Republic of China. Fortunately for her, but less so for those with the task of 'China-watching', there exists a long tradition that 'silence is golden' because this is a colony."

Yet a usually reliable source tells me that though Chinese Intelligence have a large number of agents here, there are probably no more than half a dozen Chinese Communist Party members in Hongkong, including such people as Li Chou-chih, general manager of the Bank of China, two members of the N.C.N.A. and some unidentifiable people, possibly located in a newspaper office, but more likely within the Bank of China building, which is Peking's nerve centre in the colony. There is no Communist Party in Hongkong.

Needless to say Chiang Kai-shek has maintained an Intelligence Service in Hongkong for the whole of the past quarter of a century under his Taiwan administration and, of course, before that, one directed from the mainland. This is not now regarded as much more than a vague "China-watching" operation which tries to maintain links with its agents inside China and sometimes engages in bartering of information with double-agents.

The Taiwanese Intelligence Service still employs the

Triads, as it has traditionally done for many years. But this branch of Taiwanese intelligence has also deteriorated rapidly in the past decade, as the Triads of today have changed from self-protection organizations into criminal groups involved in corruption, protection rackets, drug-smuggling and all forms of crime. In short, most of the Triads appear to have abandoned political aims and to have degenerated into common gangsters, now cynically known as the "quasi-Triads", who do more to discredit the Kuomintang forces than anything else.

After the establishment of the People's Republic in 1949 the Nationalist General Koi Sui-heong organised some eighteen sub-branches of the "14-K" Triad in Hongkong as a nucleus of secret agents and saboteurs to facilitate an eventual Nationalist return to the mainland. Today one section of "14-K" exists to spy on the Communists and to infiltrate into the trade unions but, though powerful in the 'fifties, this group's activities have declined sharply. They are probably more a help than a hindrance to the Communists as the Triads' reputation among the uncommitted population of the colony is about as low as it could be.

The situation *vis à vis* the Triads in Hongkong is today so bad that, in the summer of 1973, the Hongkong Police Triad Bureau sent out strong-arm units of Chinese detectives and police disguised as coolies and hawkers to intervene in organised battles between the armed gangs.

There is, of course, considerable speculation as to who the No. 1 man in Chinese Intelligence is in Hongkong. One authority claims that a recent defector from the mainland named the chief man as someone inside the *Wen Wei Pao* newspaper (the oldest Communist paper in Hongkong). But the consensus of knowledgeable opinion seems to be that he is Li Chu-sheng, N.C.N.A. deputy director.

Li Chu-sheng is certainly a powerful figure in the Chinese Communist ranks here, and rumour has it that he brought off something of a minor diplomatic coup by obtaining a verbal agreement with London to operate "unofficially" a representative office in the colony. Certainly Li has had diplomatic experience in the past, having been a *chargé d'affairs* in Indonesia, and he is believed to have attended the tenth Communist Party Congress in Peking, which would indicate his importance in the movement, a privilege not usually granted to a deputy director of a N.C.N.A. branch.

He came to Hongkong in May 1973, and the following month the news was leaked from London that Peking had renewed its seventeen-year-old request for diplomatic representation here. It is, as we have seen, an open secret that news gathering and dissemination is only a small part of the N.C.N.A.'s functions. Its members travel on diplomatic passports and have already the status of unofficial Peking diplomats in Hongkong.

With or without a secret agreement with London, the N.C.N.A. is operating as a consular-type office to facilitate contacts between Peking and London. Indeed in some respects there may even be some unofficial contacts on an Intelligence level between the British and Chinese Secret Services, especially as both have a vested interest in seeing the Triads stamped out. Peking certainly tolerates some double-agents who are used to exchange information on known Triad criminals or any new Triad gangster activities.

What is interesting about a diplomat such as Li Chu-sheng is that he is sixty-two years old, and therefore quite a senior official, yet he is officially the number two man in the N.C.N.A. under the director, Liang Wei-lin. Indisputably Li is in effective overall control and the N.C.N.A. in Hongkong is an important section of Chinese Intelligence.[1]

While the N.C.N.A. is the key centre of Chinese Intelligence in Hongkong, the Bank of China is where its antennae are situated. It will be recalled that centuries ago the Secret Service of Imperial China relied upon pawn-shops as centres of espionage; today, in a much more sophisticated manner, the Bank of China is known to play an invaluable rôle not merely in intelligence gathering, but in assessment of information brought in from other sources. In Hongkong a very close intelligence watch is kept on the movements of stocks and shares, especially on all those relating to the oil markets of the world.

Rumours are often planted in the colony to try to draw out information when some share movement baffles the Bank's experts. When the shares of the Thomson Organisation shot up by as much as twenty pence or more in a single day a few years ago, the N.C.N.A. took a keen interest in more than one of its branches. Not long before, Lord Thomson had made a visit to Hongkong and other centres in the Far East. The Chinese knew he was interested in North Sea oil prospects and they were following up a report, albeit a wrong one, that he was considering exploring possibilities in the region of the Spratley Islands. It would be interesting to know whether, indirectly, this quest for information by Peking led to the occupation in January 1974 of other islands in this part of the world. Certainly the Chinese were among the first to learn details of the oil prospects off these shores.

Within the Bank of China in Hongkong is one organisation that deserves some attention: it is called China Resources, the import and export section of which controls financial transactions with the mainland, allocates business and occupies four floors of the towering Bank of China building. Only one of these floors is open to visitors.

Certainly one of the offices of the Bank has been used for some very odd activities. During the 1967 riots in the colony it was used as a headquarters for anti-British activities and propaganda, though these were discreetly covered up. When Henry Kissinger, the U.S. Secretary of State, stopped over in Hongkong in February 1972, he was met by Bank of China officials and seen off at the airport by top men of the N.C.N.A.

Hongkong has the largest number of Chinese Communist banks outside China—thirteen in all, nine incorporated in China and four in Hongkong. The nine China-based banks operate a total of fifty-eight branches throughout Hongkong and the four Hongkong-registered banks have nearly a dozen offices. This multiplicity of banks is in itself significant, for traditionally in all the big spy centres of the world —Tangier in its hey-day, Geneva and elsewhere— there has been this mushrooming in the number of banks. But in the case of China the thirteen banks with all their various branches provide a ready-made network which can be used as and when wanted.

The Bank of China main building in Hongkong has thirteen floors, of which China Resources occupies floors 9–12, while floors 6, 8 and 13 have no description on the index-board beside the entrance door. Security at the Bank is very tight indeed.

Until quite recently a passport of the People's Republic was unacceptable for entry into the U.S.A., but Hongkong residents with a Certificate of Identity (C.I.) could and still can enter the U.S. if they have a valid reason. The C.I. can be obtained without much difficulty even if by refugees into the colony, and can also just as easily be forged. The forging of such certificates is one of the chores of the highly skilled forgers the Chinese Secret Service employ in Hongkong. The C.I. is especially useful for entering Thailand, the Philippines and other countries which do not as yet extend diplomatic recognition to China.

Every day at the Lo Wu crossing point, as we have seen, fifty Chinese are permitted entry into Hongkong. Over and above that a number equivalent to that of travellers into China from the colony is admitted. Obviously this is the simplest route for agents without legitimate·official covers. "Hongkong is an ideal centre for sending out agents all over Asia—even to Taiwan," a Chinese Communist supporter admitted. But he dismissed "as a C.I.A.-Kuomintang fiction" the image of China having thousands of spies all over the world. "Of course, we have tens of thousands of reliable supporters we could call upon, but if you have too many spies, like the Russians, for example, they only get blown because they can't all acquire a high standard of efficiency. Spies, like flies, if you have too many of them, can easily be caught. But you try to catch one or two flies and you will see what I mean." It was a perspicacious remark and he added, somewhat contemptuously, "China does not engage in the cocktail-party espionage tactics of the Soviet Union."

Hongkong will probably remain a key centre of Chinese Intelligence for some years to come, but it will inevitably decrease in importance as Peking's contacts with the outside world increase. What one must remember is that for many years—certainly from 1949 until the early 1960s—Peking depended enormously on Hongkong as a listening-post. With her paucity of contacts elsewhere she needed the backing of Hongkong's Intelligence centre to double-check information that came to her from such places as Geneva, Berne, Amsterdam and Brussels.

Fascinating to study are the so-called "Fat Cats of Communism" in the colony of Hongkong. They are not members of the Peking hierarchy, but they get the best out of both worlds by working with Peking and making vast profits in Hongkong.

One of the most important of these is Dr Wang Kwan-cheng (sometimes referred to as K. C. Wang). When Kinkazu Saionji visited Hongkong on his return from Peking he was the houseguest of Dr Wang in his jade-roomed luxury villa, one of the most splendid in the colony. Born in Ningpo, Chekina Province, Dr Wang is reputed to be a multi-millionaire with business interests which range from ships and emporiums to a luxury Kowloon restaurant. His occupations are listed as "chairman of the Board of Directors of Magna Development Company, Dah Yuen Real Estate Company, Chinese Arts and Crafts (Hongkong)" among others.

As chairman of the Chinese General Chamber of Commerce he occupies what has been described as "the most prestigious post in the colony, along with the British Governor-General". He makes frequent trips to China, ostensibly for business, but almost certainly not unconnected with the co-ordination of Peking's policies towards the colony.

Some time ago it was reported that Dr Wang was considering selling out and going to live overseas with his family, possibly in Canada, because of a fear of kidnapping.[2] But so far he has stayed. The relationship between Wang and China may be said to be one of mutual interdependence. The mainland could, if it wished, cut off his supplies and stop buying from him. But nobody can arrange for them to obtain hard currencies so easily as Dr Wang can and there seems

437

little likelihood of the mutually profitable relationship ending. People who know him say he is "a real Communist", despite his devotion to capitalism.

One of the original "Fat Cats" is Chen Pei-shih, who came to Hongkong in 1937, went back to the mainland during the war, and returned to Hongkong afterwards. He is the son of Chen Yu-chin, the first Foreign Minister of the Kuomintang. After World War II Chen was retained by the mainland as a barrister in numerous cases of property claims. For a long time he was regarded as Peking's "representative" in the colony, but when challenged on this he laughingly denies any such title, yet admits to having been a go-between for Peking and the Hongkong Government. His main rôle at present seems to be that of chairman of the Marco Polo Club, which is believed to be financed by Peking to bring Communist Chinese in the colony together with Westerners from various walks of life. He has Western education and manners and is half-Trinidadian, but considers himself Chinese.

Other "Fat Cats" are C. H. Kao, vice-chairman of the Chinese General Chamber of Commerce, who made a fortune out of sending medical supplies into China during the Korean War; Ho Yin, chairman of the Macao Chamber of Commerce, and Macao's representative to the People's Congress; and K. C. Jay (or Choi), a retired Bank of China official, who is now a consultant to the Bank of China and a currency broker.

C. H. Kao's sources of revenue include casinos and trading. In May 1966 he was the victim of a bomb attack, but escaped with injuries. K. C. Jay, who breeds pedigree dogs as a pastime, is said by some to rank very highly in Peking's most secret counsels.

(Macao is, of course, another important colonial outpost, which, like Hongkong, Peking tolerates and uses in the short-term. Close to Canton, opposite Kowloon (Hongkong), administered by the Portuguese, it is another spy territory of long standing. It brings to Peking many benefits from an intelligence view-point, not least of which is traffic in gold, a vital commodity in financing espionage operations. One of the more recent transactions which the Chinese Secret Service is said to be surreptitiously conducting through Macao is the smuggling of synthetic diamonds which Chinese scientists have been producing mainly for industrial purposes by a dynamic high pressure process.)

In many respects one of the most interesting of Peking's men in Hongkong is the wealthy Fei Yi-ming, proprietor and publisher of the Communist mouthpiece in Hongkong, *Ta Kung Pao*. He took part in the Communist-inspired riots in Hongkong in 1967, joining the so-called Anti-Persecution Struggle Committee's demonstration in front of Government House. Stepping out of his Mercedes to join a four-hundred-strong crowd of demonstrators, he took a copy of the "Little Red Book of Chairman Mao" from a pocket of his well-tailored Chinese-style jacket, held it up in his right hand, and shouted "Down with British Imperialism!"

This gave Mr Fei a great deal of publicity and there were some ironic comments about the fortune which he had made in the real estate business. According to a friend of his, Mr Fei is placed third in the Communist hierarchy in Hongkong. Now sixty-six years old, Fei was a correspondent of the French news agency, Havas, before World War II. It is believed that he was partly educated in France. During the war Fei was business manager of the *Ta Kung Pao* in Chunking and it was he who led this then independent newspaper to join the Communist cause. He has a wife who was prominent in the Anti-Persecution Struggle Committee, two sons studying in Hongkong and a daughter in China who was once reported to be active in the Red Guard movement.

What is abundantly clear is that Peking has a great reservoir of strength and talent among its supporters in Hongkong. Its Secret Service activities there are low-key, as in many other centres, and have avoided clashes with the authorities. Indeed the only espionage scandals to break in the colony for several years past are attributable to other powers altogether, some of them at least manufactured by the Chinese to embarrass another nation. Perhaps the subtlest of these was when in 1973 a Chinese Intelligence agent tipped off the British about two K.G.B. agents, who had been taught Chinese at the University of Vladivostock, arriving in Hongkong. In their possession were found documents containing valuable information about the Soviet espionage network in the Far East.

Of course, the Chinese had seen these documents before the British were tipped off!

35

The Opium War in Reverse 1963-1972

> One of the most remarkable things Chou En-lai said that night when talking about the demoralisation of the American soldiers [in Vietnam] was that 'some of them are trying opium, and we are helping them. We are planting the best kinds of opium especially for the American soldiers in Vietnam.'
>
> *Mohammed Heikal,* biographer of Abdul Gamal Nasser, quoting Nasser on a conversation with Chou En-lai on 23 June 1965.

THE above quotation has been seized upon by some propagandists to paint Communist China in the blackest, rather than the reddest, hue and to use it as a foolish excuse for not having diplomatic links with the most populous nation in the world. "President Nixon's visit to the Communist People's Republic of China," wrote Mr Geoffrey Stewart-Smith, M.P. in April 1973, "has led to a wave of illusory wishful thinking throughout the West about the intentions of the world's largest country. . . . For years many in the West have been perturbed by the growing amount of evidence that Mao's China is using drugs as a weapon in a subversive war against the Free World."[1]

Before we examine this allegation by a British Member of Parliament and assume that Chou En-lai has admitted as much, it is as well that we should avoid the charge of blatant hypocrisy. Looking back at the earlier chapter of this book, dealing with the Opium Wars, one should remember who started this vicious trafficking—not, let it be stated, to employ it as a secret weapon in a war against a major power, but as an inexcusable method of earning money by inflicting on a more or less defenceless nation a trade she did not want and which created much misery among her people.

If opium could be introduced into a country that did not wish it in peacetime by a so-called civilised Western Power, with the connivance of its Government, how can the British adopt an outraged critical tone towards China for copying her own tactics, not by having opium forcibly imported this time, but by exporting the stuff to try to check such a war as that in Vietnam, which threatened to go on indefinitely?

It is, of course, a fact that while the British were primarily responsible for the opium trade into China, later Americans, French and other Europeans profited from it. Can one blame China, however intrinsically disgusting the tactic may be for manipulating an "opium war in reverse"? I am sure one can guess what Sun Tzu's verdict on such an espionage tactic would be, for the use of opium in this context is very much a matter of Secret Service machinations.

After the East India Company had inflicted the curse of opium-smoking on the Chinese people, opium addiction in China grew rapidly, despite brave efforts to check it. Much later a corrupt Imperial Chinese Government in the latter days of the royal regime encouraged the private growing of opium and, particularly in South China, areas were given over to the cultivation of the opium poppy. Chiang Kai-shek made some efforts to stamp it out, but to little effect.

After the Japanese invaded China in 1937 they were the first to exploit opium-growing for subversive purposes. Not only did they make systematic attempts to encourage and spread opium addiction in those parts of China they occupied, but they also developed laboratories in Manchuria where opium was used in the production of morphine and heroin.

The Chinese Communists were already well aware

441

of the damage wrought by the Japanese tactics when they came to power and their own Intelligence Service realised far more quickly than did the Kuomintang what a deadly secret weapon opium could be. As a result of their reports on the demoralising effects of the drug on a civilian population the Chinese Communist Government launched a rigorous anti-drug campaign. They banned the import of narcotics, severely punished offenders and effectively curtailed, if not altogether stamping out, the consumption of drugs in China. Certainly they were more successful in achieving this than any previous Government.

At the same time they nationalised the growing of opium and brought it under rigorous State control. Production figures of the poppy crops became a top secret and for a long time little information was available as to what use was made of them. Strangely, bearing in mind that the Intelligence Services of the Western powers must have known something at least of how Japanese consuls set up opium dens and sold morphine and heroin in Shanghai, Tientsin, Peking and other places as a means of undermining the Chinese people, nobody in the West seems to have looked into the mystery of what was happening to Chinese opium until it was too late.

Yet the Chinese Secret Service started quite early on organising the dissemination of narcotics inside Japan. At first it was thought that this was a revenge for what had happened during the war; not for a long time was it suspected that the real target might be, not the Japanese, but U.S. Servicemen in Japan.

In his book, *The Cairo Documents,* Mohammed Heikal recalls that after Chou En-lai had made the statement to Nasser about "planting the best kinds of opium especially for the American soldiers in Vietnam," he continued: "Do you remember when the West imposed opium on us? They fought us with opium. And we are going to fight them with their own weapons. We are going to use their own methods against them."[2]

Since this revelation by one of Nasser's closest confidants, Chou En-lai has indicated to more recent questioners on this subject that China does not now pursue any such deliberate policy. Probably not: indeed it may be that the enormous international growth in the drug traffic has frightened even the Chinese by the way it has got out of hand and the realisation that it could, unless there be perpetual vigilance, boomerang back on them as it did on the West.

Estimates of the extent of China's opium crops vary. Intelligence circles in Hongkong come up with some conflicting figures. The Taiwanese allege that the mainland production of raw opium is about ten to twelve thousand tons per annum. This figure is almost certainly grossly exaggerated, even allowing for the fact that production sources have risen in Yunnan and Kweichow provinces in recent years; and so, too, one can be fairly sure is the Taiwanese Intelligence report (a copy of which I was shown) which stated that at a secret Wuhan meeting in 1968 Chou En-lai "ordered an annual target of thirty-five thousand tons production". Chou En-lai would have had rather more important tasks to perform than to set targets for opium production.

The Soviet figure concerning Chinese opium production is said to be based to some extent on Japanese reports, suggesting that as long ago as 1958 some eight thousand tons a year were produced in China. Yet even this figure is sensational when, if you consider the comment of J. H. Turnbull, who carried out an inquiry into the subject, it "represents about ten times the total world requirements for legitimate use".[3]

Production quotas for opium are set by the authorities and it is estimated that the total area of poppies in the whole country is between three-hundred and four-hundred thousand hectares. From this it is estimated that the Chinese Communist Government organises the illicit export of two thousand tons of opium a year to the non-Communist world, and this is worth about five (American) billion dollars annually to Peking.

That this is exported for sinister purposes is the considered opinion of various experts who have spent some years probing the extent of the traffic. J. H. Turnbull writes that "the production of opium drugs

443

for export on a global scale provides the Chinese with a valuable source of national income and a powerful weapon of subversion. The subversive aspects of the Chinese drugs drive have three basic aims: to finance subversive activities abroad; to corrupt and weaken the people of the Free World; and to destroy the morale of U.S. Servicemen fighting in South-East Asia. Communist subversive activities in foreign countries are mainly financed from the profits of the narcotics trade."[4]

Yet another view is that "in 1937 the Japanese imperialists . . . encouraged the cultivation and sale of opium in occupied areas [of China]. The Chinese Communists reaped in profits from this same practice in their lairs along the Shensi-Kansu-Ningsia border area. Intensifying their efforts after they seized the Chinese mainland, the Chinese Communists have made China the world's major producer of narcotics . . . to cultivate opium to pay for their military expenditures when they first launched their rebellion . . . Chinese Communist drugs are directed primarily at the United States. In addition to shipping narcotics to the United States through their international drug network, the Chinese Communists also sell narcotics directly to American soldiers stationed in South Vietnam".[5]

Two things need to be said about these reports. First of all, while their evidence is factually sound (and both sources tally closely with one another), they do tend to give a one-sided picture in that little or no mention is made of the other organisations of the world—Taiwanese Triads in Hongkong, the Mafia in Italy and the U.S.A., the "French Connection" and many others—who peddle drugs solely for commercial profit. There is some marginal evidence that the Chinese encourage such traffic by dumping drugs for others to do their dirty work for them: this would, of course, to some extent preserve the secrecy of the drugs drive for subversion. But there is equally some indication that the Chinese are well aware of the dangers of prolonging this traffic and that now, with the Americans having withdrawn from Vietnam, and an agreement made with the U.S.A., the tactics will not be repeated. It is therefore important to pin-point only what has happened in the past, or at least the recent past, and not to use this evidence to suggest that exactly the same tactics are being used today. Whether or not they are, it is absolutely certain that they have been drastically modified.

Harry Anslinger, former director of the U.S. Federal Bureau of Narcotics, stated in 1961 that: "One primary outlet for the Red Chinese traffic has been Hongkong. Heroin made in Chinese factories out of poppies grown in China is smuggled into Hongkong and on to freighters and planes to Malaysia, Macao, the Philippines, the Hawaiian Islands, the United States, or, going the other direction, India, Egypt, Africa and Europe. A prime 'target area' in the United States was California. The Los Angeles area alone probably received forty per cent of the smuggled contraband from China's heroin and morphine plants. The syndicate crowd does not object to dealing with the Reds as long as the profits are big in terms of dollars."[6]

Unfortunately American charges of Hongkong being used as a prime channel for the traffic were for a long time refuted by many British officials who should have known better. The Hongkong Government, notoriously lax and complacent in the face of growing corruption in its own Colonial Police Force, has for years turned a blind eye to the traffic or pretended it was not happening. An Assistant Chief Preventive Officer, Mr Graham Crookdale, stated: "We've never had a single seizure from China since 1949 and I've been here since 1947. We have customs posts out on the boundary and the search is quite strict. There is only one road and one rail connection, so it is quite easy to control."[7]

But in 1973 there came to light a whole series of scandals inside the Hongkong police which revealed considerable evidence of wide-spread drug-trafficking. It was conceded that there was close co-operation between the U.S. anti-drug agents and Hongkong's new Commission of Narcotics to suppress the "Hongkong Connection", which had developed into "an alternative heroin route to North and South America". Then came the admission at last from the British side: "This year [1973] the Hongkong Narcotics Police has

445

already seized three tons of drugs and razed six 'heroin factories'."

In fact for several years British officialdom, partly because of corruption in the Hongkong police, partly out of sheer complacency and a lack of wishing to know, and not least out of a desire to co-exist with the Communists at all costs, sided with the Chinese in denying this traffic, while the Soviet Union supported the Americans by publicising the fact that it was going on. Indeed, B. Bulatov wrote an article in the Russian *Literaturnaya Gazyetta* entitled "How the Chinese Communists Smuggle Opium".

Yet even in America there were defenders of the Chinese Communists against these charges. Alfred W. McCoy, Cathleen B. Read and Leonard P. Adams II wrote a book entitled *The Politics of Heroin in South-East Asia* in which they specifically denied that the Chinese Communists were involved in the drug traffic, alleging that the Taiwanese had planted these rumours and implying that the real culprits were the "C.I.A. financed remnants of Chiang Kai-shek's Nationalist Army which later became self-supporting by taking over 90 per cent of the opium shipments from the rebel Shan States of Burma".[8] But in the light of independent statistics, reports from a variety of sources and more recently admissions belatedly given by the British authorities in Hongkong, the denial in that admittedly very detailed book is unimpressive. It is not supported by any facts other than a quotation from Mr John Warner, chief of the Bureau of Narcotics Strategic Intelligence Office (U.S.A.), offering the explanation that the opium in Hongkong did not come from China, but from Bangkok, and that the real object of the Taiwanese was to use these allegations "to bar China from the U.N.". This interview was given in October 1971, when it was already rapidly becoming apparent that it was in the interests of the U.S.A. for China to be admitted to the United Nations.

The Chinese did not, however, blame Taiwan as much as the Russians for the charge that Peking was waging an "opium war" against the West. The New China News Agency lashed out in the beginning of

446

1973 with this statement: ". . . the wicked aim of Soviet revisionist and social imperialism in these low-down acts [i.e. the allegations of Peking's complicity in the world-wide smuggling of drugs] is to try through such lies to impair China's international prestige and disrupt the daily-growing friendship between the Chinese people and the people of other countries".

My own dossier on the "Chinese Connection" in the drug traffic is based on as many as thirty-seven separate reports from twenty-six individuals who have probably interviewed as many as fifty to sixty people —Chinese, Taiwanese, Communist defectors, police officers, secret agents, drug squad officers and non-Communist Intelligence officers. From Hongkong, Saigon and Bangkok comes incontrovertible evidence of traffic from mainland China. It is also clear that narcotics smuggling and espionage are closely related in many ways. This, it should be stressed, applies as much in the West as in the Far East, though for different motives. Western Intelligence Services, especially the French, have for many years employed as agents people engaged in drug-running, and it was partly because of this that the French Secret Service had to be drastically overhauled a few years ago.

As far as China was concerned the narcotics smuggling operations, when they were at their height, were controlled by the Central External Liaison Department and the Ministry of Investigation, which indicates the importance which the Secret Service attached to them. Couriers used for these operations varied from area to area, but in the main secret agents who were members of the pro-Peking China Sailors' Union in Hongkong were employed. A large shipment of heroin discovered by the New York police in January 1973 was brought in by members of this Union. The International United Front operations, controlled by the C.E.-L.D., included drug-pushing, with the aim of creating disruption and demoralisation in carefully selected target areas indicated by the C.E.L.D.

It is perfectly true that some of the narcotics entering Hongkong have come from Burma and not direct from China, but these have been carried from China's

447

Yunnan Province by agents going into Burma or Thailand and shipped from there to Hongkong, which is a prime transit port for the smuggling into the U.S.A. Sometimes the narcotics are flown from Thailand and Laos straight into Tan Son Nhut airport. Opium, refined and unrefined, also arrives in transit at Hongkong concealed in a variety of bamboo which grows only in Canton, thus leaving no doubt as to the origin of these drugs. These bamboos are legitimate export items and brought in by boat, after being floated down the river from Canton.

In August 1973, after the series of scandals in the Hongkong Police Force had been uncovered, it was firmly hinted in Washington that the U.S. authorities might invoke sanctions against Hongkong if they did not receive full co-operation in stamping out narcotic trafficking. When Congressman Lester Wolff visited Hongkong and was asked if the colonial authorities were effectively stamping out trafficking, he replied: "Narcotic traffic is getting through, so draw your own conclusions." He also pointed out that it was known that there were laboratories in Hongkong for producing drugs, but that they had not been discovered, and commented that the East coast of America had "dried up recently because of a clamp-down on poppy growing in Turkey and more control in Marseilles. All the narcotics entering the United States must be coming from somewhere else, the centre of which is Hongkong."[9]

Since then the Hongkong police have made a determined drive against the trafficking and proved conclusively that the goods come from the mainland, though this is not publicly admitted. So far, despite the earlier pretence that no drugs were getting through Hongkong, they have confiscated some eleven million Hongkong dollars, worth of narcotics.

There are reported to be seventy-two narcotics factories which process the poppies cultivated in China, though a few of these, it is thought, could be situated in Hongkong and/or Macao. The eight major cities from which exports come are listed as Mukden, Tientsin, Shanghai, Canton, Nanking, Kumming, Lhasa (Tibet) and Tihua. An intercepted Peking Radio broadcast of 1972 is interesting in that it claimed that "twenty-four million Americans now smoke marijuana and heroin addicts in the U.S.A. have increased from fifty-five thousand in 1960 to more than seven-hundred thousand in 1971."

It is calculated that, apart from their subversive value, narcotics are big business for China, earning an estimated eight-hundred million dollars in foreign exchange from the illicit drug traffic. The Soviet Union are obviously concerned about this traffic as they are exceedingly vulnerable to smuggling of drugs across their lengthy border with China, and both the U.S.S.R. and Hungary have complained about the flow of narcotics from China.

From Italian sources, diplomatic and otherwise, comes confirmation that the heroin traffic between Hongkong and Europe is master-minded by Chinese secret agents. It is even suspected that there may have been undercover deals between the Chinese and the Mafia for distribution of the stuff. But there is no proof of this and, on balance, the suggestion should be regarded with some suspicion.

Frederick Forsyth, the novelist and journalist who has examined the whole drugs traffic scene in some depth, writes that "only the Chinese are interested in using it politically. Where the others seek to make money to finance other projects, the Chinese pass down large quantities to subvert the decadent West, although its use and possession inside China is punishable by death."[10]

It is in the more or less unpoliced slum areas of Kowloon, Hongkong, that the morphine and heroin factories are situated. The finished products nearly all take an eastward route to the Philippines, Japan, Hawaii and San Francisco.

As early as 1951 it was revealed in reports from the GHQ of the Supreme Commander of Allied Powers in Tokyo, based on arrests and seizures of drugs, that large amounts of Chinese opium and heroin were reaching Japan from North Korea and Hongkong through the ports of Yokohama, Kobe, Kure and Sasebo. In 1960 considerable amounts of Chinese heroin of Hopei origin were seized in Japan. Currency earned from this traffic was deposited in the Bank of China in Hongkong and used to purchase machinery from Europe and to finance secret agents in the Far East. In Burma, Laos and Thailand Chinese agents sell narcotics at low prices to tribal leaders, and the border area of Yunnan, Burma and Thailand is a centre of this trade.

Many of the Thai police not only secretly support the Thailand Independence Movement, but the Chinese Communists as well, and they have been known to take bribes from Peking agents to let drugs through. J. H. Turnbull states that "evidence indicates that opium smuggling in Thailand is controlled by the Chinese Communists through the medium of local Triad societies". [11] Having examined this proposition, checking with various individuals, I believe that it is correct, but that the designation of "local Triad societies" is somewhat of a misnomer. Indeed, it is because this name has been used to describe some of the intermediaries in the traffic that Kuomintang forces have been blamed for it, as it is known that they use the Triads. The so-called Thai "Triads" are creations of the Communists and nothing whatsoever to do with the Hongkong Triads.

According to a Reuter dispatch from Bangkok on 30 November 1970, Communist guerrillas in Northern Thailand were "distributing free of charge an 'elixir' containing morphine to ease ailments of local villagers. Through such largesse the Communists receive sanctuaries and sources of supplies in the villages." Another report states that "Under the command of Chinese Communist espionage organisations . . . drug addicts are trained in special tasks to gather intelligence, steal documents and related data and spread rumours." [12]

This is undoubtedly what happened when the Chinese agents infiltrated South Vietnam and started to peddle narcotics to United States Servicemen. First of all Chinese heroin was sold to them at the low price of twenty dollars an ounce, as compared with a U.S. price of four thousand dollars. With morale low among certain groups of U.S. troops (and the Communists knew which troops to concentrate on) the peddling of drugs became only too easy. The result was that the number of addicts among officers and men rose from 30 per cent in 1970 to, at one time, about 60 per cent. A simultaneous drive was made to sell the stuff through agents in Thailand when U.S. troops were on leave there. Statistics show that troop casualties due to heroin addiction rose sharply after the Cambodian invasion in the early part of 1970.

The organisation of this traffic was developed and controlled by several cover companies and societies, including the Nankuang Company in Macao, the Hui-ching Company in Saigon and the Hsinfu Company in Bangkok, as well as numerous secret societies set up in Macao and Hongkong such as the Shanghai Society, the Kwantung Society and the Hainan Society. Between 1965 and 1970 it is estimated that the Chinese Communists have sold at least five-hundred million U.S. dollars' worth of narcotics in S.E. Asia alone.[13]

To preserve the maximum secrecy in cultivating opium the Chinese counter-Intelligence organisation insisted that wherever possible opium poppies were to be grown interspersed with other crops, and that taller plants, and even trees, should be planted around the crops to conceal them. Such areas are guarded day and night and no outsiders are allowed to enter. A great deal of research is also carried out in improving crops and making production less costly. Their very hush-hush narcotics export company was established in 1951 at Wan-tzu Hsiang near Macao, but when news of this leaked out to rival Intelligence Services the company was closed down, and set up in its place was the innocently named "National Special Products Trading Company" in Peiping.

There have even been efforts to extend the traffic to Cuba. One report states that opium cultivation experts were sent by the Chinese to Cuba under the euphemism of "farm technicians", the object being to grow opium in Cuba for smuggling into the U.S.A. and Latin America. This has not been entirely confirmed, however, though a Chinese Communist ship carrying narcotics was seized off the coast of Mexico in 1963.

Methods of smuggling are multifarious and ingenious. Some narcotics are camouflaged as medicines or pills; diplomatic and specialist missions are used as couriers; fishing junks from the mainland and even from Hongkong Harbour drop specially constructed buoys containing the drugs to be picked up by ships or couriers; in South Vietnam drugs were even dropped by parachute on occasions; coffins, toothpaste-tubes and plaster dolls are used for transporting the stuff.

A spokesman for the Institute of Drug Dependence, an independent charity, stated in September 1973 that "hard drug addiction in Britain increased by more than 10 per cent last year largely due to an increase in illegal imports of Chinese heroin".[14] That same year two Chinese, San Shun-li, a restaurant proprietor in Walsall, and M. Fat-li, his manager, of Redditch, were jailed at Middlesex Crown Court for nine years and eight years respectively for attempting to smuggle heroin valued at £350,000 into Britain. It was the biggest single-haul which customs officers had made in this country. The heroin, neatly packed in small plastic bags hidden in a bedding roll, came by a B.O.A.C. flight from Hongkong. Less publicity was given to the arrest of a Chinese secret agent in Hongkong, Tseung Yiming, who had been using the cover of a newspaper columnist for Chinese Communist newspapers. A bag of narcotics, tin foil and a paper tube containing morphine powder were found in his lodgings.

What is alarming is the extent to which some branches of officialdom both among the Americans and British have attempted to cover up this traffic or play it down. The U.S.A.'s change of policy towards Peking has in part been responsible for this. In recent years U.S. officials in the anti-drug squads have tended to blame the Taiwanese for trafficking that only a few years previously they were attributing to the Communists. Nobody who has studied the world drug traffic would deny that some individuals owing allegiance to the Taiwan Government have been engaged in drug smuggling, but not on a scale anything like that of the Chinese Communists. It was only after a U.S. Congressional report, published in July 1973, blamed the

British-run Hongkong police for the failure of attempts to stop the flow of drugs into the U.S.A. that the British were more or less forced to take more vigorous action. Repeatedly successive British Governments, both Conservative and Labour, had turned down demands for an independent inquiry into the alleged corruption of the Hongkong police.

Belatedly it was revealed that one senior British officer, Chief Superintendent Peter Godber, had amassed a fortune of £350,000 and then left the colony while his unexplained wealth was being investigated.* Another senior British police officer was also investigated under the bribery laws. A further sensation came when Alan Ellis, who had served as a probationary Inspector in Hongkong for eighteen months, returned to Britain and told the Colonial Office that he had been offered a "retainer" of £30 a month as a bribe from a civilian employee at his police station. He added that he had been discouraged by senior officers from taking action against people who operated drug dens, illegal gambling and brothels.

Many nations and many individuals are in the drug game solely for sordid commercial gain. It is essentially an international problem, but that should not blind one to the fact that only in the hands of the Chinese Communists has it been used almost solely as a subversive weapon and for financing, by an opium war in reverse, a great many of their espionage operations.

---

* Godber is currently facing extradition proceedings in Britain.

Chinese Espionage in the Middle East and Africa 1957-1974

If Mao's mistakes are inspired by ignorance, it is an ignorance compounded by bad reporting. The Communist movement throughout the world has at times been notorious for the way in which it has lied to its leaders by painting the situation in absurdly bright colours.
Dennis Bloodworth in *The Chinese Looking Glass*

WHILE the Chinese Secret Service under the Maoist regime has achieved spectacular gains in some spheres, it has also seriously suffered from a tendency, especially in the early 'sixties, to spread its wings too far too soon, and sometimes to lose its normal sense of caution in the remoter parts of the world.

Much of this may perhaps be forgiven as mere over-enthusiasm. On the other hand, as Dennis Bloodworth points out, "the ingratiating Chinese, ever moving with the current, is in any case inclined to tell a man what he thinks he would like to hear, rather than the unpalatable truth. And to his knack for tactful distortion may be added his isolation from the local facts of life."[1]

It would, nonetheless, be a grave error to be lulled into wishful thinking that because of this occurring in certain areas the Chinese Secret Service has over-reached itself and is guilty of inefficiency in many centres of the world. Mistakes have been made, but many of them have already been rectified. The Chinese have a gift for swift recovery from a dangerous situation: they are far less unnerved by such incidents than would be many Western powers, and cover them up much more gracefully.

For example, the Chinese espionage operations in the Congo, masterminded originally by their Belgian network, were by most standards a failure. But, rightly or wrongly, the Chinese became perturbed about the extent of Russian infiltration into Africa and the Middle East and decided that they must enter into competition even before they were ready for it. On 28 January 1973 *Agence France Presse* reported from Kinshasa that Mao Tse-tung had admitted in Peking, with brutal frankness, that he had lost a lot of money and arms in trying to overthrow the Zairese (formerly part of the Belgian Congo) President Mobutu Sese Seko. This was revealed by none other than the President himself who made known this Maoist admission upon his return from a trip to China, describing it as "a confession of Chinese interference in Zaire's political life". At the same time he announced the "sweetener" which Mao had given him along with the smoothly made confession—an interest-free loan of one hundred million dollars for agricultural development.

It had been known for a long time that the Chinese had been infiltrating the African continent and fomenting rebellions against some of the governments of the newly independent countries there, but this was the first time such a candid, official recognition had been made of what Mao's Secret Service was doing in those parts. Too often it happened that the insurgents, backed by the Chinese, were incompetent failures themselves and this ultimately brought a revulsion to Chinese tactics in many quarters in Africa. In the Congo and adjacent territories disaster followed disaster. In Burundi diplomatic recognition was withdrawn from the Chinese and their mission (suspected of espionage and acts of aggression) was expelled when the Burundi Prime Minister was assassinated and a young cultural attaché, Tung Chi-p'eng, defected and informed the Burundi Government that the Chinese were plotting a revolt by Gaston Soumialot against the neighbouring Democratic Republic of the Congo. The Chinese had had a somewhat remarkable theory that once the Congo was toppled the whole of Africa would revolt and throw out the imperialists everywhere.

In fact, as the Belgians, French, American, British

455

and Russians already understood, the Congo was about the most complicated and divided set-up in the whole of Africa in which anyone could make a successful coup. But it is by no means certain that Tung Chi-p'eng was not deliberately leaking information under orders from his masters in order to frighten and confuse. After all Burundi was not all that important, no more than a stepping-stone to the Congo, and the real Chinese headquarters for these operations was in their embassy in Brazzaville, formerly the French Congo capital city. From here the organisation of a revolt was carried out by Colonel Kan Mei, a key secret agent, who set up training camps for Congolese rebels at Gamboma and Impfondo. The object of this operation was to pave the way to power for Pierre Mulele, who had been trained in guerrilla tactics in Peking for nearly two years. But this plan was doomed to failure and in 1966 when the two Congos united the Chinese experiment had ended. Some say that the Chinese had been interested in Congolese uranium and wished to establish a monopoly in it, but, if so, it was a naïve idea.

There was also an untypically brash intervention by Chou En-lai at Dar es Salaam in June 1965, when he made the statement that the "time is ripe for revolution in Africa", though to be fair to Chou, whose mastery of language is effortless and selective, his actual words seem to have been taken out of context. Nevertheless excerpts from it were widely circulated and wildly misinterpreted and shortly afterwards five African countries ended their formal relations with China. Chou's speech also drew a blast from the forthright, British-educated and autocratic Dr Hastings Banda, Prime Minister of Malawi, that he was "less afraid of Queen Elizabeth II than I am of the Kubla Khan in Peking".

Thus the early successes of the Chinese in their drive into Africa, which had gained them recognition in seventeen countries by 1964, was by the following year seriously set back. But these mistakes were quickly realised and the Secret Service was told to play a low-profile game once more. In the succeeding years approximately 2,196 million dollars in aid was given out by China and of this about 50 per cent went to African countries. The purpose of much of this aid was to counteract Russian influence and it was conditioned by China's growing estrangement from the U.S.S.R. The key-note of the Chinese appeal to African countries has been for Afro-Asian solidarity against the super-powers, including the Soviet Union.

Colonel Kan Mai, the key figure in Chinese espionage activities in Africa in the early period of penetration from the Orient, held the rank of military attaché early on in his career. According to Huang Yungsheng, a defector to the West in 1964, Kan Mai was engaged in subversive tactics in Nepal where he had brought in a large number of agents disguised as roadbuilders, ostensibly to help the Nepalese, but actually as an advance guard for a revolt. He was also believed to have made reconnaissances in India and Tibet shortly before China invaded these territories and to have submitted some brilliant Intelligence reports. But in Africa he was not so fortunate.

The New China News Agency has been used as a vital arm of the Intelligence Service in Africa where the Chinese established offices of this news agency in Algeria, Congo-Brazzaville, Ethiopia, Ghana, Guinea, Mali, Senegal, Somalia, the Sudan, Tanzania, Tunisia, the United Arab Republic and Zambia.

It is significant that in Africa the somewhat sinisterly named "Military Section" of the N.C.N.A. has been prominent. This is a section which, though including war correspondents, is mainly the repository of those who are considered to be most trusted by the Party leaders. In other words it is a spearhead section of Intelligence. Its members receive special training and are sent to the N.C.N.A.'s own school of foreign languages. Chiang Kewilin, who worked for the agency for twelve years before defecting to Taiwan while serving with the N.C.N.A. in Cairo, stated that "Among N.C.-N.A. correspondents those of the Military Section are strongest in 'Party spirit' and highest in 'political qualification'. They are all Party members and range from 30 to 40-years-old. They have an average of more than ten years of Party membership and they are from the so-called 'old liberated areas'. They were recruited by the Communists immediately after their graduation from high schools."[2]

It is from this Military Section of the N.C.N.A. (usually after they have passed through the school of foreign languages in Peking) that the shock troops of Intelligence overseas are selected. A typical example was Li Yeh-tseng and his wife, Chen Chung-yin. Li, who had been an N.C.N.A. reporter attached to an Army unit prior to 1949, was first made chief of the war reporting team in Korea, then regional news editor of the N.C.N.A. in Peking, and after 1958 went first with his wife to the Middle East, heading the N.C.N.A. Bureau in Syria, and finally to Africa. They were both expelled from Ethiopia in 1968.

One of the chief tasks of such Intelligence agents in Africa was to send in regular reports on all Russian activities and moves and to assess the reaction to them. Some of these reports were not so much inadequate as over-zealous and conveyed too often a roseate view of how Russian influence could be countermanded by stirring up revolt. They were inspired by a white hot revolutionary fervour rather than a cool and objective logic.

But though Chinese directors of Intelligence (both regional and those in Peking) may have been misled by some of these reports, the Chinese espionage set-up in Africa and the Middle East worried the Russians and caused them to spend more time in counter-espionage against the Chinese than in doing their own real job of spying. Even in Ceylon during the elections of 1965 the K.G.B. and the Chinese Intelligence were constantly watching one another as each strove to support Ceylon's Communist Party. Both of them failed to get Mrs Bandaranaike re-elected and the new Government warned Chinese and Russians alike to reduce the size of their "diplomatic" staffs.

1965 was a bad year for China in Africa and the Middle East. The Chinese Ambassador in Tanzania was named as the ringleader in an attempt to overthrow the Hastings Banda regime in Malawi, while in June of that year it was discovered that Chinese agents, some of whom had entered Kenya illegally, had set up a large spy network and organised the smuggling of arms into that country. Later a member of the Embassy was expelled from Nairobi.

Much the same story followed in other parts of Africa in 1965–6. Four members of the United Trades' Union Congress of Zambia were sacked in 1965 for having taken bribes from the Chinese mission for promising to organise strikes. The following year, when a new military regime was established in the Central African Republic, a drive against "foreign agents" was launched and quantities of arms and ammunition were found and traced to Chinese agents who, once again, had entered the country illegally. They were expelled together with Chinese Embassy staff and members of the N.C.N.A. At the same time the Chinese were ordered out of Dahomey, which they had used as a spy headquarters for planning subversion in Nigeria, Togoland and the Upper Volta.

As though this was not enough disaster in one year, the ultimate humiliation was the overthrowing of Kwame Nkrumah, the fellow-travelling head of state of Ghana, while he was actually visiting Peking. Nkrumah was accused of having connived with the Chinese in the establishment of a number of schools for spies aimed at subverting other African nations. This was no cooked-up charge by those who had overthrown Nkrumah: in his safe was found a copy of a guerrilla warfare textbook, compiled by the Chinese. Diplomatic relations with Peking were cancelled by the new Government of Ghana, and nearly five hundred Chinese, including secret agents and military instructors, were ordered to leave the country.

But gradually this situation was to a large extent reversed. China realised that she had to become selective in her African targets and to know in which countries she could achieve the maximum influence. One of the men who helped to bring about this change was Kao Liang, chief African correspondent of the N.C.N.A., who, as his title suggests, was an experienced Intelligence operator. Today he is secretary of China's delegation to the United Nations and he has been described as "the most illustrious N.C.-N.A. correspondent". Before joining the N.C.N.A.

Kao Liang was secretary of the Communist Party Committee in Hungchao, a suburb of Shanghai. He owed his rapid promotion to his fluent English, and, according to one report, made a reputation for himself in New Dehli where the Indian Ministry of Information accused him of gross interference in India's internal affairs. Kao was shortly afterwards expelled from India and the New Delhi Bureau was closed down.

Then in 1961, after having been an assistant of Colonel Kan Mei, Kao Liang arrived in Dar es Salaam where he became not only something of a cult figure among the pro-Chinese section of the community, but one who was quickly noted for his lavish style of living, his free spending and swinging parties. Though officially head of the N.C.N.A. in Tanzania, he assumed the status of a diplomat and made frequent visits to other parts of Africa. Calling him a "key figure" in China's diplomatic activities in Dar es Salaam, Colin Legum, of the London *Observer,* said of Kao that he was "a go-between for the diplomats and their African contacts".[3]

Kao not only maintained contact with Tanzanian politicians, but with political refugees from South Africa and Rhodesia. He instigated the Chinese-inspired coup in Zanzibar in 1964, providing arms and cash for Sheik Babu, who later became Foreign Minister of the amalgamated Tanganyika and Zanzibar. Many of his expeditions from Zanzibar were kept so secret that for days and sometimes weeks he disappeared without trace. But he is reputed to have patched up Sino-Congolese relations and to have taught "at Djove in a school which instructed members of the Youth Section of the National Revolutionary Movement in military techniques".[4]

Kao Liang was probably one of the ablest overseas operators in the Chinese Secret Service and it is hard to believe that in his new rôle at the United Nations in New York he does not still maintain strong links with Intelligence. He has a personality of considerable charm and was never dismayed or even abashed when expelled from any territory. He has been thrown out of Mauritius as well as India, and no doubt the powerful Indian community in this Indian Ocean island was responsible for that.

Certainly nobody helped more to smooth China's diplomatic overtures in Tanzania. Today China is regarded as Zanzibar's best friend and is giving major support to the island to speed up industrial development, including the setting up of a cigarette factory which is now specialising in clove-flavoured cigarettes, as well as sugar and rice farms, shoe and leather factories and a tractor assembly plant. There is also a Mao Tse-tung stadium in Zanzibar which is one of the best in Africa.

China's reverses in Africa stemmed largely from ill-advised and brash attempts by her earlier agents to interfere in local politics and to promote pro-Peking revolutions. But the recovery from these reverses has been spectacular in the past five years. A large proportion of Chinese aid has been concentrated on the Tanzam Railway, which, from Peking's point of view, has the advantages of being a large prestige project and of providing a foothold in Tanzania and Zambia and a bridgehead to the adjoining territories.

So much for the political and economic gains: in fact it gave China an excuse for sending in a large number of workers and technicians and, possibly in the long run, will be a major factor for exploiting espionage tactics to aid the struggle against white minority rule in Southern Africa.

Elsewhere in Africa China's espionage task has been to check Russian influence and to spy on all Soviet missions. Thus in Somalia the Chinese learned of Soviet intentions to make a loan and promptly outstripped it with a whole series of aid projects. This was partly done to counter Soviet influence in neighbouring Ethiopia where China has had less success than the U.S.S.R.

For a while Chinese relations with Egypt under Nasser were extremely good and a deliberately low-profile approach was again adopted in Cairo and elsewhere in the country. Indeed the Chinese knew that the Russians were not popular with the Egyptians as a whole and delighted in exploiting this. But, possibly because Chinese Intelligence established its Middle

East headquarters in Damascus, it began to take an increasingly critical view of Nasser and to place its faith in extremist splinter-groups, using bookshops and trading agencies as covers for agents whose task was to co-ordinate such movements into a pro-Peking group.

Yet, though Nasser's Egypt was the first African nation to recognise Communist China, the Chinese were foolish enough to allow themselves to be implicated in an Arab Communist plot to assassinate Nasser in December 1965. The Chinese Ambassador left the country after the Egyptian police found links between the plotters and the head of the N.C.N.A., who was reported to have helped finance the coup.

Another front organisation which the Chinese sponsored in the Middle East was the Chinese Islamic Association, but this has only really made much headway in Yemen, where, in the north at least, the Chinese have been much more influential than the Russians. They have set up technical schools where the students are also taught Chinese, and helped to build a 144-mile road on which Chinese workers have toiled alongside Yemenis. There is already a kind of "cold war" between Chinese military advisers in North Yemen and Russian advisers in South Yemen. The Chinese have ingratiated themselves with the Yemenis at all levels far better than the Russians have done.

It is in the Sudan where Chinese Intelligence has perhaps played its most devious game and one which often seems to bear more relevance to Egypt and Israel than to the Sudan itself. Sudan was a focus of Soviet bloc interest and ties of all kinds were developed with President Nimeri's military government until the attempted Communist coup in July 1971, when Soviet and Bulgarian diplomats were expelled because of alleged complicity and most Soviet bloc aid schemes were suspended. The Chinese were quick to move in with new aid offers of their own in an attempt to supplant the Russians and the nature and details of these offers showed that their Intelligence had made an astute assessment of the requirements of the Sudanese.

Though the Russians have recovered some lost ground in the Sudan since then, the Chinese influence prevails quietly on the surface and underground is said to play a very deep game. In Khartoum the Chinese Intelligence Service is credited with having established some unusual links with both the French Intelligence in neighbouring territories, both north and south, and with Israel.

Attempts to unravel the truth of these machinations have, it must be confessed, failed. In the largely unreported civil war that waged for years in the Sudan there were at times some incredible groupings of rival interests of several powers—Egypt, France, Russia, Israel and China, each aided by some mercenaries.

It is perhaps significant that China has made a one hundred and fifteen million dollar interest-free loan to the Sudan. But China's attitude to the Arab-Israeli confrontation in recent years has been low-key and occasionally devious. While taking a pro-Arab stand on the restoration of certain territories from Israel, China has frequently taken the view that she dislikes the idea of either of the super-powers, U.S.S.R. and America, trying to settle this problem. The Chinese delegate did not participate in either of the Security Council's key votes of 1973, thus avoiding a veto on the two cease-fire resolutions. For a time it seemed as though China would woo the more extreme of the Palestinian guerrilla movements. Today there are signs that—possibly for a very long time—Chinese Intelligence has cautiously established links with the Israeli Intelligence in a joint effort to thwart the Russians. Certainly Khartoum and certain areas of West Africa seem to be points where undercover agents of China and Israel do make contact.

A report came to me early in 1973 that "an Israeli double-agent named———had been effectively master-minding joint Israeli-Chinese intelligence operations in Africa and that he had also been involved in a plot to kill Nasser and to have arranged the blowing-up of the U.S. Consulate in Egypt".[5] Further inquiries suggested that there had undoubtedly been such an agent, that he was of European ancestry and had worked for the Israelis inside Egypt while posing as an agent of the Arabs. It also showed that he had had frequent meetings with an N.C.N.A. man in Cairo.

After carrying out various acts of sabotage for the Israelis in Egypt he had to flee the country to avoid arrest. After going underground for a lengthy period he arrived incognito in Los Angeles and is said to have lived for a while in the Chinese quarter of San Francisco. Further investigations revealed that he was a secret member of an Israeli Communist organisation. ——'s story seemed promising and a good deal of effort went into trying to obtain it. Alas, by early 1974 he had disappeared without trace before he could be interviewed.

37

New Faces in the Secret Service 1960-1974

It is absurd that a rogue's dogs
should bark at a saint,
And there should be no news of the clay
oxen that went overseas.
Unfurl the red flags into the east wind
To turn the world scarlet.
Mao Tse-tung, writing at the height of
the Sino-Soviet dispute in January 1963

"AFTER many shady meetings with sometimes extremely shady characters and much checking and cross-checking of my notes, I find pages of material that read like a bureaucrat's report. It is a dull recital of endless people's committees . . . the structure of the Chinese Secret Service is tedious beyond belief."

So wrote one member of the "Jackdaw" research team after delving into the latest developments into the organisation of Chinese Intelligence in the past decade. There is probably no other Secret Service in the world that has so many tentacles stretching out into almost every section of Chinese bureaucracy and every aspect of Chinese life, creating in fact a wide-ranging, all-seeing upper hierarchy in the Intelligence field. It could be argued that some of these links with other organisations and ministries are tenuous and un-worthy of close examination, but to have neglected looking into them would certainly have caused some highly important evidence to be overlooked. For ex-ample, the link between the C.E.L.D. and the General Office of Information is mainly concerned with the dispersal of information. The G.O.I. is roughly equiva-lent to the British CIO (Central Information Office), but the Intelligence Service is kept closely aware of all that the G.O.I. puts out and it also occasionally uses the latter for the dissemination of "disinformation", though more often this is left to the N.C.N.A.

Closer examination revealed a further link be-tween the C.E.L.D. and the G.O.I. in that the former nominates "press officers" to the latter and these are usually intelligence agents. Sometimes over-seas a man who is known to have been primarily in intelligence work is also made press officer. Thus Kao Liang not only co-ordinates intelligence activities in New York and at the United Nations H.Q., but con-trols press relations as well.

Similarly the link between the Chinese Secret Service and the Ministry of Agriculture, which looked so un-promising—it was hard to believe that the Chinese would use "Ag and Fish" (as it was known in British Intelligence) as an annexe of the Secret Service as the British did—provided on closer examination a clue to the intensive security precautions linked with opium production.

The various Friendship Associations—China-Burma, China-India, China-United Kingdom—are also controlled to some extent by the C.E.L.D., though in a very discreet manner. Self-styled European "Maoists", for example, are not encouraged to join such associations, but merely tolerated; and in some countries, notably Britain, the indigenous Maoists are regarded as a positive embarrassment and, as one Chinese Communist told me, as "Stage Socialists and

Cultural Morons". And he added: "Put that in capital letters."

This throw-away remark might have been propaganda, but it struck me as being too spontaneous a reaction for that. Before 1965 these Friendship Associations were known as "Cultural Associations" and they were directed by the External Liaison Cultural Committee, which was superseded by the C.E.L.D. after the Cultural Revolution.

One man who worked in the Department of the Organisation of Friendship Associations was Tung Chip'eng, now in the U.S.A., who defected in Burundi as described in the last chapter. From him came the information that the co-ordination of intelligence from or through the Friendship Associations is most discreetly and effectively masterminded in Peking. Every effort is made to ensure that the chairmen and other officers of such associations are usually noted scholars or scientists in their own country. In the United Kingdom, for example, active members include university scientists and professors, economists and sometimes businessmen. Through them China gains access to foreign technology, one case being that of a British crystallographer who has made several visits to Peking.

The External Trade Promotion Committee is also a key agency for intelligence operations, especially in areas where trade offices take the place of diplomatic posts. Chi Ch'ao-ting, a Harvard Ph.D., used to be director of the China Bureau in the United States' Communist Party. This U.S.-educated Chinese was then given an appointment by Peking and became representative of the Trade Promotion Committee for Latin America. Until his death quite recently he travelled around Central and South America setting up trade offices.

The China-Japan Memorandum Trade Tokyo Office (a curiously designated organisation in which the key word is "Memorandum") has as its chief representative Hsiao Hsiang-chien, who is vice-secretary of the Association of People's Diplomacy, which is yet another annexe of the Secret Service. The Minister of External Trade is Bai Hsiang-kuo, who was formerly in the Political Work Department of the Ministry of

Defence, which is mainly in charge of the security of the armed forces. Though the extent of the Ministry of External Trade's intelligence activities is difficult to gauge, Bai is assumed to have been chosen for his experience in this field.

The most secret of all organisations in the modern Chinese Secret Service is the Investigation Bureau, on whose personnel it has been the most difficult to gather any information, but it is known that it is strongly represented overseas in every Chinese embassy, especially at the level of First, Second and even Third Secretaries. Obviously since the Cultural Revolution there have been quite enormous changes in this Bureau. Ch'ou Ta-p'eng, who was a key figure in the Investigation Bureau, appears to have disappeared since the Cultural Revolution. At one time he was regarded as an extremely important Intelligence operator and it is by no means certain that he has completely passed out of the organisation.

Ch'ou Ta-p'eng was in the "Special Services" before he became deputy director of the External Cultural Liaison Committee of the State Council, which became defunct with the Cultural Revolution. Before 1965 the Committee was obliged to submit its report to the Investigation Bureau of the Party. This committee has not been rehabilitated, but its functions have been taken over by the C.E.L.D. It should perhaps be noted that Ch'ou had been the senior officer over Tung Chip'eng.

There is a predilection in the Chinese Secret Service for using media people—journalists and radio and television personnel—for United Front operations. It would seem from all reports that Peking is able to recruit fairly prominent people of a kind able to be most effective and yet escape suspicion. This particularly applies to foreign journalists who are manipulated in a manner that is much more sophisticated than any tactics employed by the Russians: in some instances the Chinese have actually lured away from the Russians foreign journalists devoted to their cause.

The Chinese technique in recruiting such people is largely one of first letting the fly come to the spider.

Once they are assured his interest is genuine, or that he has been disenchanted by Soviet communism, or some other form of communism, then he becomes a primary target for the Secret Service. In this connection the Chinese Secret Service's primary interest has been in Australian journalists. This in itself is an interesting rebuttal of the idea held in some Western circles that the Chinese have yet to learn to discriminate. The fact is that for more than a quarter of a century Australian journalists have made an enormous impression by their diligence in research, their crusading patience and overall ability all over the world. It is no exaggeration to say that they command some of the key reporting posts in British journalism, that they are well regarded in the U.S.A. and that, despite this, they remain dedicated left-wingers, some of them openly pro-Communist, others bending over backwards to explain that they are against the Russians in Czechoslovakia and not uncritical of Communist Parties.

In 1973 Mr Gough Whitlam, the left-wing Prime Minister of Australia, in answer to questions by an interviewer after he had had a quarrel with his own Secret Service, said: "I should say there are more British than Russian agents in Australia. I would not say there are more than half a dozen Soviet agents in the country and probably not more than three Chinese." Whether Mr Gough Whitlam really meant what he said on this occasion, or whether he had his tongue well and truly in his cheek, the statement is mischievous and rather laughable.

It is mischievous because it is almost certainly inaccurate as far as the Chinese are concerned. It is laughable because, according to one highly knowledgeable Chinese now living in London, "Gough Whitlam should know that the chief man specialising in Australian Intelligence for China lives in Gerrard Street, not Canberra! Chinese espionage in Australia is masterminded and the intelligence it produces is sifted in London, as is that of New Zealand."

I should, perhaps, add that the Chinese in question is a widely travelled businessman, who is neither a Communist nor a supporter of the Kuomintang, though on balance he is friendly toward the Peking regime. "The Chinese have used their own people for espionage rather less in Australia and New Zealand than in any other countries of the world. Gough Whitlam ought to know that back in the early 'fifties a Chinese network which covered Australia was directed from London and that the Chinese Secret Service has always had something like half a dozen Australian extreme left-wing operators working for it not only inside Australia, but in London, Paris and other centres where they have managed to mute their political beliefs," continued my Chinese contact.

Further inquiries have confirmed much of what he asserted. On 13 June 1952 it was reported that Colonel C.C.F. Spry, chief of Australia's Secret Service, had asked the then Australian Prime Minister, Mr R. G. Menzies, for a complete overhaul of the security arrangements at the Woomera Rocket Range and other centres before Britain's first atom bomb was tested in the Montebello Islands. This followed reports from Canberra of serious leakages of secret information from Civil Service Departments. At the time it was widely believed in Canberra that the recipients of these leakages were the Russians, as it was well known that the U.S.S.R. had a considerable spy network in Australia. In fact, unknown to Australian security officers, the Chinese were already trying to obtain information about Woomera, which was heavily guarded and about a hundred and twenty miles from the nearest settlement.

To get inside the area without a permit was practically impossible, yet this was achieved by a Chinese conjuror and juggler who was hired to put on a show in Woomera. He was an agent of the Chinese Secret Service. Whether he obtained sufficient information to justify the risk it is not possible to say: he had no specialised knowledge, but he had almost certainly been carefully briefed as to what he should look out for. Some years later it transpired that what had prompted the Chinese to take such a risk was that Chinese agents elsewhere in the Pacific area had found a curious balloon which appeared to have come from Woomera. At first it was thought that it might be a prototype for a new secret weapon. It was, in fact, one of many balloons, filled with hydrogen, sent up from Woomera to record the secrets of a hitherto unknown atomic particle in the stratosphere, the V–1 or meson, produced by the bombardment of cosmic rays.

Nor is this the most bizarre of stories concerning Chinese Secret Service manoeuvres in Australia. Even more remarkable was a clever piece of "disinformation" which they launched on the world's press in the summer of 1973. The story that suddenly appeared in the papers was of an Australian threat to declare biological war on French vineyards if France's planned nuclear tests in the Pacific went ahead. The threat to unleash a special pesticide-proof strain of the dreaded phylloxera vine louse on France came in a telex message from a Manila hotel to the Sydney office of *The Australian*. The message, sent in the form of a news story by a young woman using a pseudonym, claimed that two Australian scientists—one from a Government research station and the other from a university —had produced this new and deadly strain of phylloxera after the previous year's nuclear tests.

The scientists, the story went on, had obtained leave of absence to get the bug into France, where it was left with a sympathiser in the Champagne region. The conspirators were reported to be back in Australia from whence they would send a signal back to France to release the bug when the tests began.

Inquiries to check this report in Manila produced the information that the young woman sending the story had obtained it from an "impeccable source", but this source was found to have been supplied with the information by a Chinese agent in Manila as a piece of "disinformation" aimed at causing the maximum amount of mischief. It was part of a plot to upset relations between Paris and Canberra which, at that time, were already strained.

What needs to be stressed more than anything else is that both the strength and the weakness of the Chinese Secret Service is that the highest of all the intelligence organisations still comes under control of the Communist Party. It would now appear that the key organisation is not so much the C.E.L.D. as the Ministry of Investigation. It is too early to assess whether this is a strength or a weakness in intelligence overall control.

At present the most important figure in this Ministry is the Deputy Minister of Investigation, Lo Ch'ingch'ang, who was formerly chief of the first section of the Social Affairs Department of the Central Committee of the Chinese Communist Party. He survived the Cultural Revolution unscathed mainly owing to his close association with Chou En-lai. He is concerned with both internal and external espionage operations.

The Ministry for Public Security has not only been tightened up and pruned, but its bureau reduced from sixty before the Cultural Revolution to twenty today. It still controls internal security, sends spies to Taiwan and includes the counter-espionage bureau, as well as having officials in every embassy abroad.

Military intelligence is technically under the Chinese General Staff and is concerned with internal and external military intelligence. It selects military attachés and also utilises non-military personnel in the embassies. Li T'ao used to be in charge of this and, at the moment of writing, as far as is known, still is, with Liu Shao-wen as his deputy.

Li T'ao, a native of Hunnan born in 1906, joined the Red Army during the Autumn Harvest Uprising of September 1927. He made swift progress, being promoted to the Political Department of the First Front Army, responsible for training conscripted workers, and later for organising and training prisoners-of-war engaged in rear services operations. He followed the Red Army to North Shensi and accompanied Chou En-lai and Yeh Chien-ying to Sian, master-minding the Sian incident which ended in the "kidnapping" of Chiang Kai-shek. Later he operated the Hengshan Guerrilla Cadres Training Centre under Yeh Chienying's command and in 1938 was made director of the Third Office of the Central Intelligence Department. In October 1949 Li T'ao was made director of the Operational Department, People's Revolutionary Military Council, and in the following year he became deputy director of the General H.Q. of the Central

Defence Committee. Appointed a general in September 1955, he was promoted to Director of the Intelligence Division of the General Staff in 1961, and, four years later, was made a member of the National Defence Council.

Liu Shao-wen, his number two, is assistant director of the Intelligence Division of the Ministry of Defence. Another native of Hunnan, born in 1905, Liu was a graduate of the Sun Yat-sen University, Moscow, and Leningrad Military and Political University. He took part in the early stages of the "Long March", serving as a secretary to the Red Army H.Q. In July 1963 he was identified as Deputy Director of the Intelligence Department of the General Staff.

At this time of writing, however, it should be noted that recent reports from the research team indicate that both Li T'ao and Liu Shao-wen have made few appearances in public recently. The last message suggested that Cha'a Cheng-wen, who was previously a deputy like Liu Shao-wen, may have been promoted to Li T'ao's position, though officially he is still identified as the chief of the Bureau of Foreign Affairs of the Ministry of Defence.

In none of the great capitals of the world has the Chinese Secret Service kept such a low profile as in London. There are varying reasons for this: one, and perhaps the most important, is that because of the easy access to Britain of Chinese agents via Hongkong, Peking is anxious to do nothing which would cause the authorities in Whitehall to clamp down on such immigration. Apart from this the other two factors which encourage the utmost caution are that the Chinese Secret Service has traditionally had a great respect for its British counterpart, and especially for British counter-espionage (M.I.5), and that they have at the same time been shocked by the extent of the infiltration of the British Secret Service by such Russian agents as Guy Burgess, Donald Maclean, George Blake and "Kim" Philby. Because of the last-named the Chinese espionage set-up in London was ordered several years ago to beware of all new contacts with Britons on the grounds that they might be agents of the U.S.S.R.

The Profumo Affair in 1963, the uncovering of the clandestine *affaire* which the British War Minister, John Profumo, was having with a young woman who was sharing her favours with a Soviet military attaché, so alarmed the Chinese Secret Service that they demanded from London a detailed report. This was used as material for a textbook giving warnings to agents on the problems which might face them in London, with particular attention being drawn to the risks of being involved with the Soviet network.

Certainly the London agents of Chinese Intelligence seem to have heeded these warnings carefully, for neither at any of their diplomatic premises in the capital, nor in the N.C.N.A., has there been an overt sign, or hint, of unusual activity.

The London headquarters of the Chinese Intelligence set-up in Britain (regardless of how it might be discreetly controlled by the diplomatic team) is almost certainly in Gerrard Street, as my contact has asserted. Indeed, Gerrard Street today is probably the most important Chinese centre in the whole of Europe. Hongkong newspapers are flown in there every day to the Hongkong Cultural and Art Centre, and delivered to various parts of Europe. Chinese from Belgium, France and Germany come to Gerrard Street to do their shopping. London's Chinatown, which at one time centred almost entirely in the East End of London, now fans out from Gerrard Street, and its population is around seventy thousand, though this figure fluctuates with the constant movement of the more itinerant members of its community.

Chinese restaurants provide listening-posts for Chinese Intelligence throughout the British Isles these days. Before World War II there were very few Chinese restaurants in Britain outside London, Liverpool and a few other seaports. Today, thanks in the beginning to an acquired taste for Chinese food by British Forces personnel returning from the Far East, Korea and Malaysia, there are now hundreds of such restaurants spread throughout the country. Of this number possibly at least fifteen per cent are used as a part of the Intelligence network, and it should be noted that the Chinese Government itself owns and runs at least one chain of Chinese restaurants in London.

The immigration of Chinese from Hongkong and South-east Asian countries into the United States and Britain provides a means of simple, legal infiltration of Chinese agents. Immigration and security officials in the United States have noted a recurring pattern: a father might have come with four or five children, usually boys in the same age group and, as soon as they are admitted, the family disperses, the youths all enter universities and establish themselves as student leaders. This trend is rather more marked in the U.S.A. than in Britain.

To estimate the number of such agents is to enter the realms of fantasy. Doubtless there are large numbers of unpaid operatives as well as paid professional agents sent in for a single mission. Chinese Intelligence operatives in countries with large Chinese communities are like the darting miniature fish in a large, crowded bowl: there are also 52,000 Chinese in Japan, 30,000 in South Korea, 150,000 in the Philippines and 3,500,000 in Indonesia. Since many of these may have relatives in China it is not difficult to exert pressure for the purpose of recruitment. In both Indonesia and Malaysia the Chinese communities occupy strong economic positions and, in the case of the former, may be said to control the domestic economy; and thus such communities provide an excellent base for penetrating the economic and industrial levels of the nation, and, through these, to obtain access to governmental and military sectors.

Great caution is shown in sending agents to Britain. Careful analysis shows that, if the final target for an agent is London, he is sometimes dispatched to Hongkong first and ordered to stay there for several years and become a British subject before being sent to Britain.

Top of all espionage target lists for the Chinese today is electronics, and in particular computers. This has applied as much in Britain as in the U.S.A. In the mid-1960s word went back from London to Peking that there was enormous scope inside Britain for telephone espionage, with the added hint that this

474

could be done for relatively no cost at all. The information supporting this contention was cleverly interpolated into a crossword puzzle worked out by a Chinese student in Britain. By substituting numbers for letters given in the crossword it was possible for the Chinese Intelligence to test the reliability of the report.

Accordingly Peking alerted a student specialising in electronics at Cambridge University and gave instructions to two other technicians working in London to test out the theory. These agents in turn discovered that a group of men, some with university degrees and others with telephone engineering experience, had evolved a system for cheating the British Post Office by making calls all over the world at local rates with the use of a "bleep", or, as they called it, "a cheat box". This exploitation of a dialling-round-the-world-for-free telephone system resulted in the conviction of a number of young Britons, but it is worth mentioning that not a single Chinese was caught. They had cleverly worked on the principle of obtaining their information not the hard way, but through the efforts of others. When the Britons were brought to trial, it was stated that "they have used and abused the telephone system both in the United Kingdom and abroad on an increasing and important scale, advancing at the same time not only their own, but others' knowledge of the system. For that purpose they exchanged information by letter about highly technical matters. The conspiracy had been going on from 1968 to October last year."

A device had been developed which defeated the Post Office system by sending signals to the Post Office machinery which would act upon them, believing them to be despatched lawfully. At the other end of the scale there was a system of cheating which consisted of a twopenny piece being attached to a fine piece of thread, thus enabling calls to be made from a public box by inserting the piece in the slot and then retrieving it. A little silver box called a "bleep box" enabled a call to be made at a local rate to almost anywhere in the world.

The Chinese obtained the full details of this system and themselves manufactured the necessary equipment, including a multi-frequency simulator, a machine for generating tones or frequencies which were used on the Australian networks, in Eastern Europe (the Communist bloc) and some parts of North and West Africa. They soon found that this enabled contacts to be established in the U.S.A. and Asia.

Through this system the Chinese, backed by all the sophisticated electronic know-how at their disposal, were able to crack the secret numbers of many organisations and governmental organisations all over the world. They not only obtained a whole list of vital numbers of the British Foreign Office, 10 Downing Street and various ministries, including links between the Home Office and the Special Branch of the Police, but also numbers inside the Kremlin and ministries in Prague and Warsaw.

If the telephone fraud racket had not been discovered by the Post Office, it is possible that the Chinese could have infiltrated all manner of secret numbers in Britain over a long period and gained intelligence of priceless value. In the end nineteen Britons were brought to trial and it was stated in court that the fraud involved three hundred and sixty group switch centres and would cost the Post Office £400,-000 to prevent such a fraud again. The Chinese immediately ceased their telephonic spying operations in Britain.

There are some grounds for believing that the Chinese revived their telephone espionage a few years later. Once again the revelation came from *Stern* Magazine. In May 1973 *Stern* alleged that "an attempt to bug the London love-nest involved in a call girl scandal probably failed because British agents apparently were electronically eavesdropping on Chinese diplomats next door". *Stern* based its report on a long statement which it claimed was made to its London correspondent by the husband of Norma Levy, the call girl at the centre of the scandal which eventually led to the resignation of two Ministers, Lord Lambton and Lord Jellicoe.[1]

The statement in *Stern* said that "microphones placed in Norma's bedroom did not work properly because of other snooping devices in the building. These

476

other bugs were probably being operated by Secret Service agents to listen in to the Chinese in the adjoining building".[2]

The flat in which Norma Levy and her husband lived was in fact next door to one occupied by Chinese diplomats, and all people calling on Norma, including Lord Lambton (who was secretly photographed while in the flat) were in full view of the staff of the Chinese Embassy at Marlborough Court, St John's Wood. The Levys' flat adjoined a six-storey block used as a residence for embassy staff, including the First Secretary, Mr Hung Lung. The second-floor flat where Mrs Levy received visitors was one of seven flats on the north side of Marlborough Court, which all abutted on the south wall of the block occupied by the Chinese Embassy staff. Five of the flats, including Mrs Levy's had balconies on their north sides which were separated by only an inch from the wall of the adjoining building. The juxtaposition would have made it easy for Chinese Intelligence officers to spy on Mrs Levy and her visitors had they wished to do so. A small hole drilled in the wall of the Embassy block and fitted with a lens would give a clear view into the flat through its northern window. A hole drilled through the brickwork of the balcony would give a view directly into the flat itself. It was equally obvious that the flat could easily have been "bugged".

From a security point of view the risks were enormous and this alone could have provided ample reasons for Lord Lambton's resignation from a sensitive position inside the Ministry of Defence. For anyone who knows the rudimentary precepts of Chinese intelligence it is impossible to doubt that the Chinese were not only fully aware of their neighbour's activities, but of the identity of her visitors. One of the first rules of Chinese intelligence is for any of their diplomat-occupied premises to be screened thoroughly: in this respect they are even more thorough than the Russians.

My Gerrard Street contact had this to say on the Lambton affair: "It would be surprising if the Chinese did not know all about the Norma Levy set-up and the visitors she received, including Lord Lambton. It would be an elementary precaution for them to check up on neighbours and on their neighbours' visitors, not least because this would be espionage on the cheap, something the Chinese are devoted to. You must also remember that the Chinese Secret Service is probably better informed on the whole call-girl set-up in London than anyone else. Until the Street Offences Act was passed, streets such as Gerrard Street and Lisle Street were riddled with brothels and it was as a result of that Act and the driving out of the prostitutes and sending them underground that the Chinese were admitted to this corner of Soho.

"Knowing full well the value of such contacts, the Chinese coming in would be the first to find out the addresses to which the demi-monde had moved. The move back to St John's Wood was natural because here was the original corner of London where Victorian gentlemen put their mistresses."

Drug-pushing in London by Chinese agents undoubtedly led to the unmasking of the head of Britain's Secret Service, Sir John Rennie, in 1973, though this has never been admitted. In May 1973 a well planned police operation cracked open the trade in Chinese heroin in Gerrard Street when at the Old Bailey seventeen people were jailed for a total of seventy-six years, including the prime pusher of Chinese heroin in London, Yuo On-yao, a 37-year-old Malaysian Chinese.

Yao, who was known as "Chinese Lawrence", supplied drugs to Charles Tatham Rennie, the son of Sir John Rennie. He was selling Chinese heroin at £200 an ounce, an enormous profit bearing in mind that he was buying it at £30 an ounce. (These at least were the figures quoted in the national press.)

Unlike the Russians, the Chinese have avoided any attempts to publicise their Secret Service. They have encouraged, through their sympathisers in the U.S.A. and Europe, the idea that they do not need to indulge in espionage. When one bears in mind the efforts of the China Lobby in the 'fifties, it will be seen that this self-denigratory policy as applied to espionage has borne remarkable bonuses in the 'sixties and 'seventies. Even the erudite authors of *Thirty-three Centuries of*

Espionage have stated that "for all its power Communist China maintains an apparatus few observers consider impressive", in referring to its Secret Service.[3]

Internally the security system is possibly more authoritarian, more ruthless and more efficient than that of the Soviet Union. There remains the still largely unexplained mystery of the death of Lin Piao, who was believed to have been the natural successor to Mao Tse-tung.

Lin Piao was vice-president and Minister of Defence in the Chinese Government and officially designated as number two to Mao. A campaign was built up against him in which he was accused of having "a lurid private life"—yet another example of Chinese Communist puritanism—and of being a "political swindler, having illicit relations with capitalist and foreign powers".

The Internal Security Service reported to Mao Tse-tung that the evil genius of Lin Piao was his "rather sinister-looking wife, who, with her down-slanting eyebrows, looked like a villainess from Chinese classical opera and appears in the report as a tireless intriguer catering to the overweening ambitions of her husband, but with ambitions of her own as well."[4]

According to the Maoists, Lin Piao plotted the assassination of Mao Tse-tung on the night of 12 September 1971, and, when it failed, attempted to flee to the Soviet Union via Ulan Bator in the early hours of the following morning.

A remarkable letter from Mao Tse-tung to his wife, Chiang Ching, dated 8 July 1966, was published in the form of extracts in *Le Monde* on 2 December 1972. There seems to be no doubt that the letter was authentic and it tallies with that of a text release by Chiang Kai-shek's Intelligence organisation in Taipei.

"Evil geniuses surge forth spontaneously," wrote Mao. "Predetermined by their class origins they cannot act other than they do. . . . Certain of his ideas disturb me greatly. . . . I could never have believed that my little books could have such magic power. Now that he has so praised them, the whole country will follow his example. . . . It is the first time in my life that I am in agreement with the others on the essence of a problem against my will. . . . You must pay great attention to his weak points, his defects and his mistakes. . . . The difference between what I say and what traitors say is that I am speaking of my own reactions whilst the traitors aim at overthrowing our party and myself."

This letter is diffuse, imprecise and open to a variety of interpretations, but it may well explain why Mao Tse-tung turned eagerly to a dialogue with the Western powers in the 1972–3 period. Mao wrote this letter as one who was not sure of either himself, his allies, his wife, or his ideology. He desperately wanted independent confirmation of his conception of China's future.

There was at this time a flood of contradictory reports and speculation over Lin Piao's disappearance. As early as April 1972 it was possible from Hongkong sources (not only Kuomintang, but U.S. and British Intelligence Services) to glean the following story.

Marshal Lin Piao, his wife, Yeh Chun, and ten other members of the Defence Ministry were named as partners in a coup to overthrow Mao. At the same time it was denied that (as had been alleged by the Chinese Communists) there were three fruitless attempts to assassinate Mao. But reports from all sources denied that Lin and his wife were aboard a Chinese plane (a purchased British Trident jet) which crashed in Outer Mongolia on the night of 12-13 September 1971.

These reports were based on the alleged seizure of documents by Taiwanese agents on the mainland and correlated independent evidence from the U.S.A. and other sources. Named as principal agents in the coup against Mao were Lin Piao; his son, Lin Li-kuo; a section chief in the Air Force, Yu Hsin-Yeh; and an Air Force political officer, Li Wei-hsien. The plan was a long-range, self-defensive reaction by Lin Piao and Army and Air Force chiefs to Mao's own moves in December 1970 and January 1971, against the growing influence of the Army under Lin Piao. Mao had then intervened in military matters by purging his former political secretary, Chen Po-ta, and re-organising the Peking Military District Command.

The Chinese Nationalists claimed they had obtained documents leaked from Peking which showed that the coup against Mao was originally planned in Shanghai by Lin Piao's son and Li Wei-hsien. Code names used in the draft of the coup were as follows: "Wu Chi Yi (571) Engineer Outline." (The Chinese pronunciation of the numerals 5, 7 and 1 is the same as for the phrase "armed uprising" in Chinese.) The codename for Mao in the documents—and confirmed by other evidence—was "B52"; for Lin Piao it was "The Chief"; for Lin's wife, "Carrier Viscount"; for the conspirators generally, "Combined Fleet". Top plotters included the Chief of the Army General Staff, Huang Yung-sheng, and the Air Force Commander, Wu Fa-hsien, who disappeared with Lin Piao.

On the facts available in the captured documents "Outline Wu Chi Yi" had not been completed in detail when Mao struck early in September. It was claimed that Li Wei-hsien betrayed the plot first to Chou En-lai and that Lin Piao's daughter, Lin Li-heng, was also an informer against her father.

Independent support for this solution of the mystery was provided by Han Suyin, the well-known China-born author, who was a close friend of Chou En-lai, after a visit to Peking. Another document, a copy of which was leaked to Hongkong, supposedly intended for circulation only among Politburo members, entitled "Chung Fa (Central Issue) No. 4" cited the resolve of the conspirators "to stop the gradual slip to an anti-revolutionary trend by a sudden change with force of arms".

"B52 [Mao] already regards us with suspicion," the Wu Chi Yi outline allegedly warned. "Therefore we must move against him rather than wait for doom with our hands well tied. . . . He is a sadist and a man afflicted with suspicion mania."

Significantly, Moscow has never offered an explanation for the 'plane crash in Outer Mongolia, nor suggested officially that Lin Piao, as also alleged, was seeking a rapprochement with the Soviet Union. But eventually Chinese Intelligence leaked their own version of the Lin Piao mystery and it was not much different from the previous account. But the Maoist version had an element of brain-washing in its carefully chosen phrases. Thus Mao apparently admitted that the "struggle" between them began at the Luchan Conference in 1970. In one passage of the leaked report Mao is claimed to have said, "Lin Piao should still be protected; after my return to Peking, I shall look for him to have a talk".

Yet despite the leakages of information and the counter-leakages, which are even more confusing, the mystery of Lin Piao's death remains largely unexplained. That it was a triumph for Chinese counter-espionage is unquestionable. Teng Ying-chao, the wife of Chou En-lai, disclosed in Peking that the American C.I.A. got to know of Lin Piao's death even before the Russians. "Their information was accurate," Madame Teng told a fourteen-member group of the American Women for International Understanding in Peking.

The mystery has been exploited by Western self-styled "Chinese specialists" of academic repute in a manner so totally devoid of logic, of genuine understanding of Chinese problems and of political objectivity that one can almost dismiss as either semi-educated or politically motivated their highly decorative tergiversations.

The death of Lin Piao must have come as an acute embarrassment to Peking if only because he and Mao had been comrades over a long period. The suggestion that Lin had been taking a pro-Russian line can be regarded as highly doubtful, merely a trumped-up excuse for getting rid of him.

Mao Tse-tung has for some few years past been in a similar position to that of General de Gaulle in the last years of his presidency. Since about 1966 there has been an underground struggle for power not only as to who was to succeed Mao, but, perhaps even more important, who would be the persons of influence around his successor. So far Mao has come out on top and preserved his authority, but this has not been without considerable humiliations.

During the Cultural Revolution even some of Mao's top assistants were at one time accused of planting secret listening devices in his bedroom, his cars, his flower-pots, sofas and other places close to where he worked or rested. According to Red Guard sources, these bugging activities lasted over ten years, the chief culprit being Yang Shang-kun, a senior Party member. Yang was purged in 1968, having been accused of turning over some of the information he obtained to Russia, and one Red Guard document in February 1968 recorded that Yang and other conspirators had "obtained sophisticated listening devices from abroad as early as 1955 and carried out activities of overhearing secret information for more than ten years".[5]

One report stated that once when Mao met some unidentified foreign guests while swimming, "Secret Agent Yang Shang-kun stripped to his waist and put on an ivory-coloured wrist-watch which was a mini-phone in disguise, so as to record the conversation secretly."

According to several reports Mao discovered some of the bugging devices and ordered investigations, yet still was unable to check this eavesdropping.

Though indications are that in the middle of the Cultural Revolution almost everyone was spying on everyone else, this state of affairs cannot be compared with that in the U.S.S.R. either between 1917–22 or in the worst excesses of Stalinist rule in the late 'thirties. Nor should this spy mania be interpreted as a revelation of uncertainty in the Chinese Secret Service.

The Russians made their greatest progress in the field of Intelligence at the very time when they were threatened from outside. To a large extent the same thing has happened with the Chinese, first in respect of the U.S.A., later in respect of Soviet Russia. But it took longer for the reality of the Soviet threat, as China rightly or wrongly saw it, to percolate down to the grass roots of Chinese communism. When it did the reaction, though delayed, was fierce indeed and, if there had been a Chinese Joseph Keeley, there would have been an anti-Soviet China Lobby in Peking. The hysteria aroused by China's own brand of anti-

Russian propaganda was the stuff of which witch-hunts are made.

Much argument centred around the question of whether the Secret Service was backed by a high enough standard of education. On the one hand the most virulent of the anti-Soviet faction demanded that "education was not enough", that only "political reliability" should be the criterion for personnel in Chinese Intelligence. The more sophisticated critics argued that a major fault in the Secret Service was that some of the personnel of the N.C.N.A. had not been of a high calibre and that much of the earlier brashness and failures in the Intelligence field in Africa and elsewhere had been due to this. Criticism was directed against the decision, taken when the higher education institutes were reopened after the Cultural Revolution, that students should be selected by the revolutionary committees, presumably on political rather than educational grounds. The Party line on this is still somewhat unclear, but it would seem that the trend is being reversed, as during 1973 the N.C.N.A. announced in a report on Peking University that the students' average age was twenty, that their courses lasted three or four years, and that the university had the final say in choosing them. Qualifying examinations were then being held for the first time since 1965.

There was probably a brief period at some date between 1965 and 1968 when the structure and indeed the purpose of the Secret Service became a subject of controversy, but this did not last long and in the end the "élitists" among the Intelligence hierarchy won.

In the histories of most other Secret Services the subject of cryptography and the development of high-speed secret messages is one that recurs from century to century. By the Chinese, whose attitude to writing is rather that of the artist than the utilitarian, cryptography has been regarded somewhat cynically.

"To ask us to evolve an effective system of codes and ciphers is like asking a painter to become a plumber," one Chinese expert in this field put to me. "If he attempted anything of this kind, it would quickly be obvious that an unskilled artisan was at work. If

484

the Chinese mind is employed in the sphere of disguising messages, it is more likely to work in invisible inks, or in an adaptation of *I Ching* and the question and answer system contained therein. You may argue that several scholars of the West have themselves analysed and interpreted *I Ching* so that this is no longer valid. The answer to that is a very hollow laugh. How many readers of the European or American interpreters of *I Ching* understand what the interpreters mean? For that matter how many of the interpreters really mean what they say?

"But the main reason why there is no special history of Chinese cryptography, as is the case with most other leading powers, is that the Chinese language and especially Chinese calligraphy make it all too complicated. Mandarin has only 400-odd speech sounds, but each of these can be spoken in four tones which means that Mandarin actually has 1,600 sounds. But there are some 30,000–40,000 characters. The disparity between 1,600 and 30,000 should demonstrate that a great many Chinese characters—which by no means look alike—are pronounced in the same way."

With radio transmission of secret messages becoming an increasingly important factor in Chinese Intelligence there has been an increasing need for simplification in sending such messages. In 1972 the well-known Peking scholar, Kuo Mo-jo, urged that steps be taken towards romanising the Chinese language. It was pointed out that if the Chinese were to abandon their characters in favour of a phonetic system using the Roman alphabet, their language would be greatly simplified "from all points of view".

It has been argued in China that the Japanese have still shown no sign of romanising their language, so why should the Chinese. Nevertheless the Japanese do use a romanised version of their language quite extensively, especially as most Japanese learn English in school today so the Roman alphabet is no longer strange to them. Any Japanese wanting to send an international telegram has to use romanised Japanese and similarly Japanese journalists have to write their dispatches from overseas in romanised form. Peking must also take cognisance of the fact that the Vietnamese largely use a romanised alphabet.

In the field of Intelligence romanised Chinese is increasingly being used, though in some very odd and abbreviated forms. The Chinese have made a belated, but very thorough study of Japanese codes and ciphers which date back to the turn of the century. Herbert O. Yardley, the celebrated American cryptographer, forecast that when the Chinese really got down to the basic details of cryptography, "they would take it much further than the Japanese". Major Yardley should know what he was talking about because when, after the Washington Naval Conference of 1922, he told how he had deciphered the messages of the Japanese Government to their delegates, he discovered that the Japanese ciphers were based on a system of irrational bigrams not very different from the Great Cipher designed by Rossingnol for Louis XIV.

The cardinal rule of Chinese espionage is that total invisibility or, perhaps more accurately, total submersion within the community in which they operate is the vital test for all their secret agents.

At the moment the emphasis is moving away from the school of "aggressive agents" towards the old concept that knowledge is power. But of all subjects that dominate Chinese Intelligence thinking none is so preoccupying, or given a higher priority, than that of computers.

A defector who is an expert in electronics and the computer world generally stated that: "The emphasis on computer intelligence has been growing since the rift with the Russians. China is not so much worried by whether some madman might get triggerhappy in controlling the computers that dictate what the nuclear weapons can do, as with what we computermen call 'the glitch'.

" 'The glitch' is the subject of innumerable probes by Chinese agents. You could define it as a monster that lies deep in the science of all computerology, something that smacks of science fiction, but which, it has been proved, actually exists. A 'glitch', you could say, is what happens when a computer goes haywire, the equivalent in the world of technology of a nervous breakdown in the human race. There is now ample evidence that computers frequently go haywire, in banking systems no less than in highly complicated analytical machines, and, worst of all, perhaps, in those computers which control the launching of nuclear missiles. If such a computer went haywire, then a world war could be precipitated through a machine going out of control and not through the intention of politicians or generals.

"To obtain the very latest intelligence on computers China will stop at nothing and spend a great deal of money."

There was the strange case of Dr Paul Yu, a Chinese graduate who went to the U.S.A. and, after a thorough training in engineering and electronics, founded his own firm, Ad-Yu Electronics, in Passaic in 1951. Starting out as a one-man operation, financed (it was believed) solely by personal and family funds, the firm began to build up an export business. The first export order came from Italy in 1954; later there was business with Britain, France, Germany, Japan, Belgium, Austria, India and South Africa. Dr Yu was said to have sold many instruments to France for Government atomic research. He established a considerable reputation in his field and had many articles published in technical journals. He held a number of contracts with the Department of Defence and did sub-contracting work for some of the country's largest electric companies.

Early in 1973 Dr Yu visited Taiwan on business. He was refused entry into Hongkong on returning from Taiwan—apparently due to U.S. pressure—and had no choice but to return to Taipei. It was alleged that he had had contacts with the Taiwanese Independence Movement. He was said to have been questioned by F.B.I. agents when he returned to Taipei in connection with a charge of allegedly violating the Federal Bankruptcy Act.

After that it is not clear quite what happened, whether he was told to return to the U.S.A., or whether he went voluntarily. But on 4 April 1973 UPI reported from Honolulu that "a Chinese electronics expert, Dr

487

Paul Yu, who committed suicide aboard an airplane on Tuesday, was wanted by the F.B.I.".

Yu was found dead in the bathroom of the T.W.A. flight 742 from Taiwan when he arrived in Honolulu. It was stated that he "committed suicide by hanging himself with his belt".[6]

This was all very curious. Yu was a naturalised American citizen, with a wife in the U.S.A. The Hongkong authorities declined to deny or confirm reports that he had been refused entry to the colony. An autopsy was carried out in Honolulu and his body was cremated almost immediately. Yet the remains were sent to one Paul Yeung in Hongkong, according to the Honolulu mortuary authorities, and not to his wife, who was then in New Jersey.

Various reports circulating at the time suggested that Paul Yu might have been a Chinese agent over a lengthy period and that the talk of bankruptcy proceedings was largely a camouflage for other inquiries. One theory was that the U.S. was afraid that Yu, who had reputedly developed a new missiles device, would pass his secrets to a foreign power, which poses the question whether Yu committed suicide, or whether he was murdered by U.S. agents. A close friend of Yu's in Hongkong states that "the Americans tried to smear Yu with having sold secrets to Russia. This was blatantly untrue. He was a true Chinese patriot and his work over the years contributed much to China's development of nuclear weapons."

There was no apparent reason for Yu's suicide: the report of his death rings strangely untrue.

China's strength in her Secret Service as in all else will continue to depend on the extraordinary reserves of talent to be found in her nationals, exiled or otherwise, all over the world. This strength will undoubtedly become more obvious over the next twenty years and it will almost certainly change the direction of her policy-making. But while Mao is still at the helm, while the old school of "Long March" veterans continues to dwell on the past rather than the future, the fruits of what the Intelligence Service has garnered will not become apparent to the Western World. There is nothing so conservative as an ageing revolutionary and it is this stark truth with which young China is living and trying to come to terms. There is a risk that impatience may breed intolerance, as happened during the Cultural Revolution, and this would not only set back the work of the Secret Service, but lose China many new, if lukewarm, allies. But the most recent signs suggest that the risks are being appreciated and that Peking is marking time and consolidating.

If the Chinese Communists can consolidate without further internal dissention, they will owe a greater debt to their Secret Service than to any other of their institutions.

Postscript:

Recent Developments
1974

ONE of the more fatuous arguments of complacent observers in Britain and Western Europe for advancing the thesis that the Chinese Secret Service is extremely limited in its operations in the West is that none of the Sino-British or Sino-French societies are used as "fronts" for intelligence activities.

This is absolutely true, but the deductions are faulty. The Chinese do not operate like the Russians: they have seen how similar societies backed by the Soviet Union have often led merely to an unmasking of intelligence networks. Not only do the Chinese regard such societies with a certain amount of suspicion, but they suspect the *bona fides* of the membership.

"When we examine the credentials of these members we often find that they are the same people who support Anglo-Soviet and Franco-Soviet societies," I was informed by a Chinese Communist. "Do you wonder why we are suspicious?"

As far as Britain and Western Europe is concerned, pro-China societies are tolerated rather than used. One member of the "Jackdaw" team reports: "The Chinese in the Embassy in London have to be dragged to meetings of Sino-British societies. They attend with great reluctance. They even find them a bore."

But behind all this is a desire by the Chinese today to play intelligence operations in Europe in a very low key. The Chinese are fervent supporters of the Common Market; they desperately want to see it succeed —so much so that they would go to great lengths even in the field of espionage to harass or snub anti-Common Market politicians. They have a black list of such people. The Chinese see a United Europe, preferably politically integrated, as a safeguard against both Russian and American domination.

Contrary to general belief, the Chinese are today much better informed than they were on both the British Conservative and Labour Parties. Realistically, they pay little attention to the Liberal Party, and they dislike and mistrust the Labour Party. They have a quite astonishingly detailed dossier on the present Prime Minister, Harold Wilson, and claim to have confidential reports on at least fifteen influential members of the Labour Party whom they believe to be secret supporters and informants of the Soviet Union.

Great changes in the intelligence hierarchy are now taking place. Because of their firm belief that the threat from the U.S.S.R. is still a grave one, the Chinese have begun to bring in younger men. K'ang Sheng is now understood to have retired completely, and it has been the new and younger men who have in the past year strengthened China's intelligence links with the U.S.A., with whom there is now a modest exchange of information on an unofficial level.

Some alarm has been caused by the discovery that the Illegals Directorate of the K.G.B., which selects, trains and sends out agents to live in foreign countries under false names, has in recent years been concentrating on China. But all the indications are that the K.G.B. is finding it increasingly difficult to keep such agents in China for long. In dealing with these "Illegals", the Chinese have forced the Russians to use their China specialists in the U.S.A. in the hope of discovering intelligence on China there.

This is in itself a considerable tribute to the efficiency of China's counter-espionage and, in fact, the Chinese Secret Service has not only kept itself informed on these Russian "specialists" in the U.S.A., but kept the Americans in the picture as well, actually naming Viktor Krasheninnikov, a Russian diplomat in Washington, as head of the "Chinese section" of Soviet intelligence in the U.S.A.

But so blinded were both the C.I.A. and the U.S. State Department to the true facts of life *vis-à-vis* China in the early 'sixties that the K.G.B.'s "disinformation" activities helped enormously to shape the U.S.A.'s policies towards China. Dean Rusk persisted in his hostility towards Peking and one must remember that both Presidents Kennedy and Johnson continued to listen to Russian warnings about the "perfidious Chinese" and opposed their admission to the United Nations.

Then the Russians played this gambit once too often. In September 1969, the K.G.B., through Victor Louis, the correspondent of the London *Evening News*, slapped down what then seemed to be the trump card in the "disinformation" game: he indicated that the Soviet Union was considering a pre-emptive nuclear strike against China—in other words, to rob China of her nuclear weapon. At the same time K.G.B. officers stationed at Russian embassies in Europe and America backed this up with hints that the Russians were considering such a surprise attack.

The first impact of this "disinformation" gambit was undoubtedly in favour of the Russians. It impressed the Americans, gave some of the U.S. "hawks" the idea that in this sphere Russian co-operation could simplify America's problems in her Far East policies. The Chinese were temporarily forced to acknowledge the implied threat and to enter into new negotiations with the Soviet Union on the Sino-Russian border disputes.

But it was after September 1969 that the Chinese Secret Service went into action to counteract the K.G.B. ploy. They started to leak information to the Americans on Soviet Russia, sometimes to the C.I.A., sometimes to the State Department. It was an uphill operation, and could never have been made successful but for the aid of the Secret Service.

The first main Chinese effort was to persuade the Americans not only that the idea of a Russian nuclear strike on China was solely a K.G.B. fantasy aimed at creating panic and discord, but that it was intended deliberately to sabotage any possibility of a Sino-American agreement and to give the U.S.S.R. an advantage in the S.A.L.T. talks. When this failed to impress the State Department, some details of other K.G.B. disinformation tactics in the Far East were passed on to the C.I.A. Much of this in the early stages proved to be merely information which the C.I.A. already had, including the report that Lee Harvey Oswald, the assassin of President Kennedy, had applied for Soviet citizenship in 1959. Then the Chinese gave the Americans a real break-through in supplying details of the Soviet espionage set-up in Hongkong which eventually led to the collapse of that network.

From that moment the Chinese were able to start secret talks with the U.S.A. and these paved the way for the visit of President Nixon to Peking and the beginning of some measure of agreement between the two countries. That the talks and the events leading up to this visit were so cleverly concealed from the outside world was in no small measure due to the Chinese insistence on adequate security measures.

But there was more to it than this. The Chinese Intelligence Service had compiled a detailed dossier on Dr Henry Kissinger, mindful of the fact that in 1968 he had been appointed Assistant to the President of the United States for National Security Affairs. Reports from agents in the U.S.A., in Europe and particularly through Chinese agents who had links with the Israeli Secret Service, convinced the powers that be in Peking that Kissinger was their man. Noting that Kissinger was a Jew and that in recent years the U.S.S.R. had become markedly anti-semitic, the Chinese decided to open up direct negotiations with Kissinger himself.

As Kissinger had been a professor at Harvard University and had long before acquired a reputation as an authority on foreign affairs, a great deal of the material for the secret Chinese dossier on him had come from students in Harvard. The aim of the Chinese then became two-fold. First it was to pin-point more clearly Russian plans to encircle and isolate China, showing how since the loss of East Pakistan, in 1971, Russia had aimed at counteracting China's close relations with Western Pakistan and had sponsored a coup in Afghanistan. The Soviet aim, insisted the Chinese, was still to have a port on the Indian Ocean. Secondly, it was to show how the K.G.B. was setting out to spread smears on Dr Kissinger himself.

None of this has been an easy task, and it would have been well nigh impossible but for the Chinese Secret Service. The unofficial alliance between China and the United States which exists today is vital to both countries, but it has been brought about despite the fanatical opposition of the left-wing Chinese Radicals. Where the Chinese scored initially was by being able to tip off the U.S.A. that the K.G.B. had concocted forged documentation to the effect that the American Secretary of State, Dr Kissinger, was, under the code name of "Bor", a member of a secret section of Soviet Intelligence.

For the past six years it has been Henry Kissinger, not President Nixon, whom the Soviet Union has been out to destroy. The K.G.B. believe that, if they can destroy Kissinger, they will also destroy the Sino-American accord. On the other hand, Nixon is still regarded as a potential ally against China—this is why in the Soviet press there has been practically no mention of Watergate. But the K.G.B. campaign against Kissinger, sustained by some enemies of Kissinger within the C.I.A. for quite a time, has been totally sabotaged by the Chinese whose detailed evidence on this vicious and totally untrue piece of disinformation has finally baulked the Russians.

It was through their Swiss network that the Chinese picked up—as early as 1964—evidence that the K.G.B. was passing on to the C.I.A., through a double-agent, disinformation that Kissinger, as "Bor", had

494

been an agent of O.D.R.A., a section of Soviet Intelligence controlled from Poland. With their usual painstaking efforts the Chinese checked and double-checked and finally obtained through another double-agent the full details of the K.G.B. smear on Kissinger. All this was passed on to the Americans.

How useful a part this work of Chinese Intelligence played in paving the way to an unofficial alliance with the U.S.A. is not easy to assess, but it should not be underestimated. The smears manufactured against Kissinger by the K.G.B. were planted on a double-agent in the U.S.A. who had over the years supplied the C.I.A. with a long list of K.G.B. and G.R.U. agents, including Colonel Kolon Molody and Peter and Helen Kroger, Stig Wennerstrom of Sweden and George Blake of Britain. His intelligence had been of the utmost importance to the U.S.A. Thus, initially, some U.S. Intelligence chiefs were inclined to accept this planted K.G.B. story on Kissinger as authentic.

There are indications in the spring of 1974 that the N.C.N.A. organisation is in the process of being remodelled. "Jackdaw" reports from various centres, after monitoring N.C.N.A. dispatches, suggest that factually the N.C.N.A. is much more accurate and objective than similar news agencies controlled by the Russians. Polemics are indulged in, but they are as a general rule separated from the facts. Before N.C.N.A. correspondents are sent abroad it is impressed upon them that they must develop the will not to be affected by certain types of information that may have a demoralising effect and to withstand propaganda. At the same time they are urged to learn to analyse situations, to make accurate interpretations. Alan P. L. Liu, who is an authority on the N.C.N.A., puts it this way: "One of the main functions of N.C.N.A. correspondents abroad is to supply the 'master of the house' in Peking with the information necessary to act effectively and efficiently in world affairs. In that sense N.C.N.A. correspondents abroad are Peking's intelligence officers."

The reliability of N.C.N.A. correspondents as agents is perhaps best exemplified by the fact that not a single one of them has been known to defect. This is an impressive record. (Chiang Kewelin, the one defector linked with the N.C.N.A. and already mentioned in this book, was not a correspondent but merely a cable operator in the N.C.N.A. office in Cairo.)

In the early years of the development of the N.C.-N.A., many correspondents were left alone for years to prove themselves. But for some years now each overseas office has been inspected by an official from Peking every year and the personnel have been graded according to his findings.

There are signs that the N.C.N.A. today seems anxious to impress the outside world with at least the accuracy of its reporting, if not the objectivity of its work. Clearly, too, the activities of the N.C.N.A. are developing in an altogether lower key and the strident polemics of the early 'sixties have begun to disappear. The monitoring of foreign broadcasts and news agencies has been greatly extended. The N.C.N.A. headquarters in Peking employs more than two thousand people and monitors broadcasts of nearly fifty stations all over the world. A special top secret analysis of this monitoring is supplied to the C.E.L.D.

In the first six months of 1974 the skirmishes between the rival Secret Services of China and Russia have taken some unusual forms. According to a Kremlin decree issued in February the Far Eastern command district of the K.G.B. was given one of the country's top awards, apparently for "preparations against possible Chinese attack", which the Chinese point out somewhat slyly is "not as gallant as it sounds, because the Far Eastern District of the K.G.B. is on the Russian side of the Sino-Russian border".

China has recently had to strengthen its intelligence set-up in Tibet where Soviet agents have been stirring up trouble for some time. It was as a result of intelligence reports of the Russians sending armed infiltrators into Tibet that military reinforcements were dispatched there last March. These forces include specially trained anti-subversive squads who come directly under orders from Peking.

Meanwhile Peking's support for Communist insurgents along the Laos-Thailand border and in Burma is as strong as ever. It is estimated that among the Thao-Lao inhabitants these insurgents number two and a half thousand and appear to be concentrating on building a political infrastructure. There are about the same number in the northern area and just over one thousand in the south.

A recent report (May 1974) stated that the Governor of Chieng Rai province in Northern Thailand claimed that the Chinese were directing the tribal insurgents in that region. Some two hundred Chinese agents of the Meo region had been sent into Northern Thailand.

In Macao, however, if the army coup in Lisbon raised hopes for independence for Portugal's colony in the Far East, they were premature. China has no more intention of intervening here than she has of taking action in Hongkong. Not even the Macao Communists want the colony to be annexed to China. Peking's influence here has in any case steadily increased just as that of Taiwan has decreased, and in effect Communist China controls the commerce of Macao, its trade unions, schools and newspapers to a remarkable degree. As far as intelligence goes China has an agent in every worthwhile organisation in Macao.

Much of the credit for tightening up the operations of the C.E.L.D. is undoubtedly due to Keng Biao, who was born in 1903 in Hunan and graduated at the Whampoa Military Academy. During the Northern Expedition he served with Yeh Ting's troops and joined the Communists. In 1949 he was appointed deputy commander of the 19th Army Group; the following year he became ambassador to Sweden, and then in quick succession he was ambassador to Denmark, minister to Finland and ambassador to Pakistan before being made a vice-minister at the Ministry of Foreign Affairs in January 1960. His exact rôle in the field of intelligence has latterly been more obscure and other and younger men have come forward, but Keng Biao's experience and knowledge of the outside world is greatly respected and it is significant that in September 1963 he was sent as a special envoy to Burma.

Whether Keng Biao had anything to do with it or not, it was during 1963 that the Chinese had a tip-off from Rangoon that the K.G.B. had set up a new section called "The Twelfth" specially designed to try to trap and win over Chinese diplomats and to mount a long-term project to infiltrate the Chinese Embassy in Moscow.

"The Twelfth" appears to have been a dreadful failure from the very beginning. It was swiftly nullified by the Chinese themselves.

Supplementary Notes
to Chapters

CHAPTER 1

1 See *Sun Tzu on the Art of War: the Oldest Military Treatise in the World,* translated from the Chinese with introduction and critical notes by Lionel Giles, Luzac, London, 1910, and *The Principles of War by Sun Tzu,* a R.A.F. Publication, Ceylon, 1943.

2 Cited in *Makers of China,* by Bernard Martin and Shui Chien-tung.

3 An interesting comment appears in the works of Huai-nan Tzu: "When sovereign and ministers show perversity of mind, it is impossible even for a Sun Tzu to encounter the foe." This is the earliest direct reference to Sun Tzu as Huai-nan Tzu died in 122 B.C.

CHAPTER 2

1 This translation is a summarised version of Giles and Machell Cox's interpretation of Sun Tzu.

2 Sun Tzu: chap. xiii. This chapter of Sun's work covers the whole of his observations on espionage.

3 *Sun Tzu and the Art of War,* Giles.

4 See *The Principles of War,* R.A.F. Publication.

5 This refers to incidents during the Shang dynasty, founded in 1766 B.C. Its name was changed to Yin by P'an Keng in 1401 B.C.

499

CHAPTER 3

1   The extent of this empire was remarkable for those days. In the north and north-west it was protected by the Great Wall of China and the Yellow River. Within its borders were the Yangtze River and the Si River and on the east it was bounded by both the Yellow Sea and the South China Sea.

2   See foreward by C. J. Jung to *The I Ching or Book of Changes,* trans. by Richard Wilhelm and Cary F. Baynes. Another excellent source on this subject is the trans. of *The Book of Changes,* by John Blofeld.

3   Cited by Bernard Martin & Shui Chien-tung in *Makers of China.*

CHAPTER 4

1   See *The I Ching or Book of Changes,* Wilhelm & Baynes.

2   *Ibid.*

3   See *San Kuo or The Romance of the Three Kingdoms,* trans. by C. H. Brewitt-Taylor, 1925.

4   *Ibid.*

CHAPTER 5

1   Pan Chao also travelled considerably. She spent 20 years working on her histories, but on occasions accompanied her brother on his missions. The histories she wrote either with her other brother, Ku, or on her own, totalled ten volumes. Mao Tse-tung mentions her *Han Shu* as one of the works he studied as a young man.

2   Also referred to as Wutse Tien.

3   See *The Empress Wu,* C. P. Fitzgerald.

4   A curious prophecy said to have been put into the Bronze Urn was that the "regal flower" of China, the peony, would grow better in Loyang than in Sian, then the capital. This was backed up by evidence suggesting that the royal gardeners had neglected the cultivation of the peony

500

and had failed to take steps to improve its development. The Empress then commanded that all the flowers in the Imperial gardens should bloom on a certain day in mid-winter. All was astonishingly successful except for the peonies, which all bloomed late. By Imperial decree all the thousands of pots of peonies were banished to Loyang which became almost the sole centre for peony flowers after that and, so it is said, flourished better for it.

5　See *The Empress Wu,* Fitzgerald.
6　*Ibid.*
7　Wang An-shih's influence with the Emperor was so great that, in contrast to almost every other regime, when the all-powerful Reminders criticised him to the Emperor, the latter demoted them.

CHAPTER 6

1　See *The Mongols: A History,* Jeremiah Curtin.
2　See "Kublai Khan: A Mongol Emperor" in *Makers of China,* by Bernard Martin and Shui Chien-tung.
3　The rôle of the eunuchs was one that lasted right until the end of the monarchy in 1912 and something of its sinister nature was summed up in the *Book of Odes* as:

> "Never will misfortune cease
> While there shall be at court
> The wife and the eunuch."

In many respects the eunuchs, while developing their own secret service, actually held back the evolution of a more comprehensive system.
4　A memorial stone in the Moslem cemetery (Cheng Ho was a devout Moslem) outside Chuanchou on the Fukien coast bears the following inscription: "Admiral Cheng Ho, Imperial Emissary and Head Eunuch, in command of the mission to Hormuz in the Western Seas, 16th of the 5th moon in the 15th year of Yung-lo [1417] held a prayer meeting here to pray for Allah's

protection. This stone was dedicated by Pu Ho, the governor."

5 There are two modern translations of Chin P'ing Mei, one by Bernard Miall, the Bodley Head, London, translated from a German version, and the revised version of Col. Clement Egerton's *The Golden Lotus,* 4 vols., Routledge, 1972. An earlier translation of this ancient Chinese novel, attributed to a Confucian scholar named Wang Shih-cheng, is "Metal Vase Plum Blossom". It recounts the adventures of Hsi Men and his six wives, of whom the most alluring and cunningest is the Golden Lotus.

6 *The Golden Lotus,* Egerton.

7 See *A Documentary Chronicle of Sino-Western Relations* (1644–1820) by Fu Lo-shu, 2 vols., University of Arizona Press, Tucson, 1966.

8 *Relations et Epistolas Fratrum Minorum Saeculi XVIII, Sinica Franciscana,* ed. by Anastasius van den Wyngaert, Florence, 1936.

9 *A Documentary Chronicle of Sino-Western Relations,* Fu Lo-shu.

10 *Ibid.*

11 See *Description géographique, historique, chronologique et physique de l'Empire de la Chine,* by J. B. du Halde, vol. 4, Paris, 1753.

CHAPTER 7

1 The security system of the Forbidden City in which the Emperor himself resided was quite the most formidable in the world at this time. To some extent it remained so until late in the nineteenth century. There were actually 3 cities running in concentric circles, the innermost being the Forbidden City, closely guarded with grey brick walls 40 feet high and 40 feet thick surrounding it and a moat 40 feet wide. Encircling the Forbidden City was the Imperial City, which was also walled, and on the outer perimeter of Peking was a third city with a 50 feet high wall that extended for a circumference of 15 miles. The main permanent inhabitants of the Forbidden City,

apart from the Emperor and his immediate retinue, were the concubines, eunuchs, certain ladies of high rank and the messengers, servants and some guards. All but those who were permanently resident in the city had to leave it at night, and male visitors all had to leave the Forbidden City at sunset and this applied even to the Emperor's brothers.

2 See *Makers of China*, by Martin and Shui Chientung.

3 See *The Importance of Living*, by Lin Yutang. As always with Chinese scholars, Lin Yutang amplifies and qualifies his theory of China having a "lyrical philosophy". To understand Lin Yutang writing in the twentieth century is to grasp better how Europeans were bemused by the Chinese way of life in the eighteenth century. In referring to his own "personal testimony" Lin Yutang says: "I should have liked to call it a 'Lyrical Philosophy', using the word 'lyrical' in the sense of being a highly personal and individual outlook. But that would be too beautiful a name and I must forgo it, for fear of aiming too high and leading the reader to expect too much. . . . Sometimes when one is drunk with this earth one's spirit seems so light that he thinks he is in heaven. But actually he seldom rises 6 feet above the ground."

4 *Makers of China*, Martin and Shui Chien-tung.

5 See *The China Helpers: Western Advisers in China, 1620–1960*, by Jonathan Spence.

6 Cited by Bernard Martin and Shui Chien-tung in *Makers of China*.

7 See *East Asia: The Modern Transformation*, in *A History of East Asian Civilisation*, vol. 2, by John K. Fairbank, Edwin O. Reischauer and Albert M. Craig, Allen & Unwin, London, 1965.

CHAPTER 8

1 See *The Importance of Living*, by Lin Yutang.
2 The Chinese have shown a flexibility in the utili-

sation of secret societies that is not paralleled, or even understood in the West. Secret societies in China have always adapted themselves to the times: thus in the nineteenth and twentieth centuries they have generally adapted themselves to contemporary problems which means they have opposed foreign interests.

3   The *Hai Lu* (*A Maritime Record*) was compiled by Yang Ping-nan, *circa* 1820, and appears to have been based on the records of an interpreter, Hsieh Ch'ing-kao who had travelled widely in S.E. Asia in the latter part of the eighteenth century. He seems to have made a point of interviewing sailors, merchants and other travellers and to have made meticulous notes of everything of interest he could elicit from them.

4   See *A History of East Asian Civilisation,* vol. 2, *East Asia: The Modern Transformation,* by Fairbank, Reischauer and Craig.

CHAPTER 9

1   Cited in *A Universal History of Infamy,* by Jorge Luis Borges, translated by Norman Thomas di Giovanni, Allen Lane, 1972. For 13 years the Widow Ching was the scourge of the China seas and her fleet of ships comprised 6 squadrons, each flying a banner of a different colour. Her code of rules included these decrees: "The punishment of the pirate who abandons his post without permission will be perforation of the ears in the presence of the whole fleet; repeating the same, he will suffer death. . . . Commerce with captive women taken in the villages is prohibited on deck; permission to use violence against any woman must first be requested by the ship's purser, and then carried out only in the ship's hold. Violation of this ordinance will be punishable by death."

2   See *Trade and Diplomacy, Fairbank,* p. 69.

3   See *The Opium War Through Chinese Eyes,* by Arthur Waley, Macmillan, New York, 1958.

4   Cited from *Chinese Repository,* vol. 5, 1837, by S. Wells Williams in *The Middle Kingdom,* London and New York, 1848.

5   This letter to Queen Victoria is cited in *East Asia: The Modern Transformation,* by Fairbank, Reischauer and Craig. It is clear from other sources that Lin Tse-hsu did not send off this letter in any fit of petulance or without considerable meditation. Jonathan Spence writes in his book, *The China Helpers*: "Lin Tse-hsu drafted a letter to Queen Victoria in which he requested her help in ending the opium trade and he asked Parker to check it for him." This is a reference to the American medical missionary, Dr Peter Parker, who became a close friend and adviser to Lin Tse-hsu.

6   Parker's attitude towards the Chinese ultimately underwent a change. Reflecting on his six years in China, he recorded in 1840, writes Jonathan Spence in *The China Helpers*: "My Christian feelings are much less ardent now than then." He went back briefly to America and then returned to China, intending in his own words to prevail on the Manchu Court "to modify its ancient policy so as to afford a government that shall meet the popular demand and correspond to the progress of the nineteenth century." After that he seems to have lost the trust of even his Chinese friends, not surprisingly when he openly urged the U.S.A. to annex Taiwan to act as a bargaining counter to Britain's possession of Hongkong and Singapore.

CHAPTER 10

1   See *Makers of China,* Martin and Shui Chientung.

2   See article entitled "Empress of the Manchu Decline", by J. Dean Barrett, in *Orientations,* August 1972.

3   See *Makers of China,* Martin and Shui Chientung.

4   See *The Dragon Empress,* by Marina Warner, Weidenfeld & Nicolson, 1972.
5   See *Empress of the Manchu Decline,* by J. Dean Barrett, *Orientations,* August 1972.
6   Hongkong *China Mail,* 22 May 1862.
7   See *Makers of China.*
8   See *Empress of the Manchu Decline,* by J. Dean Barrett, *Orientations,* August 1972.
9   Cited as an extract from a dispatch from the British Consul in Peking, dated 23 June 1871, in a *Colonial Police Intelligence Report* from Hongkong in 1872.
10 See *Makers of China.*
11 Quoted from a letter from Frederick Townsend Ward to Vernon C. Davidson, 31 December 1871. Warner's statement is interesting, but in fairness it should be admitted that he was a disreputable character in some respects, as the Shanghai *North China Herald* in August 1860, stated that: "The first and best item . . . is the utter defeat of Ward and his men before Tsinggpu. This notorious man has been brought down to Shanghai not, as was hoped, dead, but severely wounded in the mouth, one side and one leg. . . . It seems astonishing that Ward should be allowed to remain unpunished, and yet not a hint is given that any measures will be taken against him."

CHAPTER 11

1   This is the anglicised version of this poem-essay given by Lin Yutang in 1937 in his book *The Importance of Living.*
2   See article entitled "Secret of the Orchid", by Richard Hughes in the "Spectrum" column of the *Sunday Times,* 21 October 1973.
3   See *Importance of Living,* Lin Yutang. This quotation is contained in a footnote on page 171. Lin Yutang implies that the vital question in the Chinese search for knowledge—and this concerns espionage as much as anything else—is

"the one and eternal question: 'How are we going to live?' "

4 See *The Dragon Empress,* Marina Warner.
5 See *East Asia: The Modern Transformation,*
   Fairbank, Reischauer and Craig.

CHAPTER 12

1 See *From Opium War to Liberation,* by Israel
   Epstein, New York World Press, Peking, 1956.
2 Anson Burlingame was American Minister to
   China and a great supporter of Frederick Townsend Ward. In 1867 he acted as Chinese envoy
   to the Western powers, an agreement voluntarily
   entered into by the Chinese Government.
3 See *The Life of Gordon,* by Demetrius C. Boulger, Fisher Unwin, London, 1896.
4 See *Gordon of Khartoum, Martyr & Misfit,* by
   Anthony Nutting, 1966.
5 See *A History of the British Secret Service* and
   A History of the Russian Secret Service, both by
   Richard Deacon, on the career of Sidney Reilly.
6 See *From Opium War to Liberation,* Epstein.
7 Cited in *Makers of China,* Martin and Shui
   Chien-tung.

CHAPTER 13

1 See *The China Helpers,* Spence.
2 See *Kidnapped in London,* by Sun Yat-sen, The
   China Society, London, 1969: extract from the
   foreword by Kenneth Cantlie.
3 See *Kidnapped in London,* Sun Yat-sen, Simkin,
   Marshall, Hamilton, Kent & Co., London, 1897.
4 *Ibid.*
5 *Ibid.*
6 *Ibid.*
7 *Ibid.*
8 *Ibid.*
9 See *The Life of Gordon,* Boulger.
10 *Ibid.*
11 See *Kidnapped in London,* Sun Yat-sen.
12 Sir Halliday Macartney sent a letter to *The*

Times, dated 24 October 1896, protesting against that paper's leading article on the kidnapping of Sun. Here he repeated his story, stating: "I repeat what I have said before—that in this case there was no inveiglement. The statement of Sun Yat-sen [*sic*]—or to call him by his real name, Sun Wen—that he was caught in the street and hustled into the Legation by two sturdy Chinamen is utterly false. He came to the Legation unexpectedly, and of his own accord, the first time on Saturday, the 10th, the second on Sunday, the 11th."

CHAPTER 14

1 See *China's Entrance into the Family of Nations; the Diplomatic Phase, 1858–1890,* by Immanuel C. Y. Hsu, Harvard University Press, 1960.
2 See *From Opium War to Liberation,* Epstein.
3 See *Indiscreet Letters from Peking,* by B. L. Putnam Weale, London, 1900.
4 See *The Dragon Empress,* Warner.
5 See *These From the Land of Sinim,* by Robert Hart, Chapman & Hall, London, 1901.
6 *Ibid.*
7 *From Opium War to Liberation,* Epstein.
8 Extract from a letter from Sidney Reilly to "E.C.F.", dated 3 December 1902.

CHAPTER 15

1 See *From Opium War to Liberation,* Epstein, in which the author states: "The information and ideas of Tung Meng Hui reflected, in part, the great effect in Asia of the example of the Russian Revolution of 1905. Its organ, *Min Pao,* printed articles on the Russian movement in almost every issue. The attention of progressive Chinese, hitherto fixed on the American and French revolutions of the eighteenth century, was now attracted to this great upheaval of their own times."
2 Cited by J. Lust in an article entitled "The Supao Case: An Episode on the Early Chinese Na-

tionalist Movement" in the 1964 *Bulletin of the School of Oriental and African Studies,* London.

3 *Ibid.*
4 *Ibid.*
5 See *The Chinese Abroad,* by Harley F. McNair, Shanghai, 1927.

CHAPTER 16

1 See *The Importance of Living,* Lin Yutang.
2 *From Opium War to Liberation,* Epstein.
3 Cited by Epstein in *From Opium War to Liberation* and quoted as an extract from a memorandum by the Black Dragon Society, issued in 1915.

CHAPTER 17

1 The document setting out these 21 demands was written on paper watermarked with drawings of cannon and warships, a deliberate hint of the threat of power.
2 Cited by Bernard Martin and Shui Chien-tung in *Makers of China.*
3 See *Two-Gun Cohen,* by Charles Drage, Jonathan Cape, London, 1954.
4 *Ibid.*

CHAPTER 18

1 In *From Opium War to Liberation,* Epstein makes the point that "the result of the strike taught another lesson. No previous struggle, whether of the Chinese peasantry fighting by itself, or of the Chinese capitalists, had been able to wrest the slightest concession from imperialism. But the resolute, united fight of the seamen and other workers in Hongkong won a 15–30 per cent. wage increase and the legislation of their trade union, which had previously been outlawed by an ordinance of the British Governor."
2 See *The Mask of Merlin: A Critical Biography of David Lloyd George,* by Donald McCormick, Macdonald, London, 1963.

3   See *The Eyes of the Navy; A Biographical Study of Admiral Sir Reginald Hall,* by Admiral Sir William James, Methuen, London, 1955.

4   Lincoln's book was *The Autobiography of an Adventurer,* under his full name of Ignatius T. T. Lincoln, translated by Emile Burns, Leonard Stein, London, 1931. Originally published in the U.S.A. in 1916, it only covers his career up to World War I and its objects would seem to be two-fold: first, to threaten the British Government with scandalous revelations if he was not treated with leniency, and, secondly, as pro-German propaganda.

5   See *Disgrace Abounding,* by Douglas Reed, Jonathan Cape, London, 1939.

6   Cited by the New York correspondent of the London *Daily Chronicle,* 20 January 1916.

7   See *The Self-Made Villain*: A Biography of *I. T. Trebitsch Lincoln,* by David Lampe and Laszlo Szenasi, Cassel, London, 1961.

8   Cited by Gerald Bowman in an article entitled "The Man From Paks", in the London *Evening News* of 30 August 1954.

9   London *Times,* 3 March 1926.

10 Cited from a review of *The Self-Made Villain,* Lampe and Szenasi, by H. D. Ziman, in the *Daily Telegraph,* 24 November 1961.

11 Wu Pei-fu sent in troops to capture the headquarters which the railway union workers had set up in Kiangan, near Hankow. The workers' leaders who were arrested included two leading Communists, one of whom, Lin Hsiang-chien was shot, while the other, Shih Yang, was tortured to death.

12 The whole story of this affair has never been told in full, but the London *Pall Mall Gazette* gave a detailed report under the heading of "German Plots with China" on 23 September 1927.

13 See *The Morning Deluge: Mao Tse-tung and the Chinese Revolution,* by Han Suyin, Jonathan Cape, London, 1972.

14 Cited by Epstein in *From Opium War to Libera-*

tion. It has been alleged that this letter was a forgery, but all evidence points to its being genuine, whether or not it was written at the request of Borodin.

CHAPTER 19

1 See *The Morning Deluge,* Han Suyin.
2 See *The China Helpers,* Spence. It should be noted that at this time Borodin's closest Chinese associate was Chang T'ai-lei, a member of the Central Committee of the Communist Party, who actually lived in Borodin's house.
3 London *Daily Express,* 11 February 1927.
4 *Ibid.*
5 *Ibid.*
6 *Ibid.*
7 Central News message, 16 November 1927.
8 *Daily Express,* 8 May 1934.
9 See Department of State (U.S.A.) documents, 893.00/8502, 16 February 1927, report from Canton Consul-General Douglas Jenkins, and 893.00/8427, Minister MacMurray to State, 24 March 1927.
10 See *The China Helpers,* Spence.

CHAPTER 20

1 See *The China Lobby Man: the Story of Alfred Kohlberg,* by Joseph Keeley, Arlington House, New York, 1969.
2 *Ibid.*
3 See *From Opium War to Liberation,* Epstein.
4 *The China Lobby Man,* Keeley.
5 See *The Morning Deluge,* Han Suyin.
6 *The China Lobby Man,* Keeley.
7 *Ibid.*

CHAPTER 21

1 See *Biographic Dictionary of Chinese Communism, 1921–65,* Klein and Clarke.
2 Cited by a Chinese defector to the author.

3   See *The Communist International*, New York special number, 13: 151, February 1936.
4   See *The Espionage Establishment*, by Wise and Ross.
5   See *A Secret War: Americans in China, 1944–45*, by Oliver J. Caldwell, Southern Illinois University Press, 1972.
6   See *The Morning Deluge*, Han Suyin.

CHAPTER 22

1   See *From Opium War to Liberation*, Epstein.
2   See *A Secret War*, Caldwell.
3   *Ibid.*
4   See *Liberty Magazine*, New York, 21 January 1939.
5   See *Biographic Dictionary of Chinese Communism*.
6   See *A Secret War*, Caldwell.
7   From a review of *A Secret War*, by Miles Copeland, who was an officer of the wartime O.S.S. and a management consultant to the C.I.A.

CHAPTER 23

1   See *The Stilwell Papers*, edited by T. H. White, New York, 1948.
2   See *A History of the Russian Secret Service*, Richard Deacon, and also *The Shanghai Conspiracy*, by Maj.-Gen. Charles A. Willoughby.
3   Cited by the *Daily Worker*, New York.
4   Cited in *Thirty-three Centuries of Espionage*, Rowan and Deindorfer, Hawthorn Books, Inc., New York, 1967.
5   *New York Times*, 1946.
6   See *A Secret War*, Caldwell.
7   *Ibid.*
8   *Ibid.*
9   See *The Amerasia Papers: Some Problems in the History of U.S.-China Relations*, by John Stewart Service.
10 See *A Secret War*, Caldwell.

CHAPTER 24

1   See *The China Lobby Man: The Story of Alfred Kohlberg*, by Joseph Keeley.
2   *Ibid.*
3   *A Secret War*, Caldwell.
4   Testimony in closed hearing before the Hobbs sub-committee of the House of Representatives, 10 March 1946, as published in *Congressional Record*, 22 May 1950, pp. 7438–40. See also Senate Committee on Foreign Relations, State Department Employee Loyalty Investigation (Government Printing Office), 1950, pt. 2, pp. 2502–5.
5   *A History of the Russian Secret Service*, Richard Deacon, Frederick Muller, London, 1972.

CHAPTER 25

1   See *Biographic Dictionary of Chinese Communism*.
2   See *Journal of International Affairs*, vol. 26, no. 2, 1972.

CHAPTER 26

1   Dispatch by David Bonavia from Peking, *The Times*, 21 January 1974.
2   *Ibid.*
3   Dispatch from Clare Hollingworth in Peking, *Daily Telegraph*, 23 January 1974.

CHAPTER 27

1   *Daily Telegraph*, 15 October 1963.
2   Based on statements from two scientist defectors.
3   *Ibid.*
4   See *The Wind and Beyond*, by Theodore Van Karman and Lee Edson.
5   *Ibid.*
6   See *The China Cloud*, by William L. Ryan and Sam Summerlin.
7   See article by Dick Wilson, entitled "China's Nu-

clear Effort", in the *Far Eastern Review,* Hong-kong, 19 August 1965.

8 *Los Angeles Times,* 13 September 1955.

9 See *The Espionage Establishment,* Wise and Ross.

CHAPTER 28

1 Article entitled "Putting Teeth into the Law", by Kazuo Kuroda in the *Japan Times,* 4 December 1965.

2 Article entitled "Japan is a Target for Espio-nage", by Tazuo Furuya, in *Keizai Orai,* March 1969.

3 The phrase "aggressive espionage" is one that is frequently used in Chinese Intelligence work and it dates back to Sun Tzu. One of the main objec-tives of such aggressive tactics by agents is to win recruits for the Secret Service either through this kind of propaganda act, or by terrorising a whole neighbourhood.

CHAPTER 29

1 This is not a typical plot in the recruiting of agents by the Chinese and Chu's last sentence should be treated with considerable reserve.

2 See *Plain Speaking: Conversations with Harry S. Truman,* by Merle Miller, Gollancz, London, 1974.

3 *Washington Post,* 18 March 1973. See story by Thomas O'Toole, entitled "Downey: A C.I.A. Agent in from the Cold".

4 Cited by Jeremy Campbell, Washington Corre-spondent in the London *Evening Standard* of 28 June 1971.

5 *Sunday Times* of London, 17 January 1971.

CHAPTER 30

1 Published in September 1972.

2 See *The Filipino in the Seventies,* by Father Charles J. McCarthy.

3 See *Philippines: the need for a new Society,* by Judith Stowe. Conflict Studies, August 1973.

CHAPTER 31

1 See *The Case of Richard Sorge,* by F. W. Deakin and G. R. Storry.
2 Miao Chen-pai was reported to be "still undergoing intensive daily interrogation by American Intelligence officials", it was reported in the London *Daily Telegraph* of 20 September 1966. At the same time it was stated that "some of the information he has made available became known today as a result of an interview his American custodians allowed him to have with an American journalist." But the gist of this interview told one nothing new whatever: it contained such generalities as "Peking did not want to become entangled with the United States and expose China's limited war potential" and "Peking's practice has been to use economic aid, however limited, to curry favour with non-Communist governments even when such tactics might actually strengthen a government against possible Communist insurgency."
3 See *China Spy,* by George Watt.

CHAPTER 32

1 A good deal of the material in this chapter has come from sources which must remain anonymous, but all of which was checked and cross-checked by members of the "Jackdaw" research team (see Introduction). An interesting point concerning the investigation in Sweden is that whereas an absolute blank was drawn on Chinese espionage in Sweden having been detected by the Swedish secret police, there was abundant evidence of Soviet spying. The Stockholm newspaper *Svenska Dagbladet* stated on 28 January 1974, that the number of "East bloc" spies in Sweden was "about 2,000", and added that Swedish security was reasonably well informed

on the matter. The team's impression was that the Swedish authorities would be extremely embarrassed if it was thought Chinese spies were operating on their territory and that they would tend to hide the discovery of such agents for fear of offending the Russians.

CHAPTER 33

1 This early part of the chapter has been compiled with the help of a study of Dutch police records of this period.
2 It has been impossible to check whether this is the professor's real name and the probability is that it is an alias.
3 One member of the "Jackdaw" research team states that the Chinese first obtained information on this nerve gas in Prague more than four years previously and that this was one reason why the N.C.N.A. were expelled from the Czech capital. Another member seems to think from various conversations that Liao Ho-shu had tipped off the C.I.A. on this discovery.
4 Some evidence suggests that the micro-film contained information that was worth far more than the capsule of gas.
5 Remarkably enough the facts unearthed in this whole affair, checked by various members of the "Jackdaw" research team, tally with an account of the Hsu Tsu-tsai incident entitled *De Chinese Affaire,* published as a paperback in Holland in 1969, and written by three well-known Dutch journalists, Link van Bruggen, Harry van Seumeren and Fritz de Blauw. This book is said to be based "75 per cent. on facts and the rest on deductions on the authors' part and part on police deductions." What gives this book an even greater authenticity is that it was written when the Chinese engineers were still under siege and long before Liao had defected.
6 Cited in "Mao Spy Chief handed to C.I.A.", in the London *Daily Express,* 5 February 1969.

7   At the time of writing (January 1974) the Ambassador to The Hague is Hao Te-chung, and the First and Second Secretaries respectively are Li Mao-lai (who is also *chargé d'affaires*) and Lo Chun-ching. There are two other attachés—Lu Chiu-tien and Tsai Liu-hai.

CHAPTER 34

1   There is continual re-grouping of agents inside the N.C.N.A. here and this has been most marked since the Cultural Revolution in 1967. A severe purge then resulted in the dismissal of the N.C.N.A. director in Peking, Wu Leng-hsi, and three of the five deputy directors. The Hongkong *Standard* of 26 August 1973, speculated that Li's official title "is believed to be First Director in charge of Chinese Affairs".

2   See Hongkong *Standard,* 17 June 1972.

CHAPTER 35

1   In a foreword to *Chinese Opium Narcotics: A Threat to the Survival of the West,* by J. H. Turnbull, Foreign Affairs Publishing Co., Richmond, Surrey, U.K., 1972.

2   See also London *Sunday Telegraph,* 24 October 1971.

3   See *Chinese Opium Narcotics: A Threat to the Survival of the West.*

4   *Ibid.*

5   See *The Chinese Communist Plot to Drug the World,* published by the World Anti-Communist League, China Chapter, February 1972.

6   See *The Murderers,* by Harry J. Anslinger, Farrar, Straus & Cudahy, New York, 1961.

7   Cited in *The Politics of Heroin in Southeast Asia,* by Alfred W. McCoy, with Cathleen B. Read and Leonard P. Adams II, Harper & Row, New York, 1972.

8   *Ibid.*

9   See *South China Morning Post,* 18 August 1973, article entitled "U.S. Sanction Threat to HK over drugs", by Harold Chang.

10 See article entitled "The Poppy Path to Death",
    by Frederick Forsyth, London *Sunday Telegraph*
    magazine, 11 and 18 August 1973.
11 See *Chinese Opium Narcotics,* Turnbull.
12 See *The Chinese Communist Plot to Drug the
    World,* World Anti-Communist League.
13 See *Stars and Stripes,* Pacific issue, 27 November
    1971.
14 *Daily Telegraph,* 9 September 1973.

CHAPTER 36

1 See *The Chinese Looking Glass,* Bloodworth.
2 See article entitled "Ideology and Information:
   Correspondents of the New China News Agency
   and Chinese Foreign Policy Making," *Journal of
   International Affairs,* vol. 26, no. 2, 1972.
3 See the London *Observer,* 27 September 1964.
4 Cited in "Ideology and Information" article in
   the *Journal of International Affairs,* vol. 26, no.
   2, 1972.
5 From a member of the "Jackdaw" research team.
   Information obtained quite independently by another team member in Hongkong was that the
   Chinese Communists first established undercover
   links with a member of the Israeli Secret Service
   through contacts originally supplied by Morris
   Cohen, Chiang Kai-shek's former Intelligence officer. This is not so improbable as Cohen's earlier
   career would suggest as latterly Cohen was used
   as a go-between by Chiang with Peking.

CHAPTER 37

1 Cited in the London *Evening Standard,* 29 May
   1973.
2 *Ibid.*
3 See *Thirty-three Centuries of Espionage,* Rowan
   and Deindorfer.
4 See "The Lin Piao Case", by Wilfred Burchett,
   Far Eastern Review, Hongkong, August 1973.
5 See dispatch from Charles R. Smith, U.P.I. correspondent in Hongkong, 29 May 1973.
6 Honolulu *Star Bulletin,* 5 April 1973.

Bibliography

AMIOT, Fr. Joseph: *Les Treizes Articles de Sun-tse,* trans. from the Chinese, Paris, 1782.

ANSLINGER, Harry J.: *The Murderers,* Farrar, Straus & Cudahy, New York, 1961.

BARNETT, A. Doak: *Cadres, Bureaucracy and Political Power in Communist China,* Columbia University Press, New York and London, 1967.

BLOFELD, John: *The Book of Changes,* trans., Allen & Unwin, London.

BLOODWORTH, Dennis: *The Chinese Looking Glass,* Secker & Warburg, London, 1967; Farrar, Straus & Giroux, New York, 1970.

CALDWELL, Oliver J.: *A Secret War: Americans in China,* 1944–5, Southern Illinois University Press, 1972.

CH'EN, Jerome: *Mao and the Chinese Revolution,* Oxford University Press, London, 1965.

CHEN, Theodore H. E.: *Thought Reform of the Chinese Intellectuals,* Hongkong University, 1960.

CHIANG YEE: *Chinese Caligraphy: An Introduction to the Aesthetic and Technique,* Methuen, London, 1938.

COMBER, Leon: *Chinese Secret Societies in Malaya,* Donald Moore, Singapore.

CRANMER-BYNG, J. L.: *Lord Macartney's Embassy to Peking in 1793,* trans. from official Chinese documents, University of Hongkong.

CURTIN, Jeremiah: *The Mongols: A History,* Little, Brown, Boston, 1908.

DEACON, Richard: *A History of the British Secret Service,* Frederick Muller, London, and Taplinger Publishing Co., New York, 1969; *A History of the Russian Secret Service,* Frederick Muller, London, and Taplinger Publishing Co., New York, 1972.

DRAGE, Charles: *Two-Gun Cohen,* Jonathan Cape, London, 1954.

EPSTEIN, Israel: *From Opium War to Liberation,* New World Press, Peking, 1956.

FAIRBANK, John K., REISCHAUER, Edwin and CRAIG, Albert M.: *A History of East Asian Civilisation,* vol. 2; *East Asia: The Modern Transformation,* Allen & Unwin, London, and Houghton Mifflin, Boston, 1965.

FITZGERALD, C. P.: *The Empress Wu,* the Cresset Press, London; *Revolution in China,* the Cresset Press.

FO LO-SHU: *A Documentary Chronicle of Sino-Western Relations, 1644–1820,* 2 vols., University of Arizona Press, Tucson, 1966.

GILES, Lionel: *Sun Tzu on the Art of War: the Oldest Military Treatise in the World,* trans. from Chinese, Luzac, London, 1910.

GREENE, Felix: *The Wall Has Two Sides,* Jonathan Cape, London, 1962.

HANS SUYIN: *The Morning Deluge: Mao Tse-tung and the Chinese Revolution: 1893–1953,* Jonathan Cape, London, 1972.

HEIKAL, Mohammed Hassanein: The Cairo Documents, The New English Library, London, 1972; Harper & Row, New York, 1971.

HIBBERT, Christopher: *The Dragon Awakes: China and the West, 1795–1911,* Longman, London, 1970.

KEELEY, Joseph: *The China Lobby Man: the Story of Alfred Kohlberg,* Arlington House, New Rochelle, N.Y., 1969.

KLEIN and CLARKE: *A Biographic Dictionary of Chinese Communism: 1921–65,* Harvard University Press.

LAMPE, David and SZENASI, Laszlo: *The Self-Made Villain: A Biography of I. T. Trebitsch Lincoln,* Cassel, London, 1961.

LIN YUTANG: *The Importance of Living,* Heinemann,

London, 1938; *My Country and My People,* Commercial Press, Shanghai, 1936.

LO KUAN-CHUNG: *San Kuo,* or *The Romance of the Three Kingdoms,* trans. by C. H. Brewitt-Taylor, Chas. E. Tuttle, Rutland, Vermont and Tokyo, 1925.

MAO TSE-TUNG: *Selected Military Writings of Mao Tse-tung,* Foreign Languages Press, Peking; China Books, New York; *Strategic Problems in the Anti-Japanese Guerrilla War,* Foreign Languages Press.

MARTIN, Bernard, and SHUI CHIEN-TUNG: *Makers of China: Confucius to Mao,* Basil Blackwell, Oxford, 1972.

MCCOY, Alfred, with READ, Cathleen B., and ADAMS, Leonard P., II: *The Politics of Heroin in Southeast Asia,* Harper & Row, New York, 1972.

MORGAN, W. P.: *Triad Societies in Hongkong,* Government Press, Hongkong.

ROWAN, Richard Wilmer and DEINDORFER, Robert G.: *Secret Service: Thirty-three Centuries of Espionage,* Hawthorn Books, New York, 1967.

RYAN, William L., and SUMMERLIN, Sam.: *The China Cloud,* Hutchinson, London, 1969.

SCHIFFRIN, Harold Z.: *Sun Yat-sen and the Origins of the Chinese Revolution,* University of California Press, Berkley, Los Angeles, and London, 1970.

SERVICE, John Stewart: *The Amerasia Papers: Some Problems in the History of U.S.-China Relations,* Center for Chinese Studies, 1971.

SPENCE, Jonathan: *The China Helpers: Western Advisers in China,* 1620–1910, Bodley Head, London, 1969.

SUN TZU: *The Principles of War by Sun Tzu,* a Royal Air Force publication, Colombo, 1943.

SUN YAT-SEN: *Kidnapped in London,* The China Society, London, 1969.

TURNBULL, J. H.: *Chinese Opium Narcotics: A Threat to the Survival of the West,* Foreign Affairs Pub. Co., Richmond, Surrey, U.K., 1972.

VAN BRUGGEN, Link, with VAN SOUVERON, Harry, and DE BLAUW, Fritz: *De Chinese Affaire,* Periodiekenpers, Apeldoorn, Holland, 1966.

VON KARMAN, Theodore, and EDSON, Lee: *The Wind and Beyond: Theodore von Karman, Pioneer in Aviation and Pathfinder in Space,* Little, Brown, Boston, 1967.

WALEY, Arthur: *The Opium War Through Chinese Eyes,* Allen & Unwin, London; Dufour Editions, Chester Springs, Pa., 1966.

WARNER, Marina: *The Dragon Empress,* Weidenfeld & Nicolson, London, 1972.

WATT, George: *China Spy,* Johnson, London, 1972.

WHITE, T. H.: The Stilwell Papers, New York, 1948.

WILHELM, Richard: *The I Ching or Book of Changes,* 2 vols. trans. from German by Cary F. Baynes, Routledge & Kegan Paul, London, 1951.

WINT, Guy: *Asia: A Handbook,* Anthony Blond, London, 1965.

WISE, David, and ROSS, Thomas D.: *The Espionage Establishment,* Random House, New York, 1967.

WU, Aitchen K.: *China and the Soviet Union,* John Day, New York, 1956.

Index

TWENTIETH CENTURY WAR
from
🅱️🅱️
BALLANTINE BOOKS

S S PANZER BATTALION
Leo Kessler   **$1.25**

THE THOUSAND-MILE WAR
Brian Garfield   **$1.95**

THE RISE OF THE LUFTWAFFE
Herbert Molloy Mason, Jr.   **$1.95**

**HUNTERS FROM THE SKY: THE
GERMAN PARACHUTE CORPS**
1940-1945 Charles Whiting   **$1.75**

THE LUFTWAFFE WAR DIARIES
Cajus Bekker, TRANSLATION by
Frank Ziegler   **$2.25**

▼ **Available at your local bookstore or mail the coupon below** ▼

THE
BENCHWARMERS
THE PRIVATE WORLD
OF THE
POWERFUL FEDERAL JUDGES
BY JOSEPH C. GOULDEN

THERE ARE NO GUIDELINES FOR THEIR SELECTION— AND VIRTUALLY NO LIMITS TO THEIR POWER

Now at last a book that takes a hard, close look at these individuals, the system that they represent, and its effects for good and for evil on America and us all.

"A TOTALLY ABSORBING, FRIGHTENING EXPOSE!"
—Fort Wayne Journal-Gazette

"TO BE READ WITH BOTH FASCINATION AND HORROR."
—Chicago Sun-Times

$1.95

➤ Available at your local bookstore or mail the coupon below ➤

NONFICTION BESTSELLERS
from
BB
BALLANTINE BOOKS

▼ Available at your local bookstore or mail the coupon below ▼